Adherent

Adherent

First Edition
ISBN 978-1-77262-082-5

Printed by Gauvin in Gatineau, Quebec, Canada

Conundrum Press
Wolfville, NS
www.conundrumpress.com

Conundrum Press acknowledges the financial support of the Canada Council for the Arts, the province of Nova Scotia and the government of Canada toward its publishing activities. The author acknowledges the support of the Ontario Arts Council in the creation of this work.

NOVA SCOTIA Canada

Canada Council for the Arts Conseil des Arts du Canada

ONTARIO ARTS COUNCIL
CONSEIL DES ARTS DE L'ONTARIO
an Ontario government agency
un organisme du gouvernement de l'Ontario

Adherent

Chris W. Kim

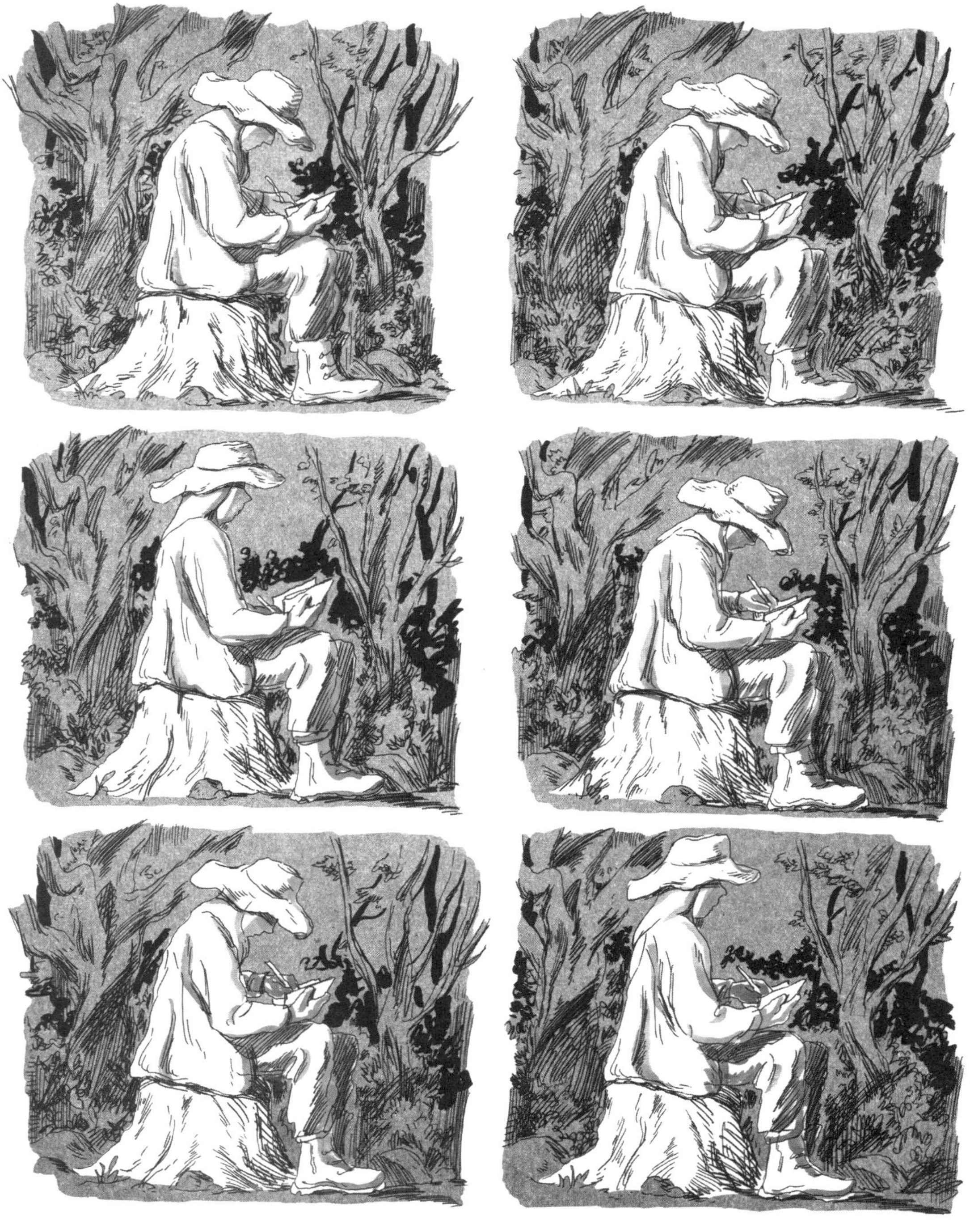

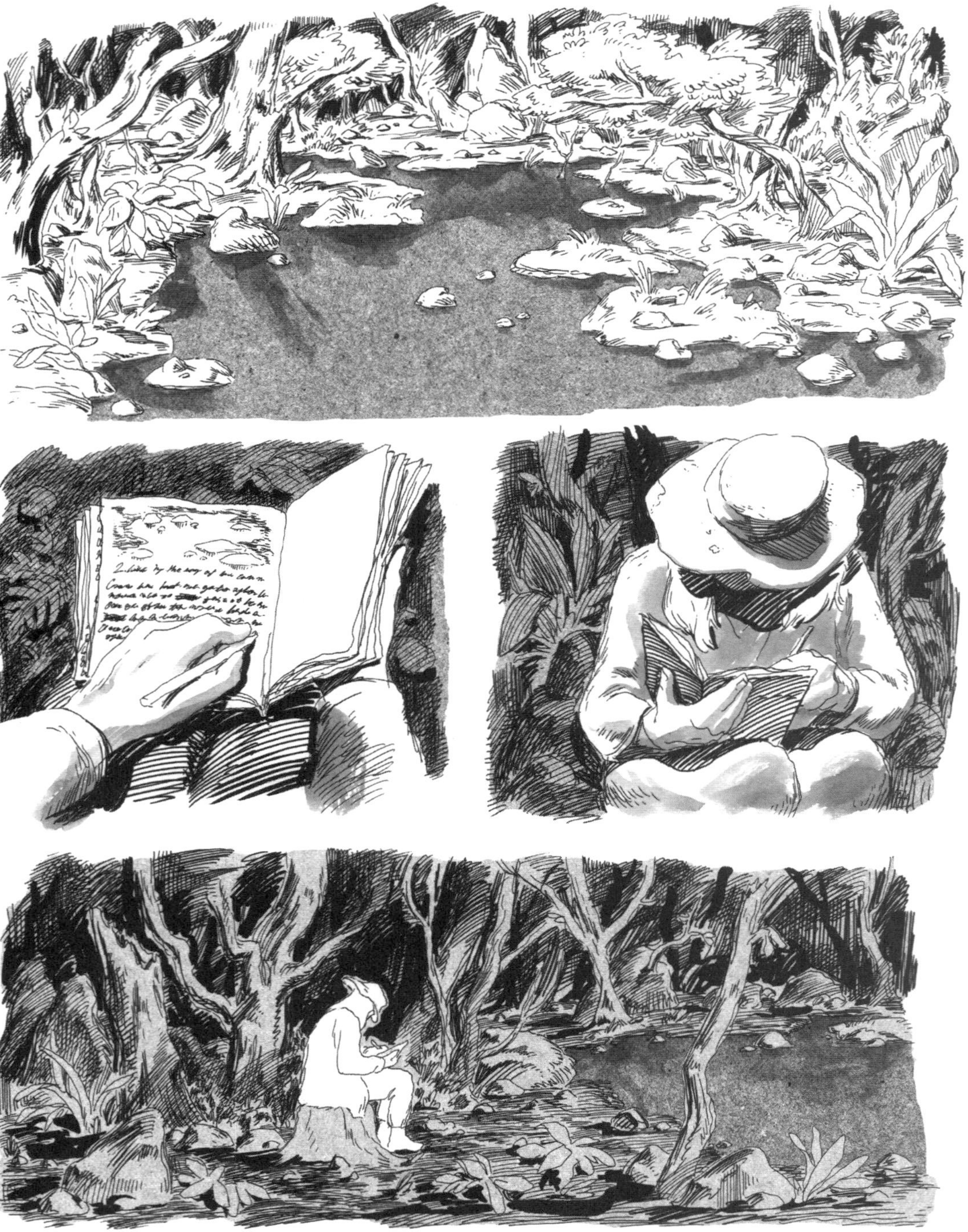

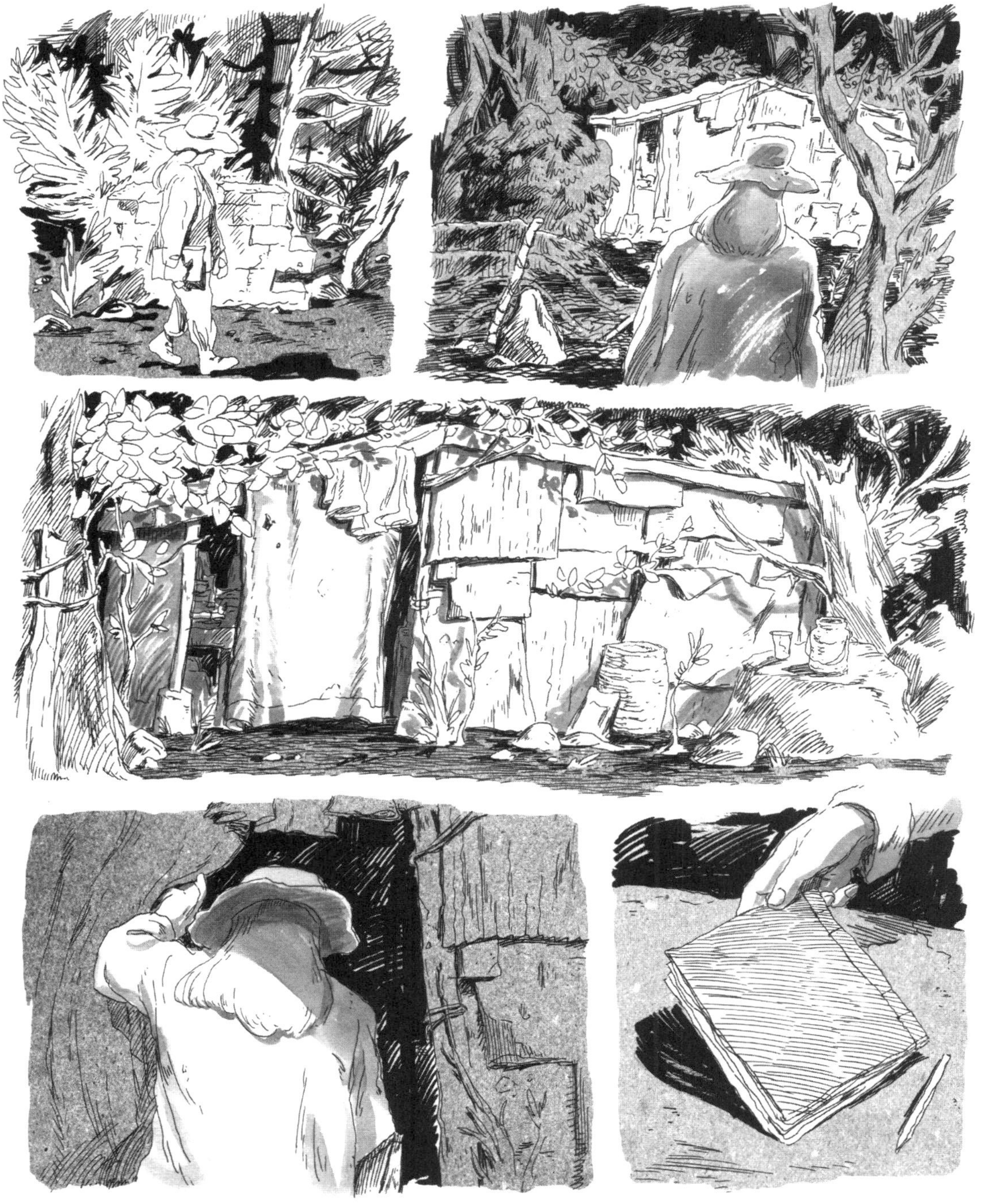

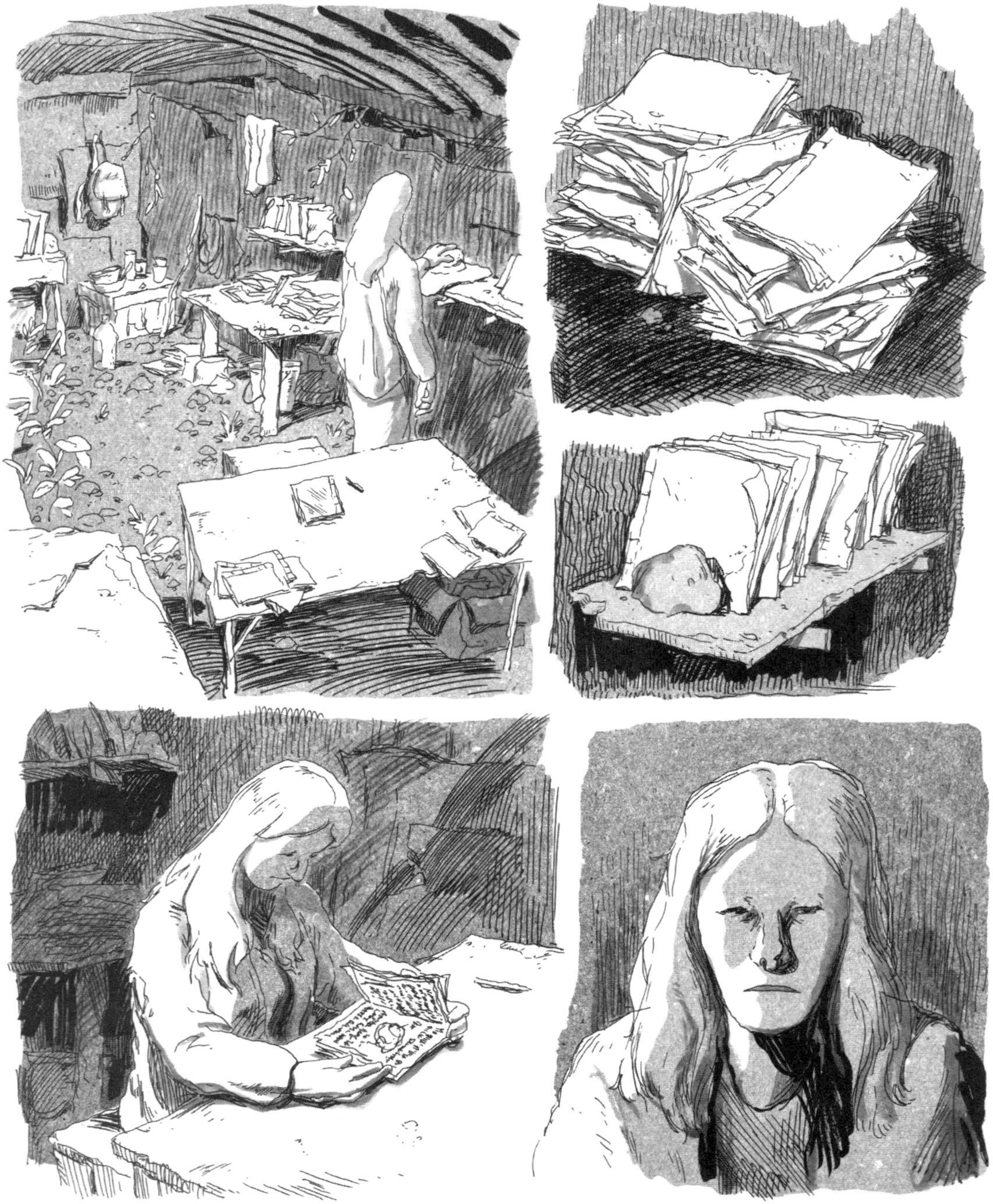

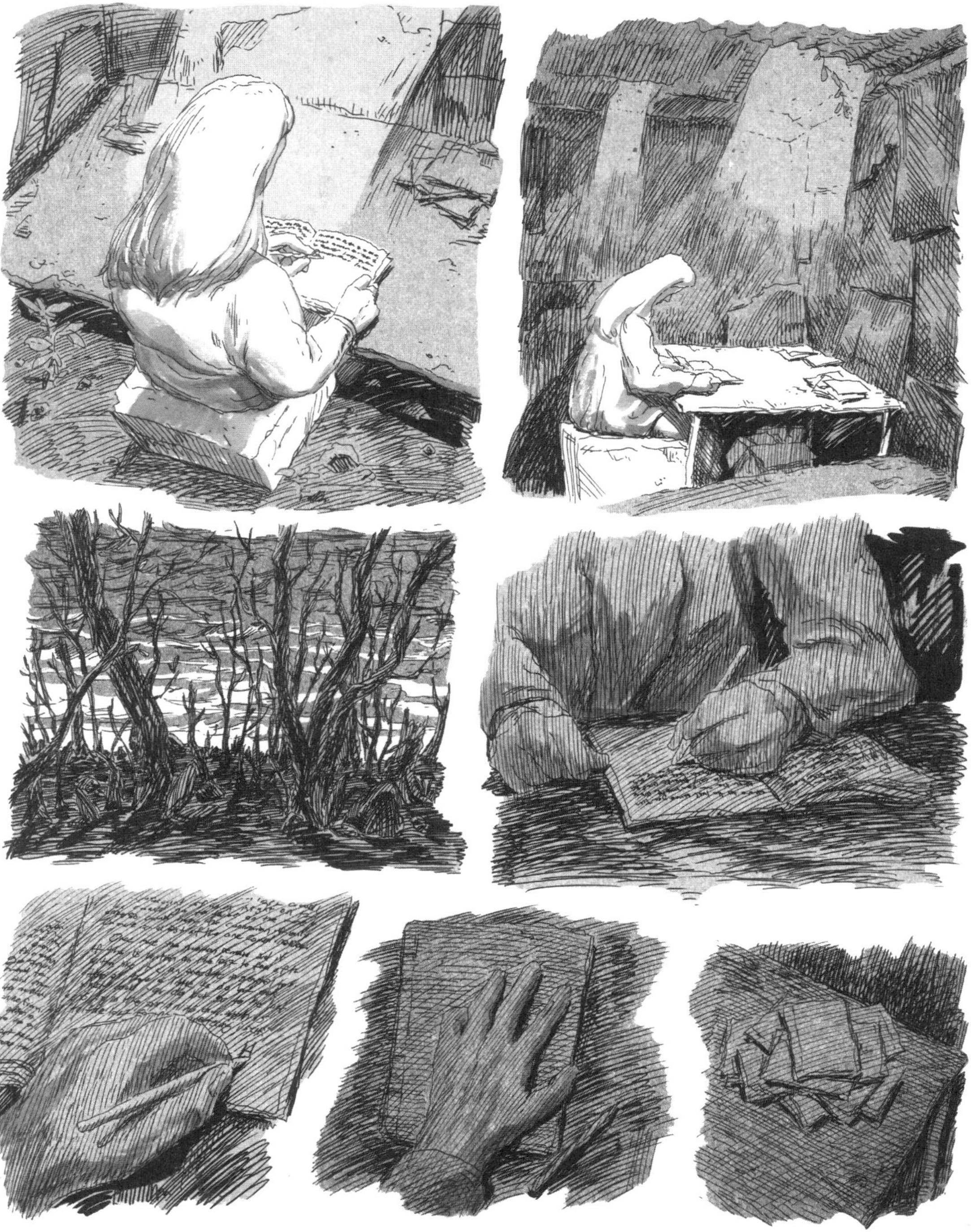

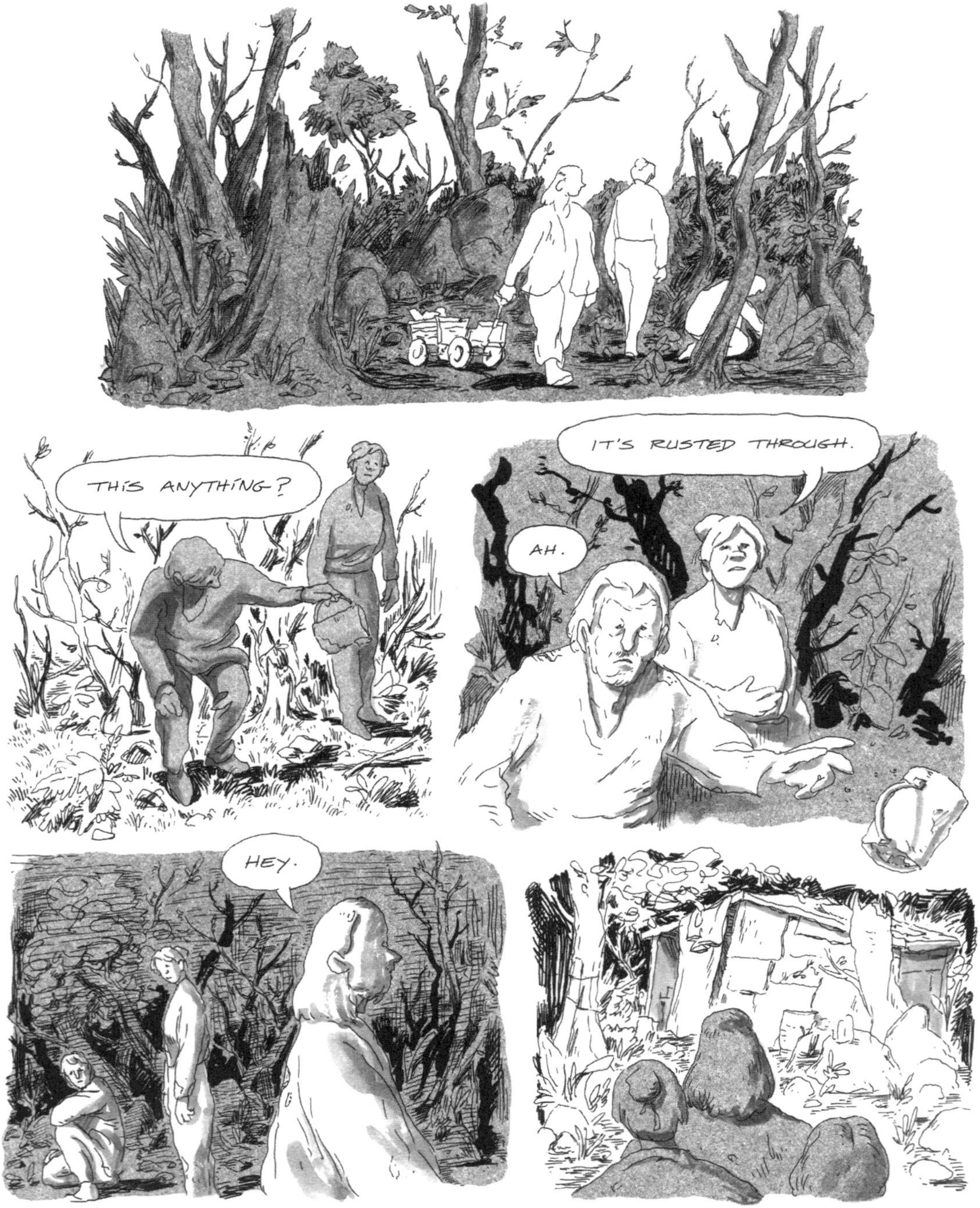
THIS ANYTHING?
IT'S RUSTED THROUGH.
AH.
HEY.

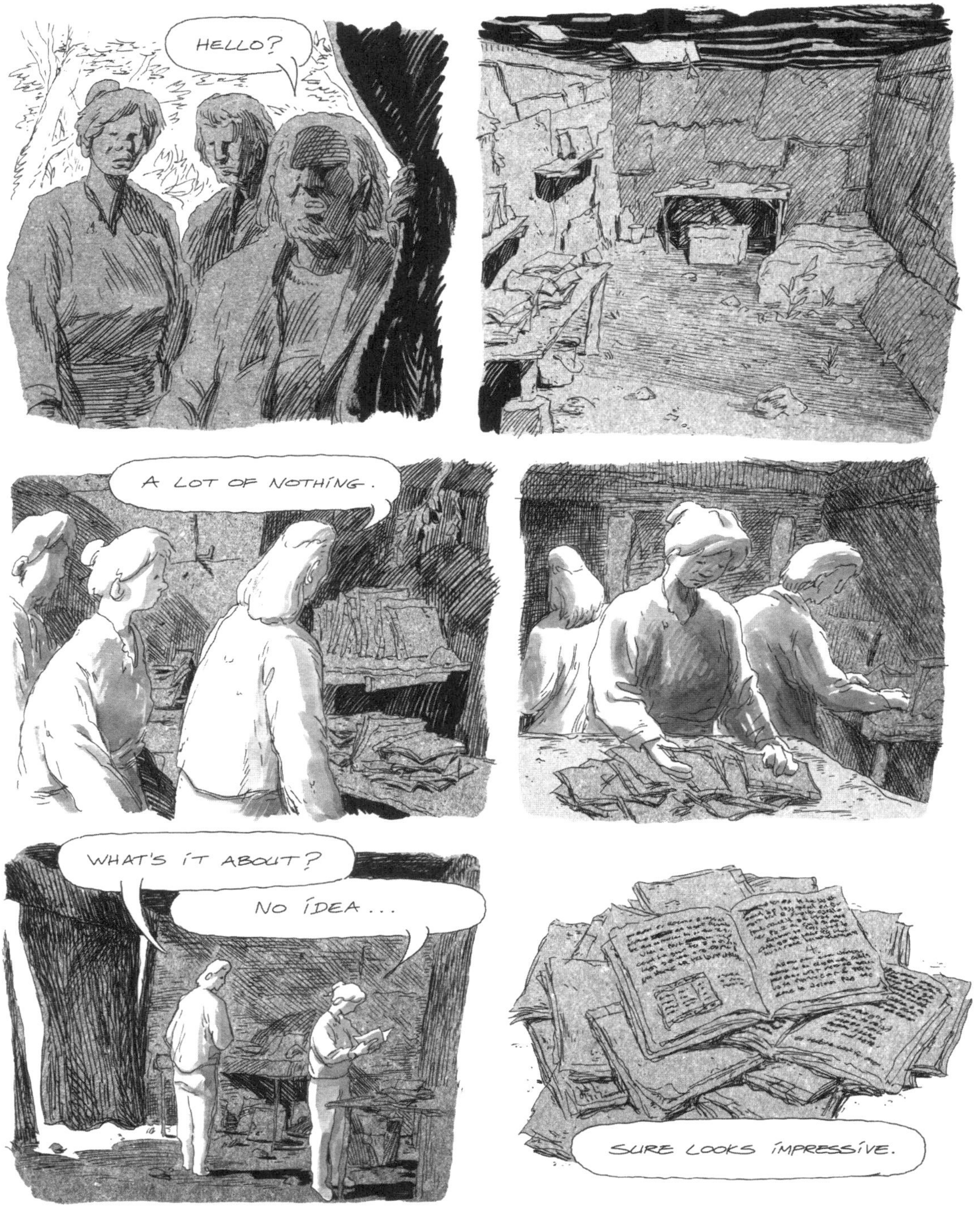
HELLO?
A LOT OF NOTHING.
WHAT'S IT ABOUT?
NO IDEA...
SURE LOOKS IMPRESSIVE.

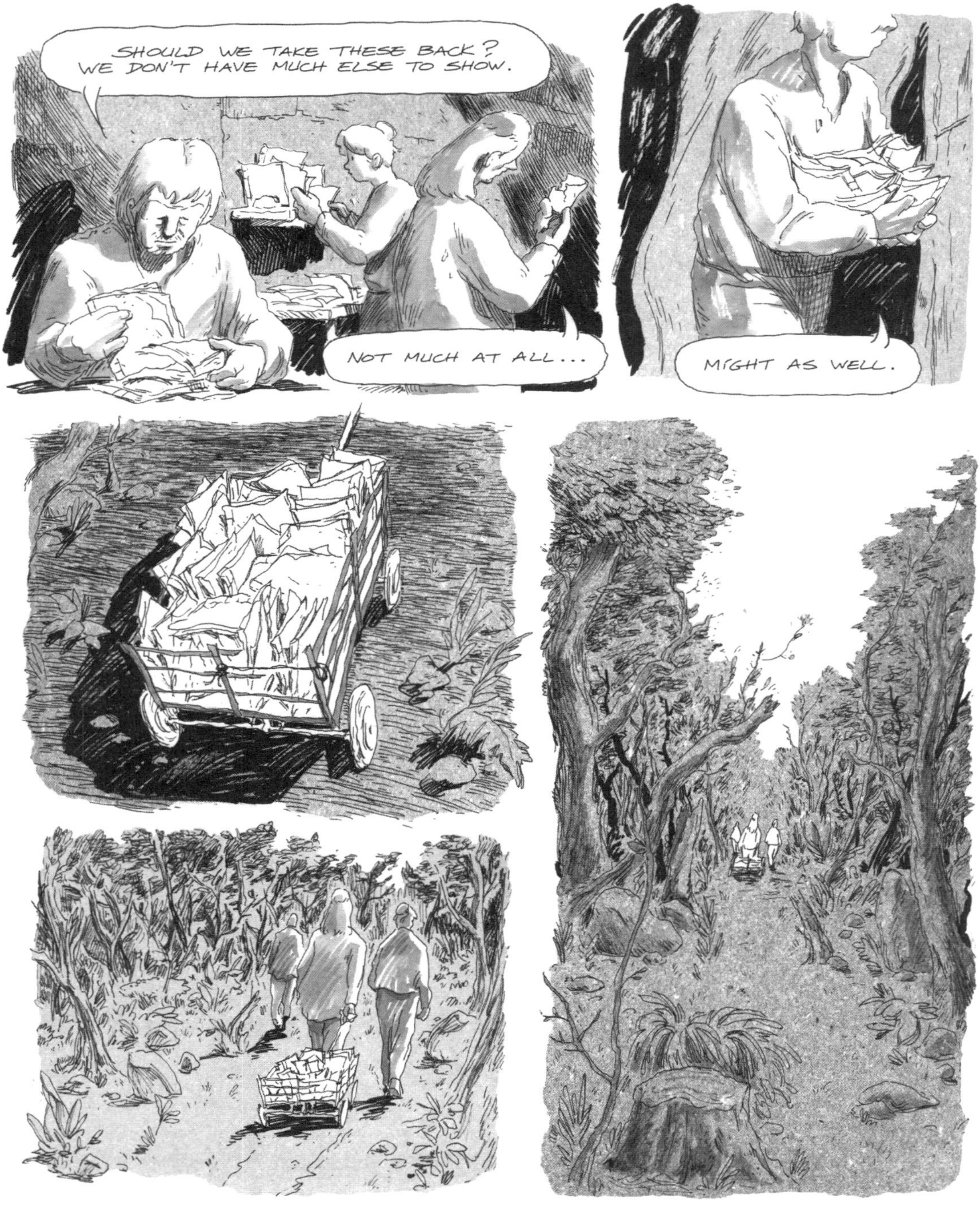
SHOULD WE TAKE THESE BACK? WE DON'T HAVE MUCH ELSE TO SHOW.
NOT MUCH AT ALL...
MIGHT AS WELL.

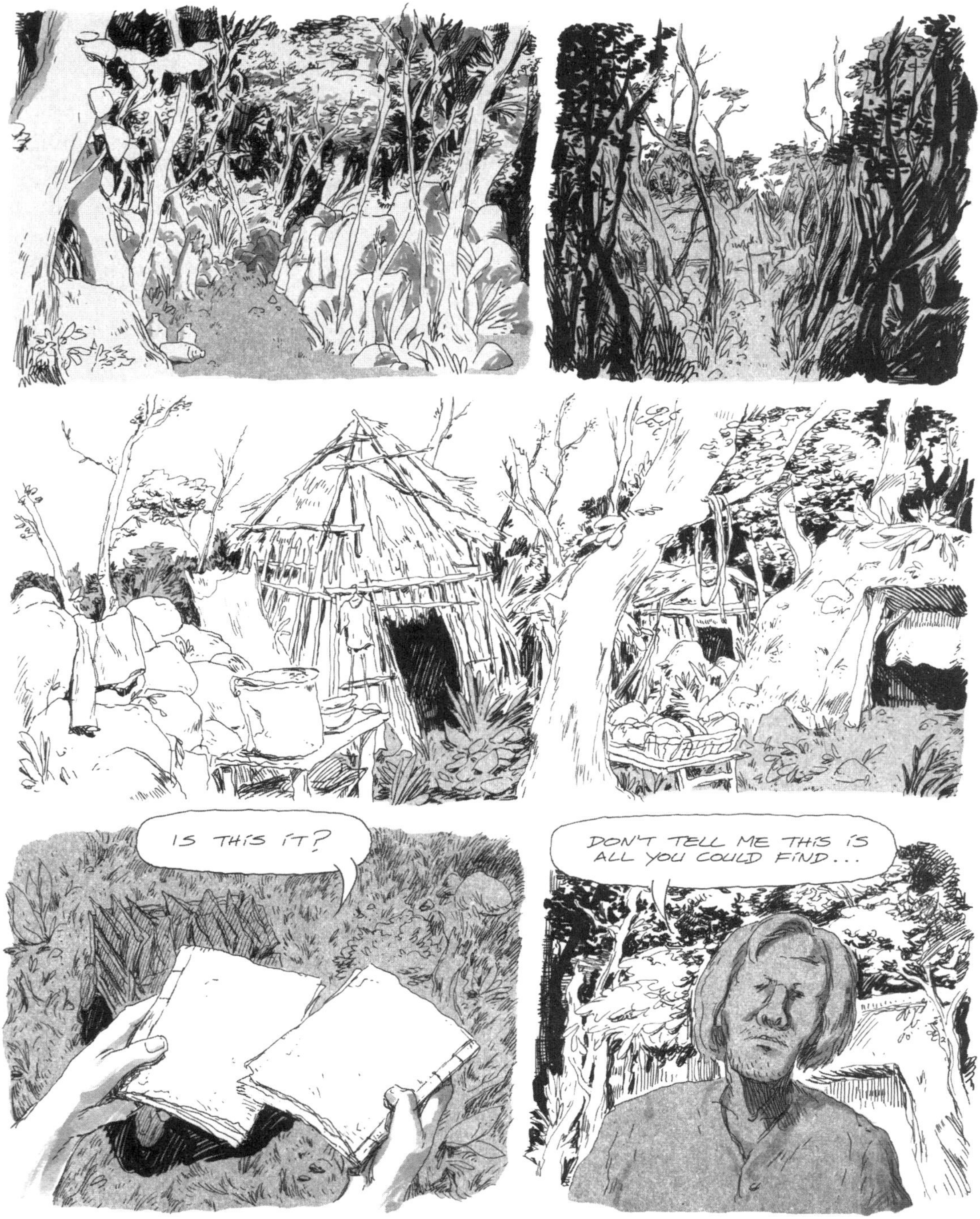
IS THIS IT?
DON'T TELL ME THIS IS ALL YOU COULD FIND...

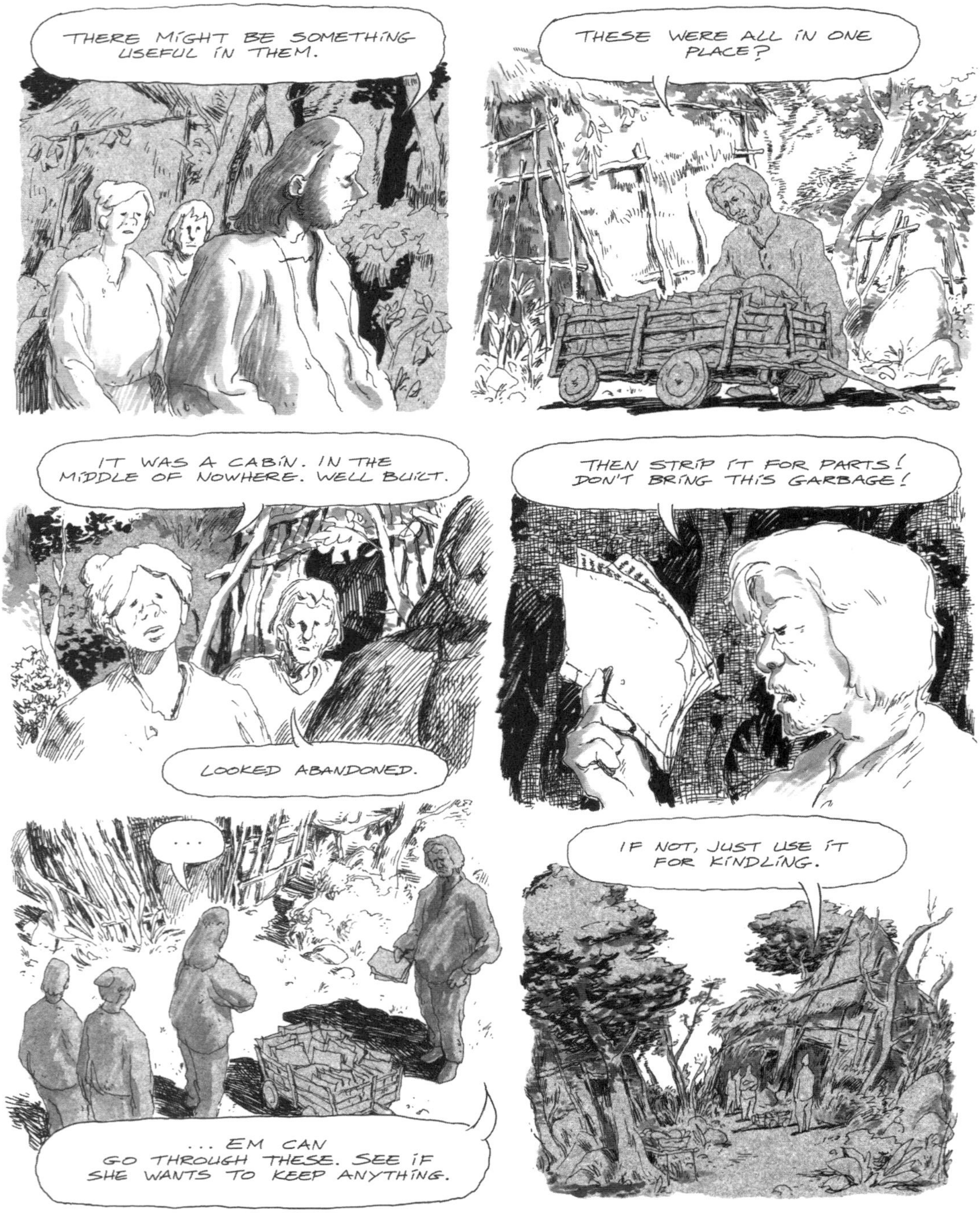
THERE MIGHT BE SOMETHING USEFUL IN THEM.
THESE WERE ALL IN ONE PLACE?
IT WAS A CABIN. IN THE MIDDLE OF NOWHERE. WELL BUILT.
LOOKED ABANDONED.
THEN STRIP IT FOR PARTS! DON'T BRING THIS GARBAGE!
...
... EM CAN GO THROUGH THESE. SEE IF SHE WANTS TO KEEP ANYTHING.
IF NOT, JUST USE IT FOR KINDLING.

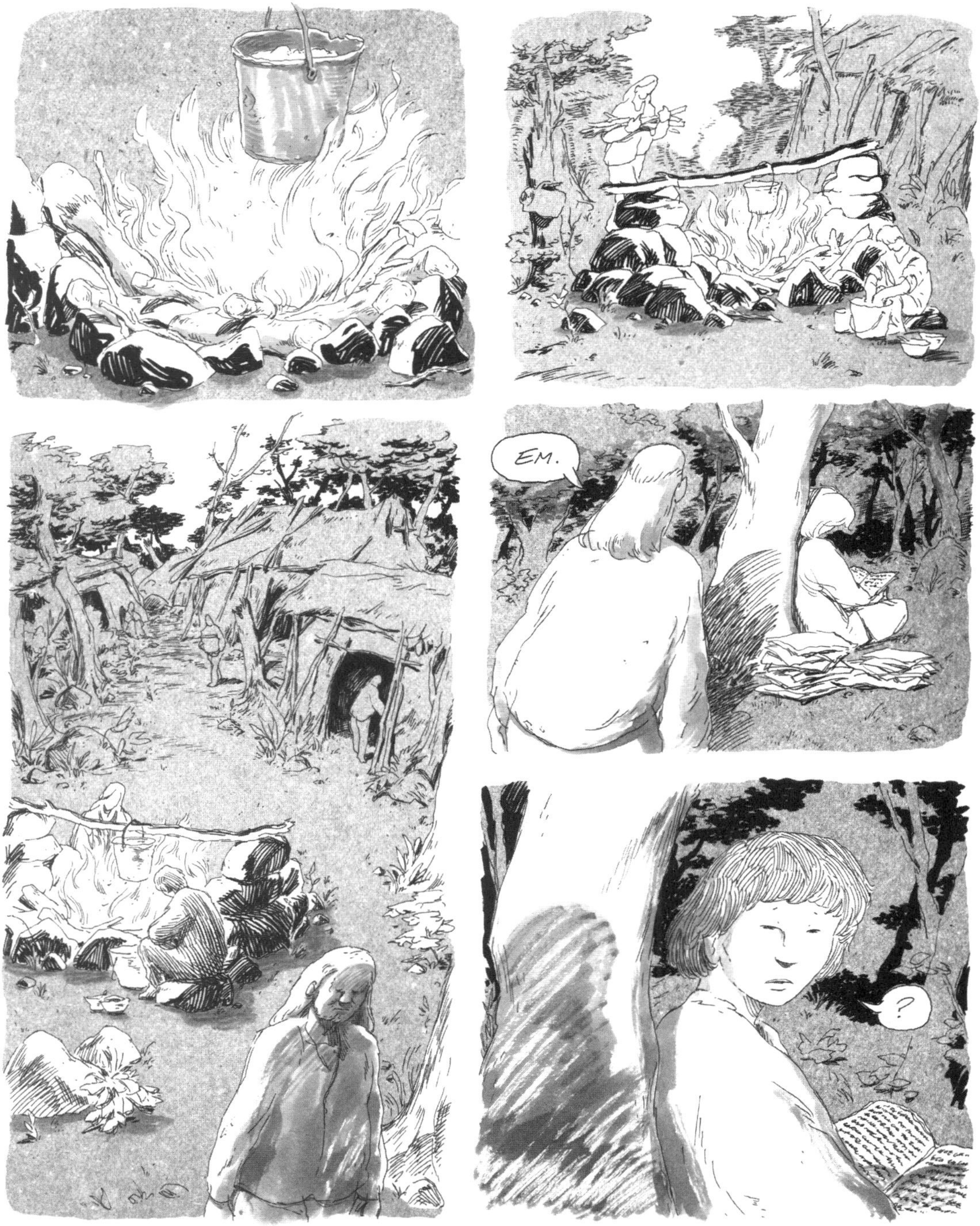
EM.
?

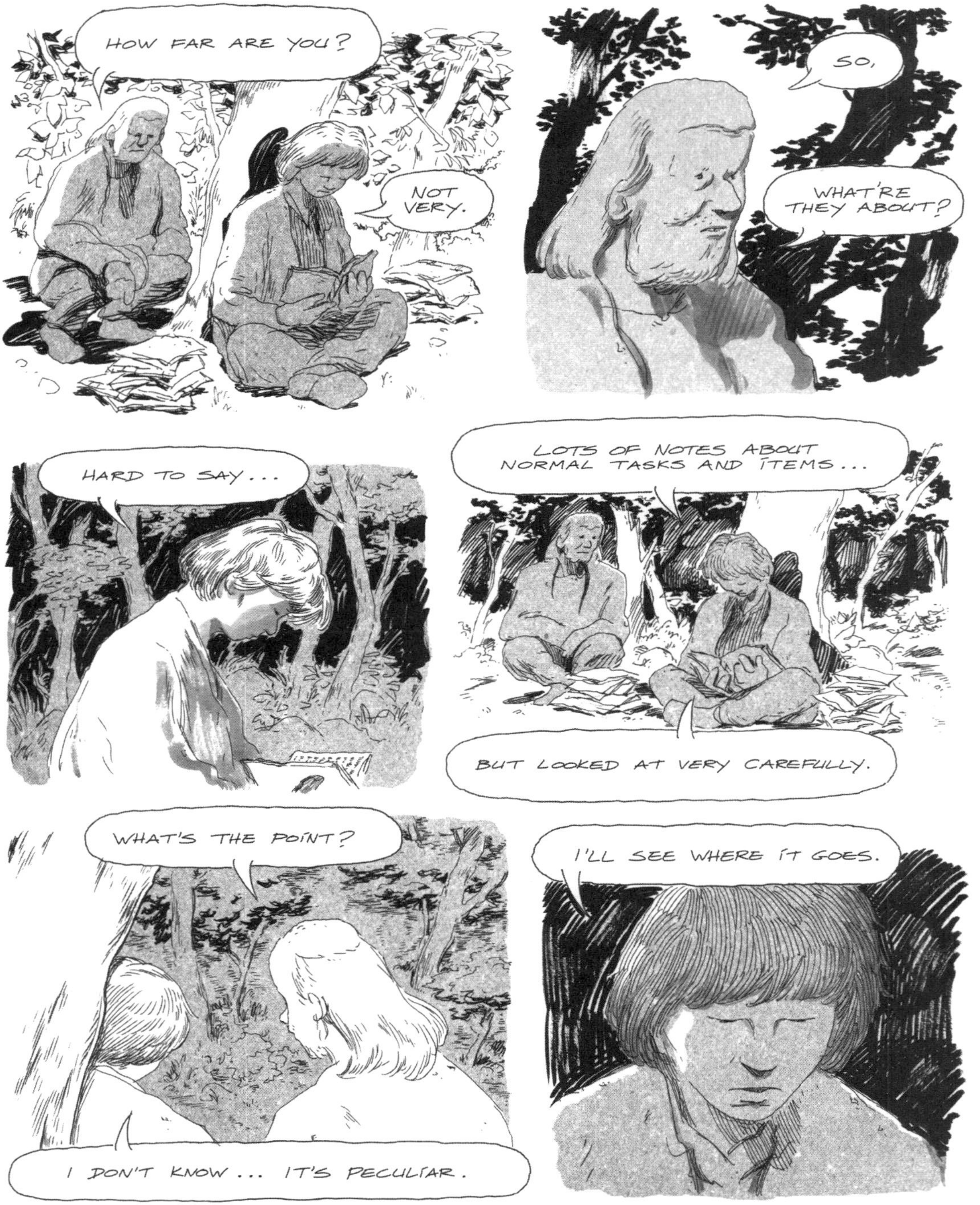
HOW FAR ARE YOU?
NOT VERY.
SO,
WHAT'RE THEY ABOUT?
HARD TO SAY...
LOTS OF NOTES ABOUT NORMAL TASKS AND ITEMS...
BUT LOOKED AT VERY CAREFULLY.
WHAT'S THE POINT?
I DON'T KNOW ... IT'S PECULIAR.
I'LL SEE WHERE IT GOES.

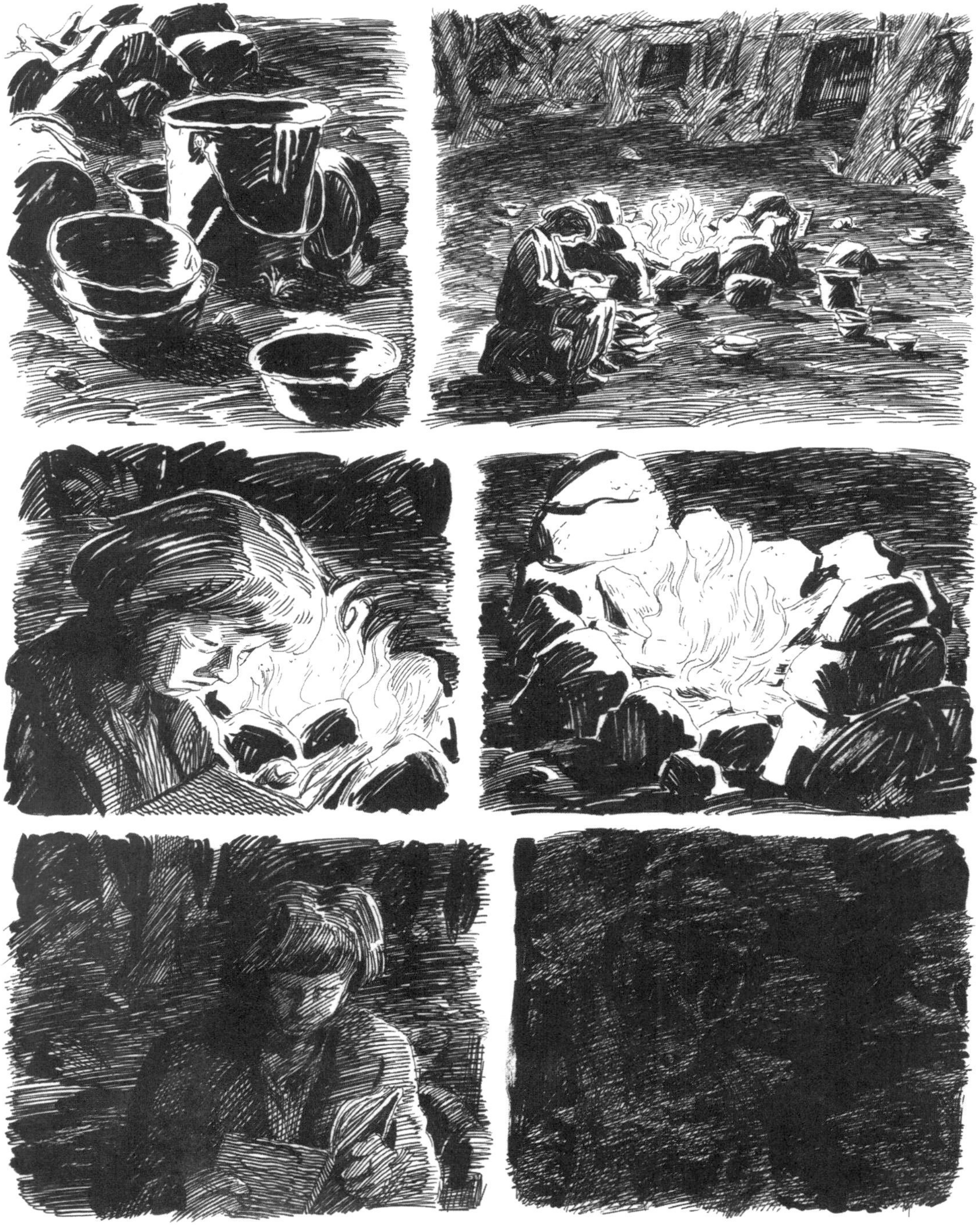

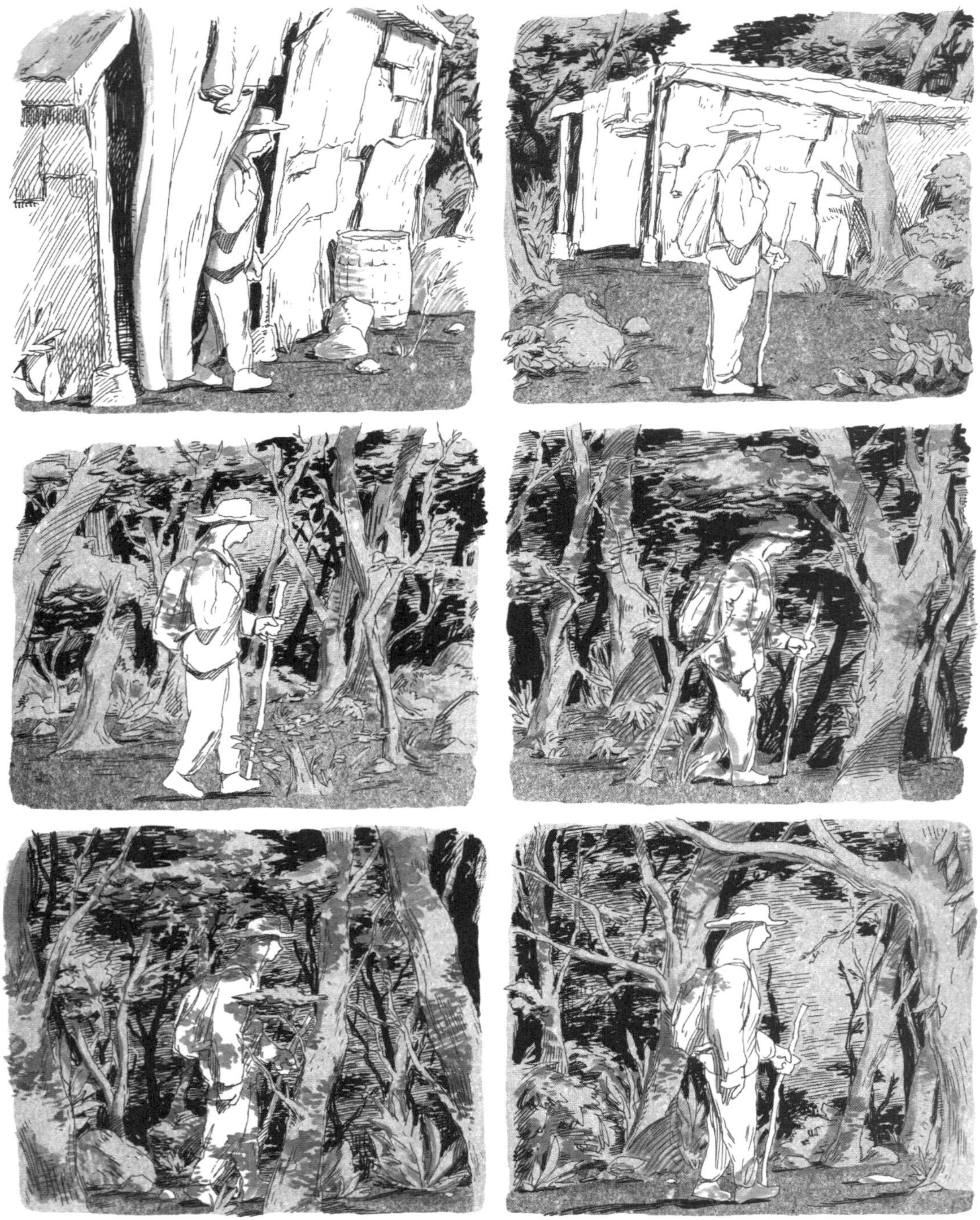

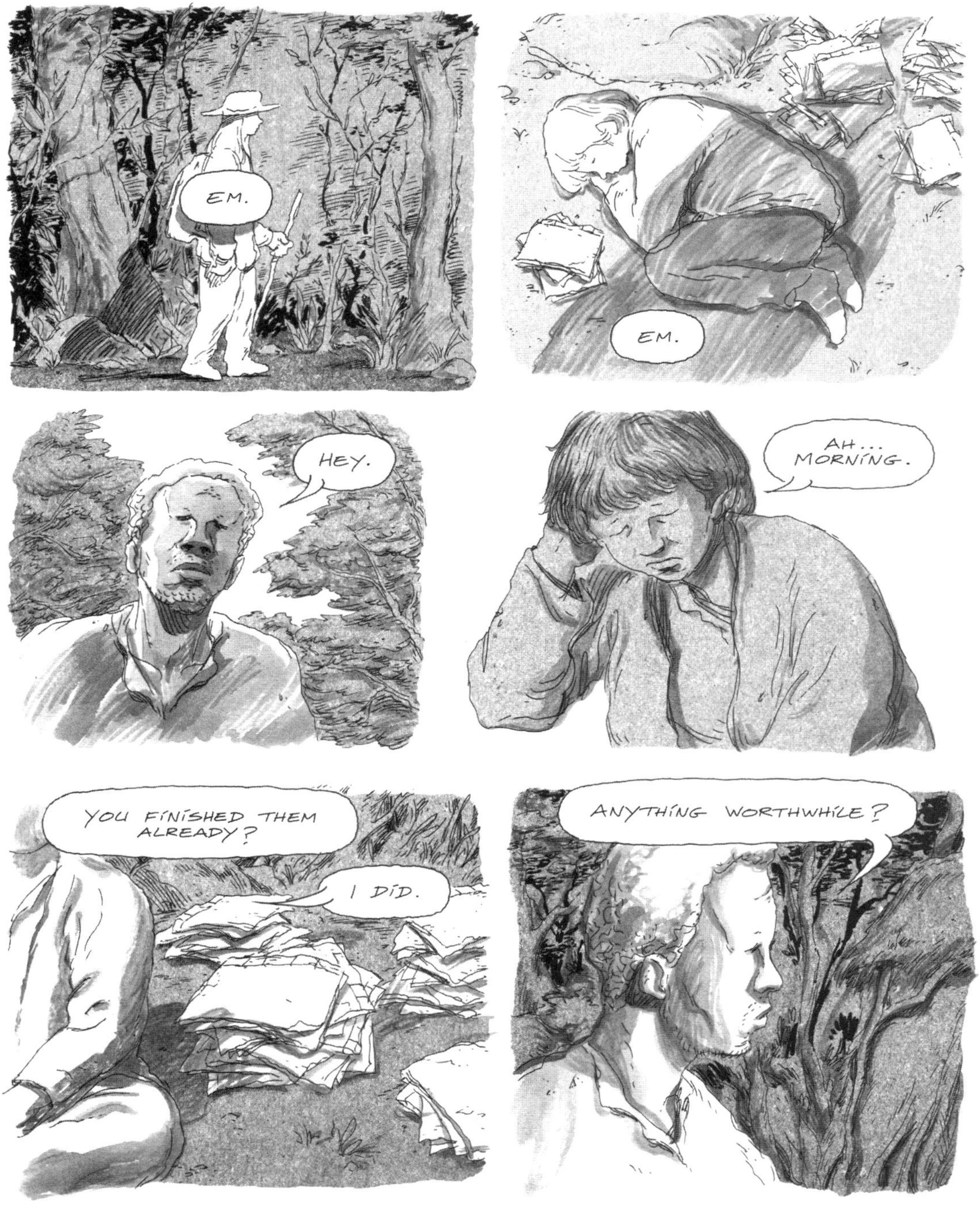
EM.
EM.
HEY.
AH... MORNING.
YOU FINISHED THEM ALREADY?
I DID.
ANYTHING WORTHWHILE?

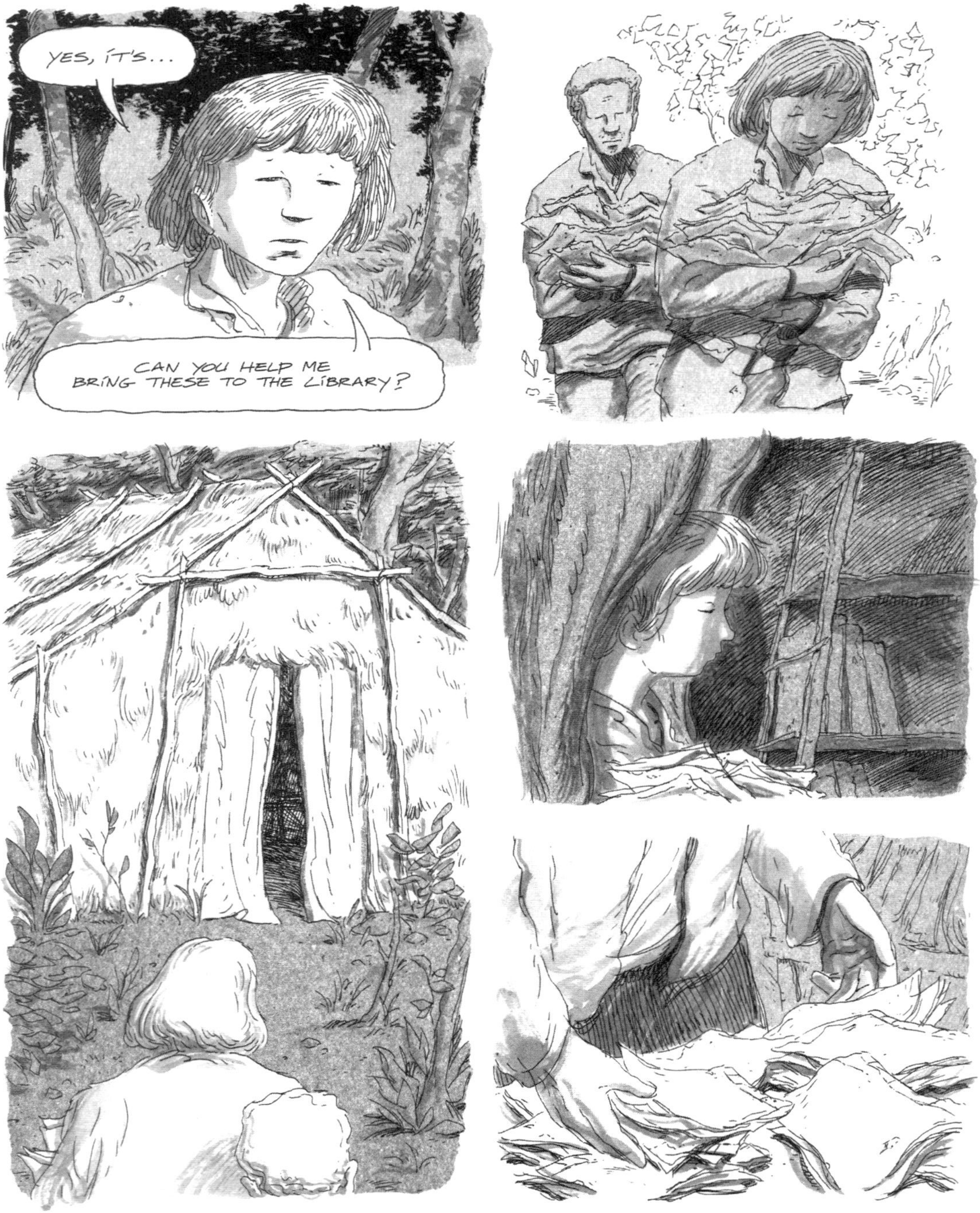
YES, IT'S...
CAN YOU HELP ME BRING THESE TO THE LIBRARY?

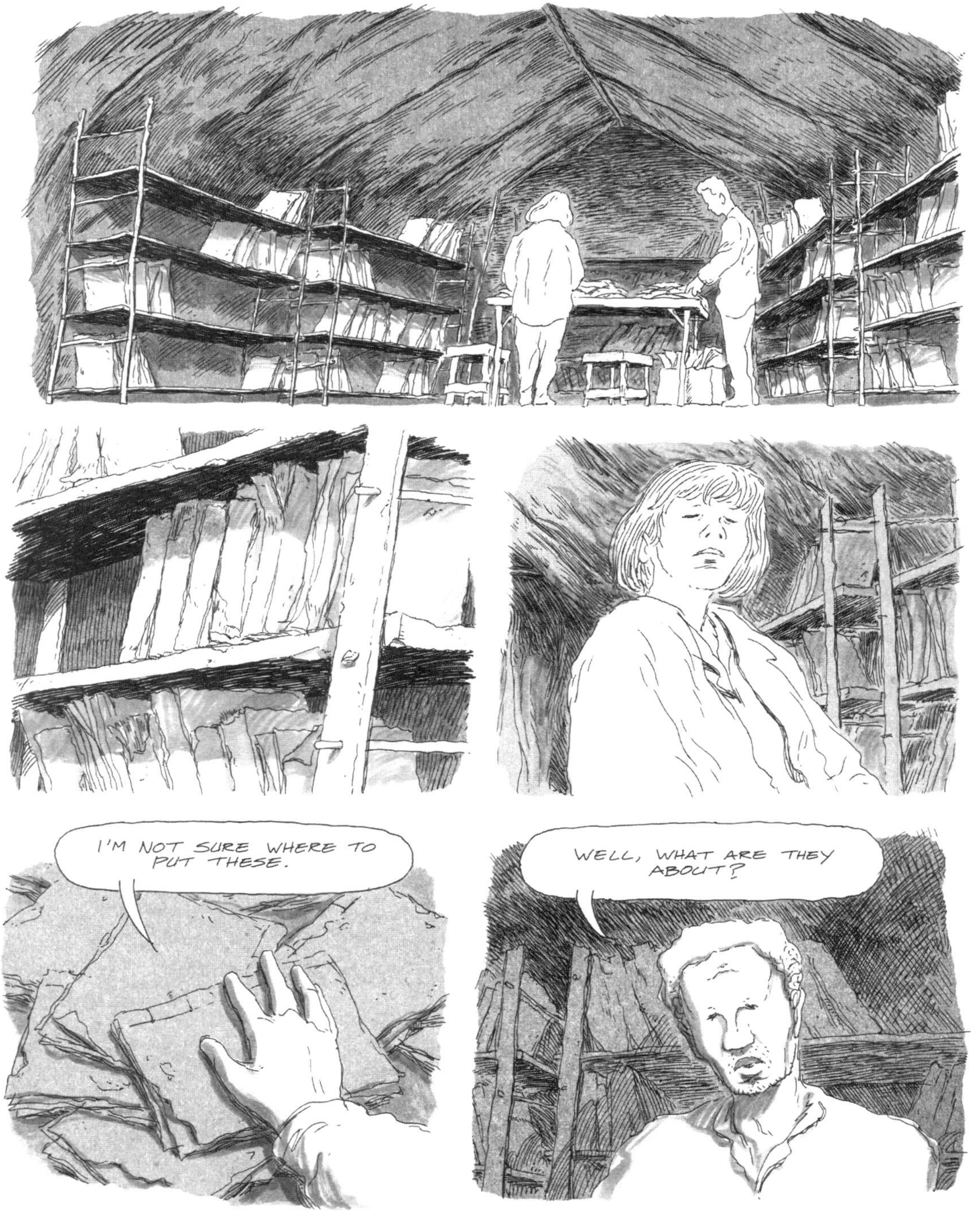
I'M NOT SURE WHERE TO PUT THESE.
WELL, WHAT ARE THEY ABOUT?

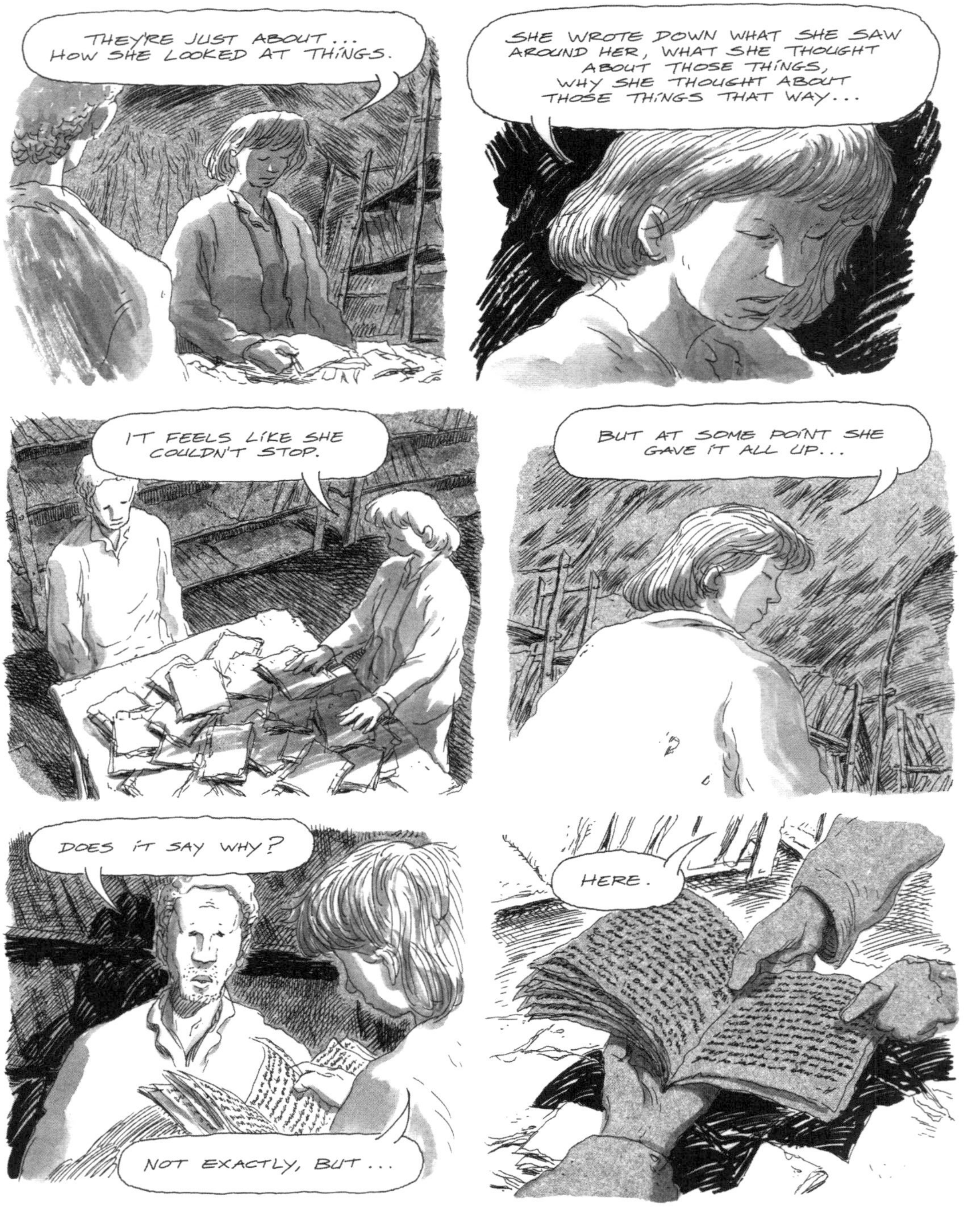
THEY'RE JUST ABOUT... HOW SHE LOOKED AT THINGS.
SHE WROTE DOWN WHAT SHE SAW AROUND HER, WHAT SHE THOUGHT ABOUT THOSE THINGS, WHY SHE THOUGHT ABOUT THOSE THINGS THAT WAY...
IT FEELS LIKE SHE COULDN'T STOP.
BUT AT SOME POINT SHE GAVE IT ALL UP...
DOES IT SAY WHY?
NOT EXACTLY, BUT...
HERE.

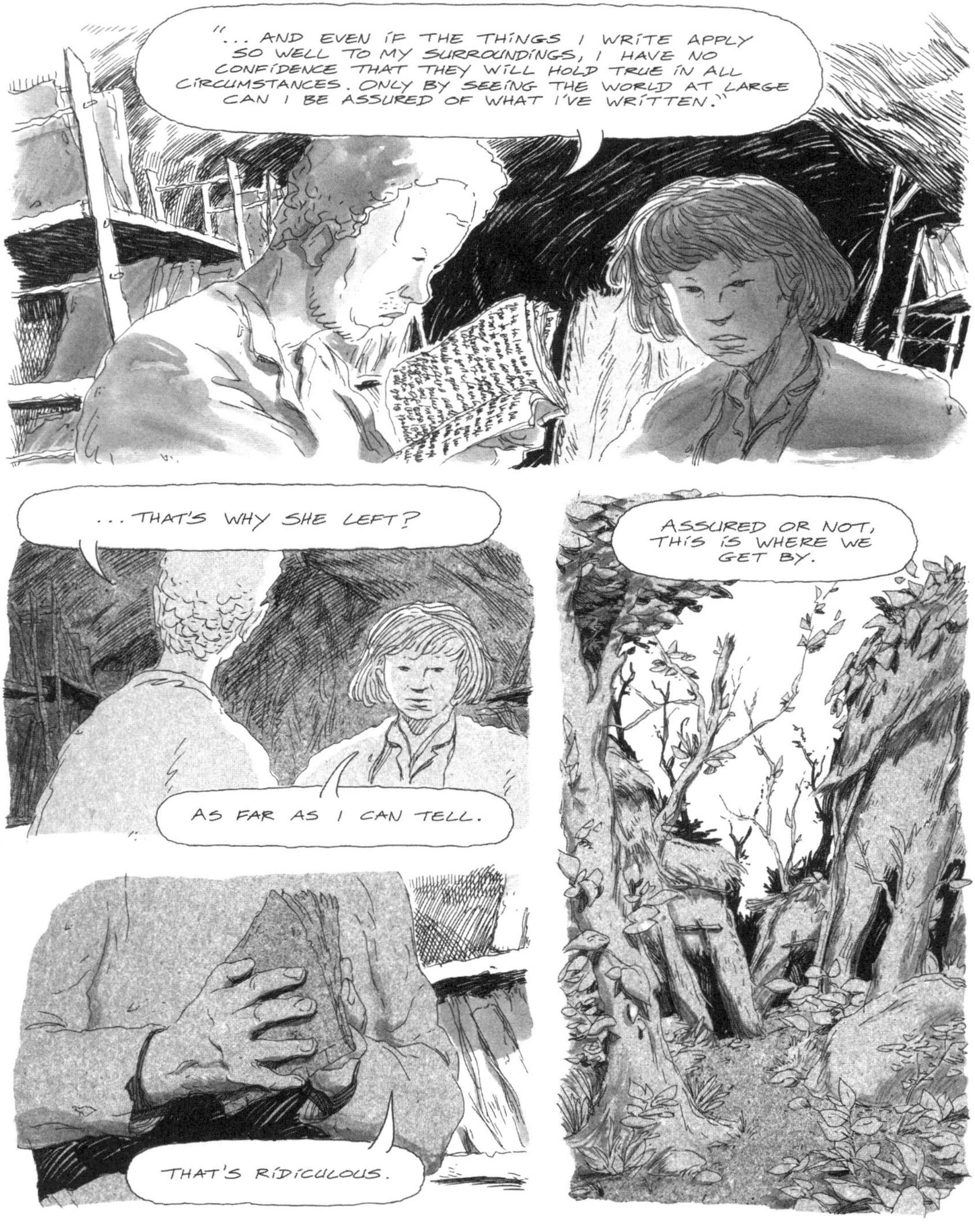
"... AND EVEN IF THE THINGS I WRITE APPLY SO WELL TO MY SURROUNDINGS, I HAVE NO CONFIDENCE THAT THEY WILL HOLD TRUE IN ALL CIRCUMSTANCES. ONLY BY SEEING THE WORLD AT LARGE CAN I BE ASSURED OF WHAT I'VE WRITTEN."
... THAT'S WHY SHE LEFT?
AS FAR AS I CAN TELL.
THAT'S RIDICULOUS.
ASSURED OR NOT, THIS IS WHERE WE GET BY.

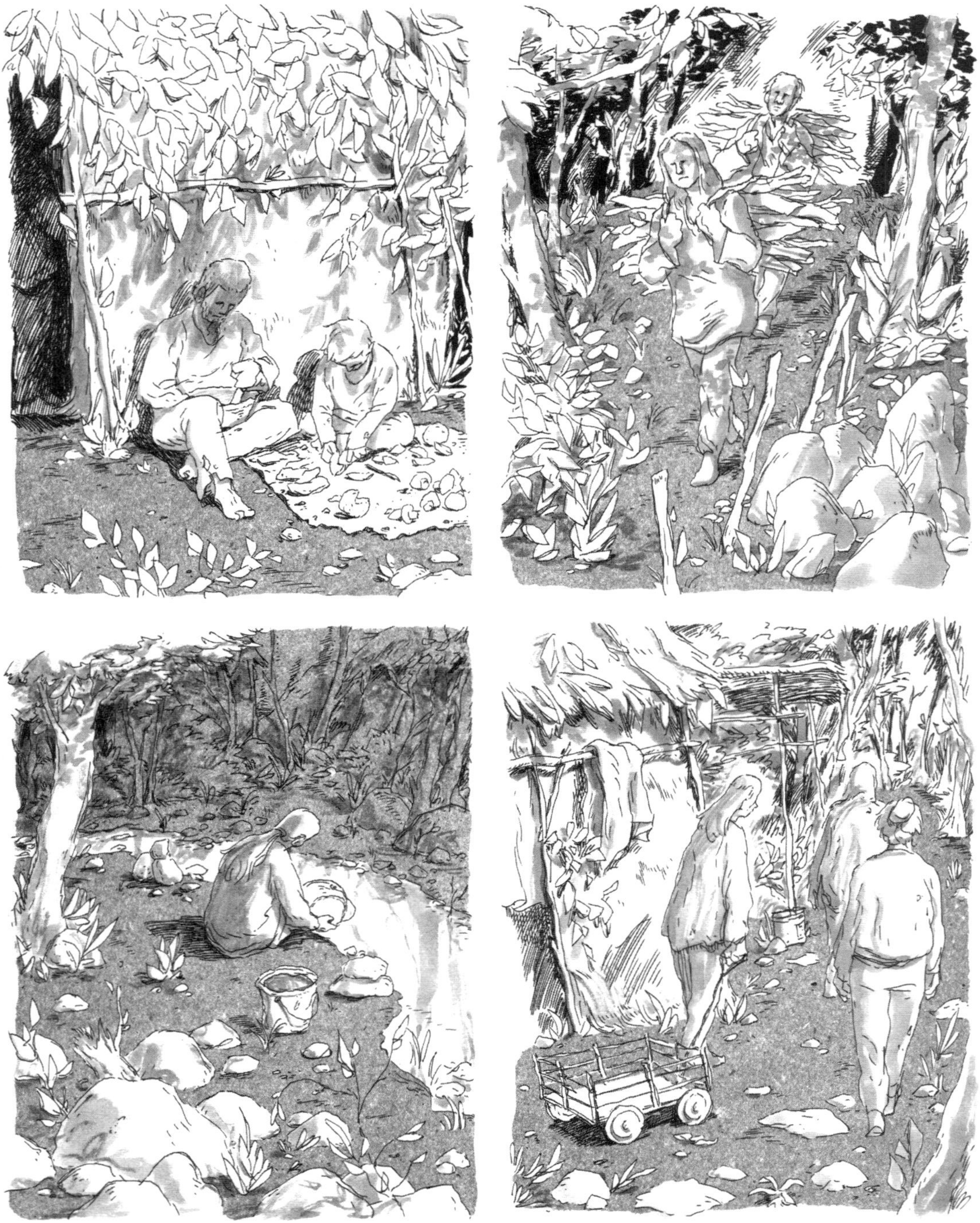

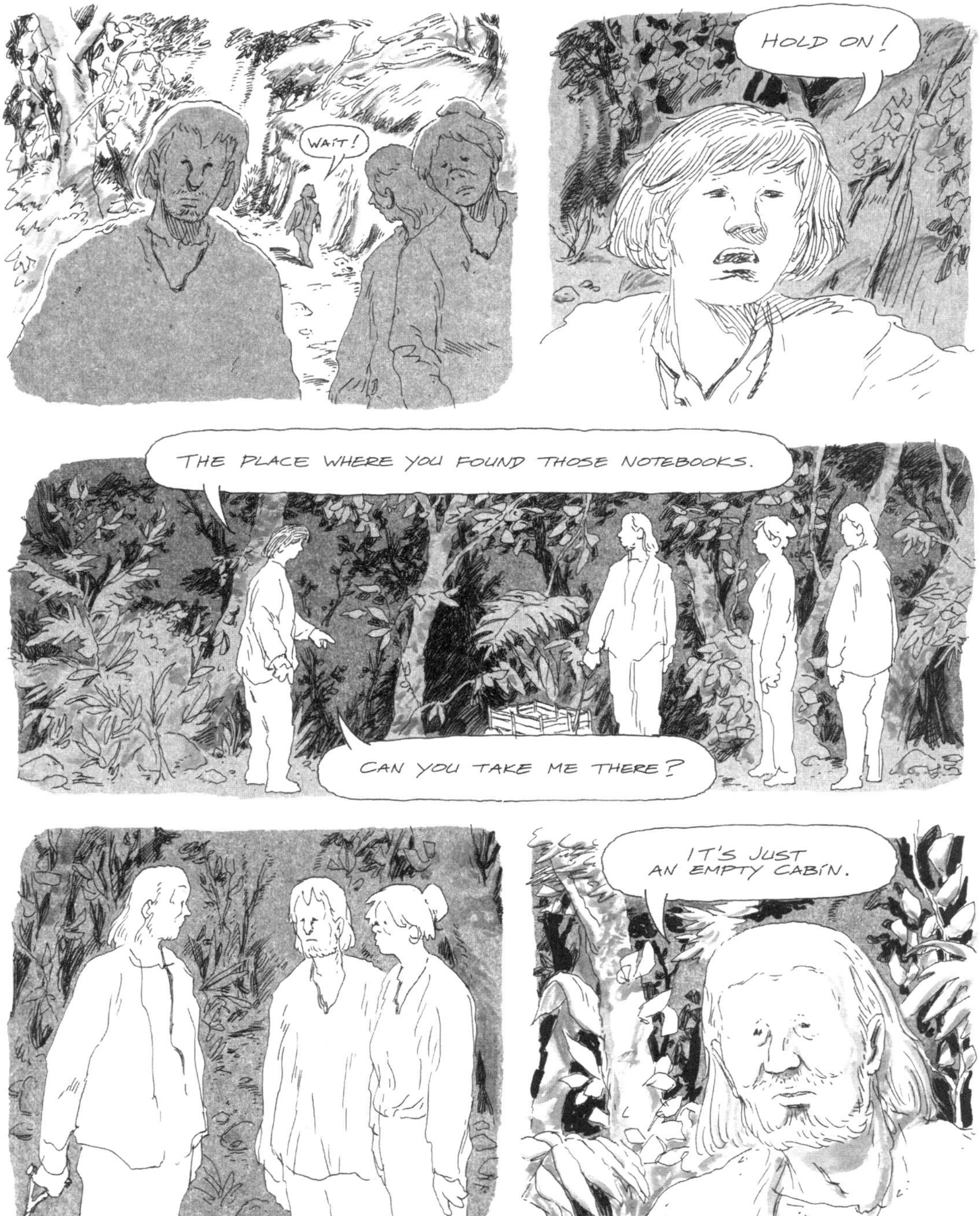
WAIT!
HOLD ON!
THE PLACE WHERE YOU FOUND THOSE NOTEBOOKS.
CAN YOU TAKE ME THERE?
IT'S JUST AN EMPTY CABIN.

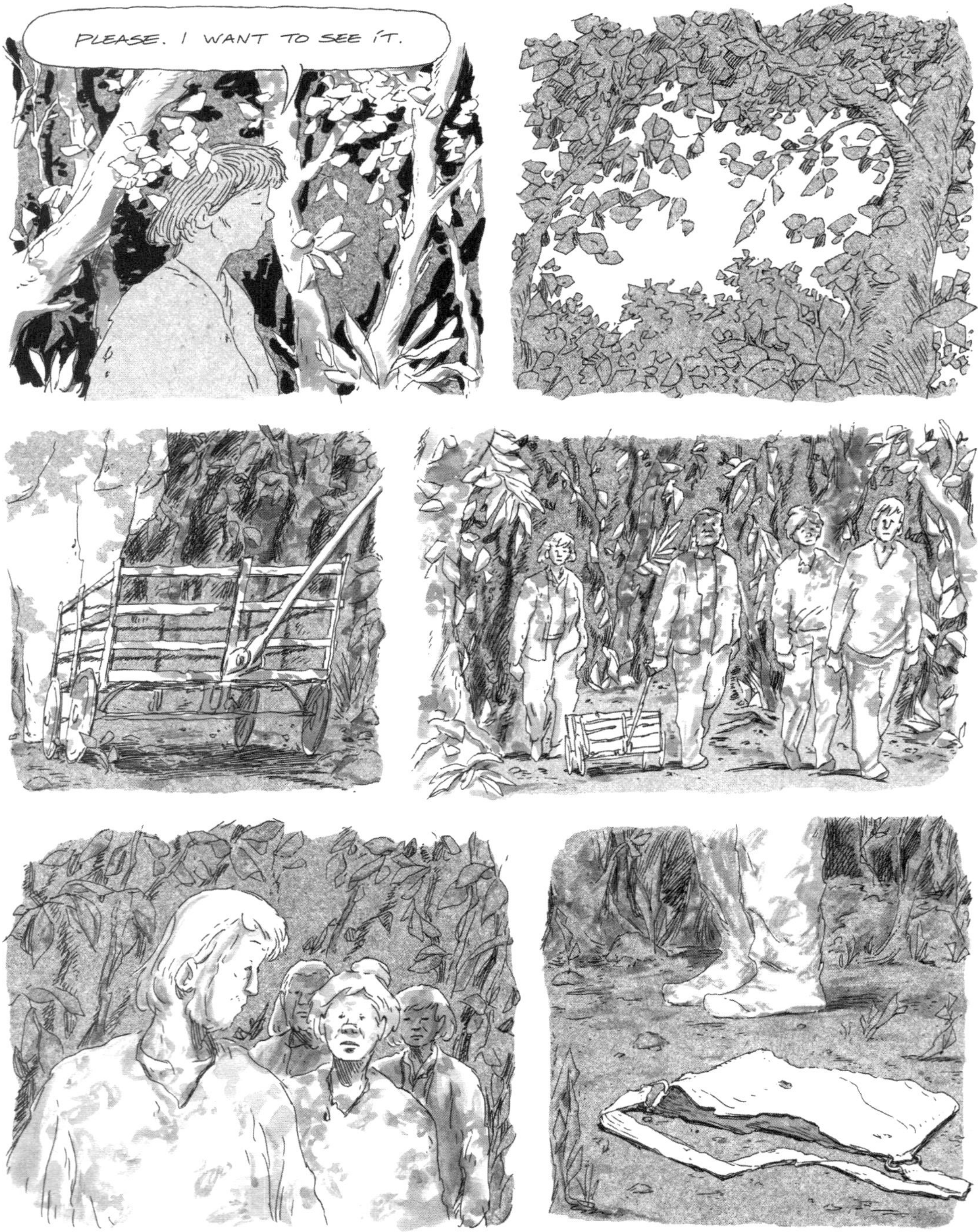
PLEASE. I WANT TO SEE IT.

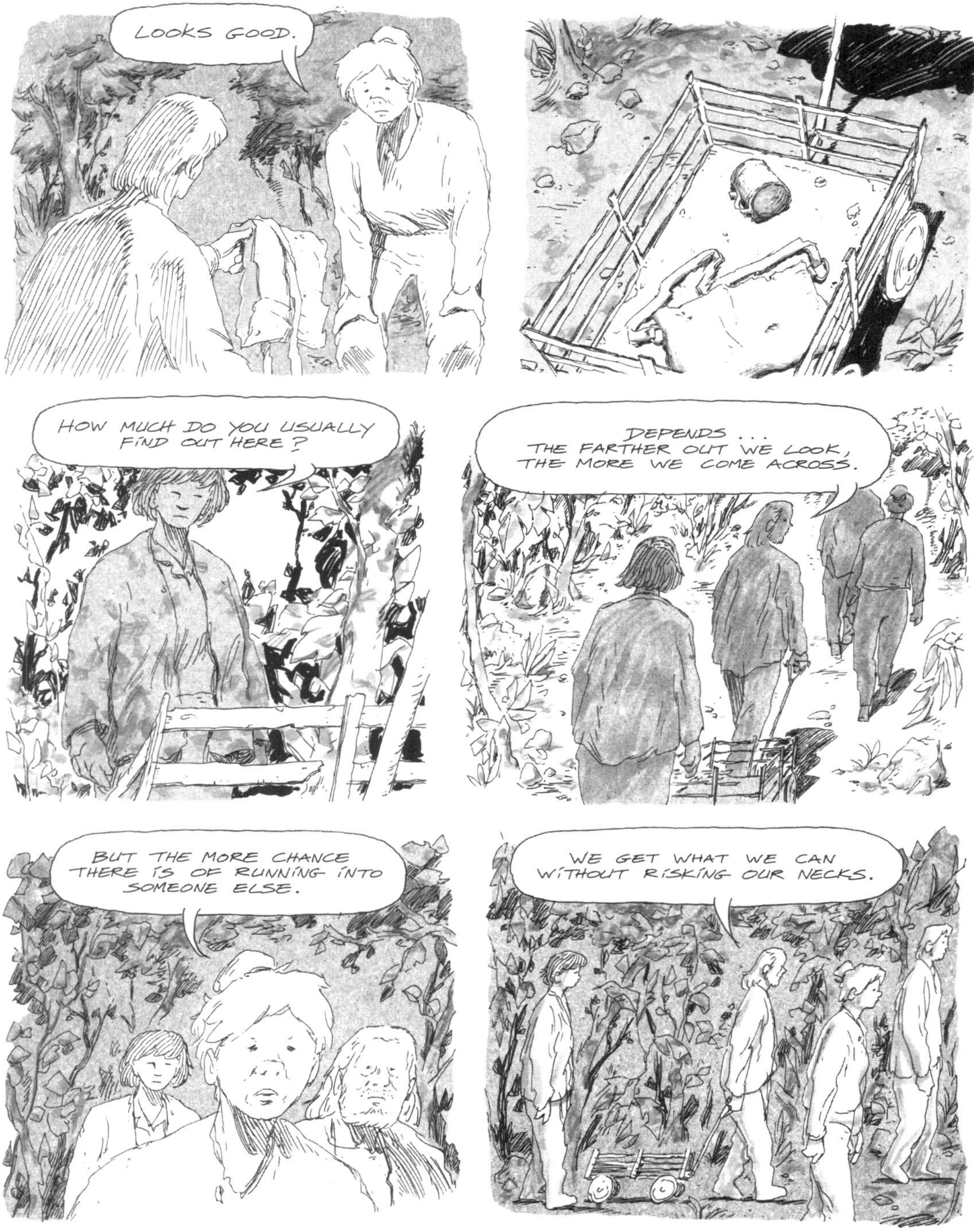
LOOKS GOOD.
HOW MUCH DO YOU USUALLY FIND OUT HERE?
DEPENDS ... THE FARTHER OUT WE LOOK, THE MORE WE COME ACROSS.
BUT THE MORE CHANCE THERE IS OF RUNNING INTO SOMEONE ELSE.
WE GET WHAT WE CAN WITHOUT RISKING OUR NECKS.

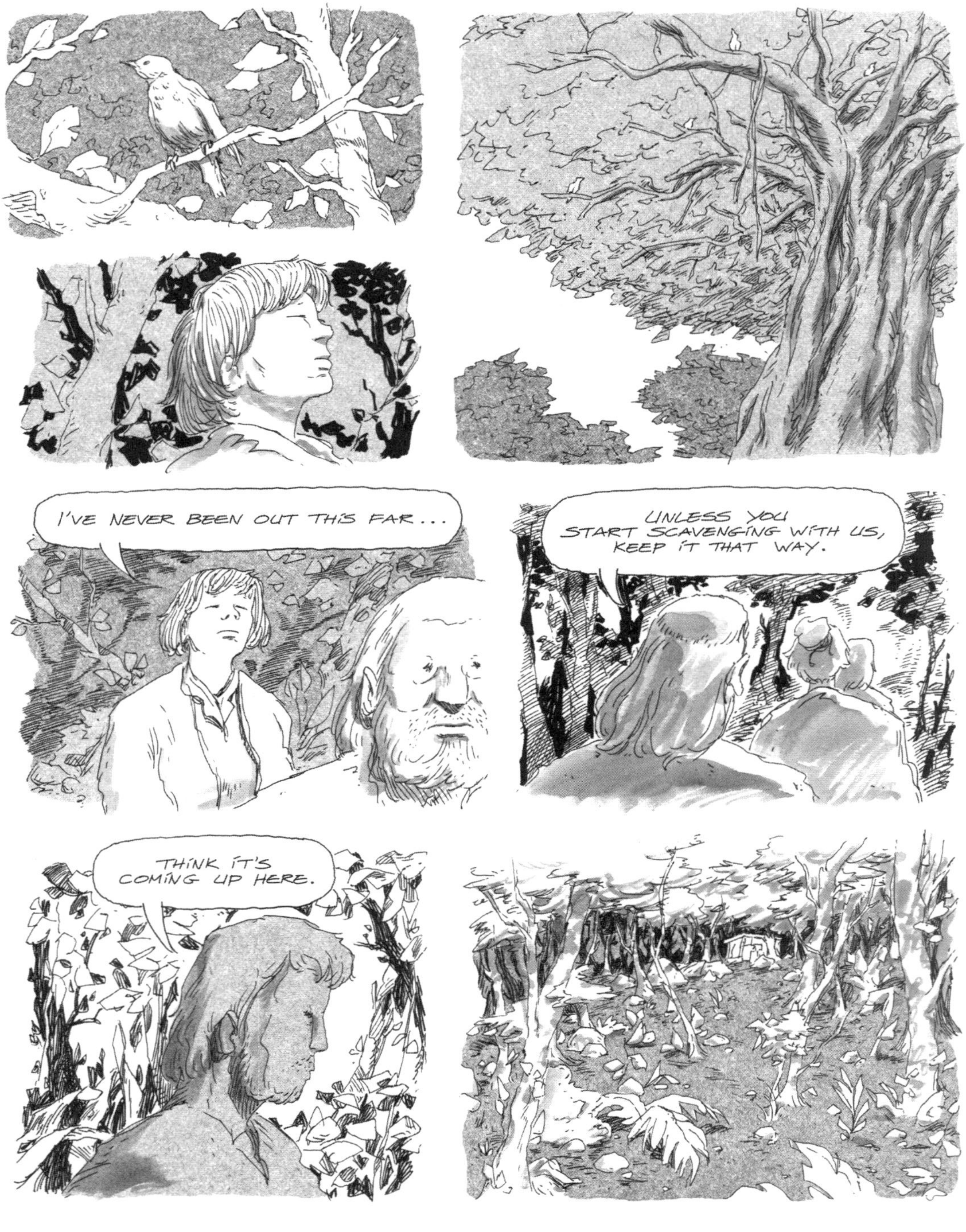
I'VE NEVER BEEN OUT THIS FAR...
UNLESS YOU START SCAVENGING WITH US, KEEP IT THAT WAY.
THINK IT'S COMING UP HERE.

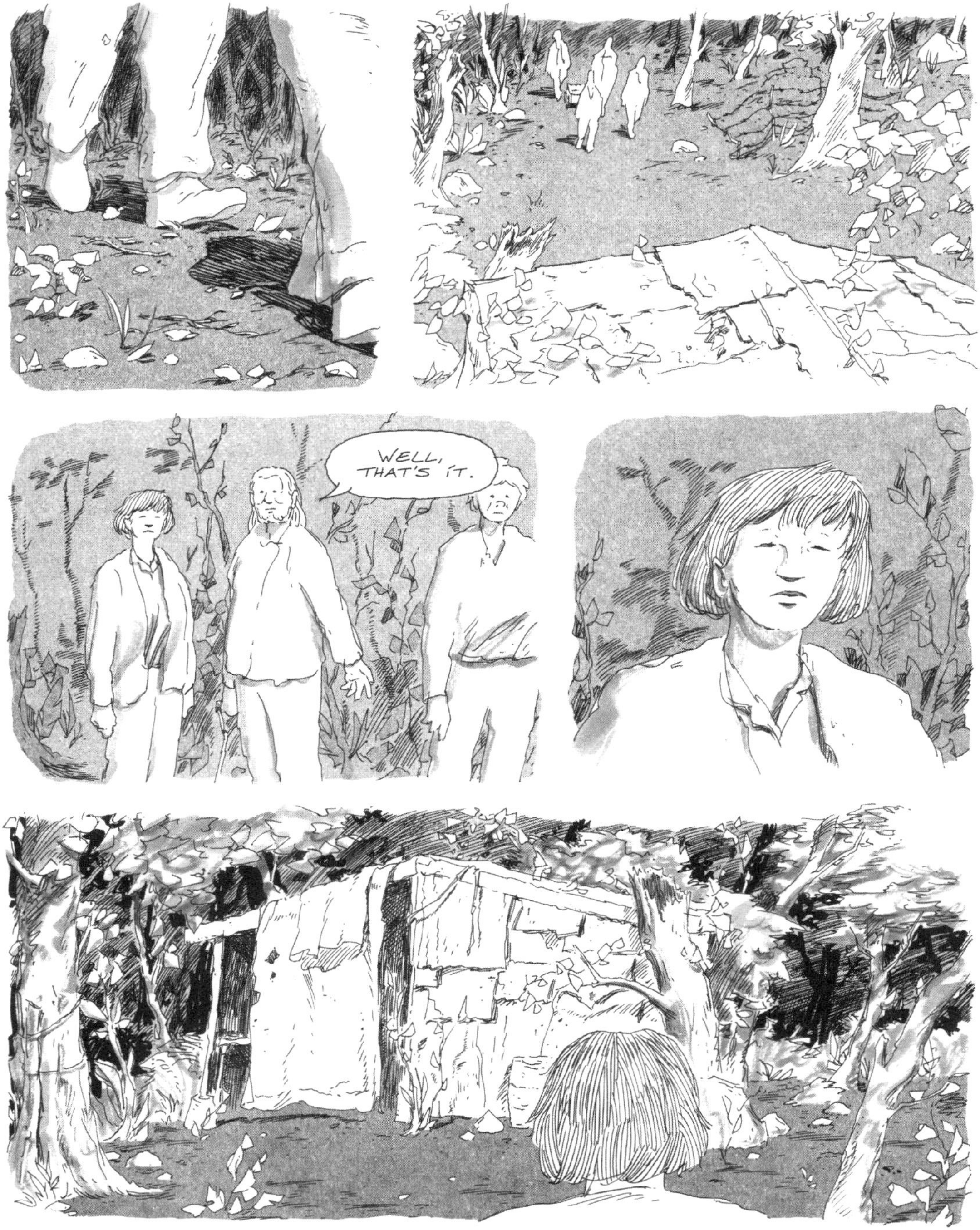
WELL, THAT'S IT.

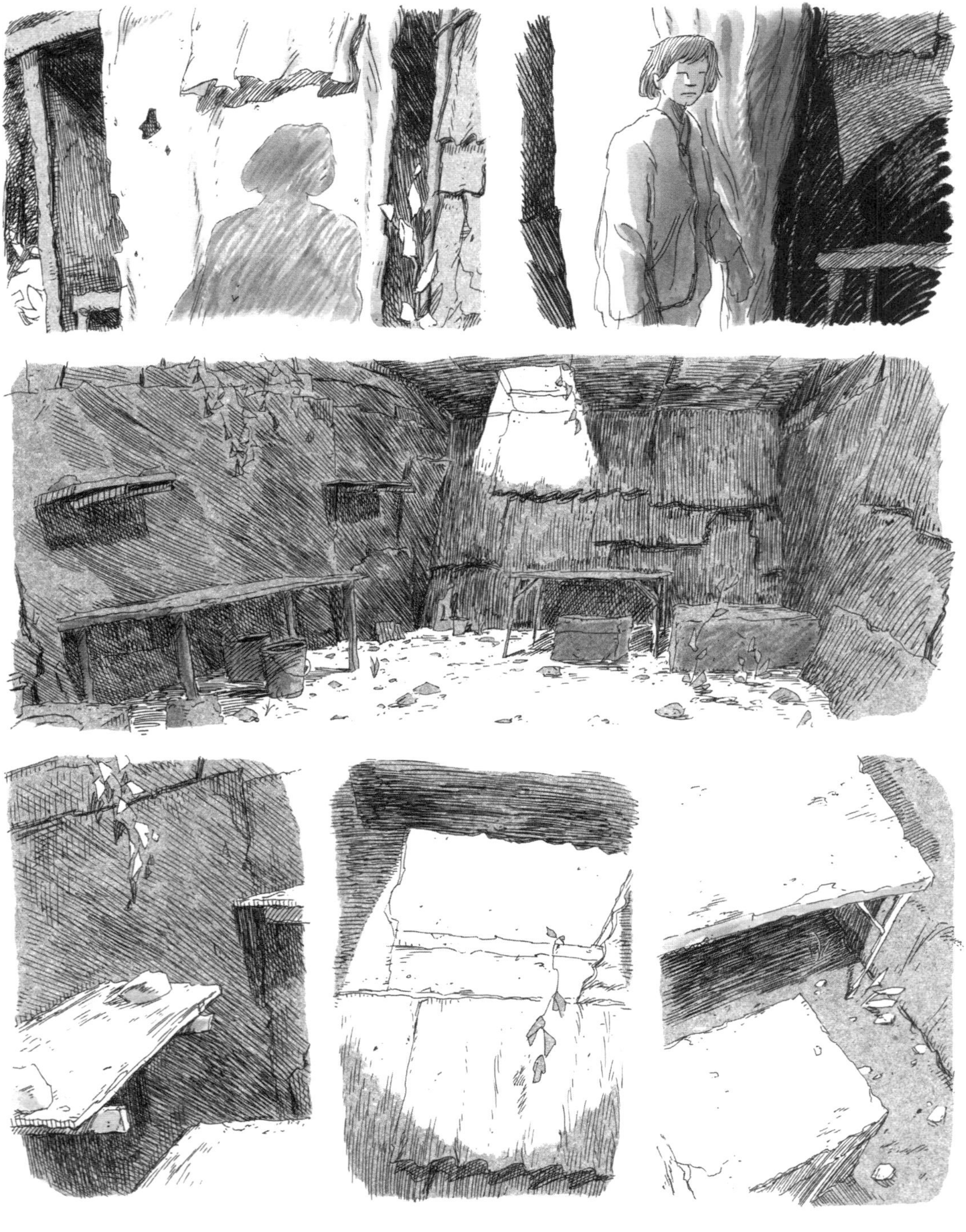

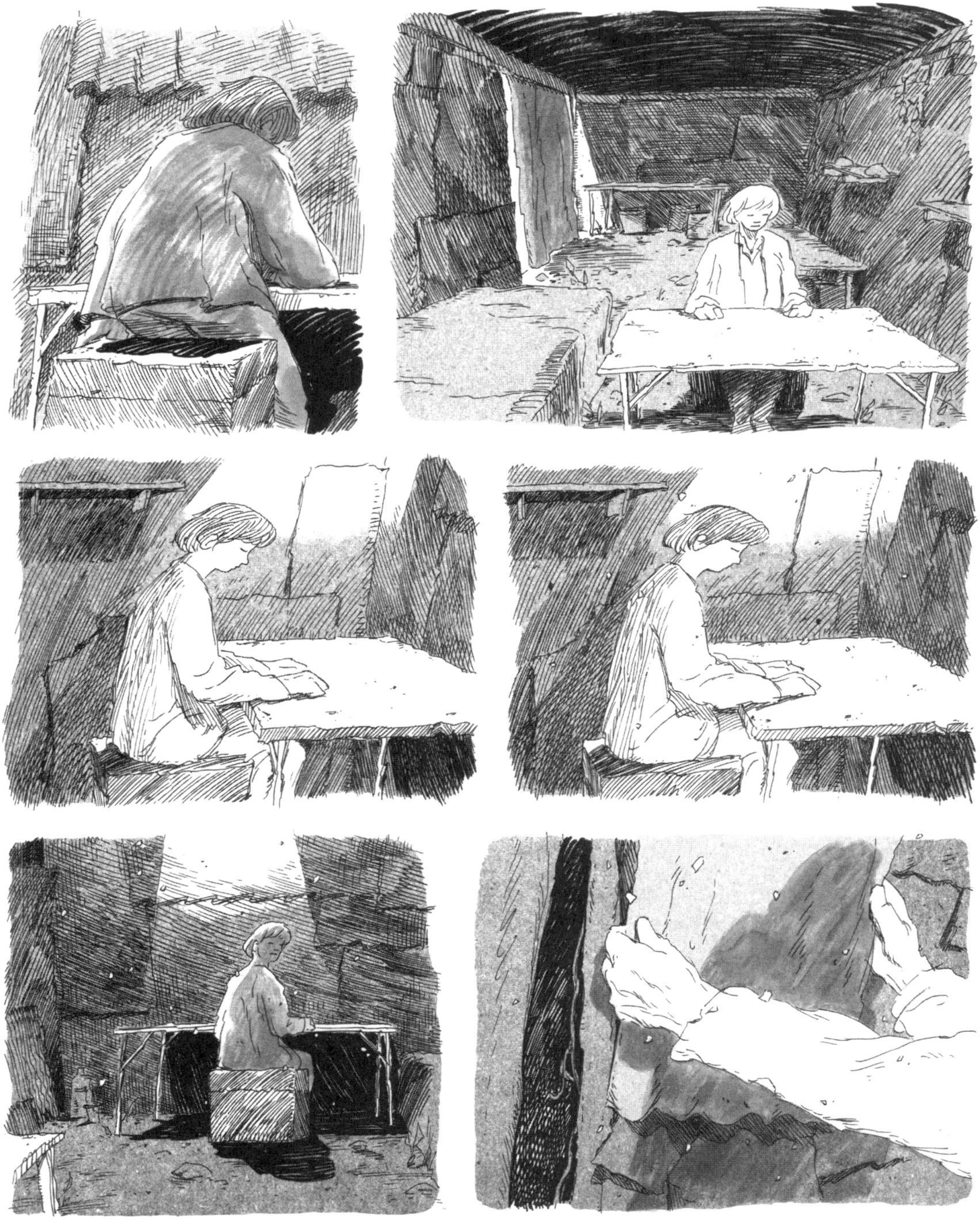

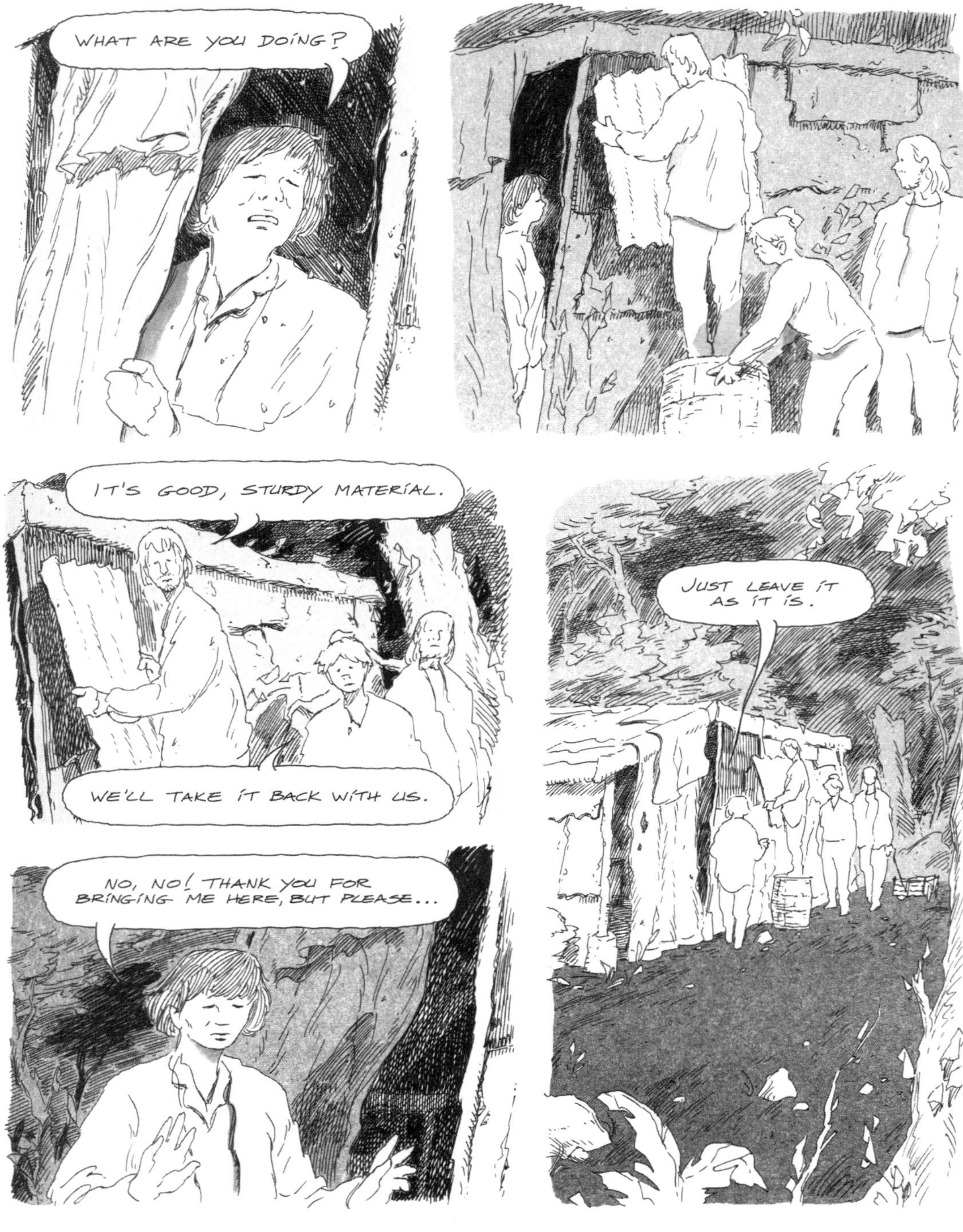
WHAT ARE YOU DOING?
IT'S GOOD, STURDY MATERIAL.
WE'LL TAKE IT BACK WITH US.
NO, NO! THANK YOU FOR BRINGING ME HERE, BUT PLEASE...
JUST LEAVE IT AS IT IS.

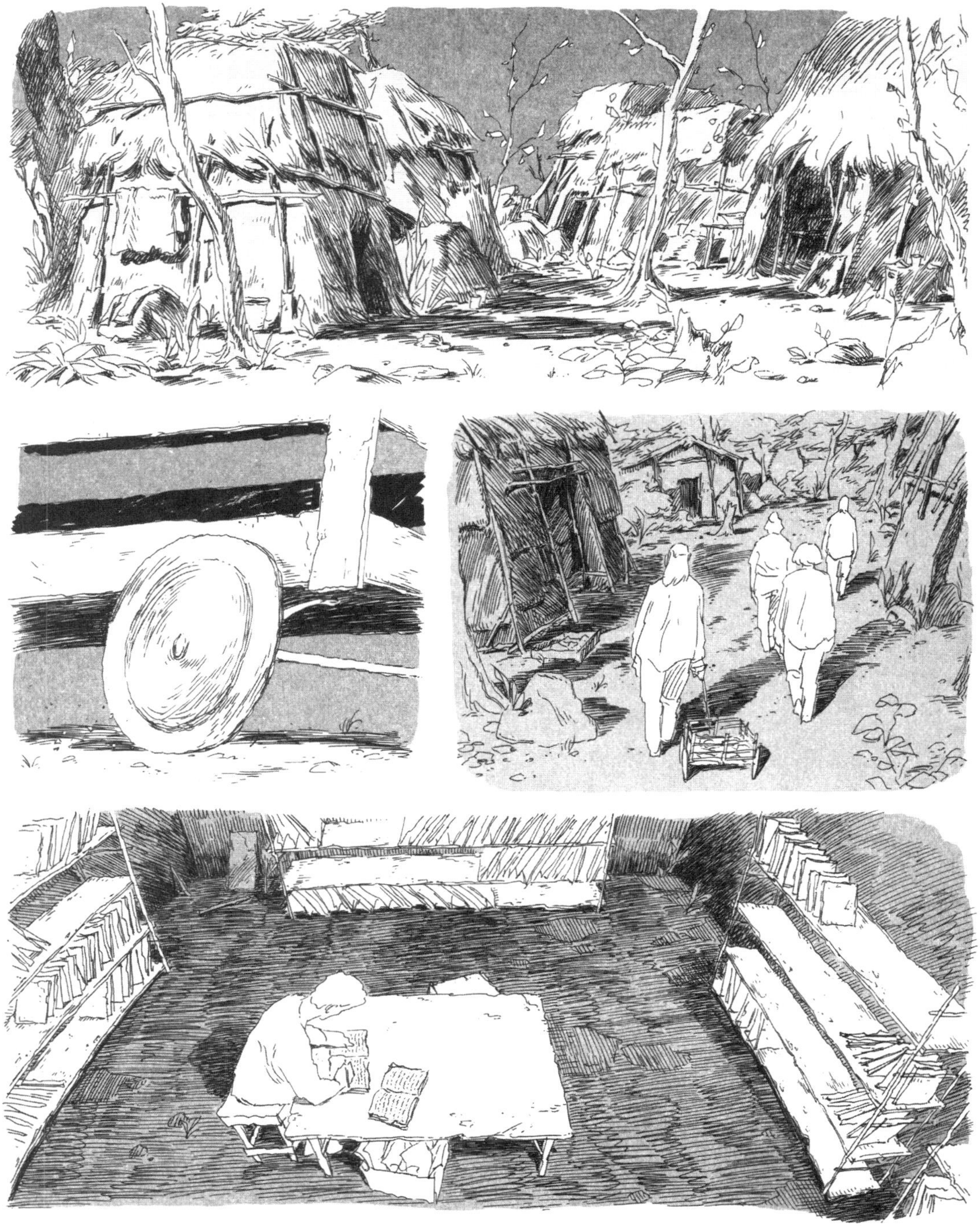

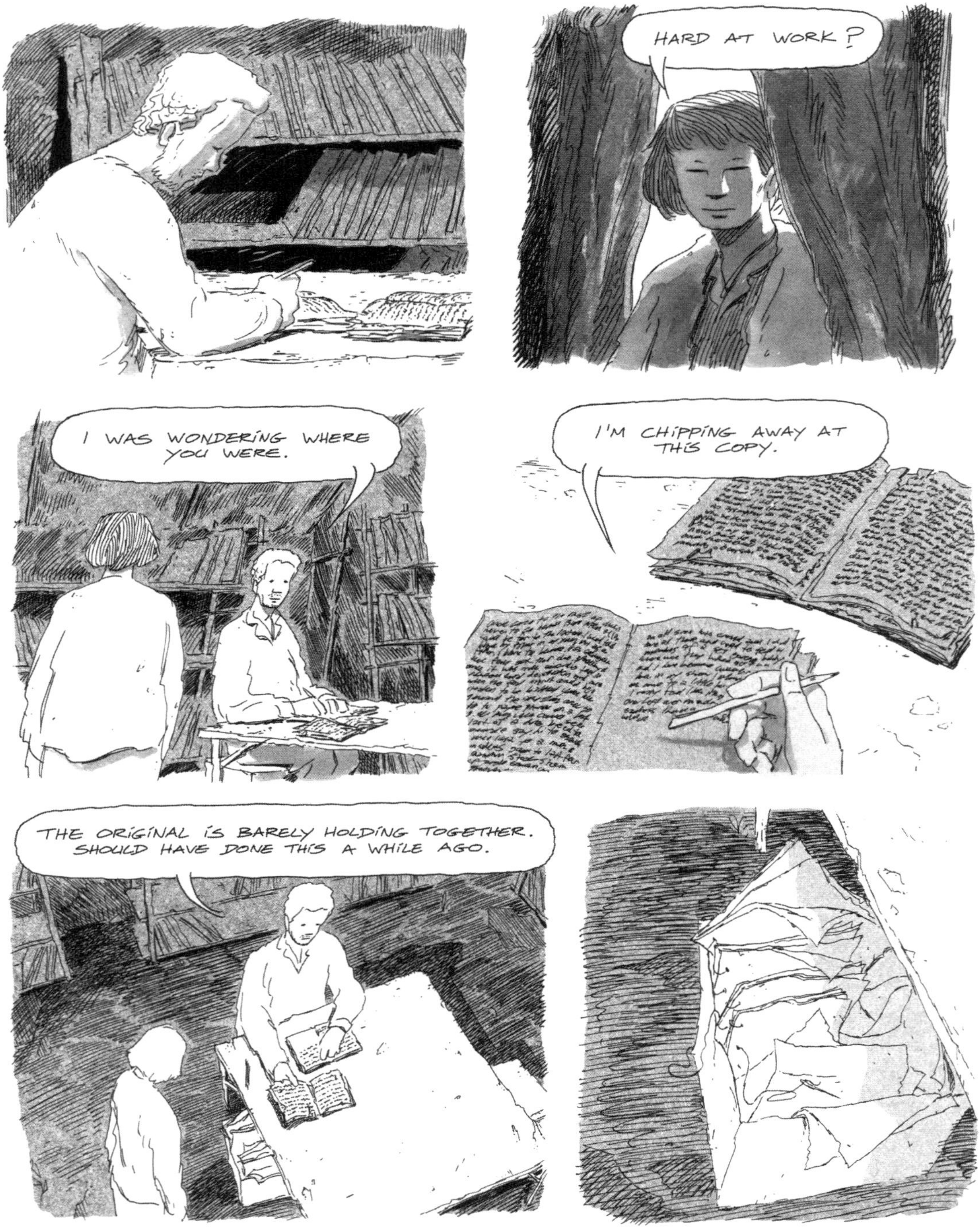
HARD AT WORK?
I WAS WONDERING WHERE YOU WERE.
I'M CHIPPING AWAY AT THIS COPY.
THE ORIGINAL IS BARELY HOLDING TOGETHER. SHOULD HAVE DONE THIS A WHILE AGO.

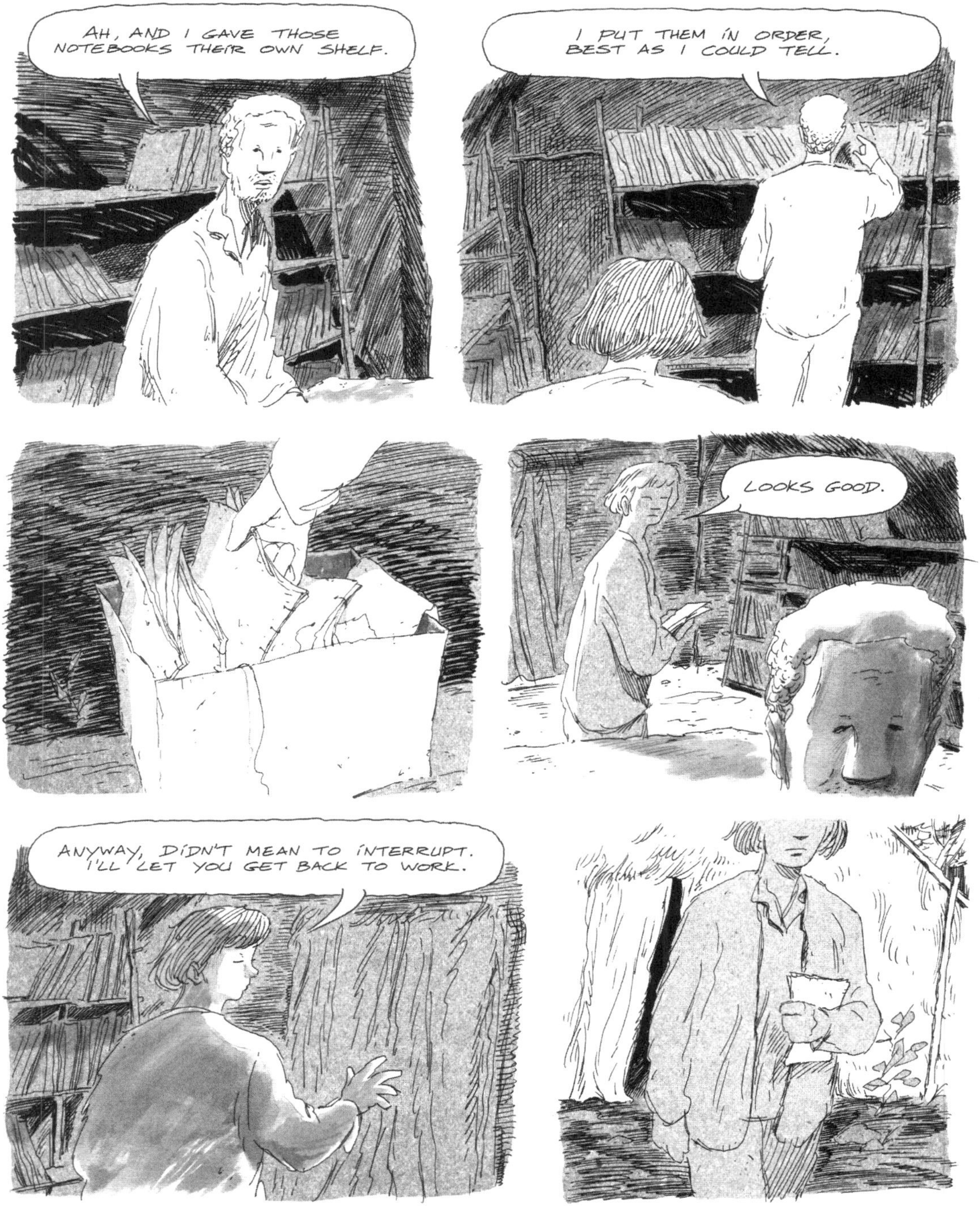
AH, AND I GAVE THOSE NOTEBOOKS THEIR OWN SHELF.
I PUT THEM IN ORDER, BEST AS I COULD TELL.
LOOKS GOOD.
ANYWAY, DIDN'T MEAN TO INTERRUPT. I'LL LET YOU GET BACK TO WORK.

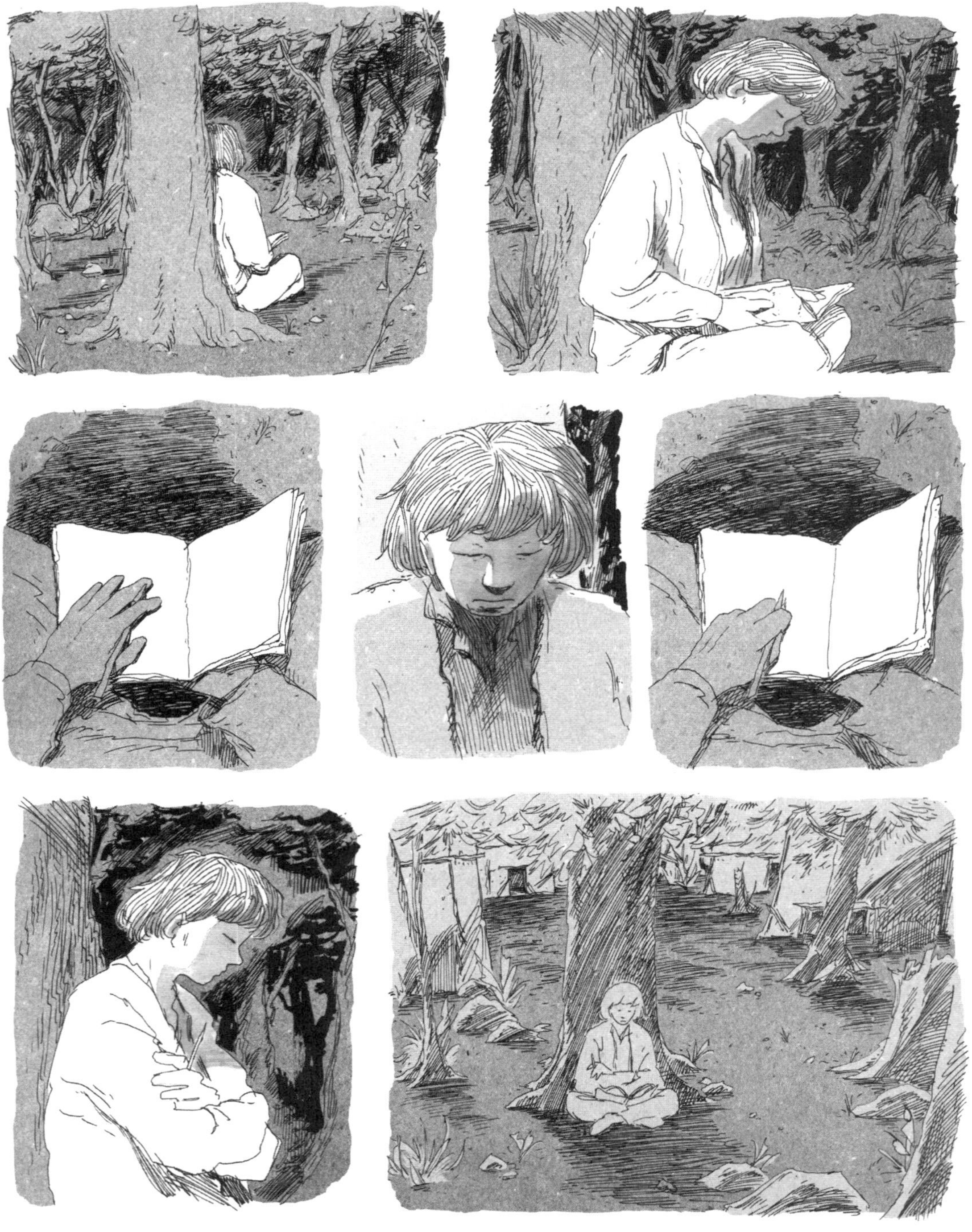

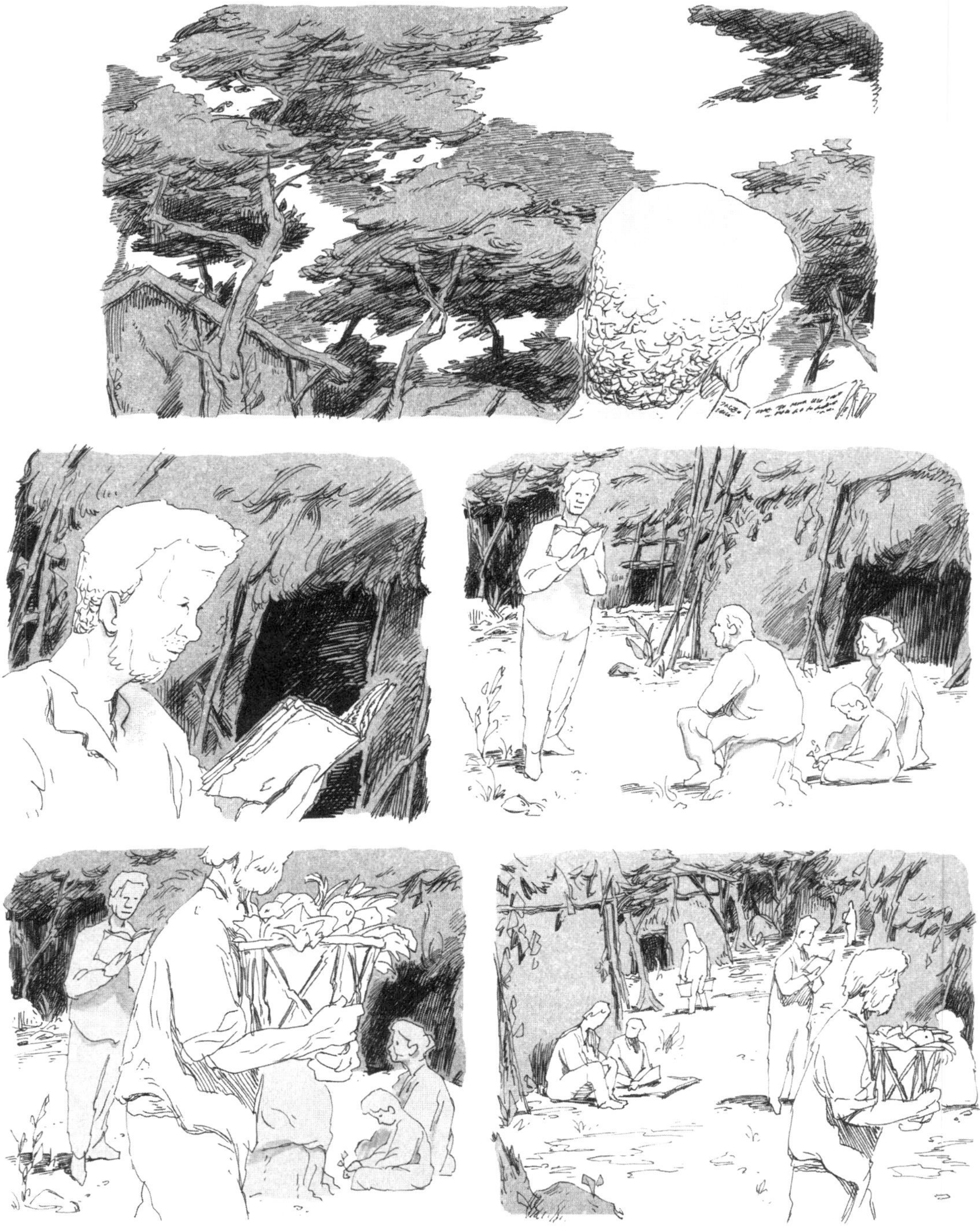

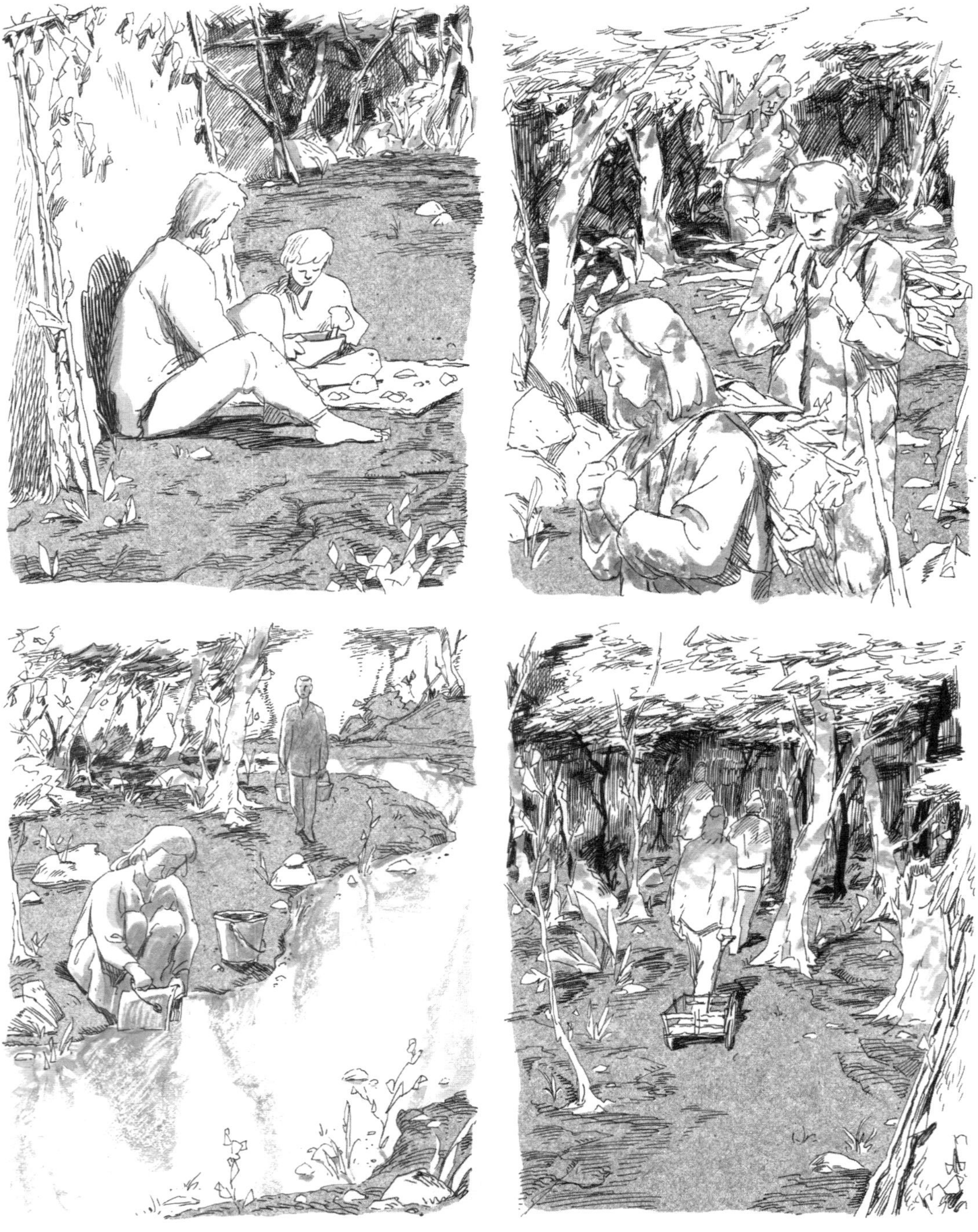

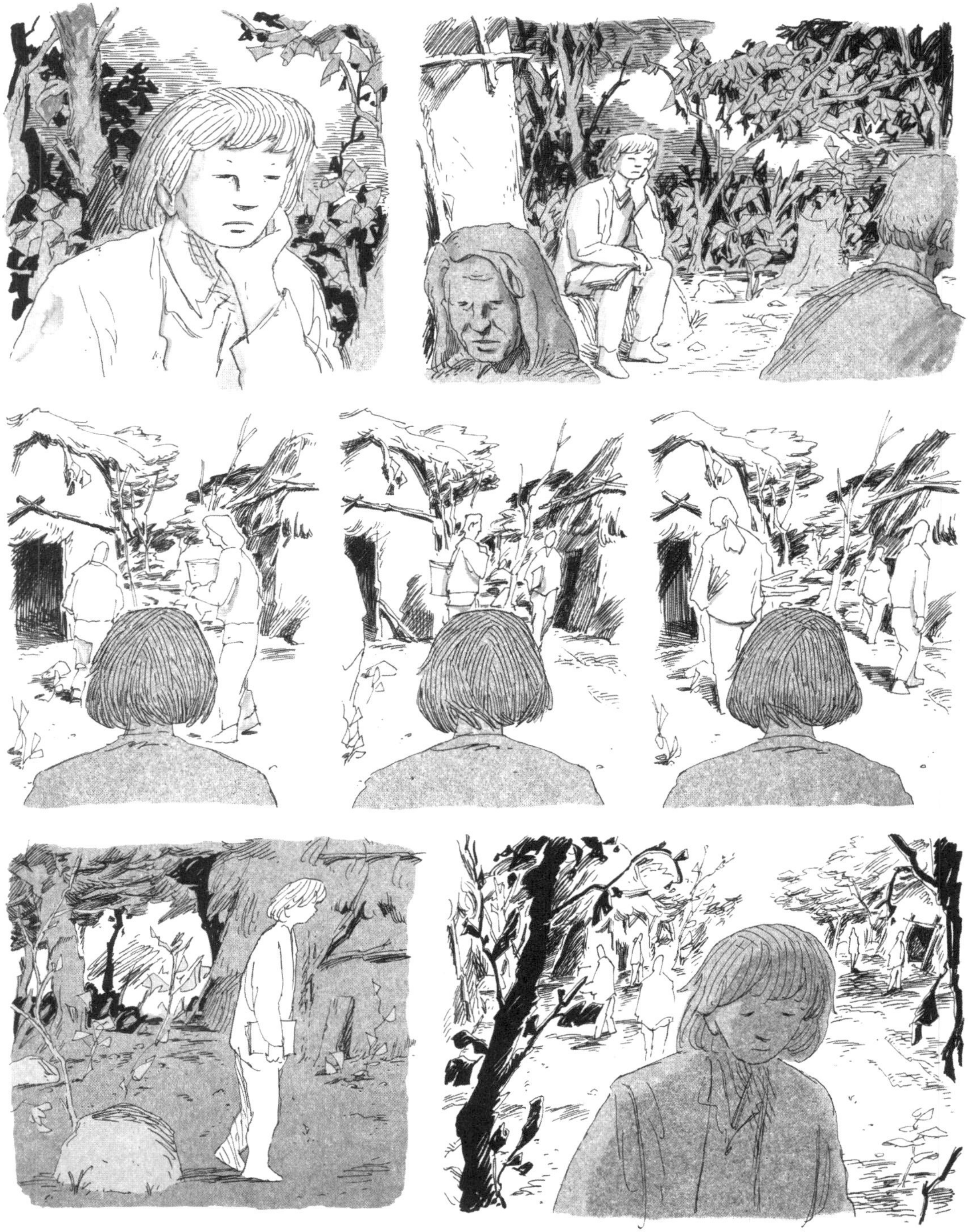

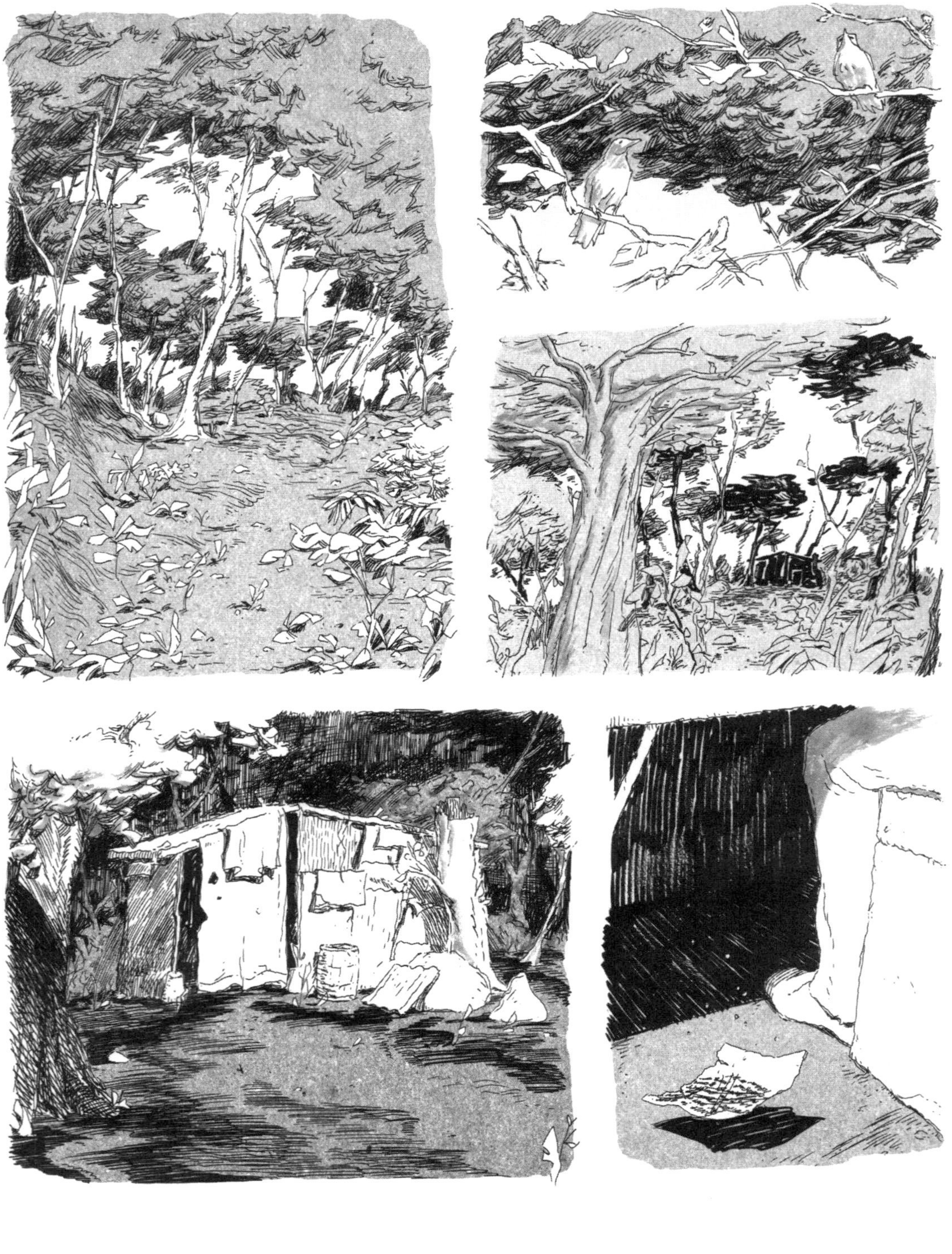

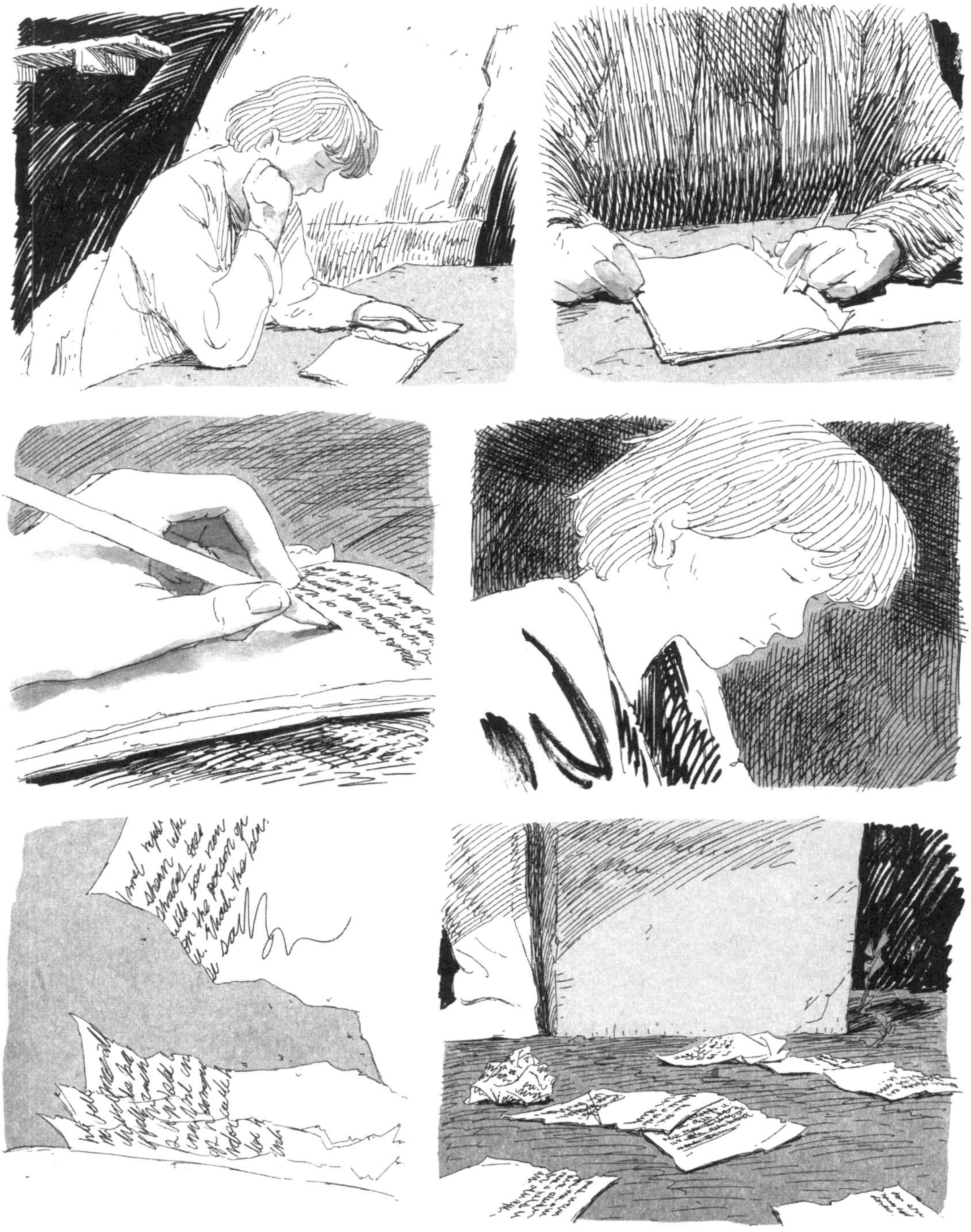

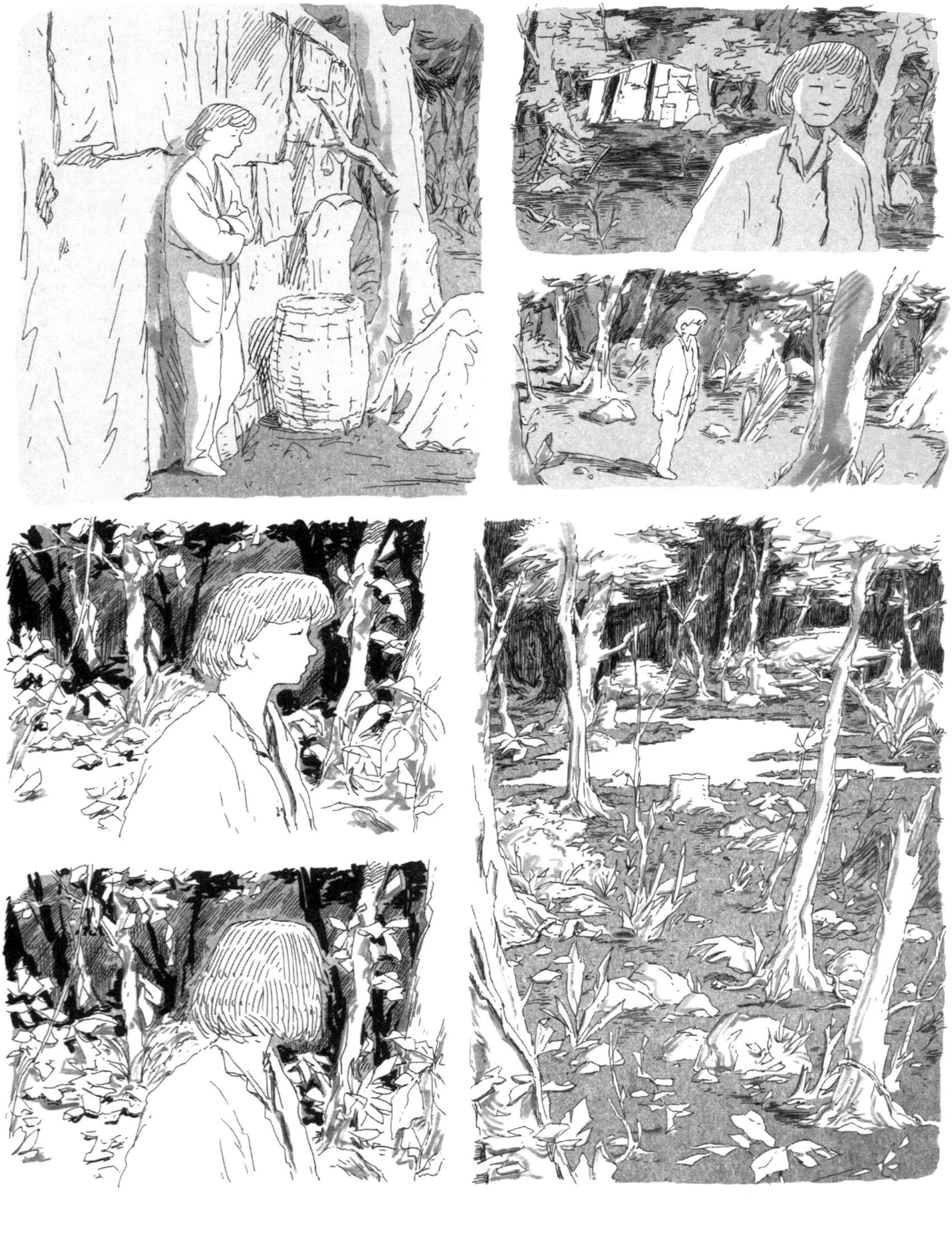

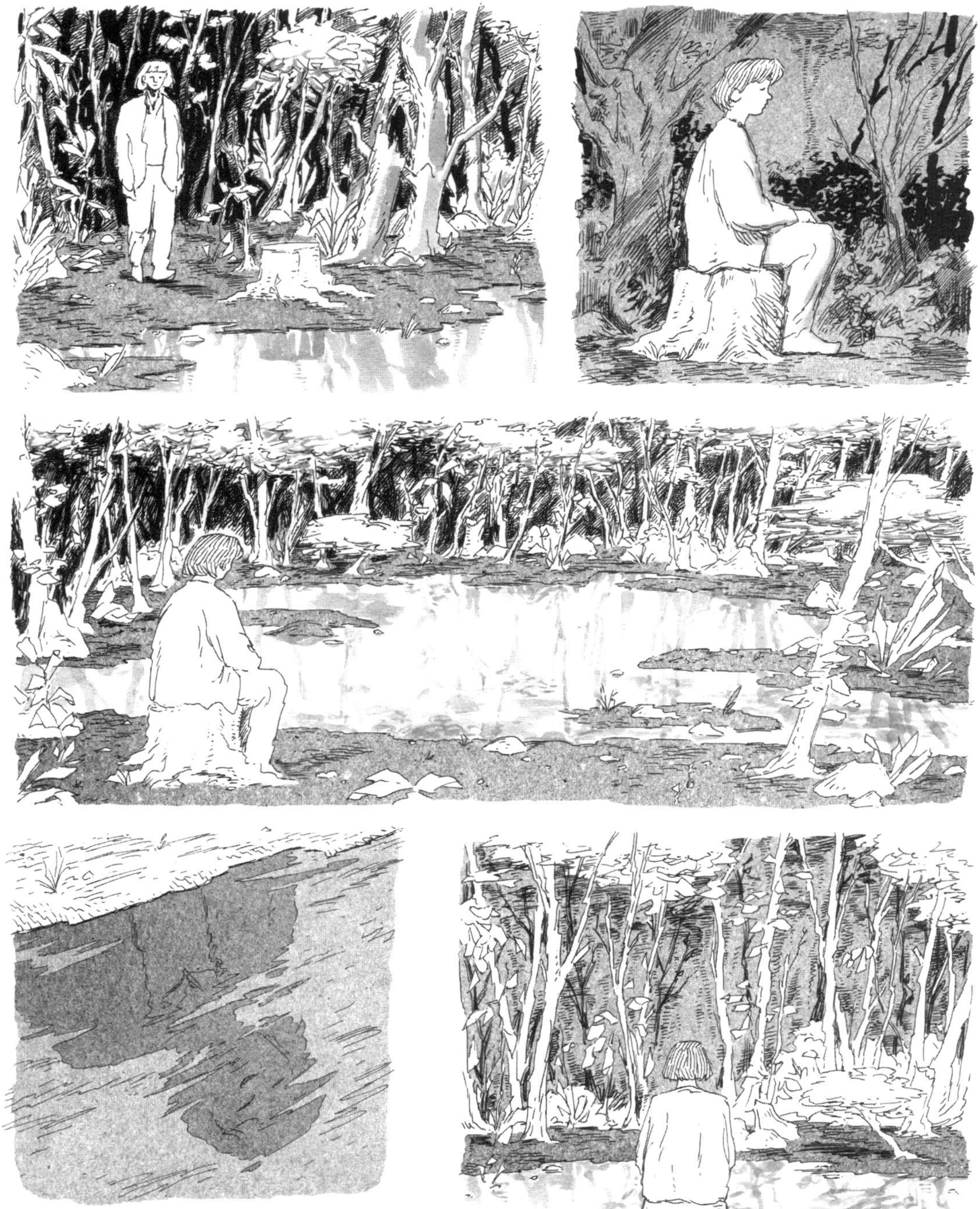

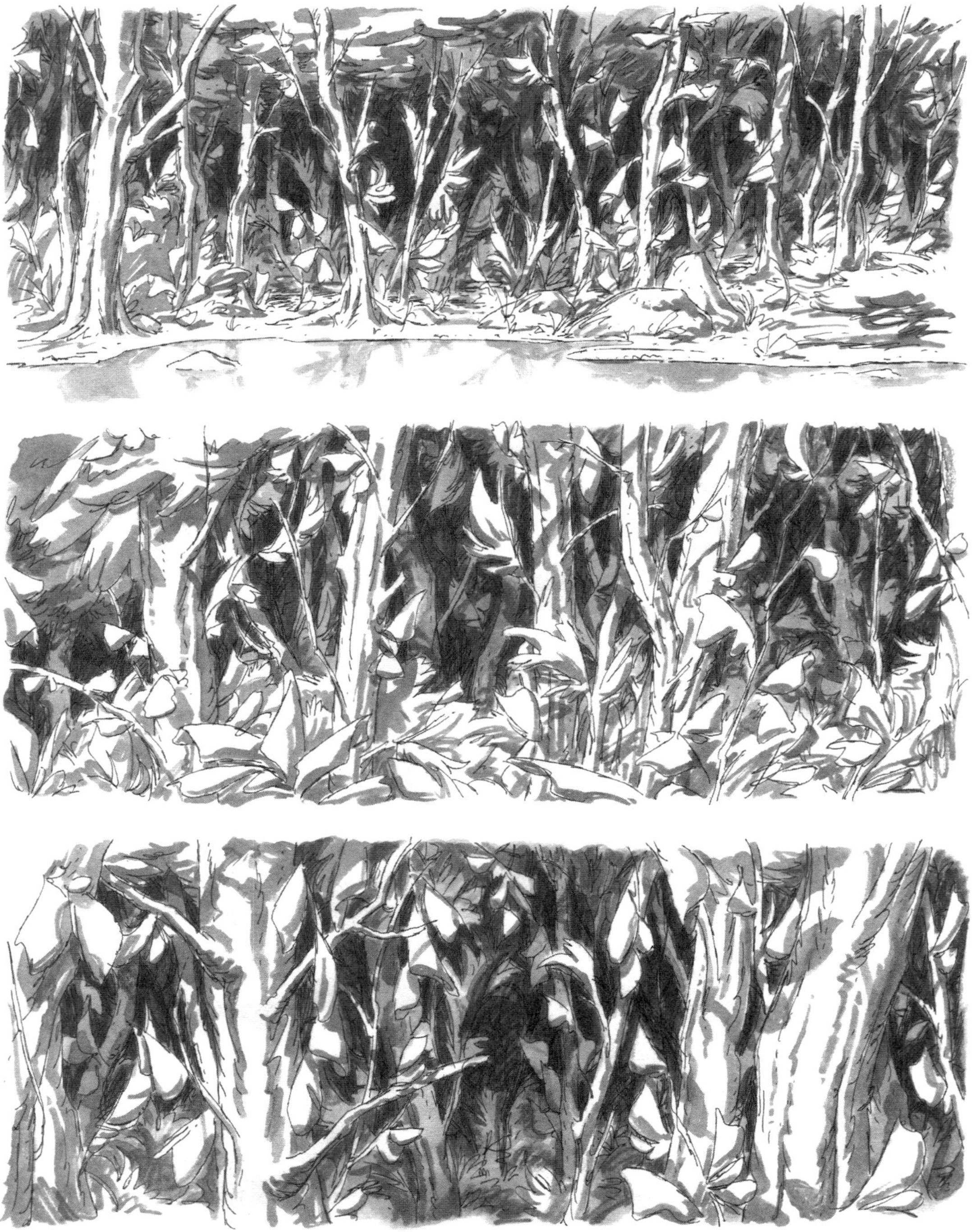

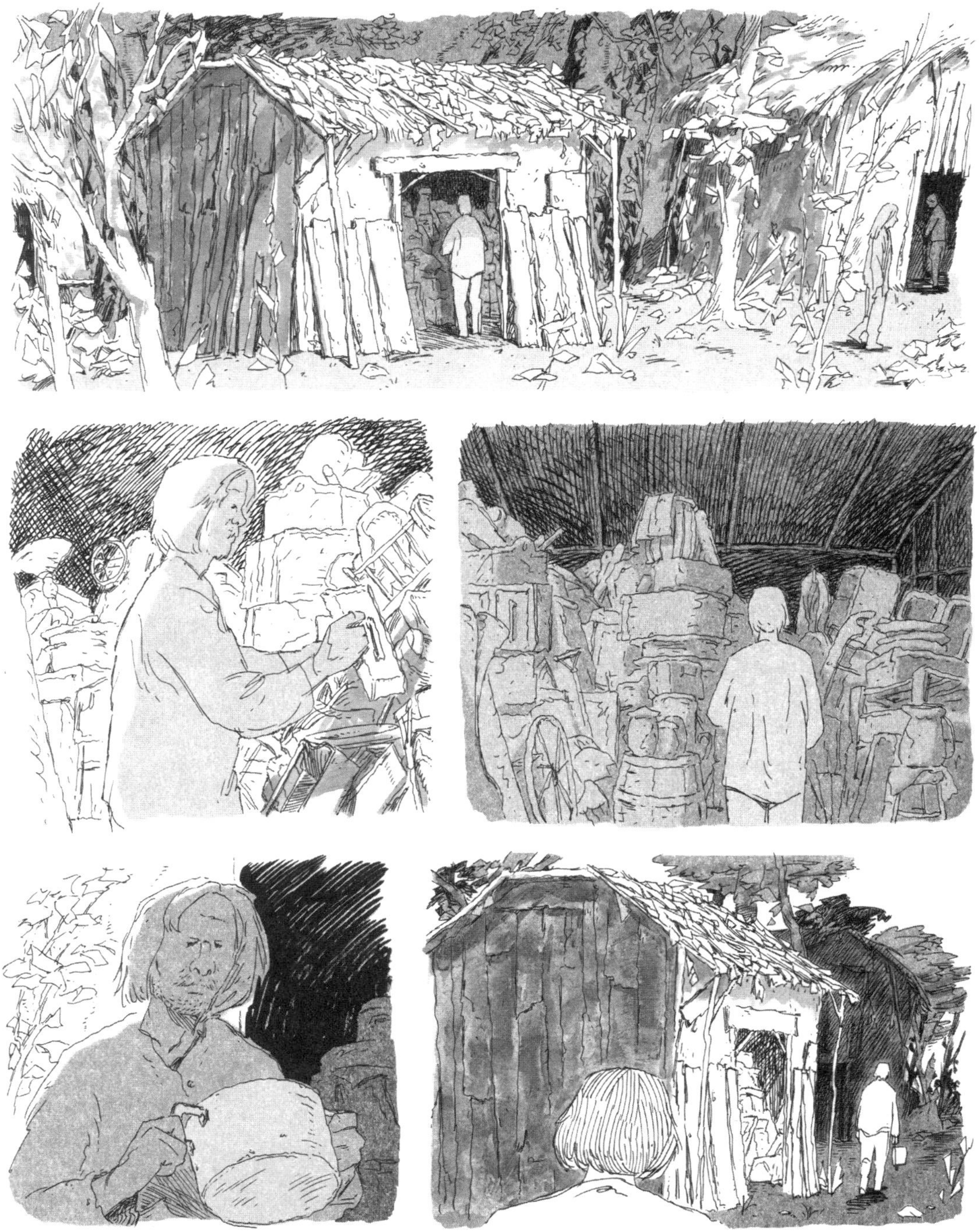

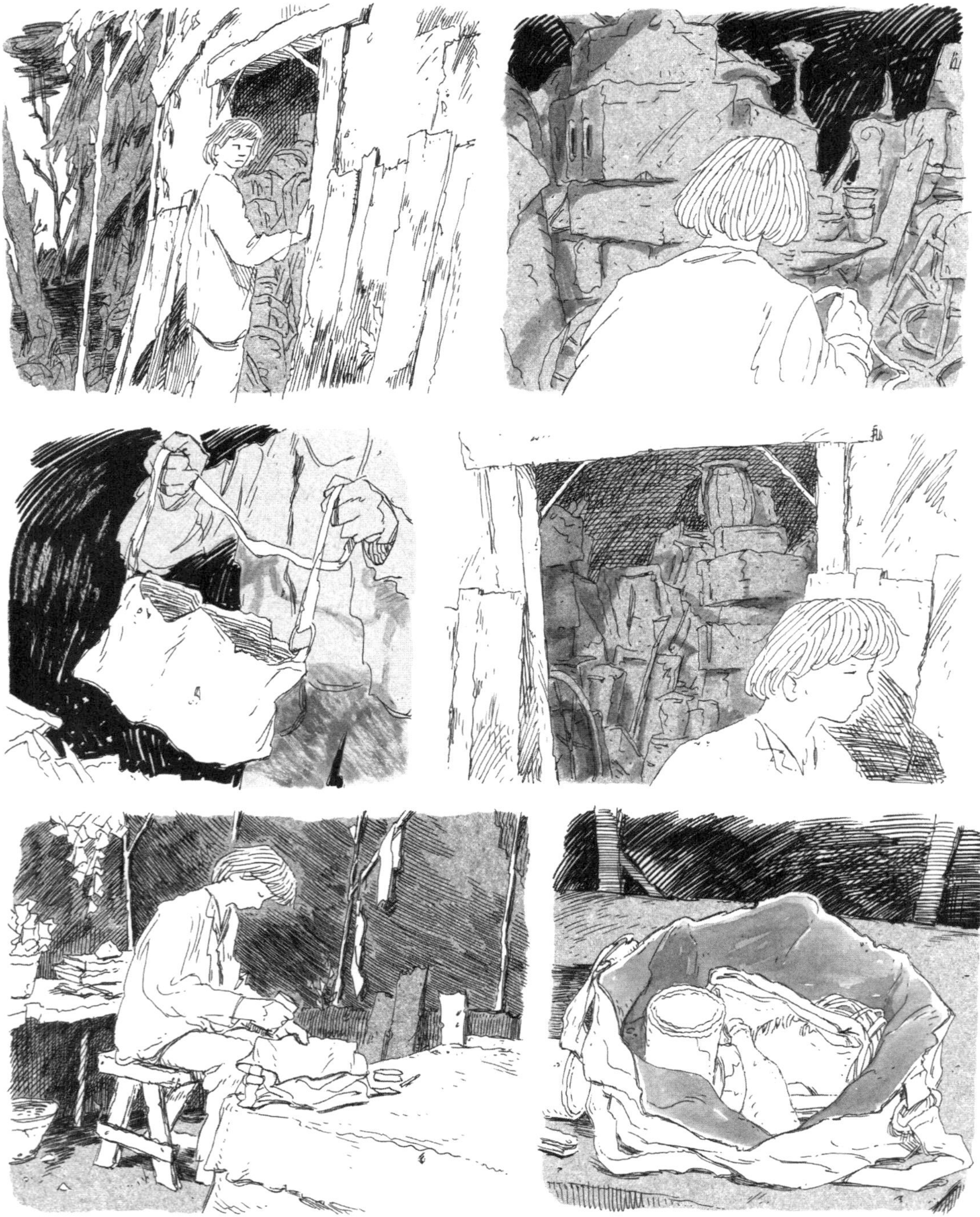

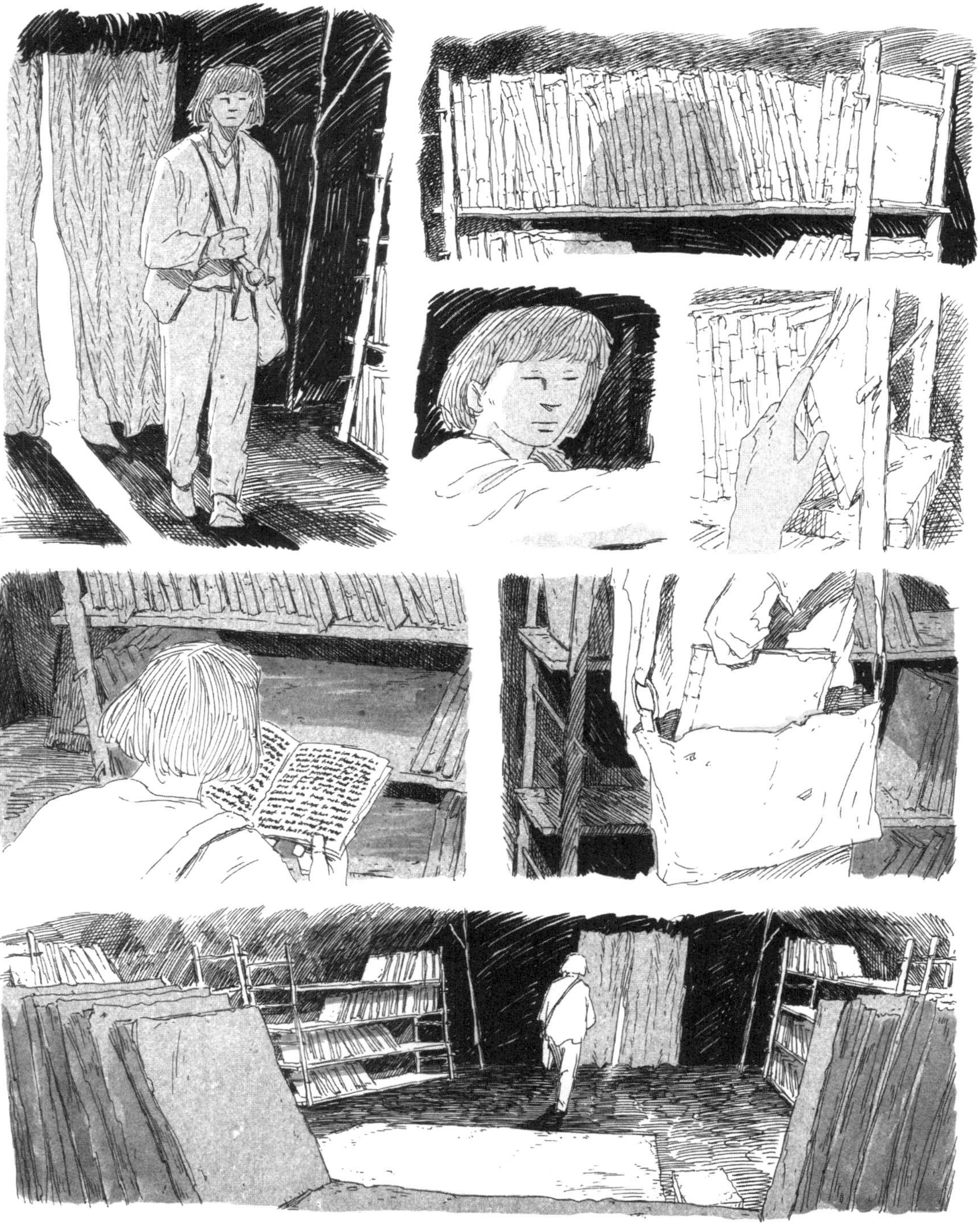

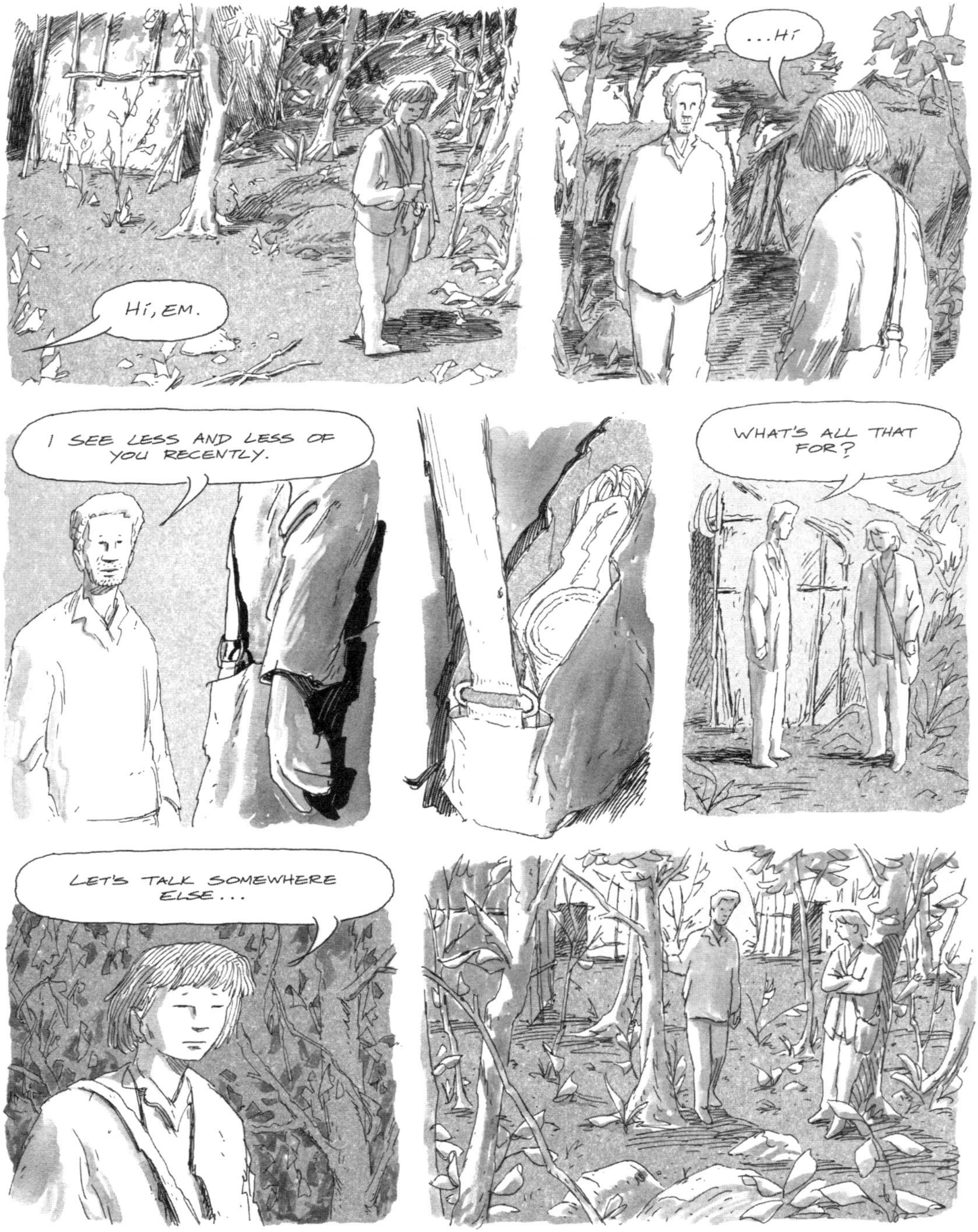
HI, EM.
...HI
I SEE LESS AND LESS OF YOU RECENTLY.
WHAT'S ALL THAT FOR?
LET'S TALK SOMEWHERE ELSE...

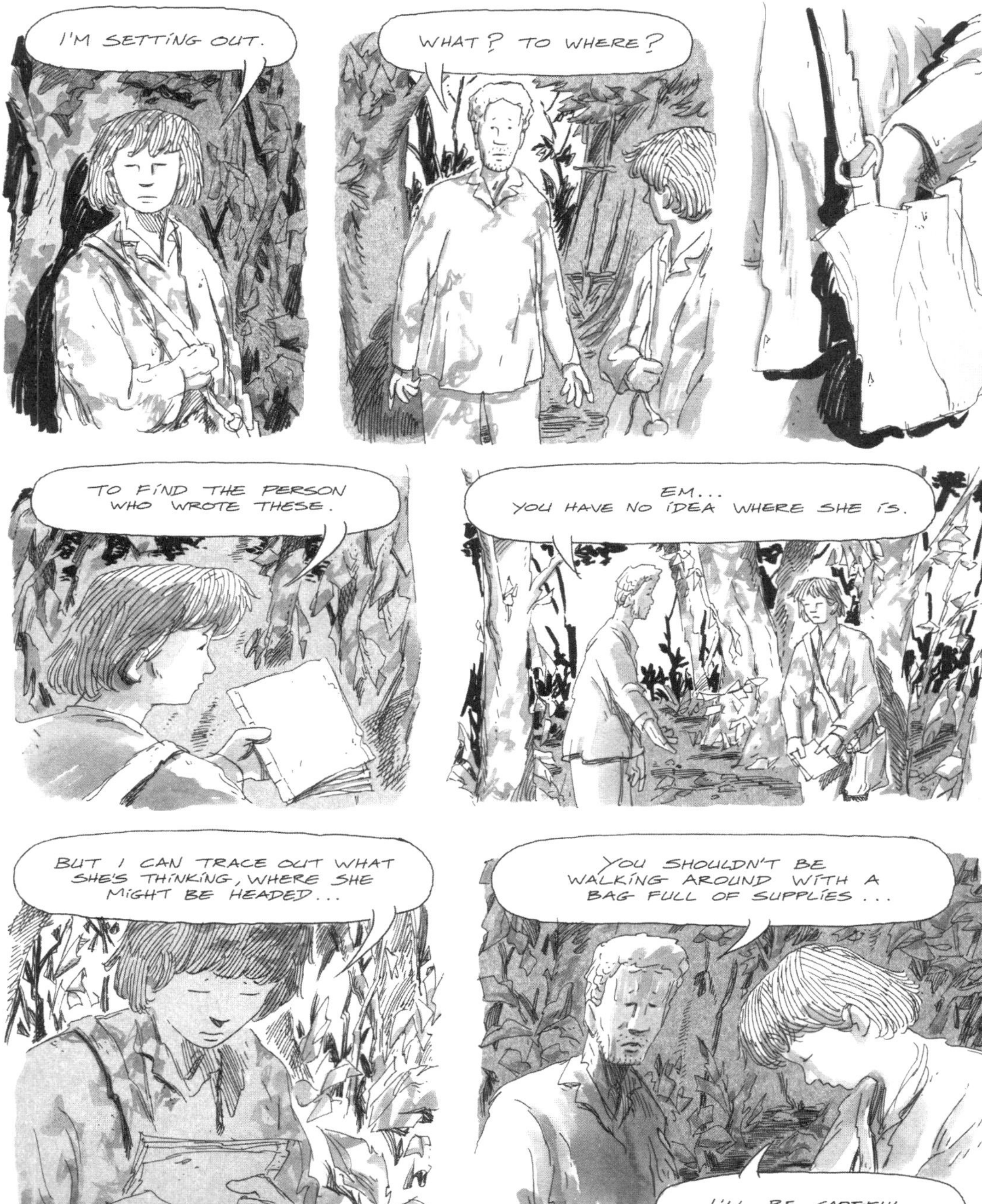
I'M SETTING OUT.
WHAT? TO WHERE?
TO FIND THE PERSON WHO WROTE THESE.
EM... YOU HAVE NO IDEA WHERE SHE IS.
BUT I CAN TRACE OUT WHAT SHE'S THINKING, WHERE SHE MIGHT BE HEADED...
YOU SHOULDN'T BE WALKING AROUND WITH A BAG FULL OF SUPPLIES...
I'LL BE CAREFUL.

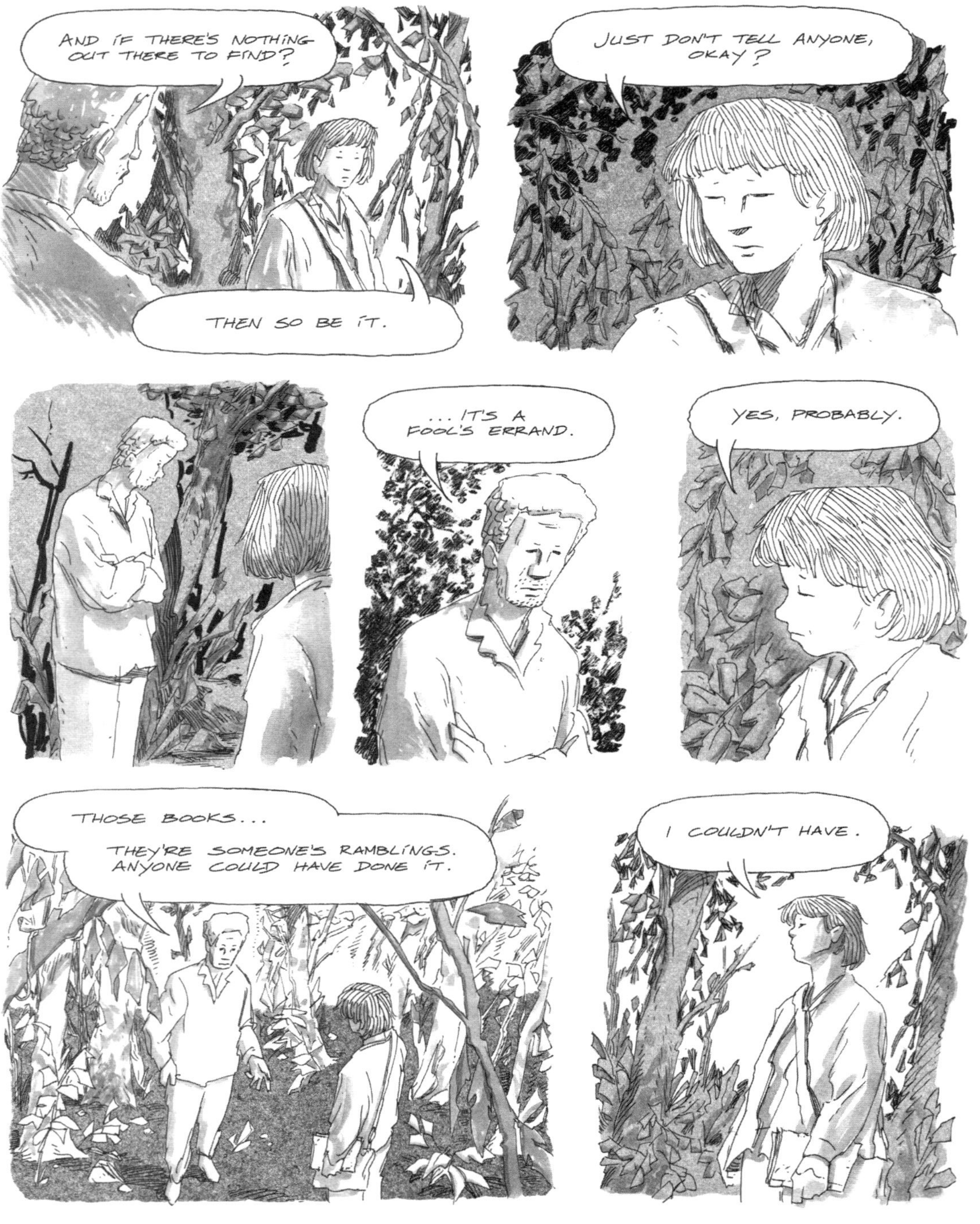
AND IF THERE'S NOTHING OUT THERE TO FIND?
THEN SO BE IT.
JUST DON'T TELL ANYONE, OKAY?
...IT'S A FOOL'S ERRAND.
YES, PROBABLY.
THOSE BOOKS...
THEY'RE SOMEONE'S RAMBLINGS. ANYONE COULD HAVE DONE IT.
I COULDN'T HAVE.

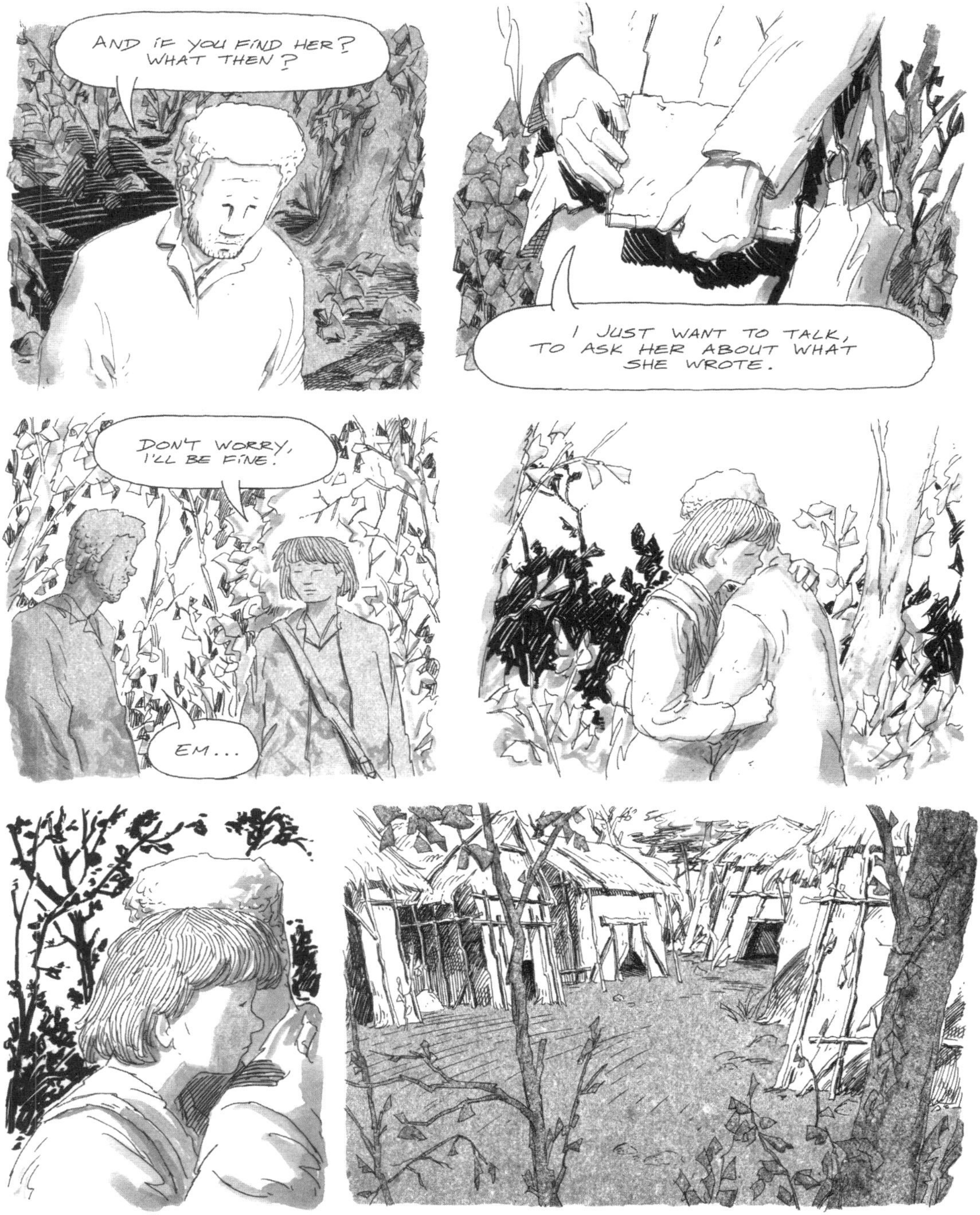
AND IF YOU FIND HER? WHAT THEN?
I JUST WANT TO TALK, TO ASK HER ABOUT WHAT SHE WROTE.
DON'T WORRY, I'LL BE FINE.
EM...

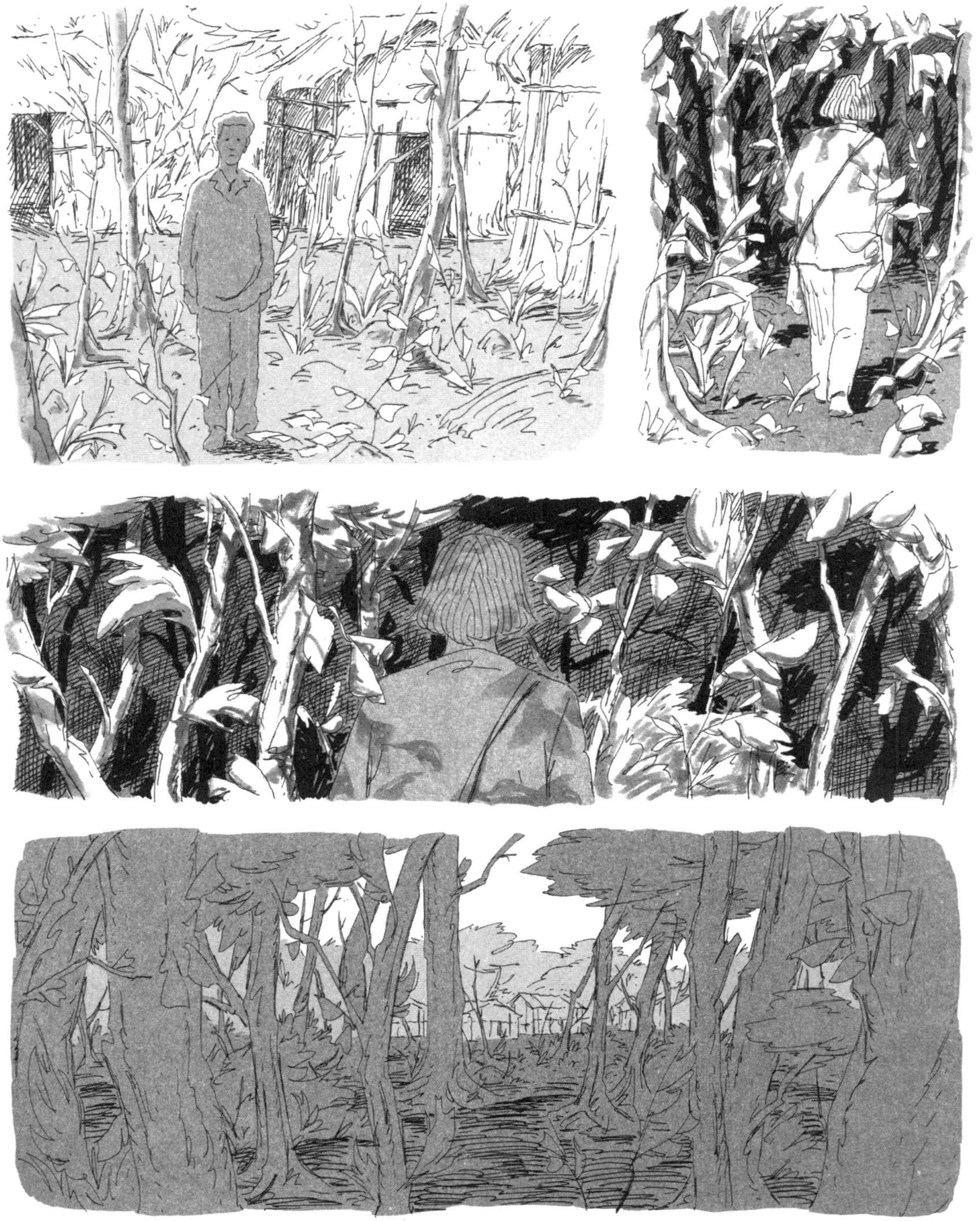

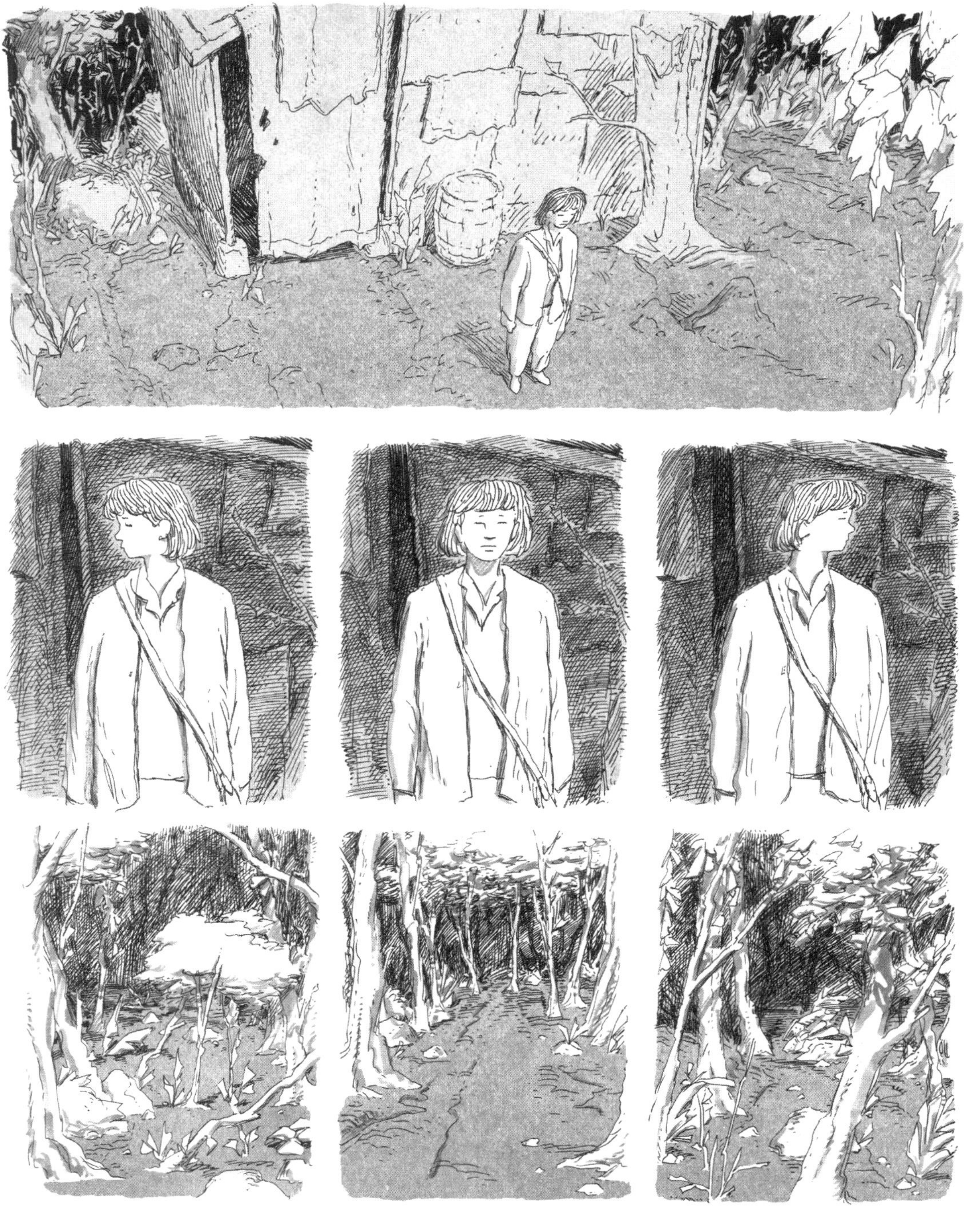

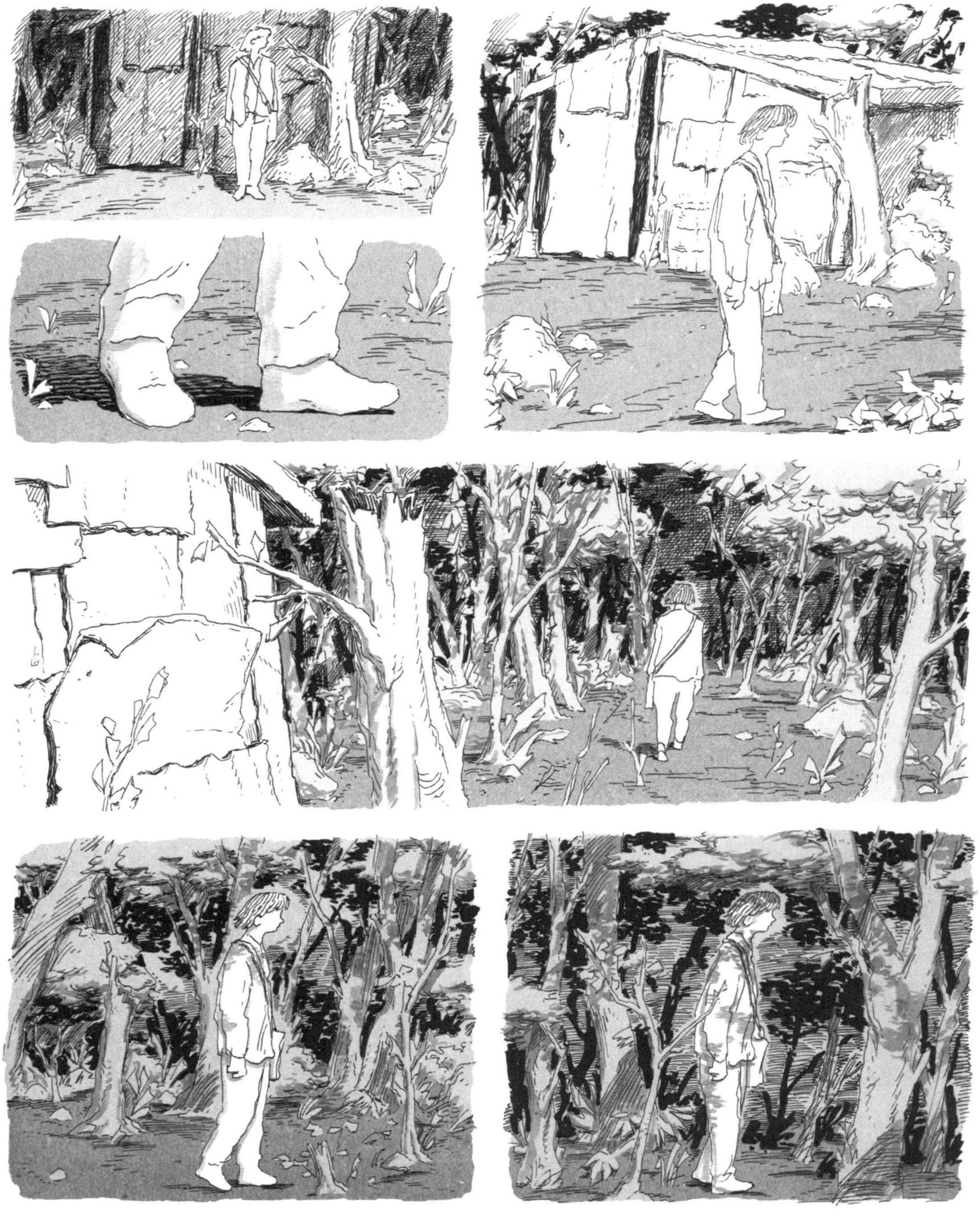

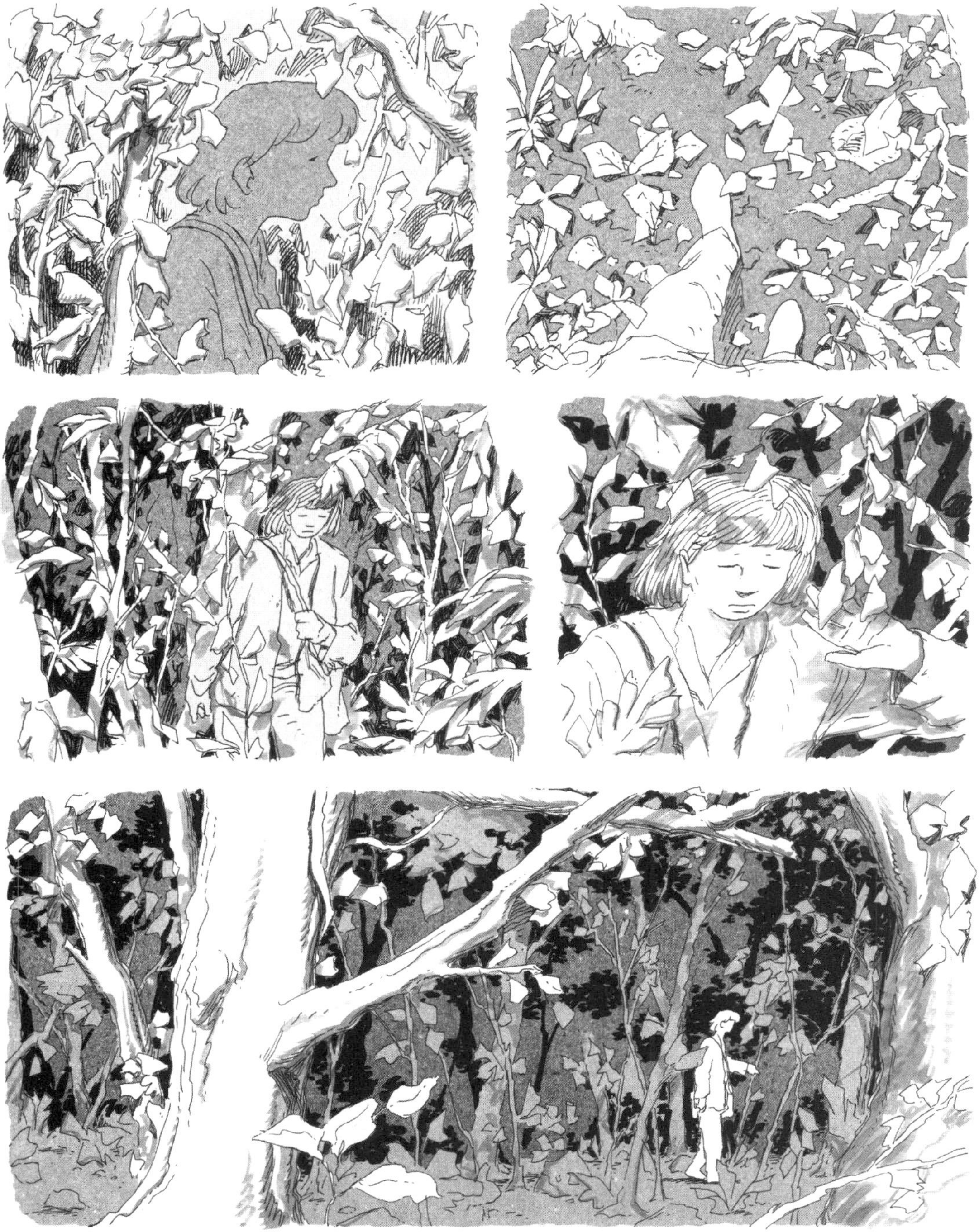

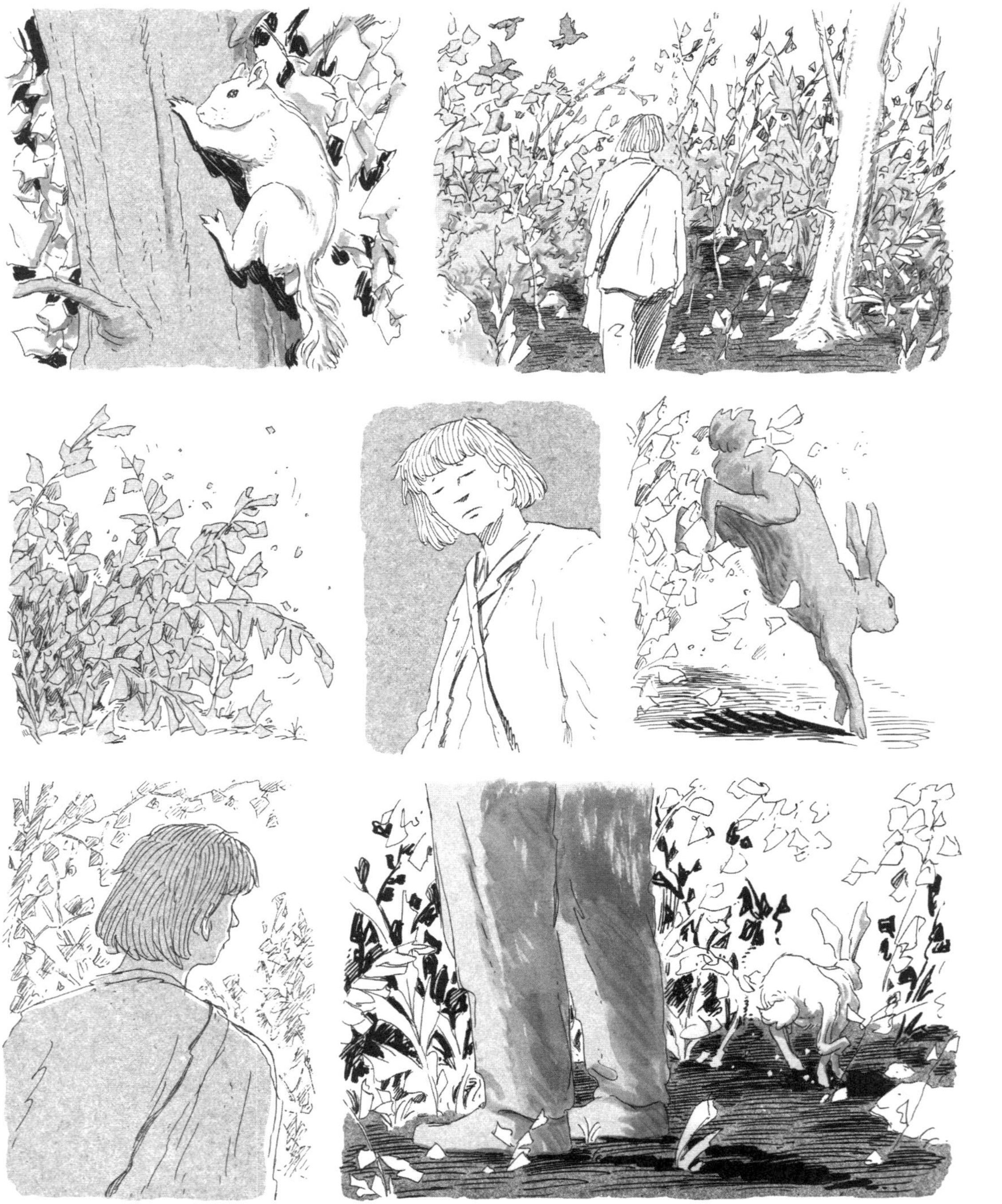

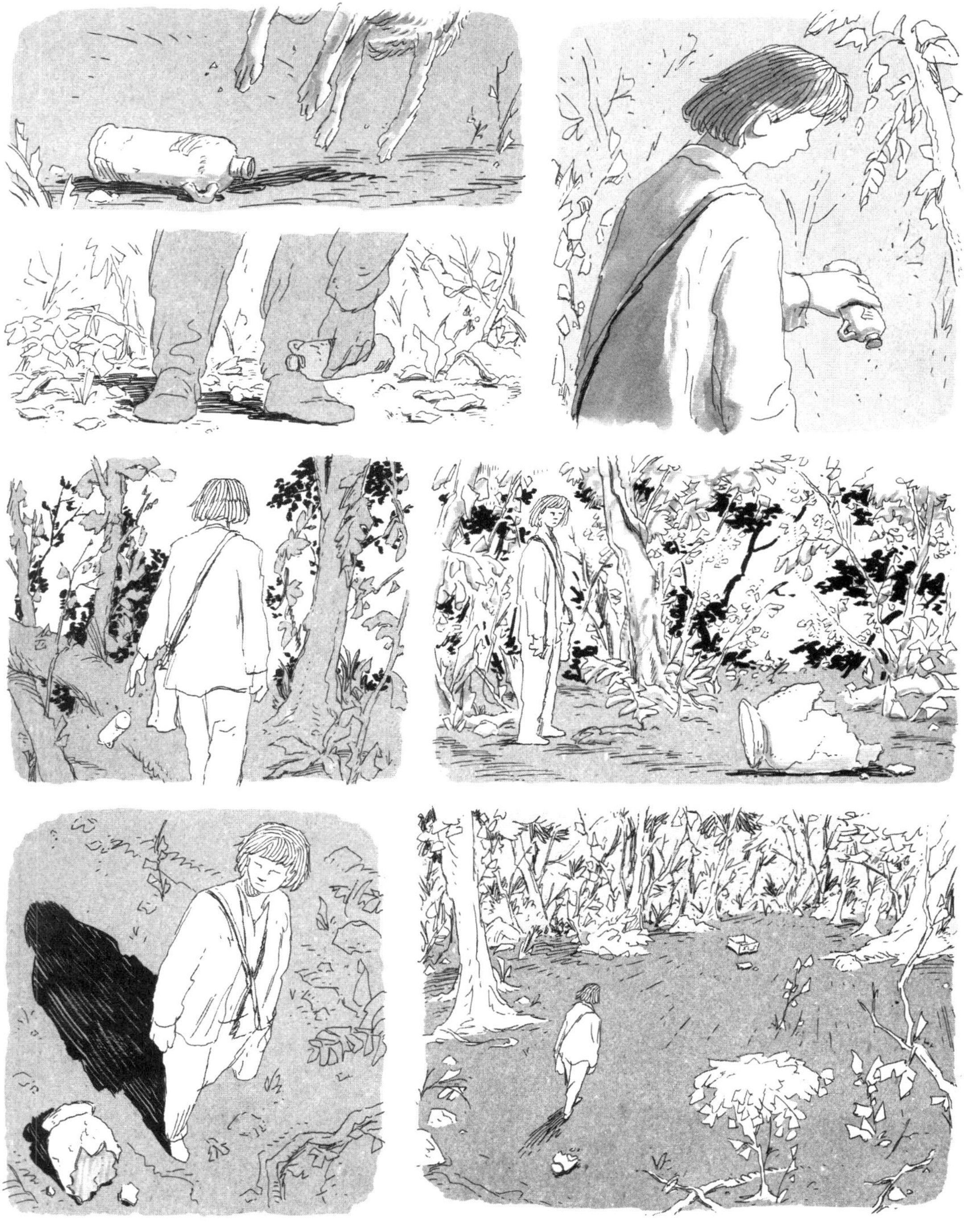

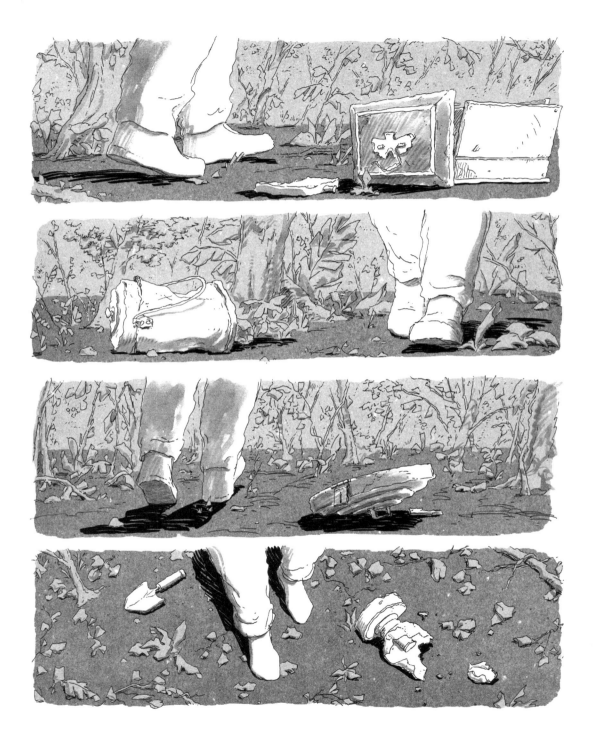

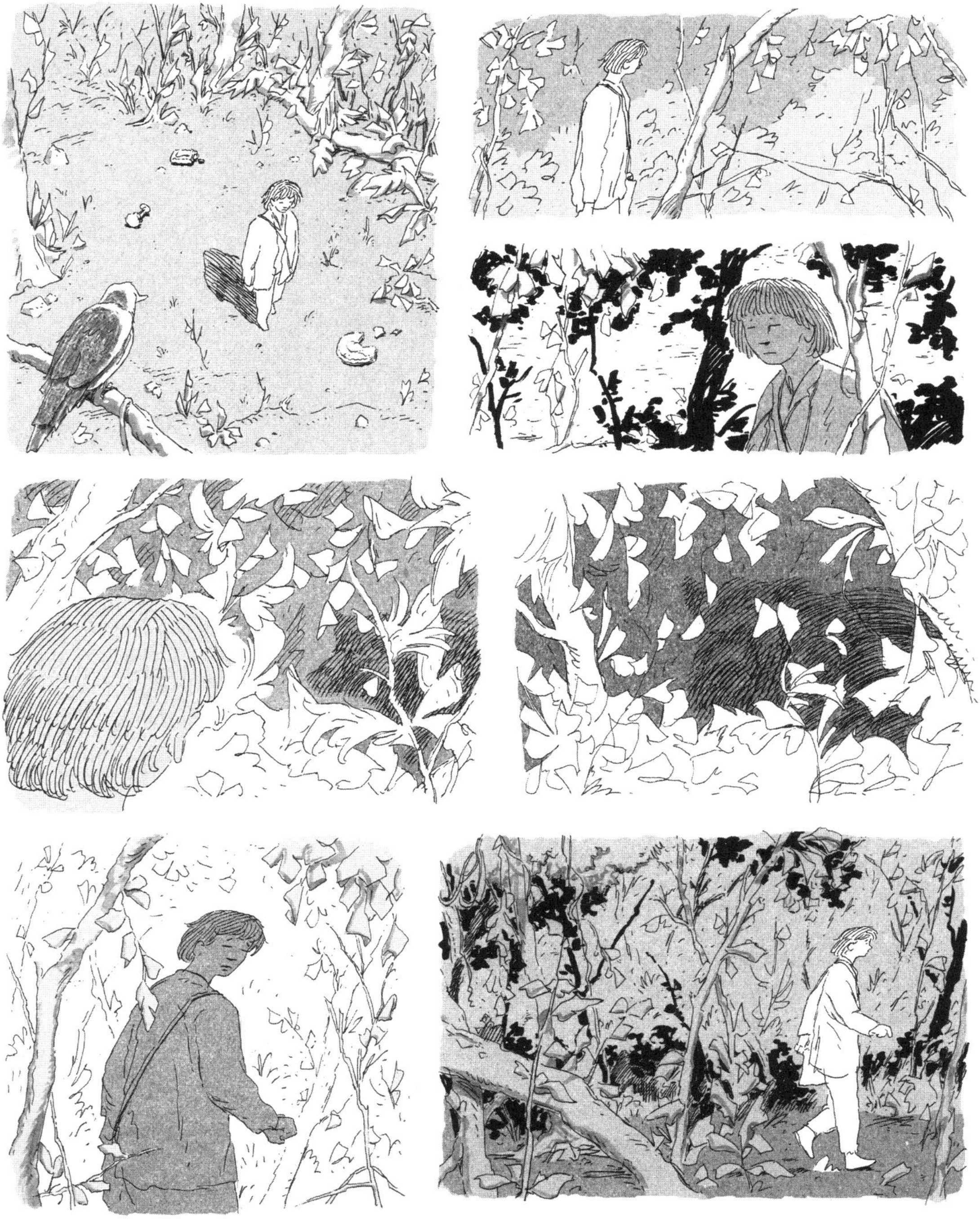

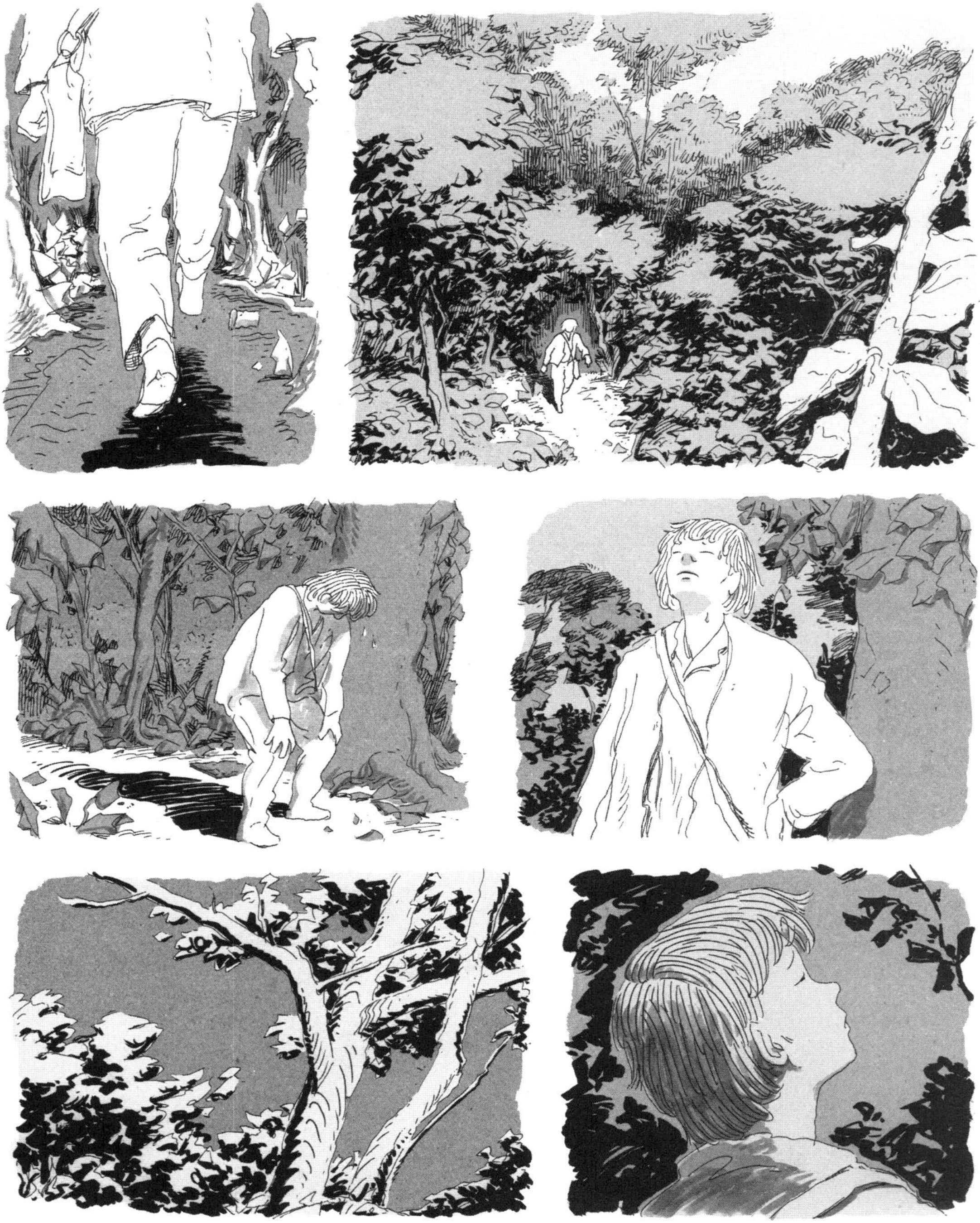

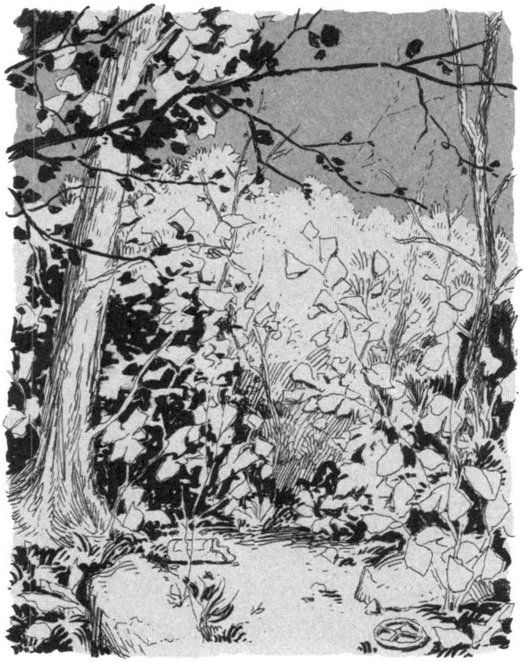

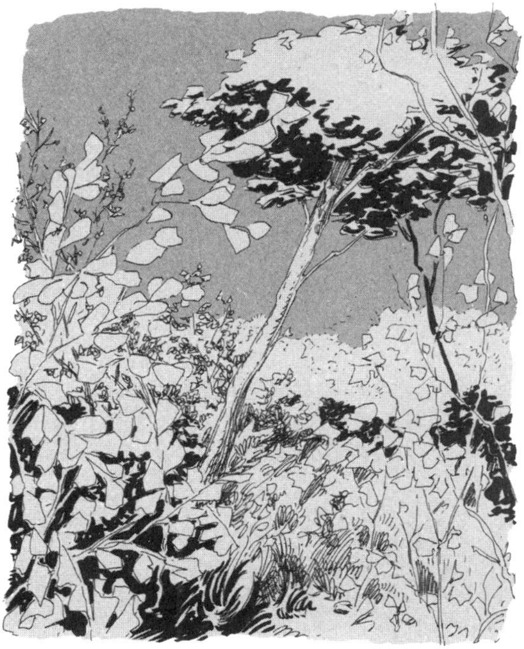

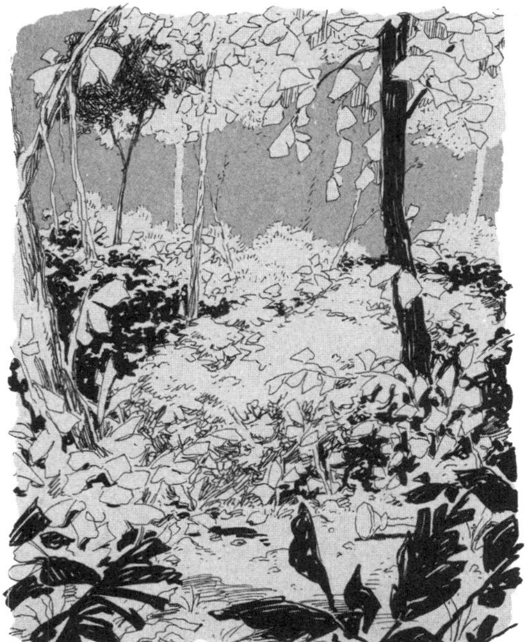

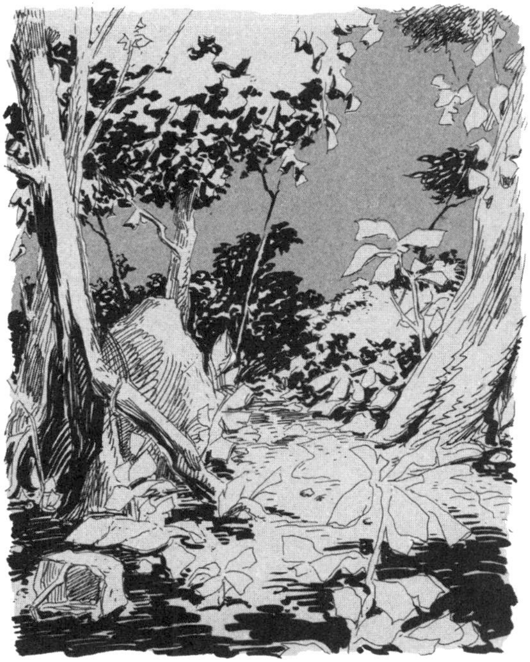

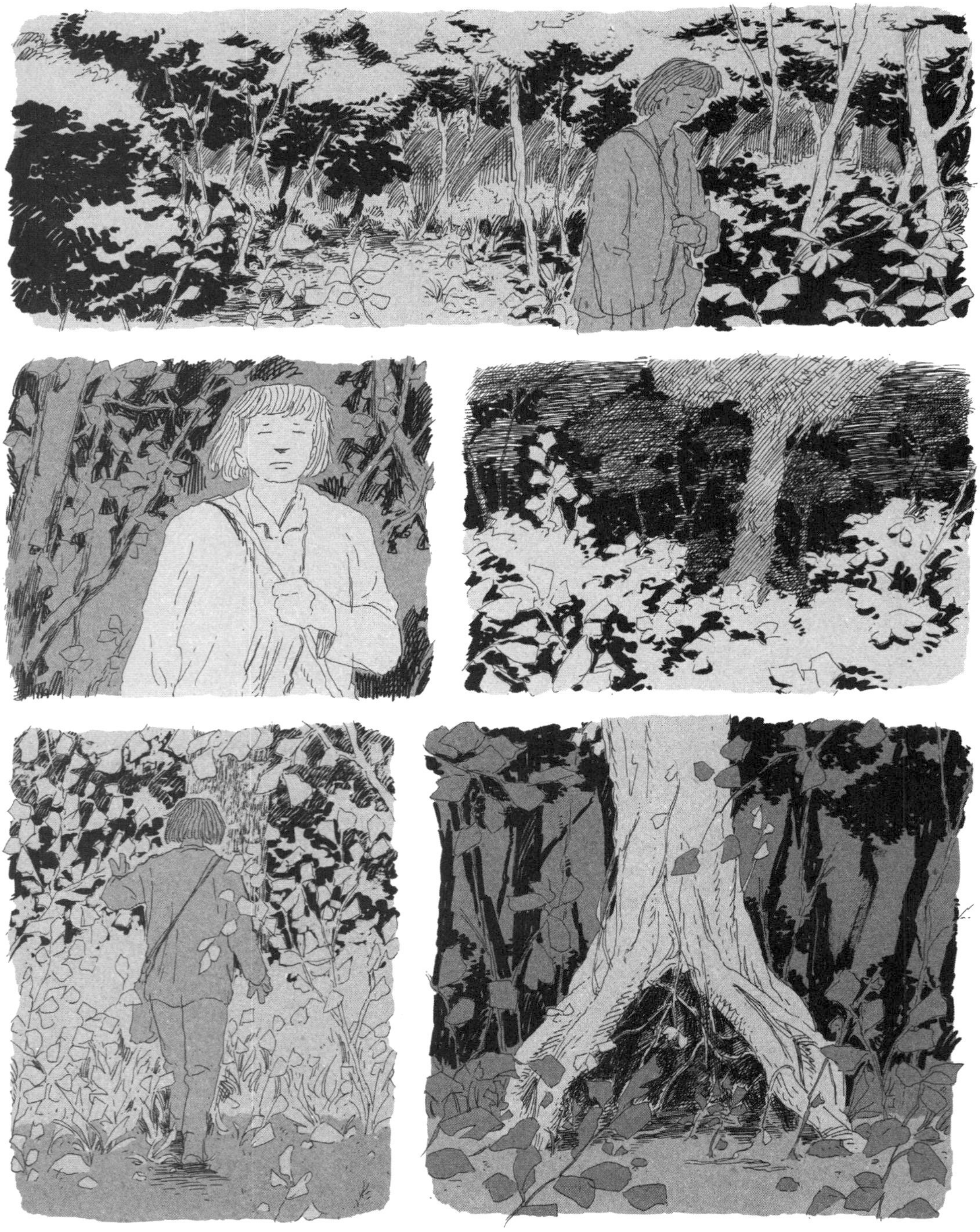

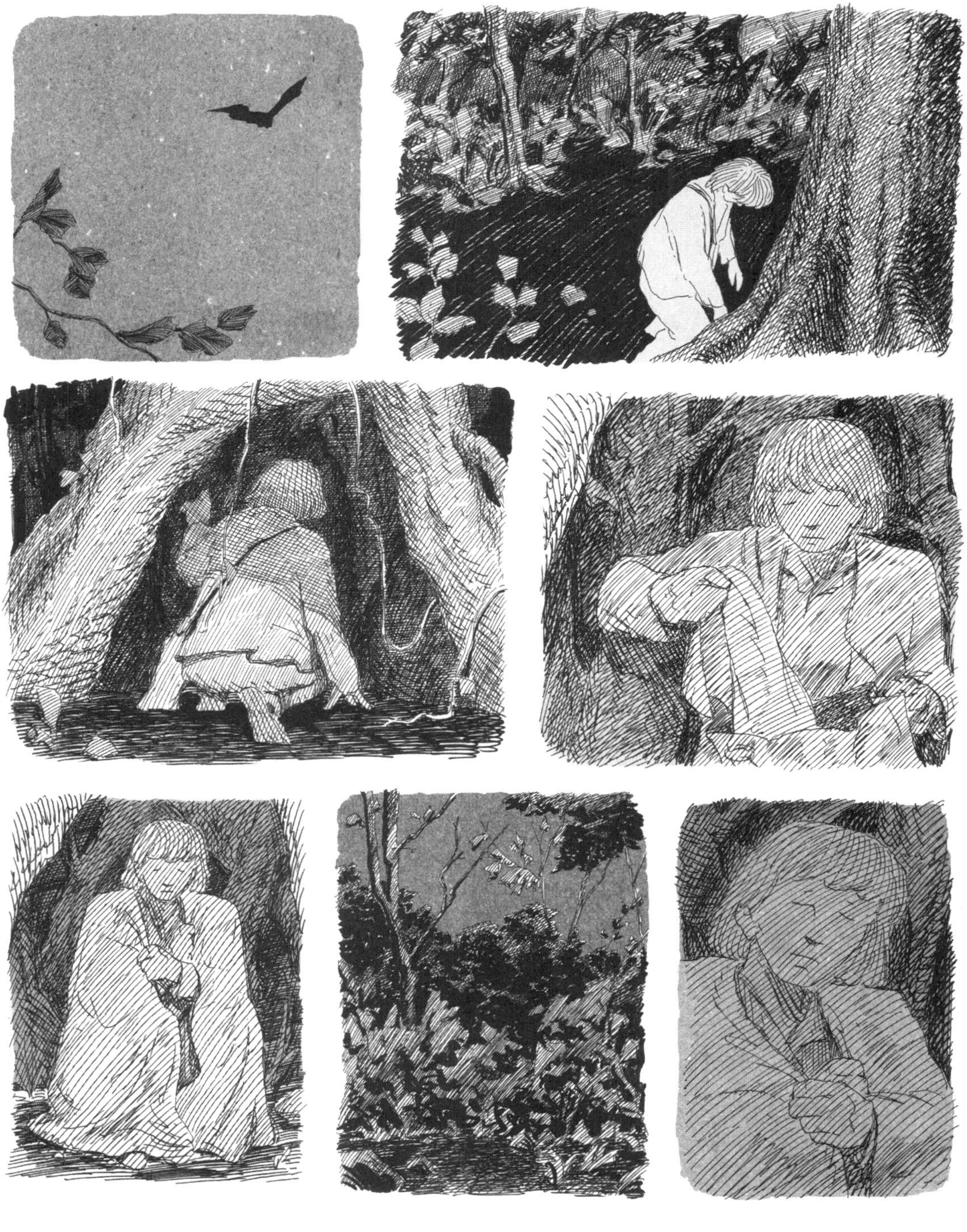

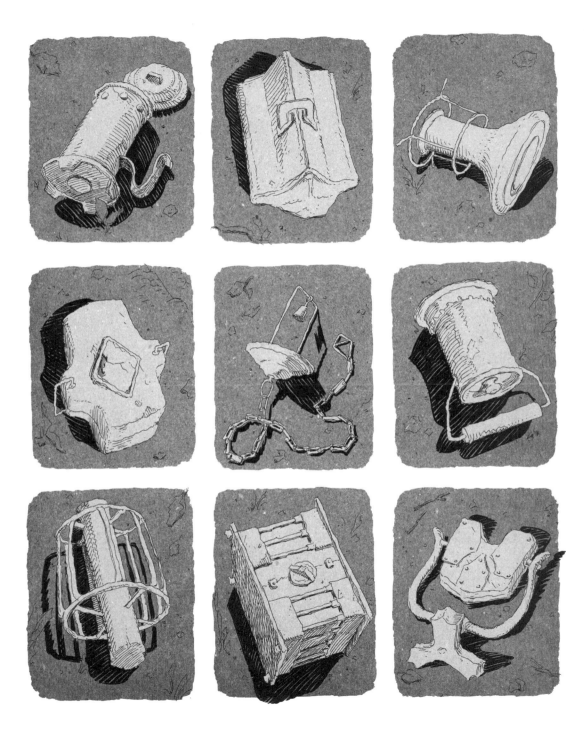

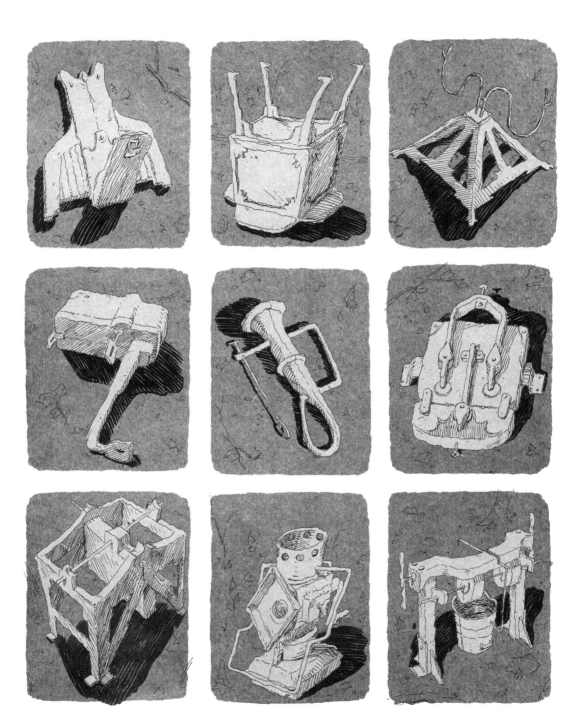

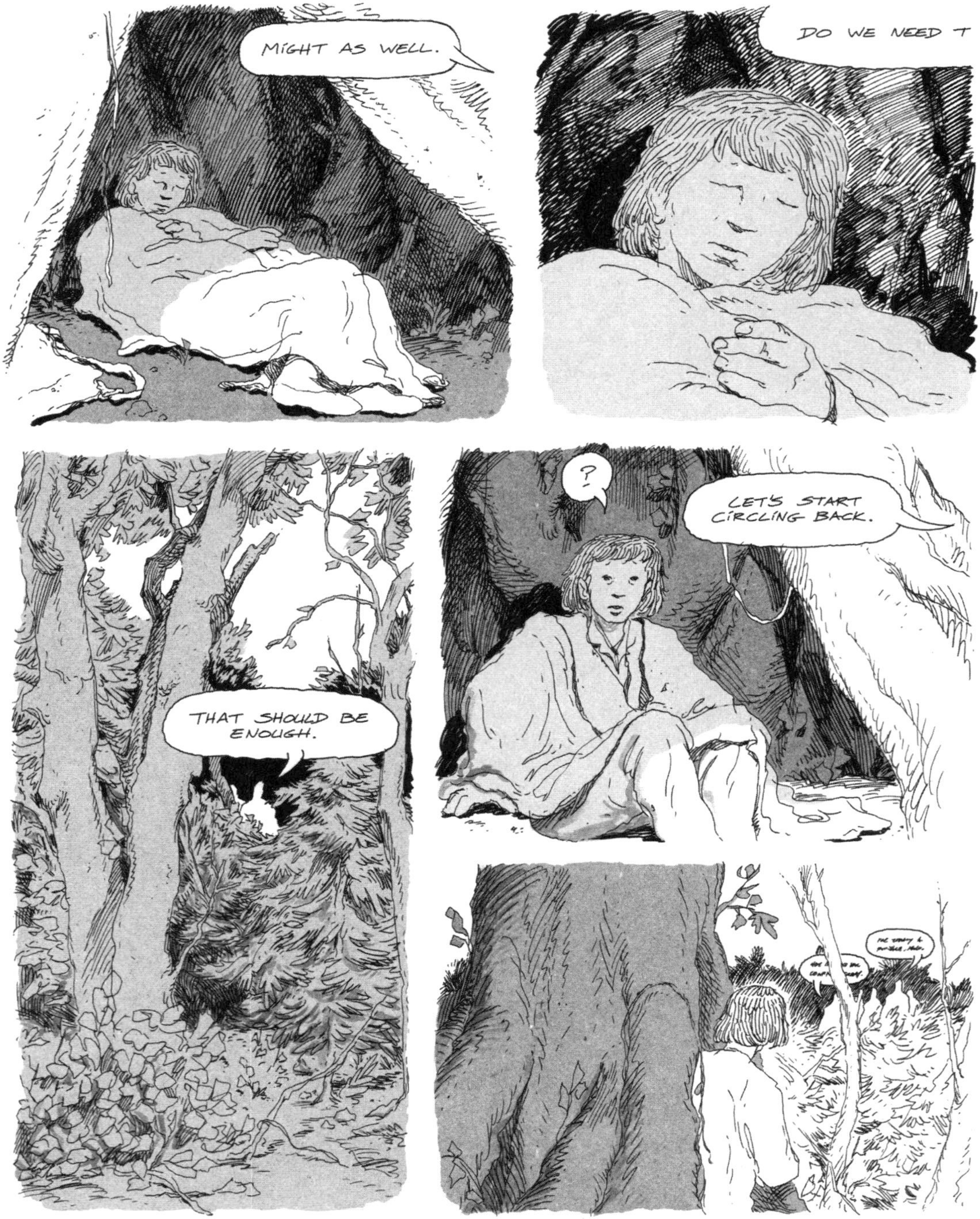
MIGHT AS WELL.
DO WE NEED T
THAT SHOULD BE ENOUGH.
?
LET'S START CIRCLING BACK.

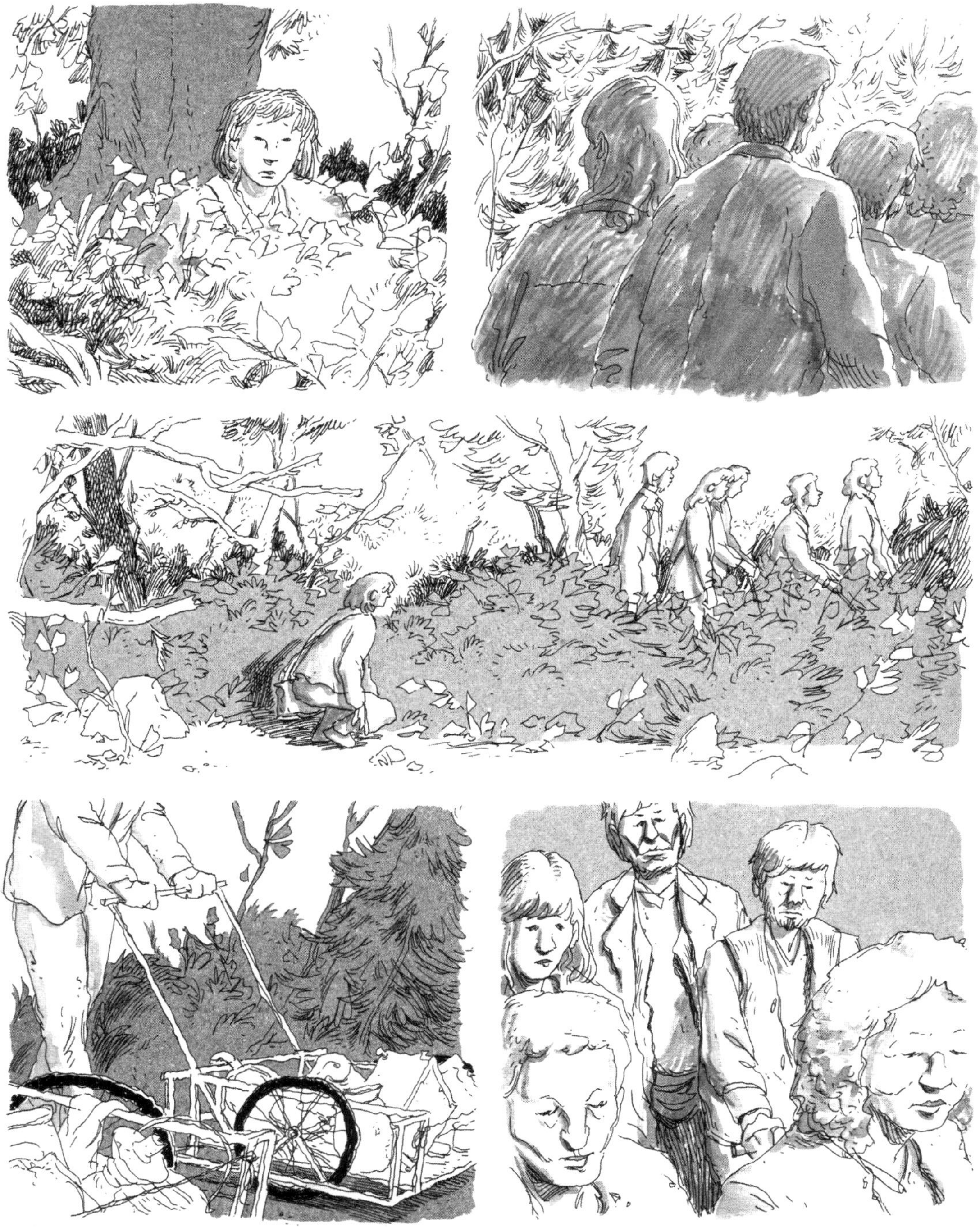

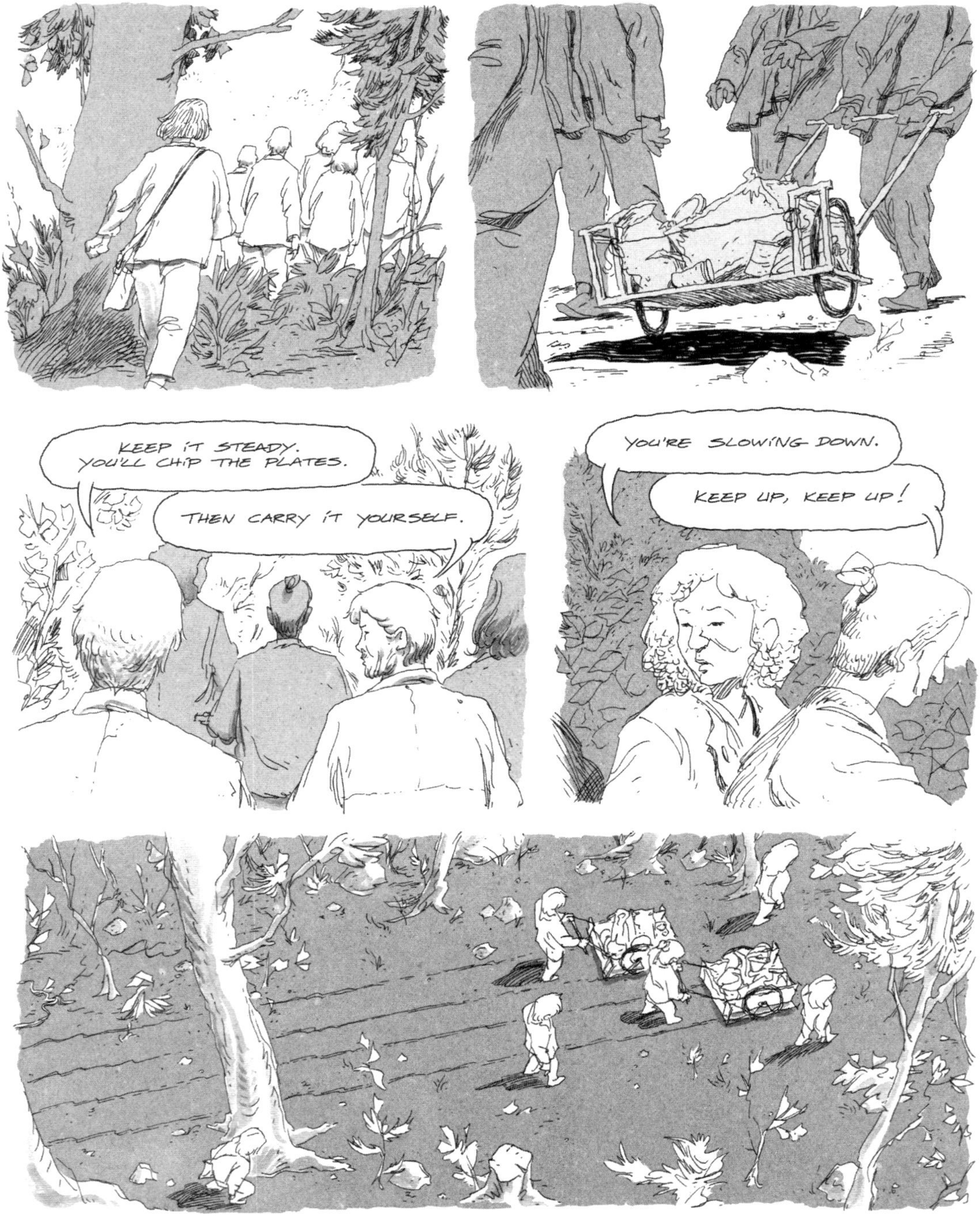
KEEP IT STEADY. YOU'LL CHIP THE PLATES.
THEN CARRY IT YOURSELF.
YOU'RE SLOWING DOWN.
KEEP UP, KEEP UP!

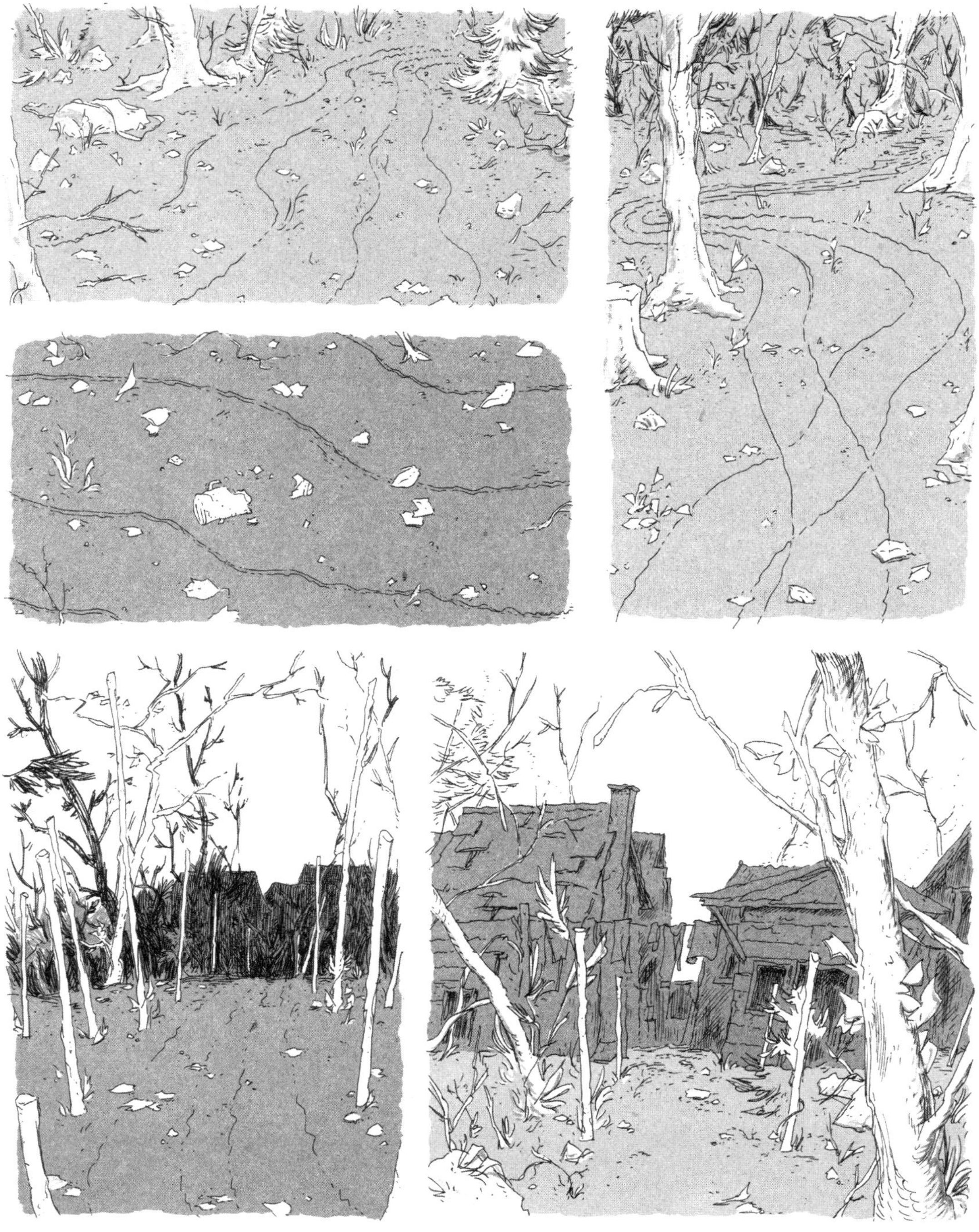

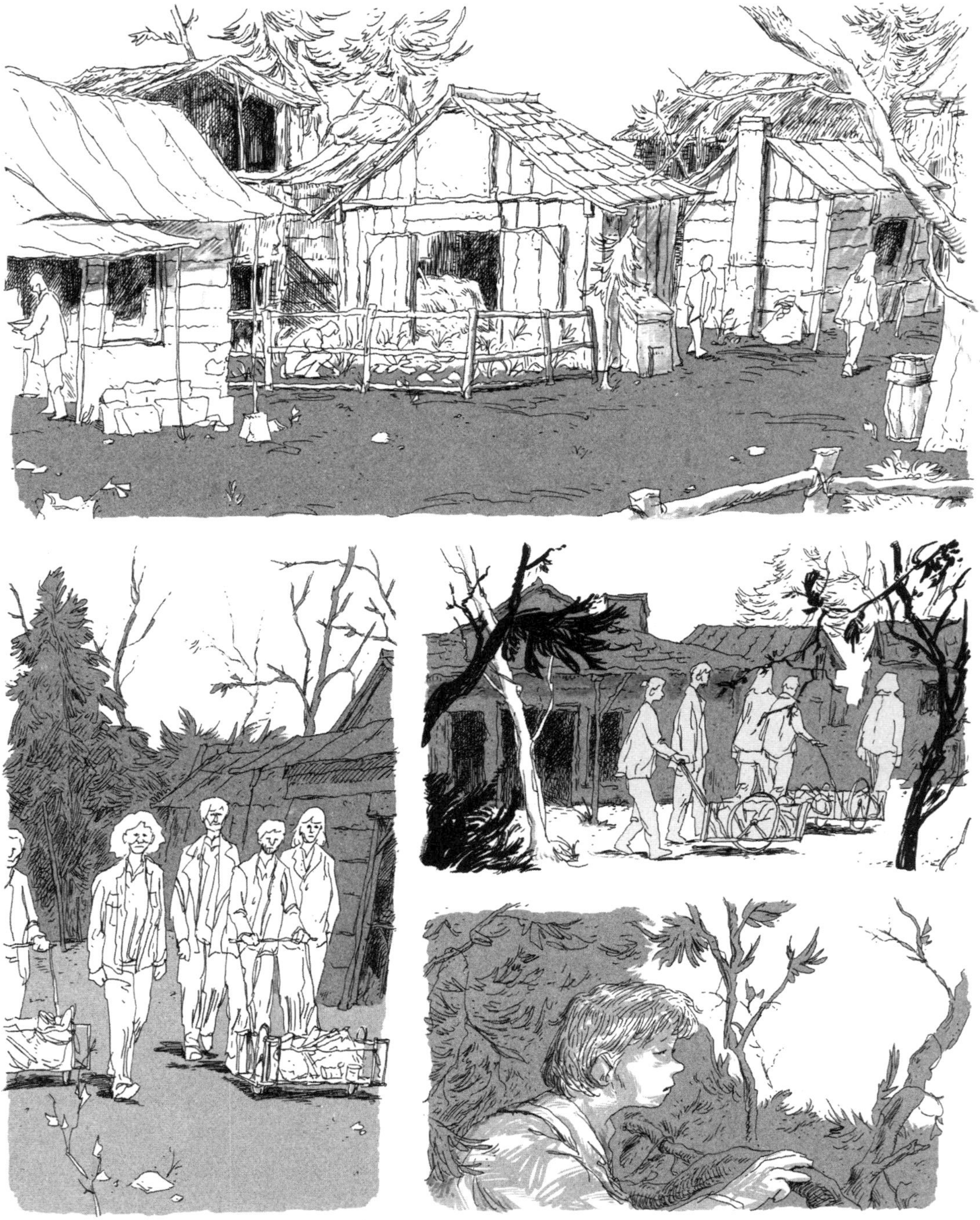

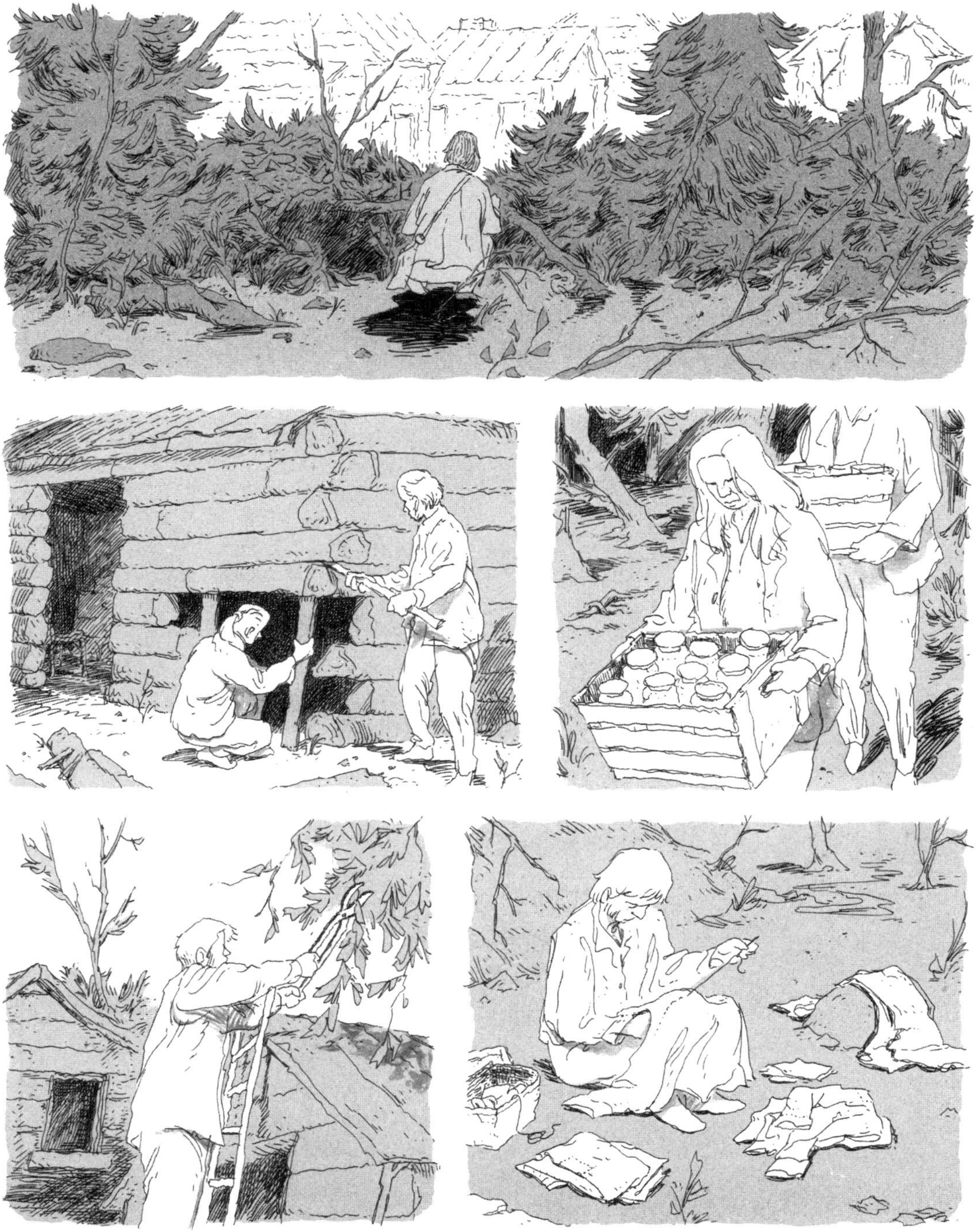

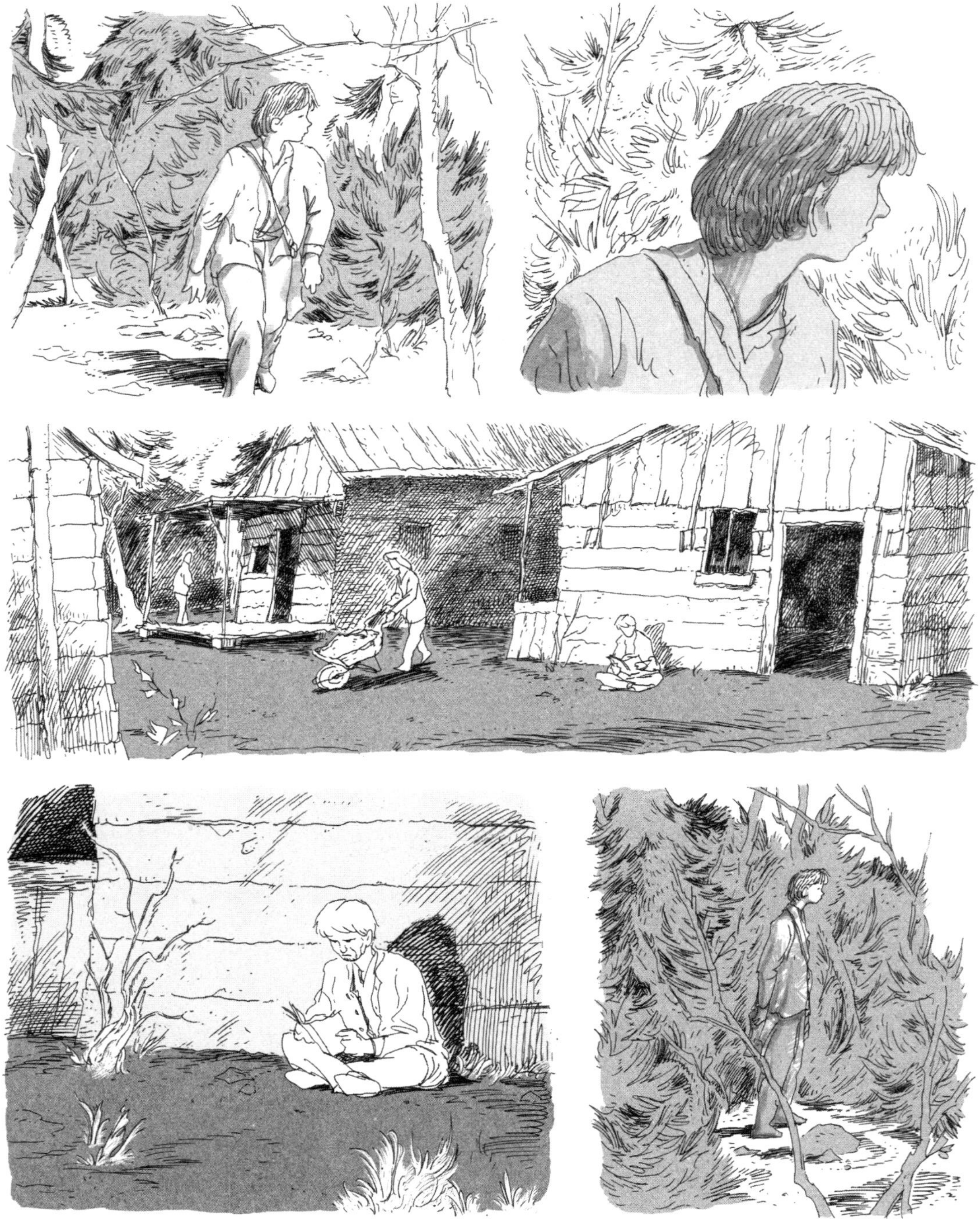

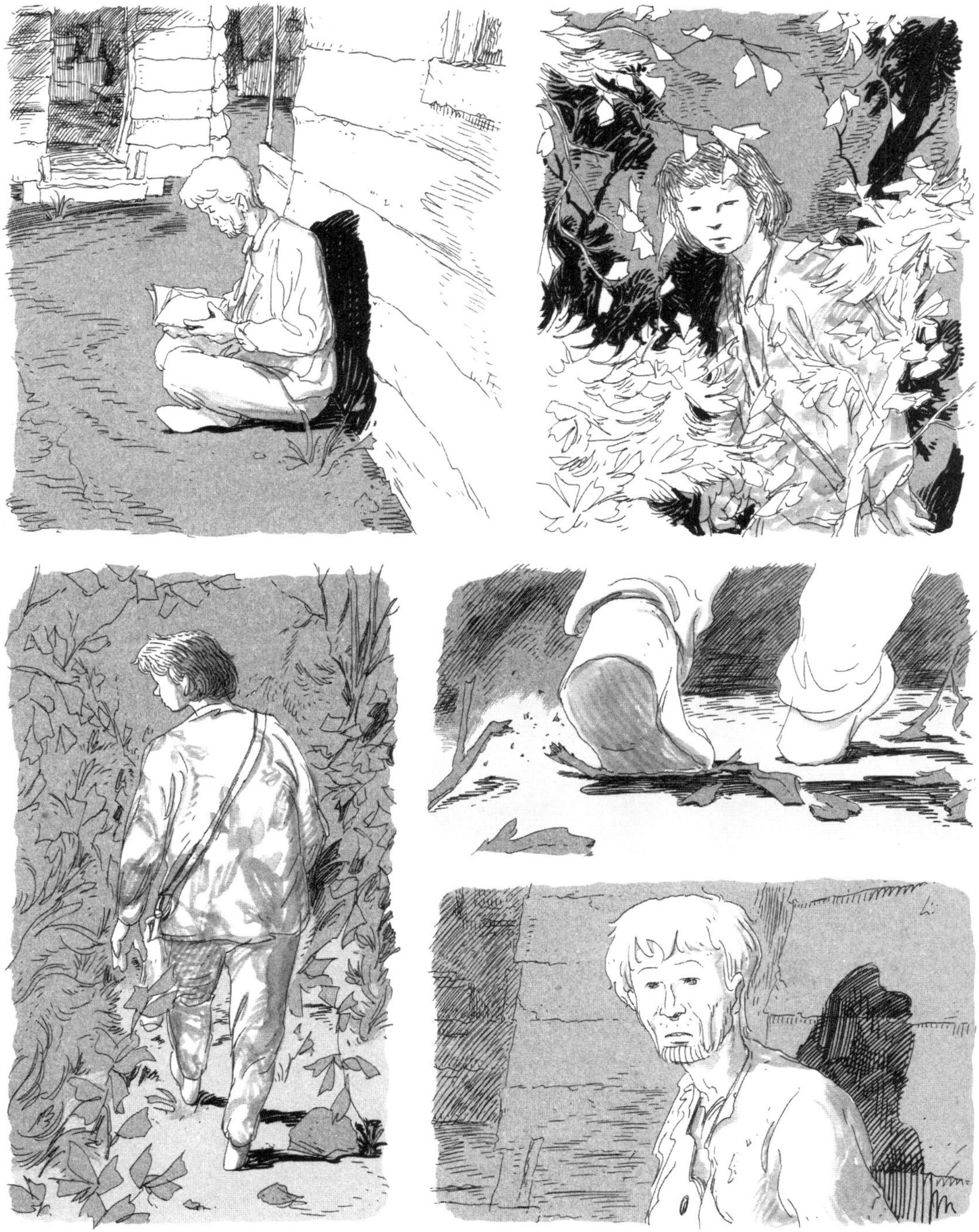

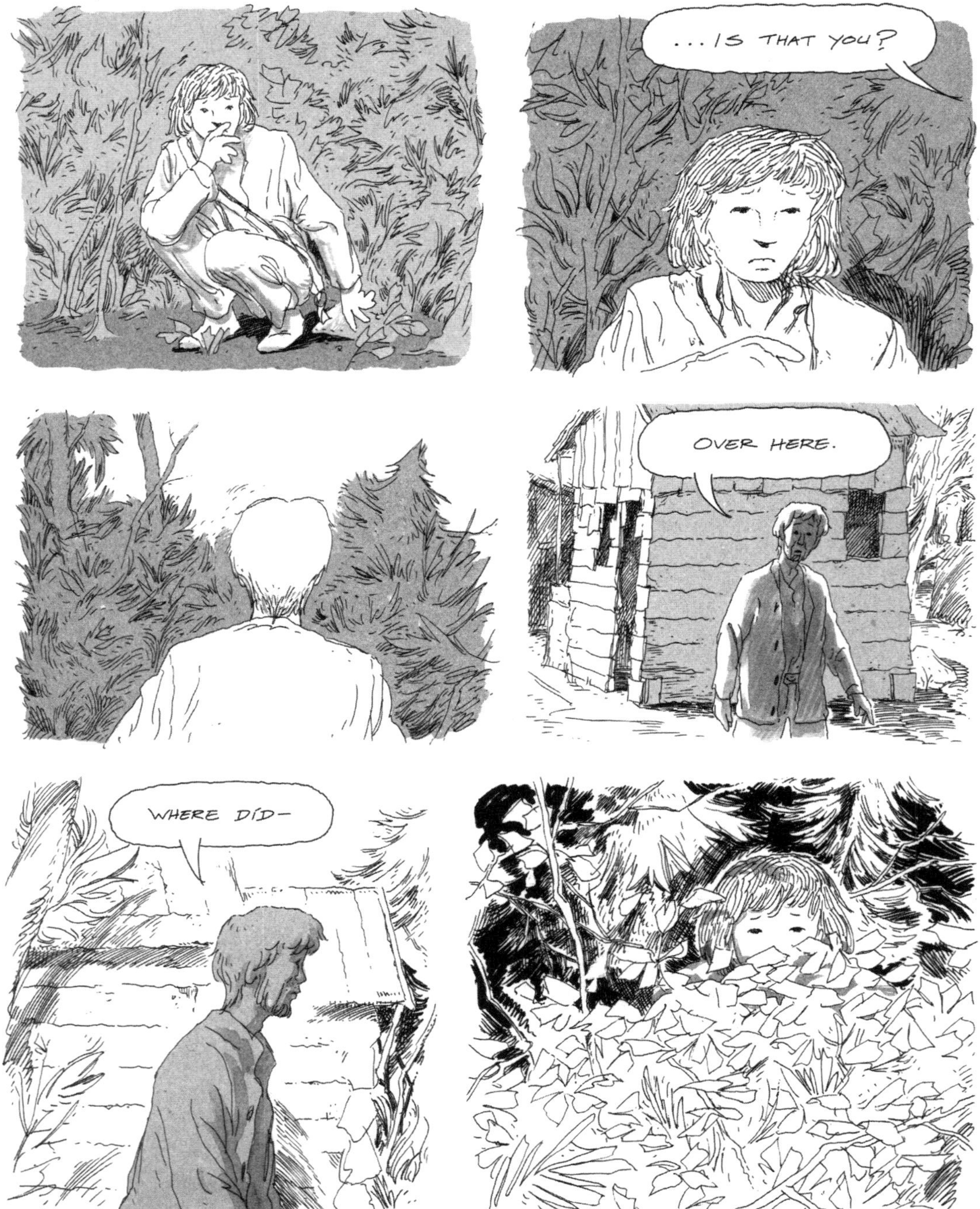
...IS THAT YOU?
OVER HERE.
WHERE DID—

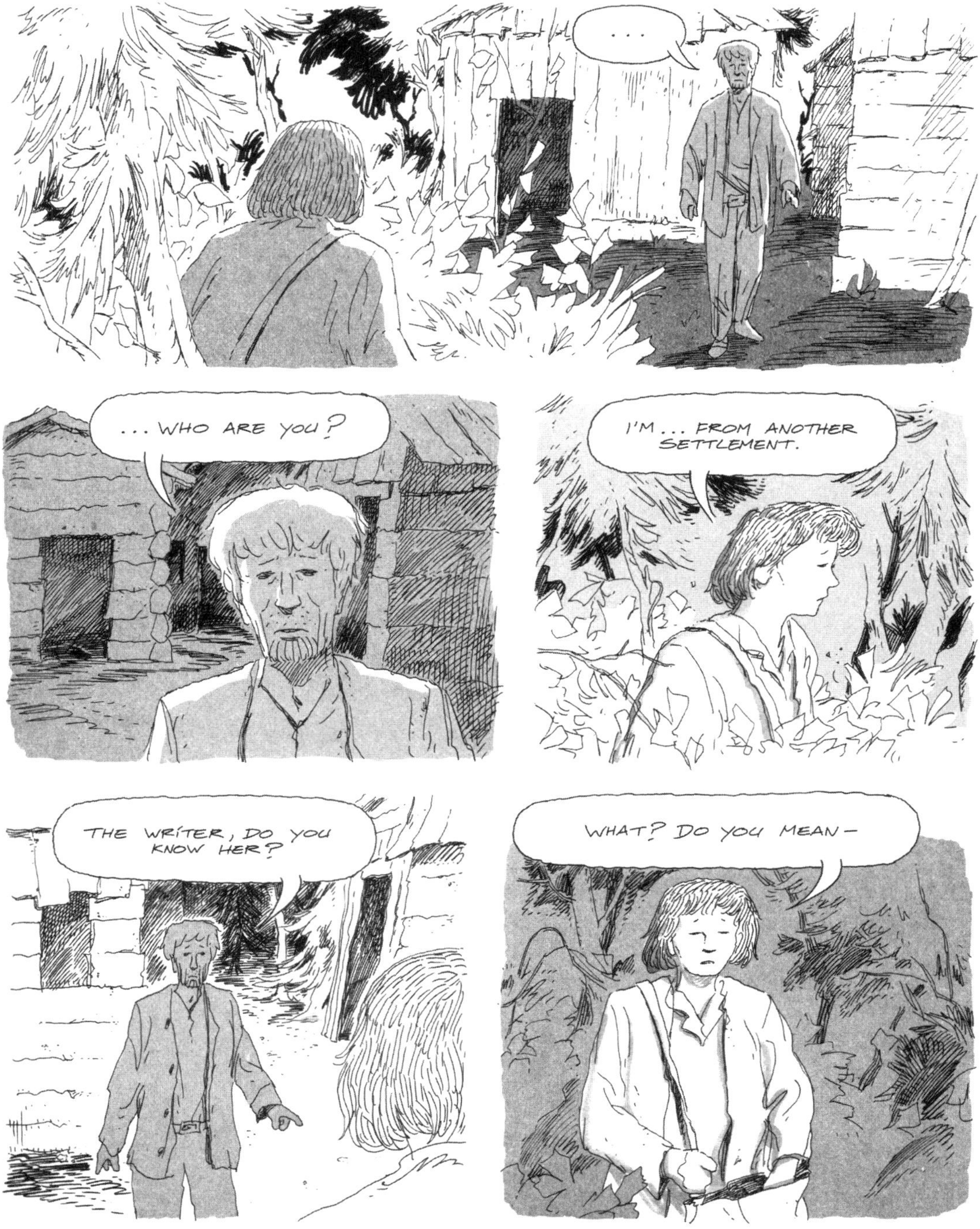
. . .
. . . WHO ARE YOU?
I'M . . . FROM ANOTHER SETTLEMENT.
THE WRITER, DO YOU KNOW HER?
WHAT? DO YOU MEAN—

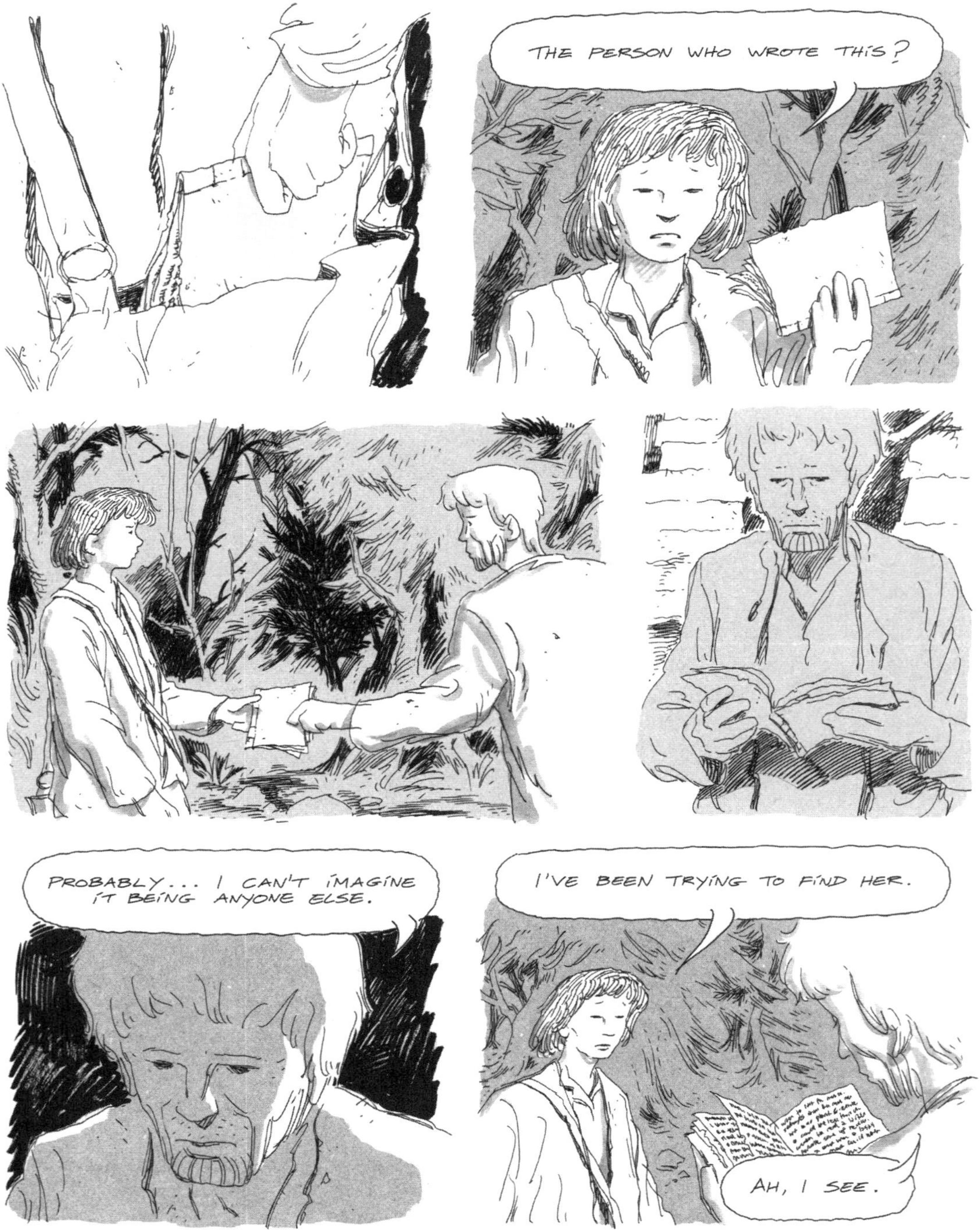
THE PERSON WHO WROTE THIS?
PROBABLY... I CAN'T IMAGINE IT BEING ANYONE ELSE.
I'VE BEEN TRYING TO FIND HER.
AH, I SEE.

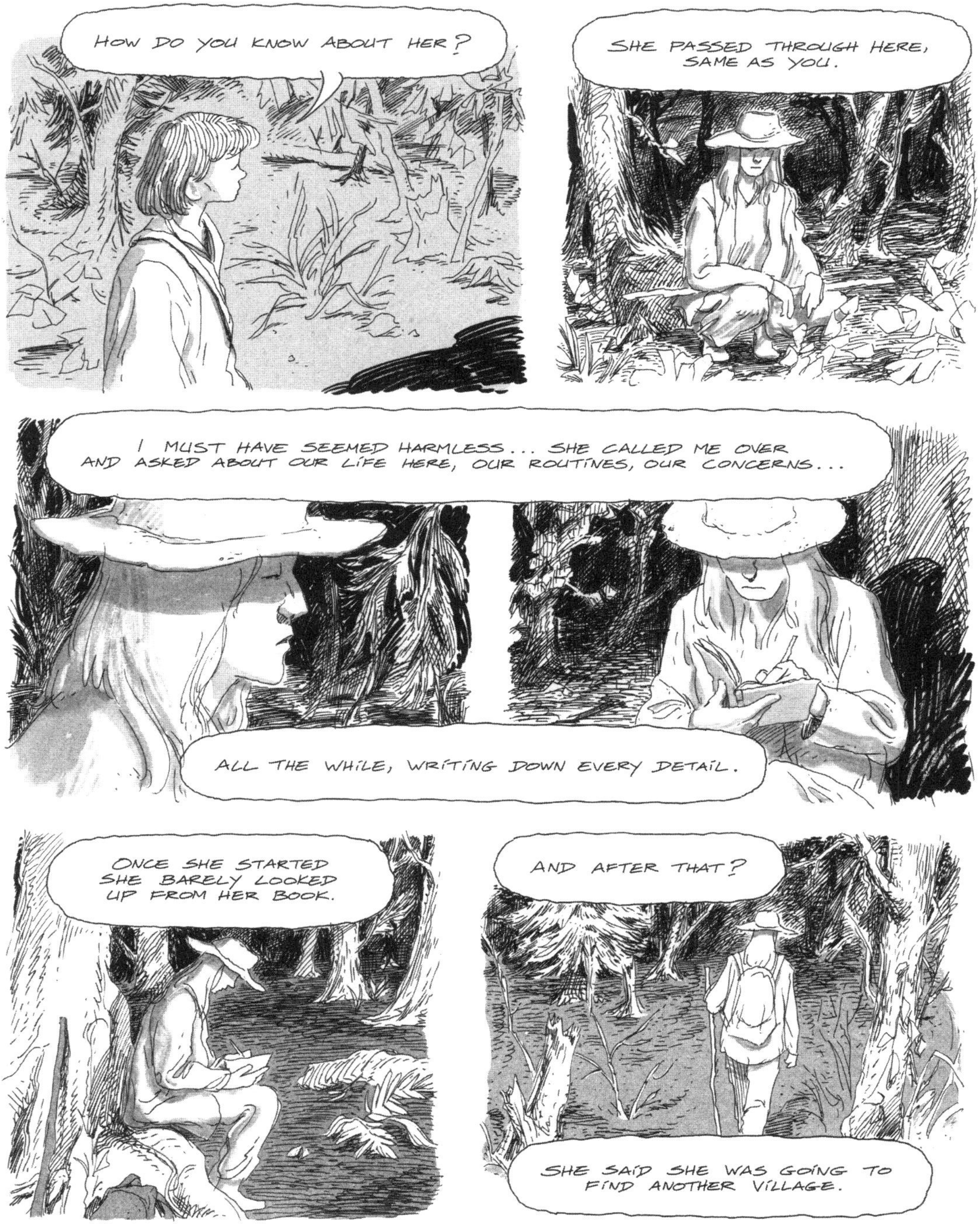
HOW DO YOU KNOW ABOUT HER?
SHE PASSED THROUGH HERE, SAME AS YOU.
I MUST HAVE SEEMED HARMLESS... SHE CALLED ME OVER AND ASKED ABOUT OUR LIFE HERE, OUR ROUTINES, OUR CONCERNS...
ALL THE WHILE, WRITING DOWN EVERY DETAIL.
ONCE SHE STARTED SHE BARELY LOOKED UP FROM HER BOOK.
AND AFTER THAT?
SHE SAID SHE WAS GOING TO FIND ANOTHER VILLAGE.

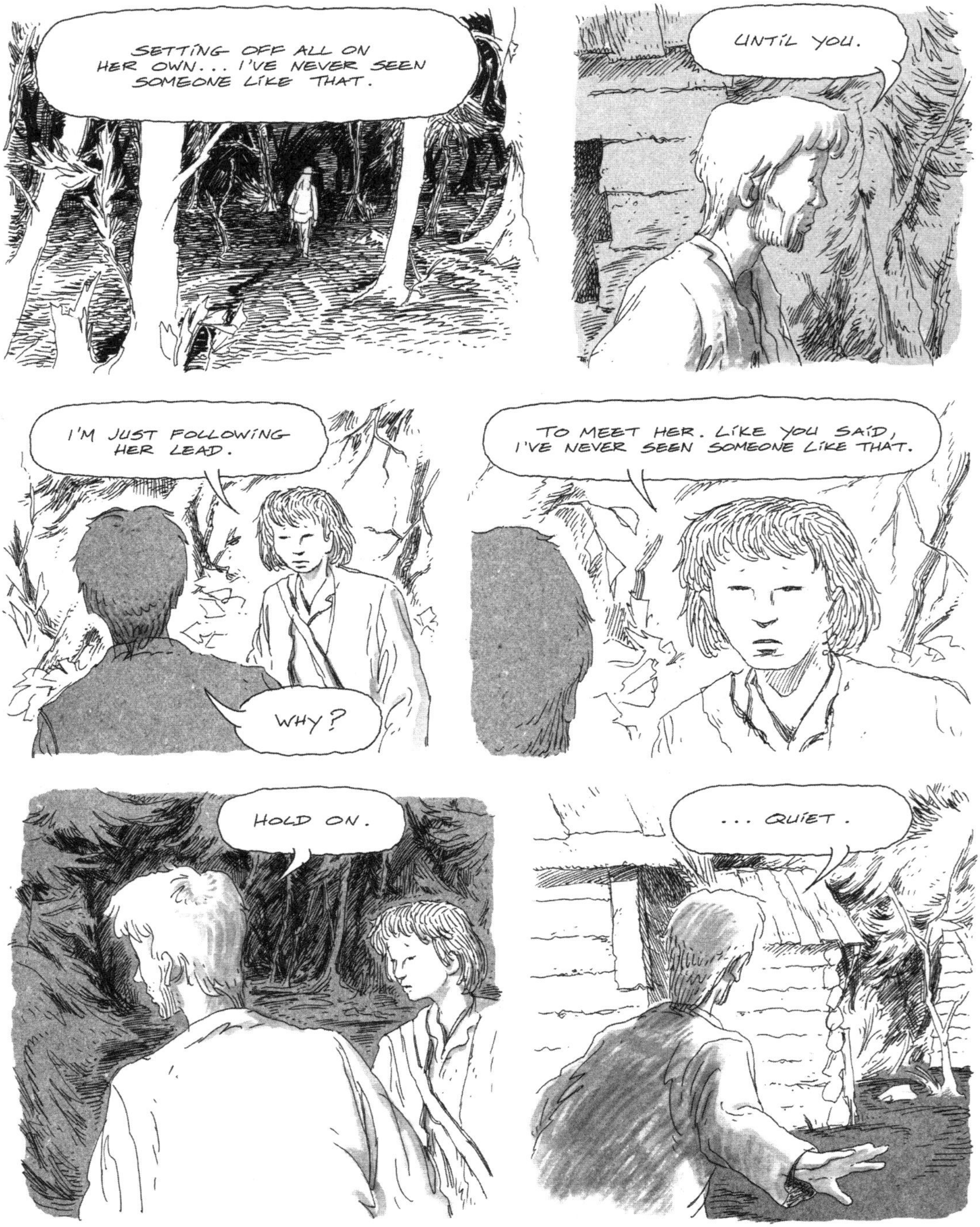
SETTING OFF ALL ON HER OWN... I'VE NEVER SEEN SOMEONE LIKE THAT.
UNTIL YOU.
I'M JUST FOLLOWING HER LEAD.
WHY?
TO MEET HER. LIKE YOU SAID, I'VE NEVER SEEN SOMEONE LIKE THAT.
HOLD ON.
... QUIET.

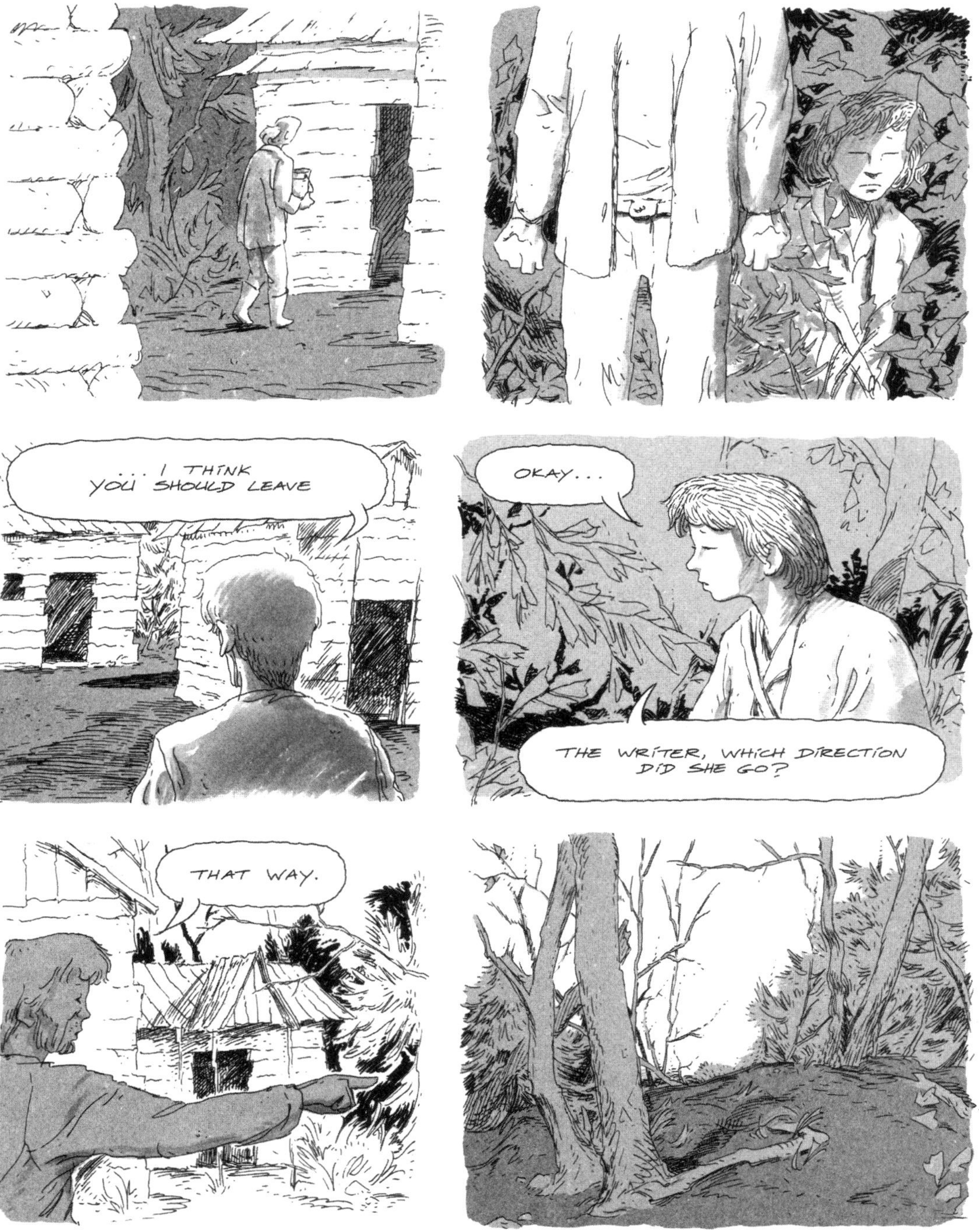
... I THINK YOU SHOULD LEAVE
OKAY...
THE WRITER, WHICH DIRECTION DID SHE GO?
THAT WAY.

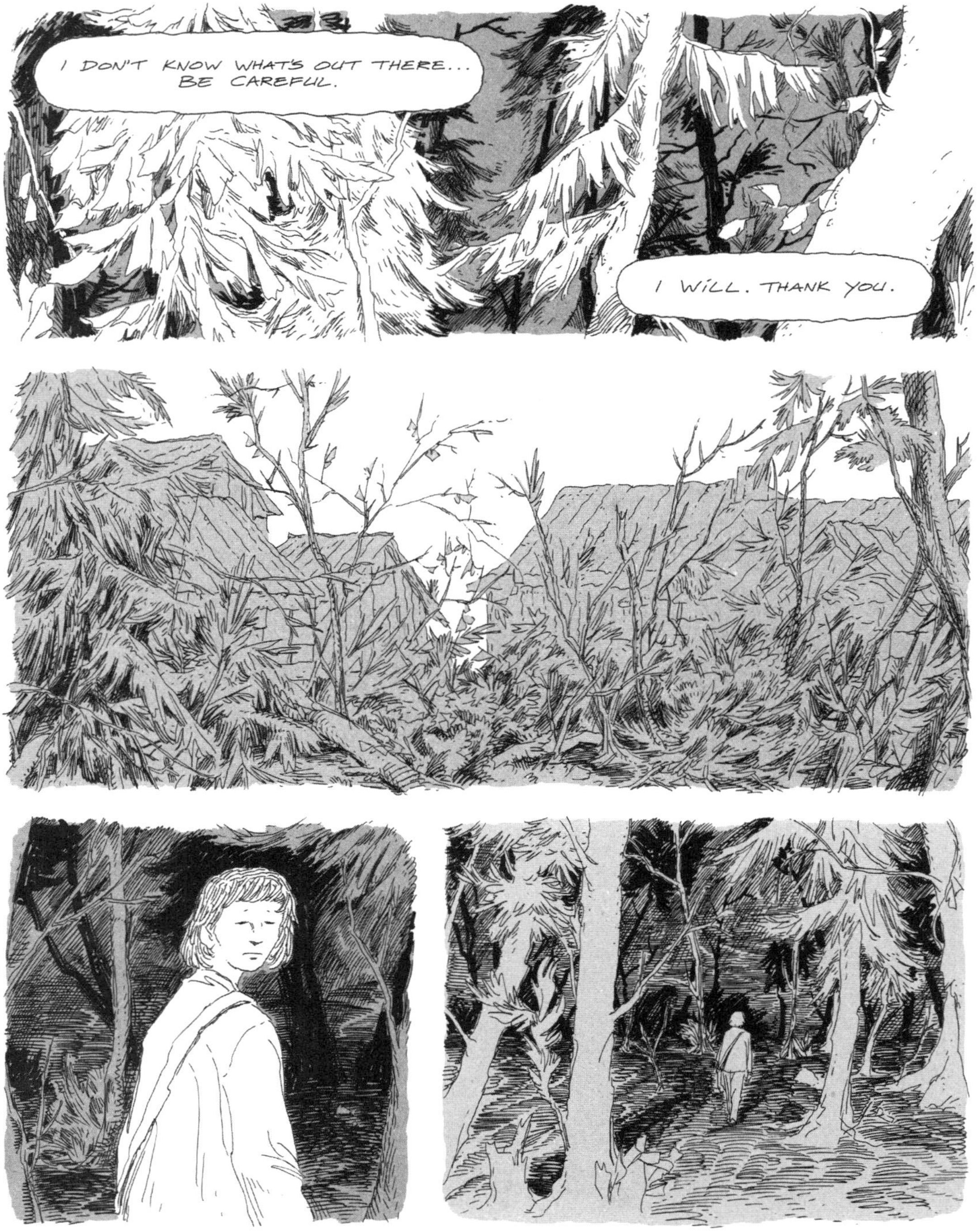
I DON'T KNOW WHAT'S OUT THERE... BE CAREFUL.
I WILL. THANK YOU.

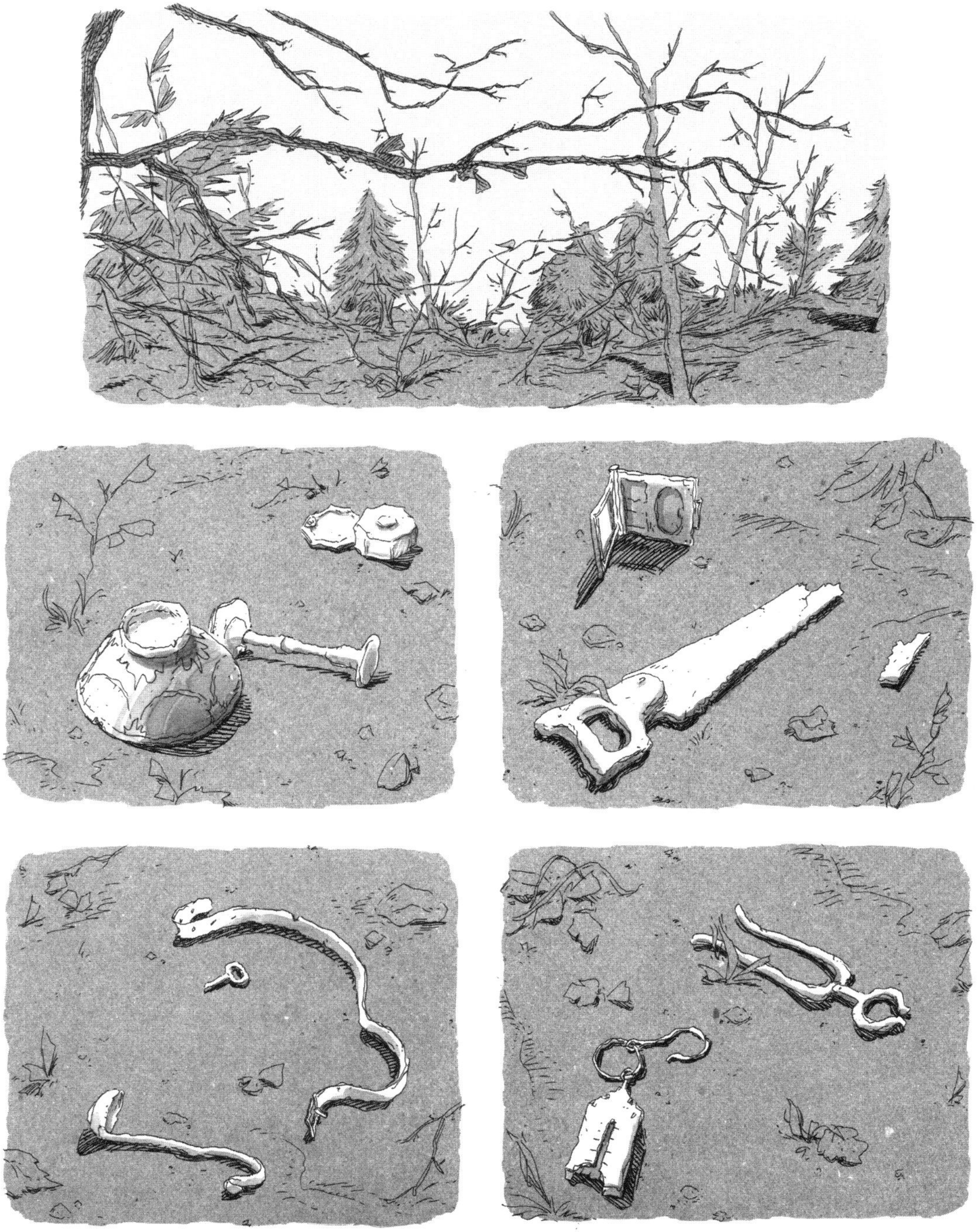

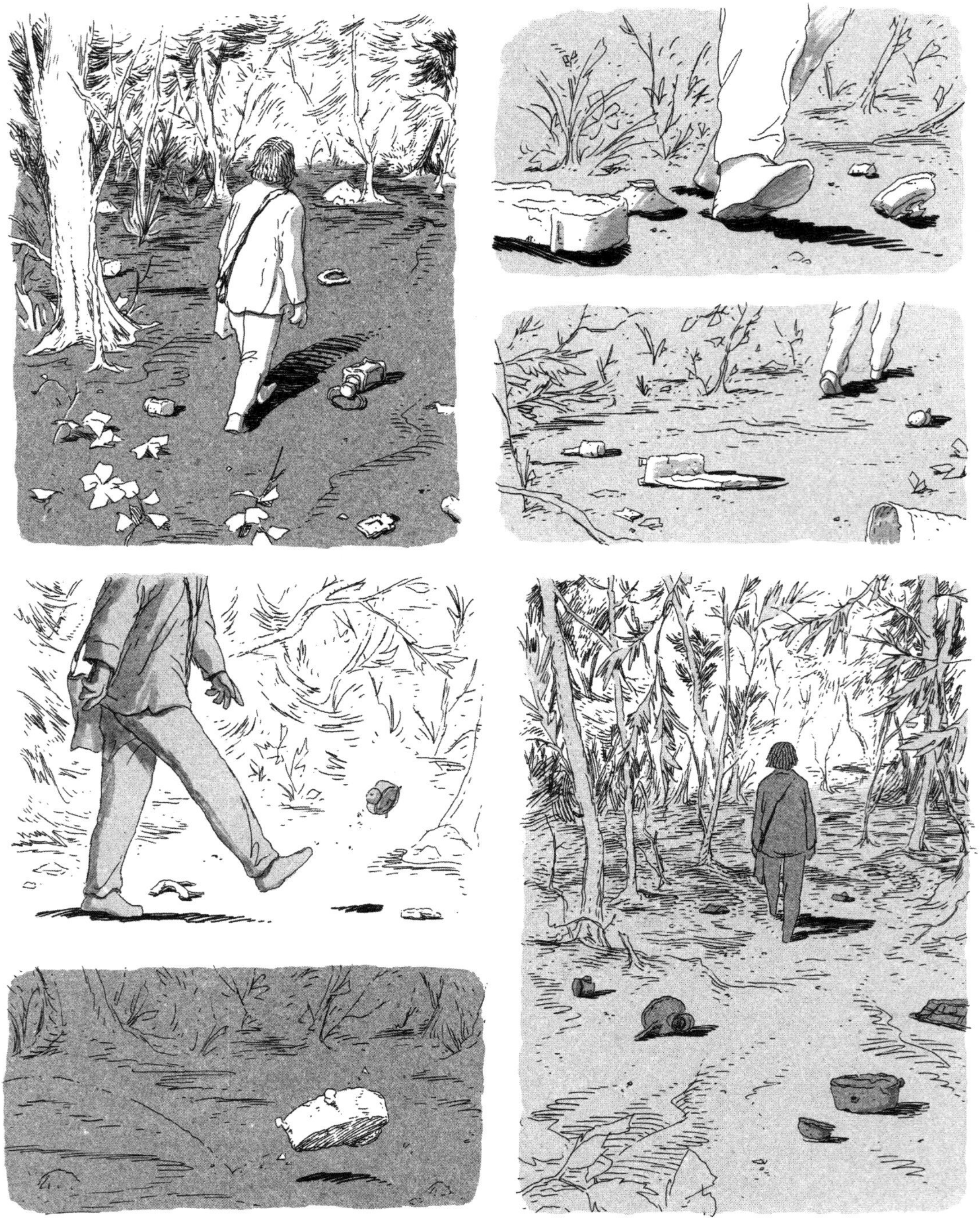

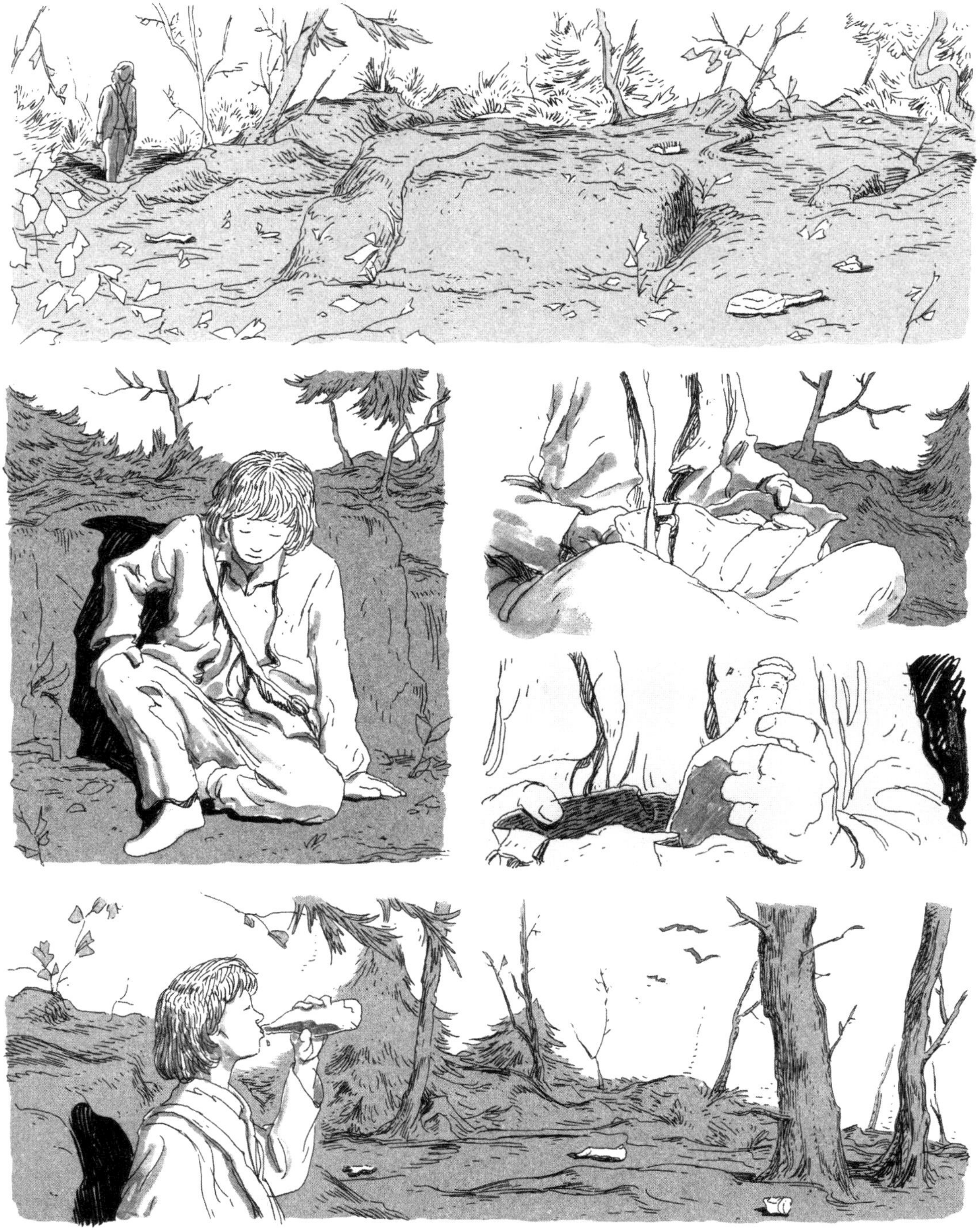

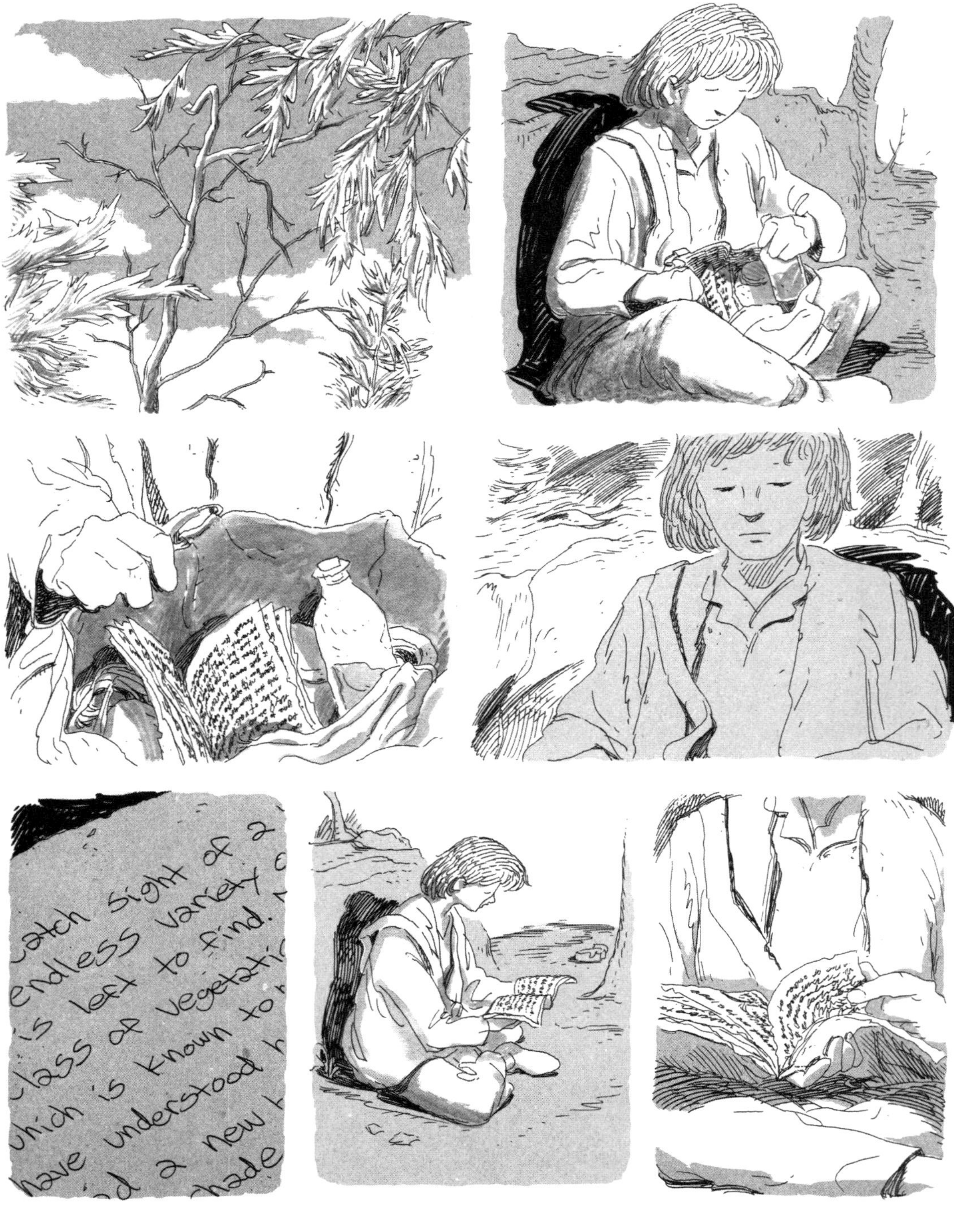
catch sight of a
endless variety
is left to find.
class of vegetati
hich is known to
have understood
d a new
shade

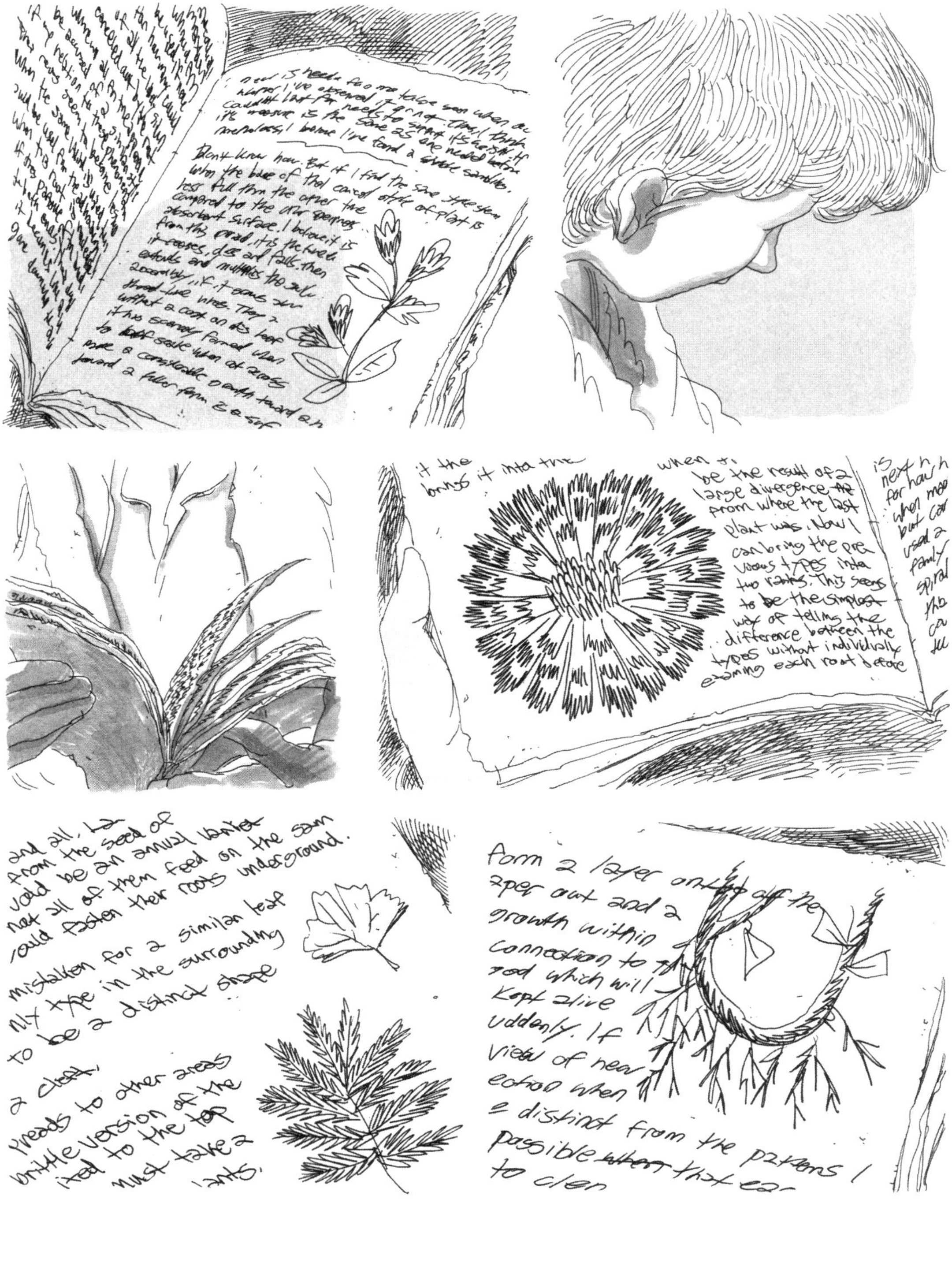

it the
brings it into the
when it
be the result of a
large divergence
from where the last
plant was. Now I
can bring the pre
vious types into
two ranks. This seems
to be the simplest
way of telling the
difference between the
types without individually
examining each root before
and all, La
from the seed of
vold be an annual
nat all of them feed on the sam
vould fasten their roots underground.
mistaken for a similar leaf
nly type in the surrounding
to be a distinct shape
a clea
preads to other areas
brittle version of the
ixed to the top
must take a
lants.
form a layer on
aper out and a
growth within
connection to
ood which will
kept alive
uddenly. If
view of near
when
e distinct from the patterns I
possible that ea
to clen

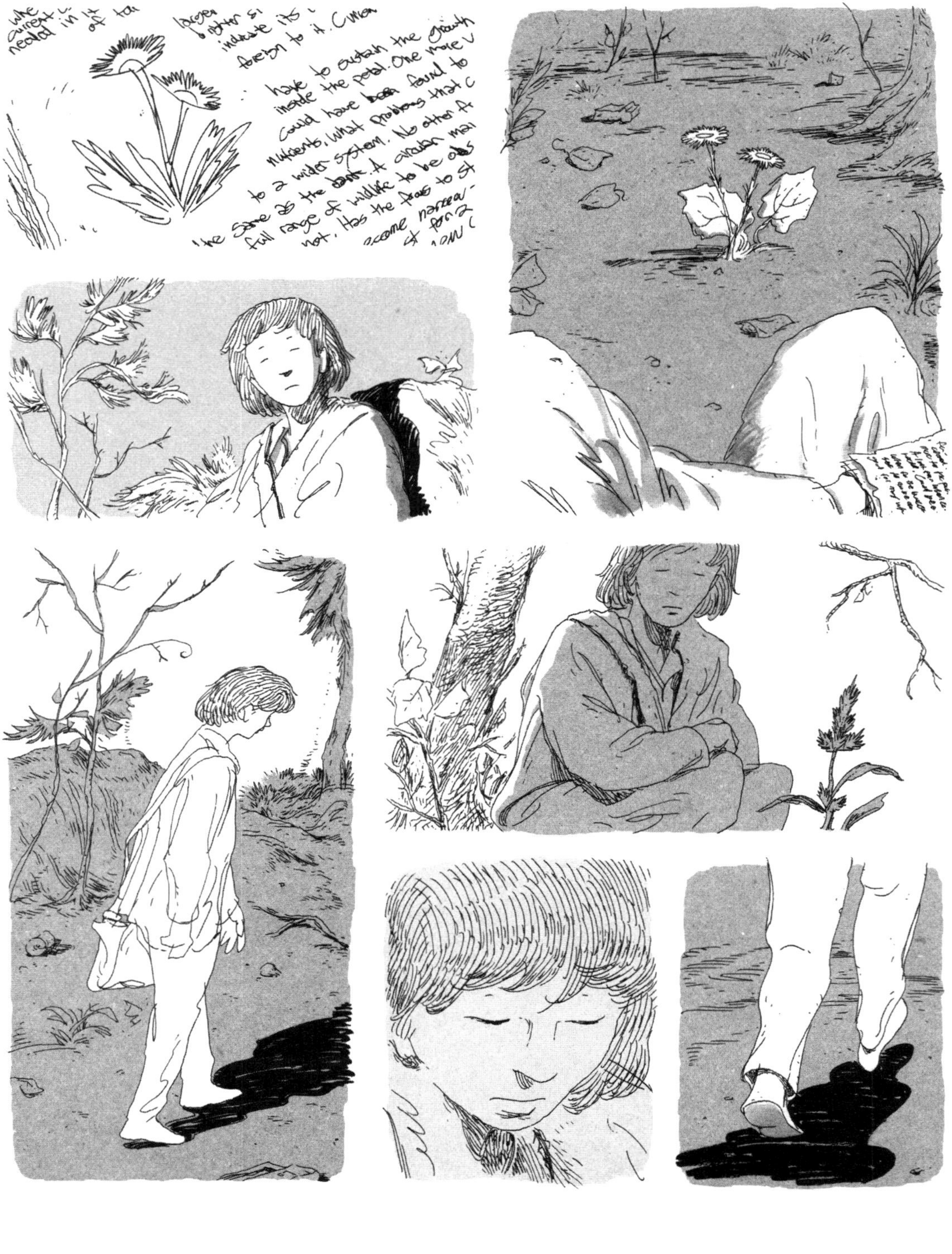
have to sustain the growth
inside the petal. One more
nutrients, what problems that
to a wider system. No other
full range of wildlife to be

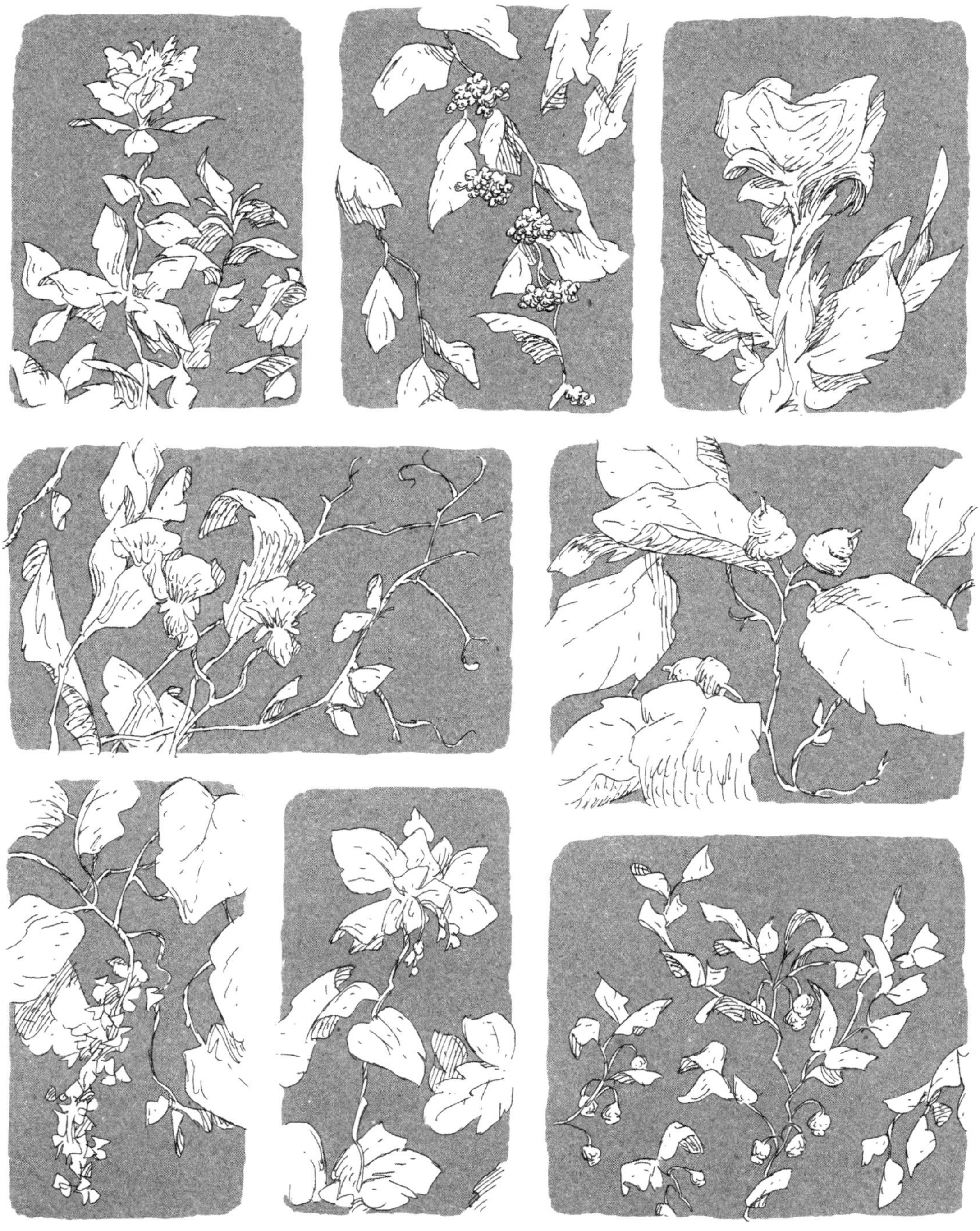

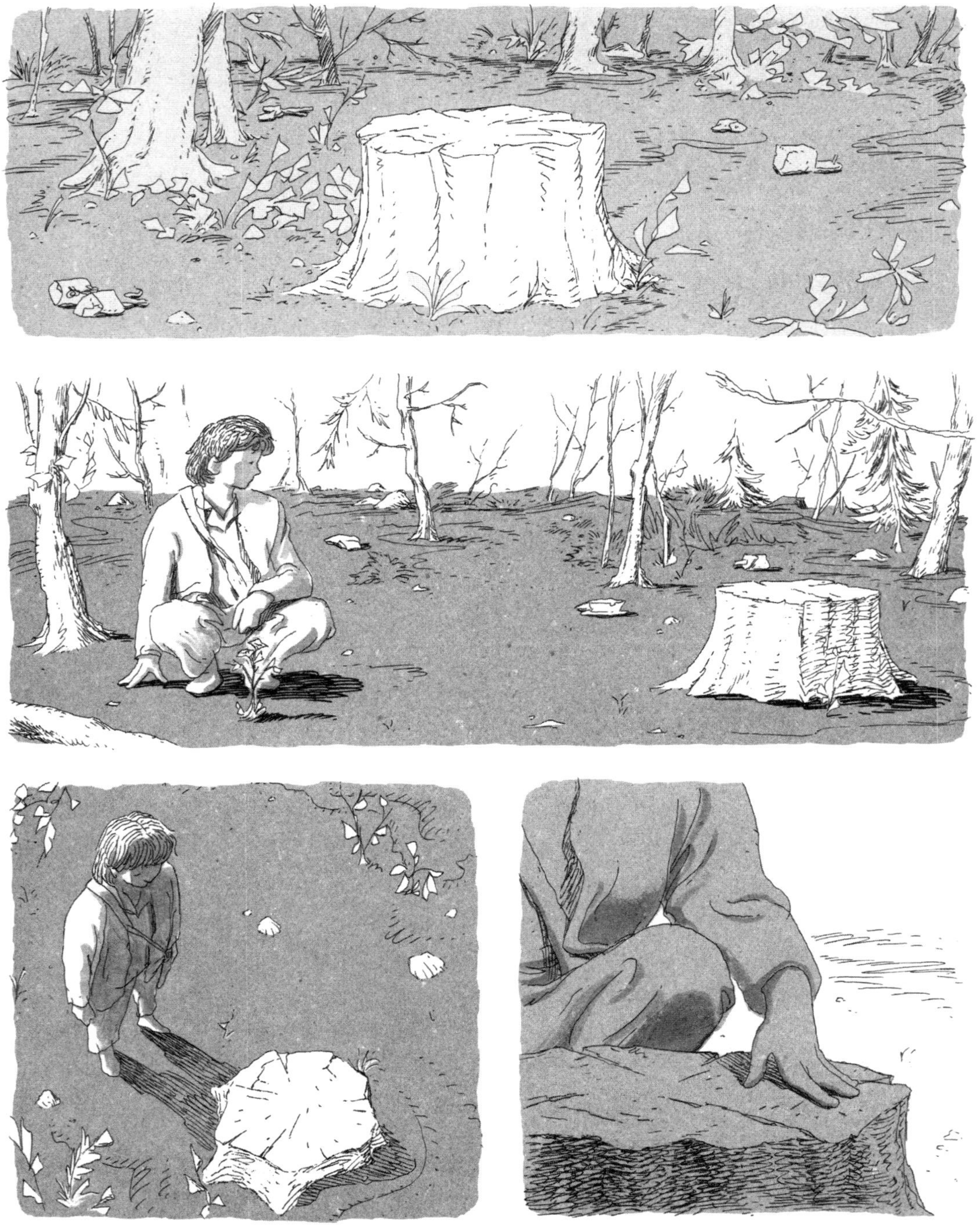

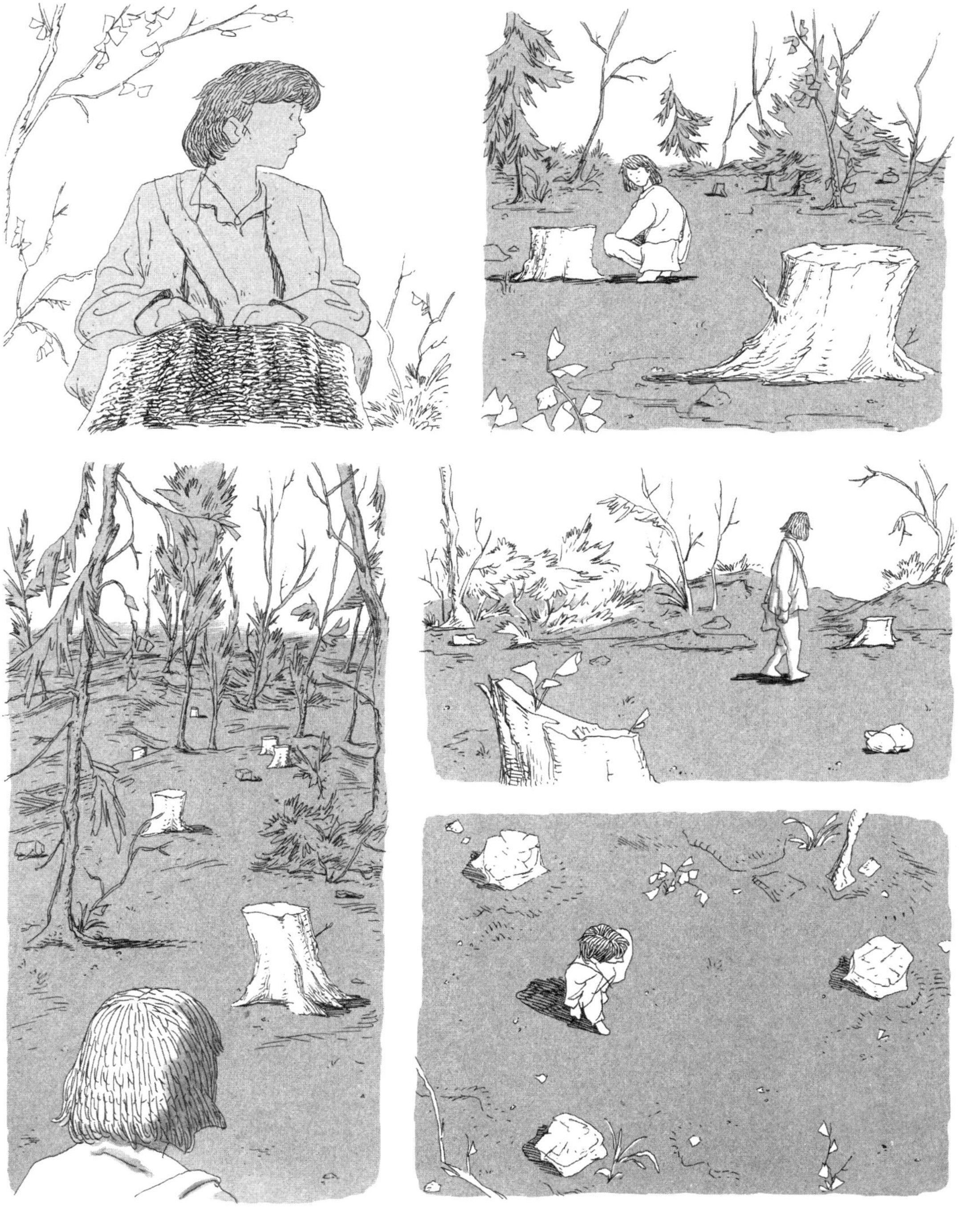

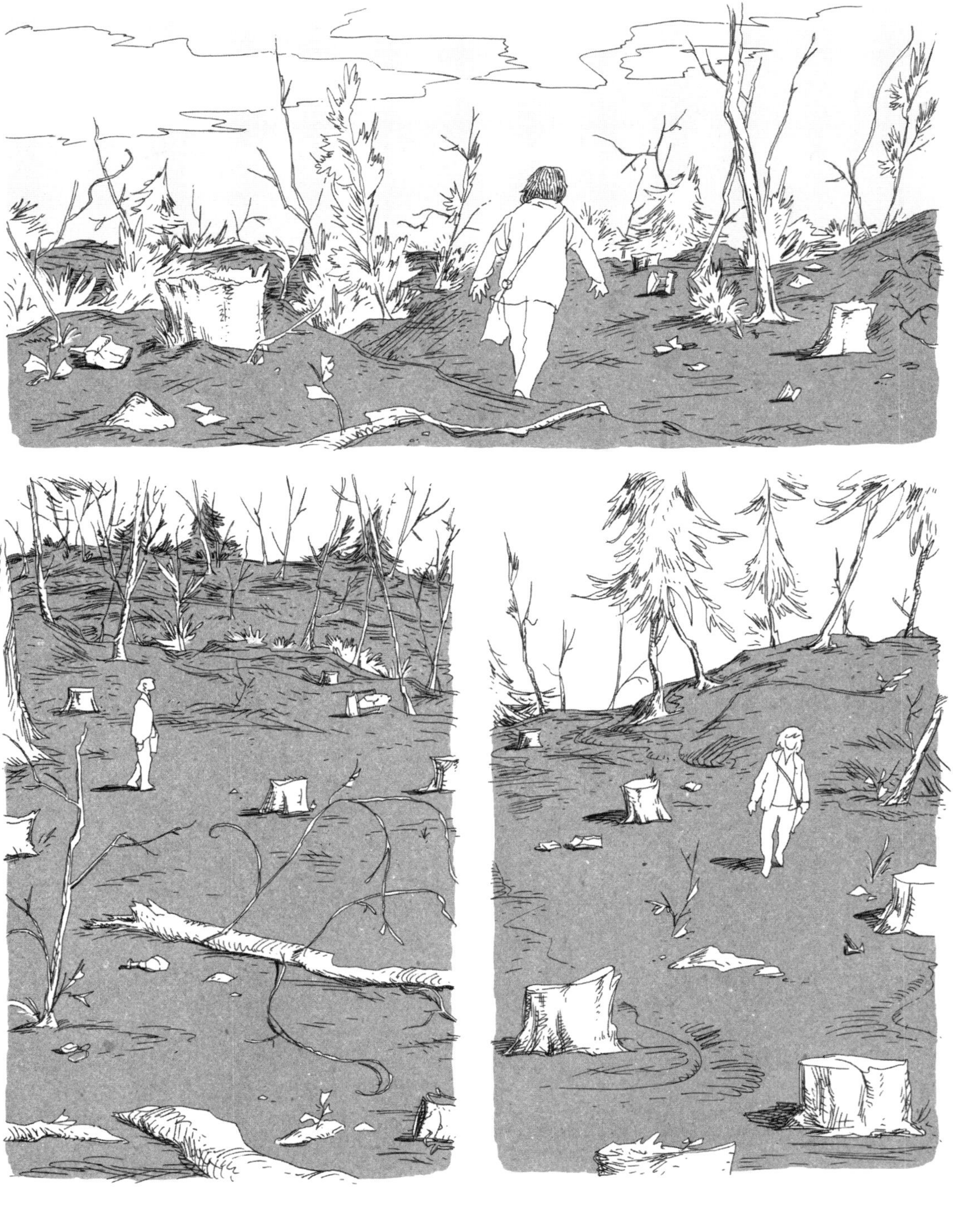

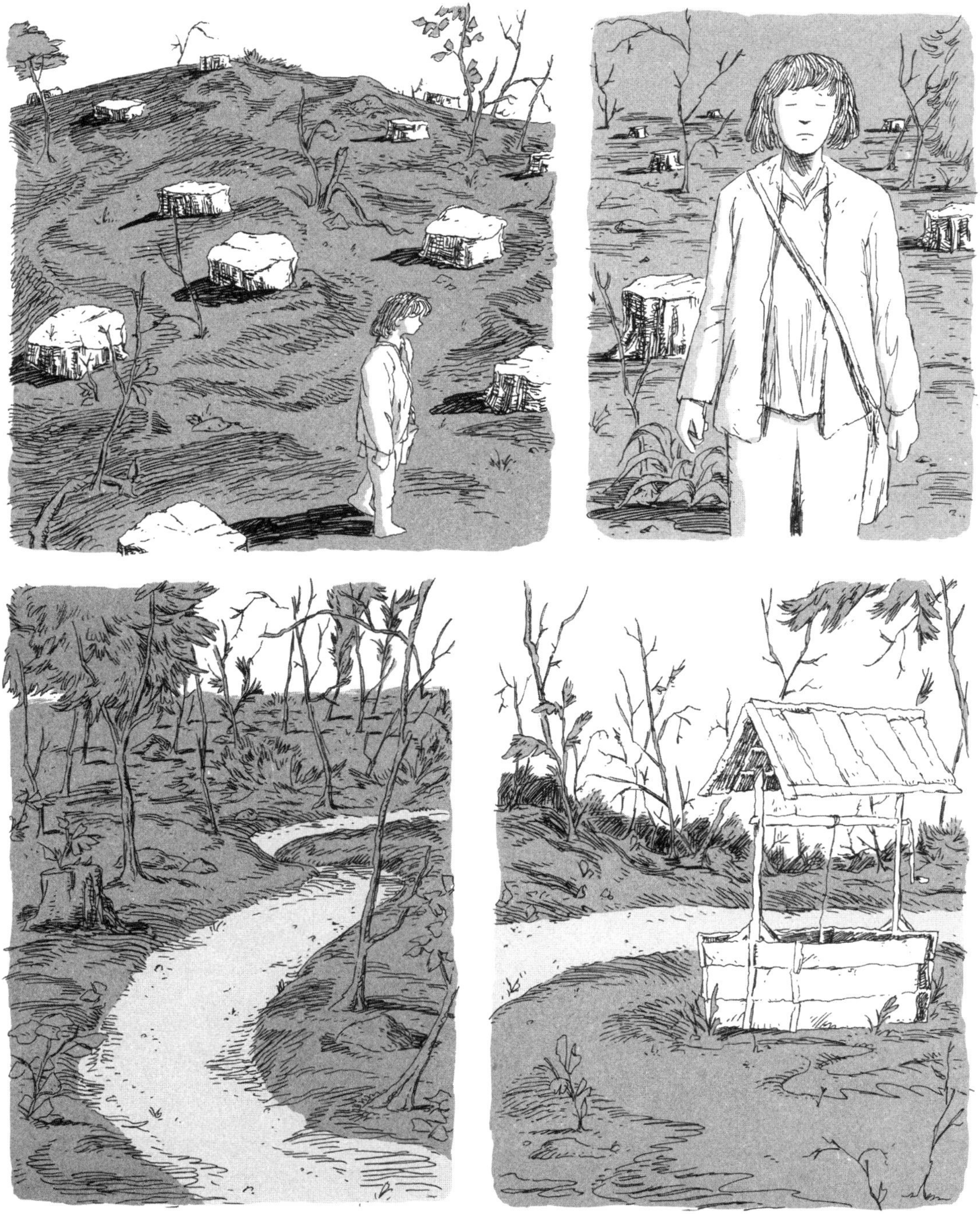

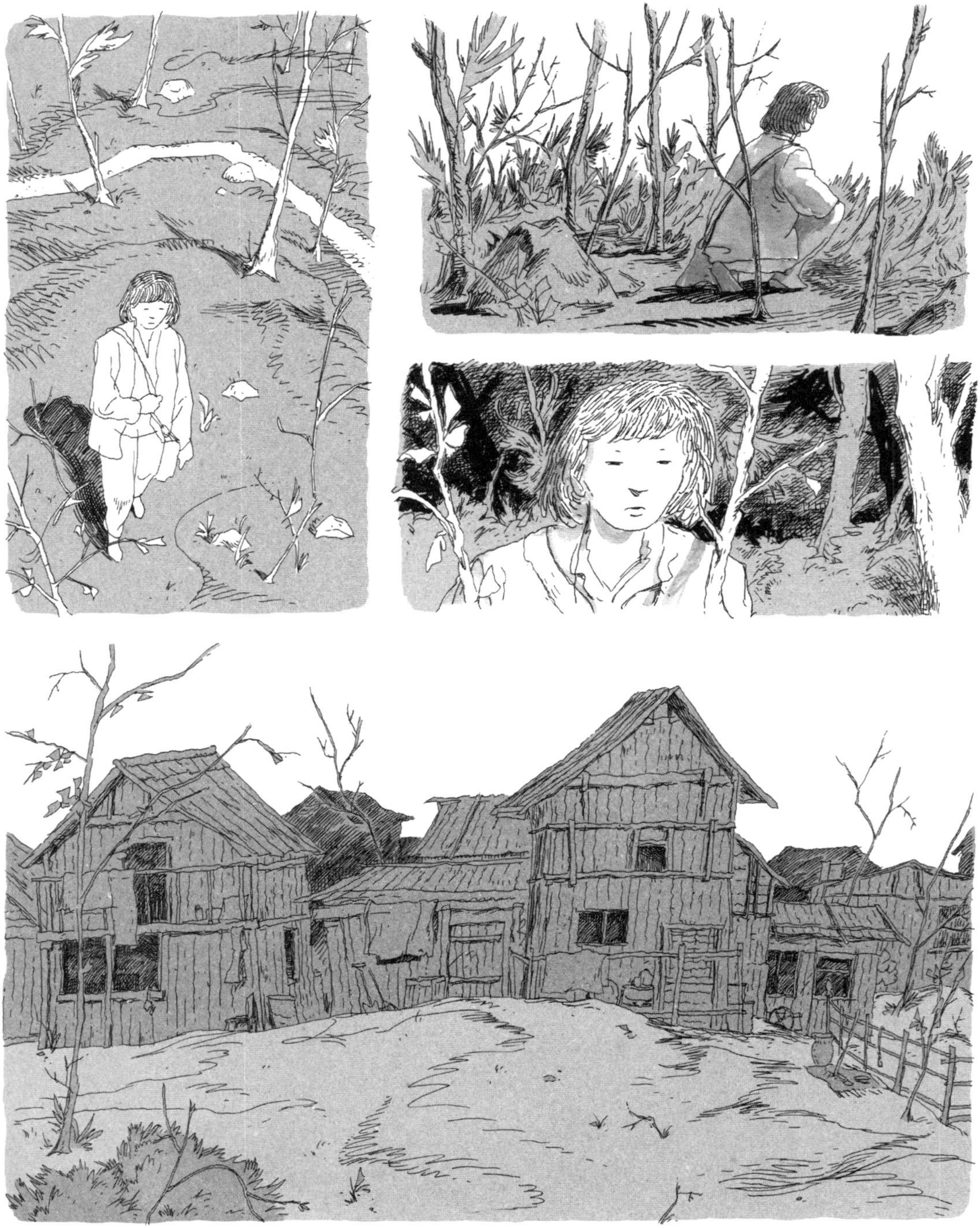

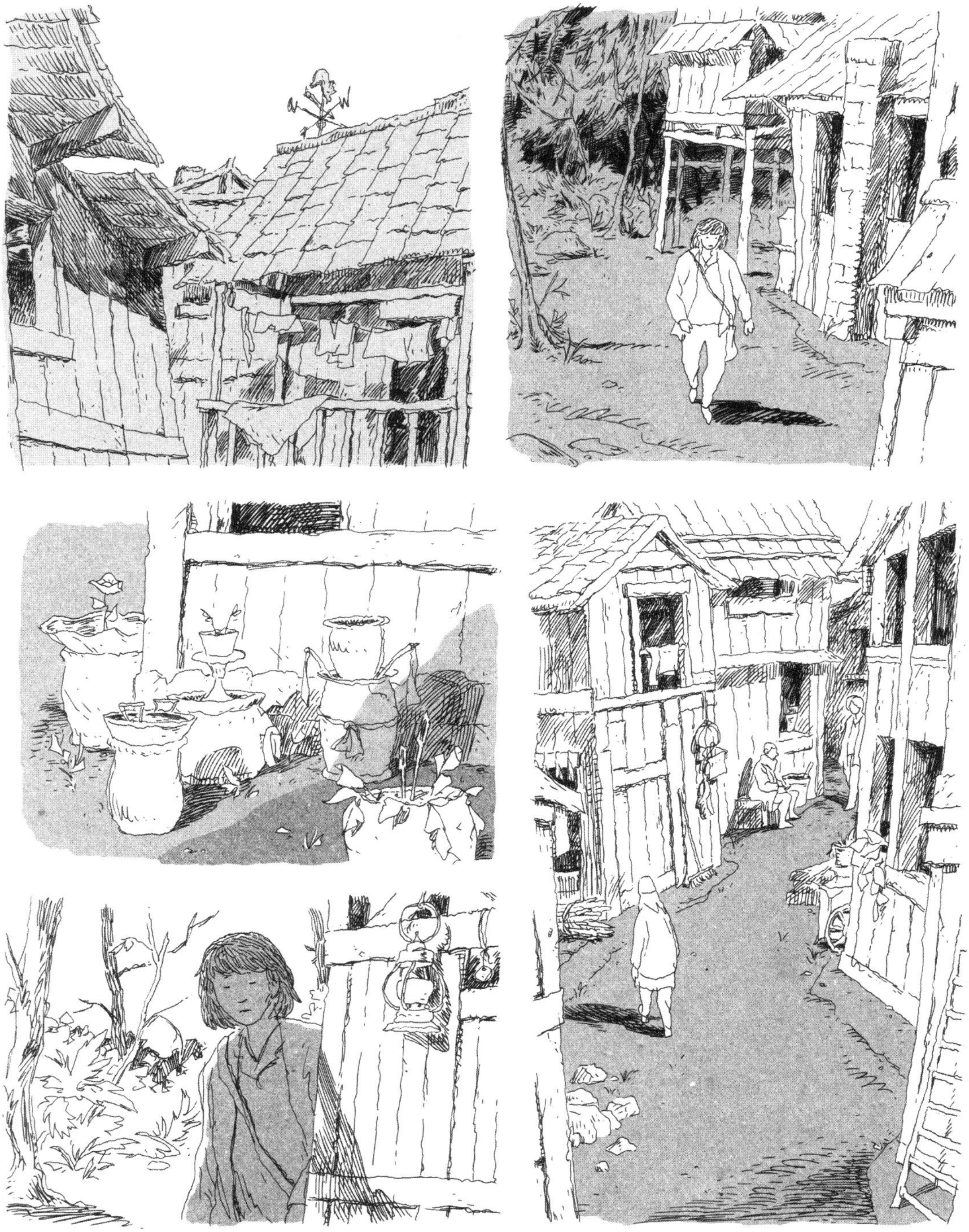

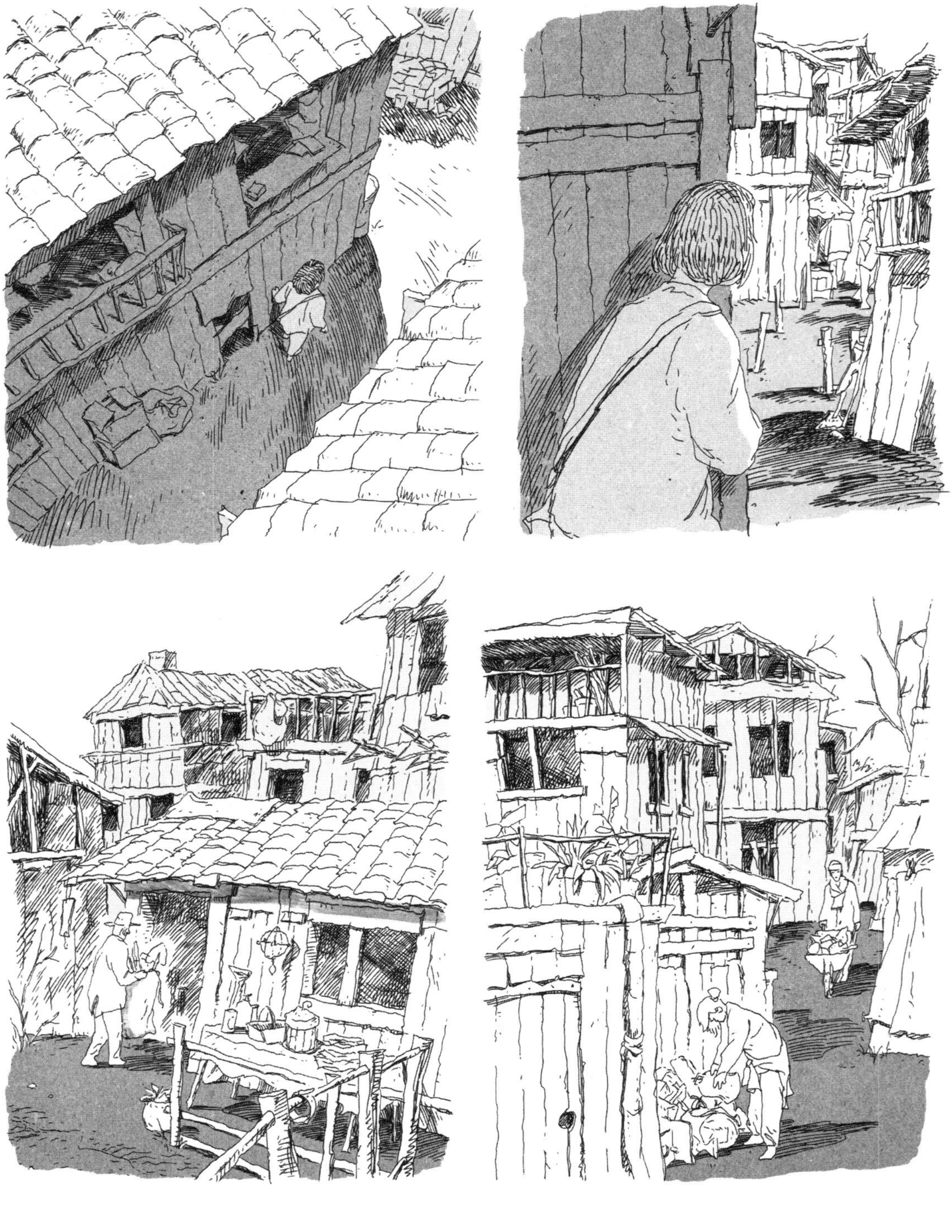

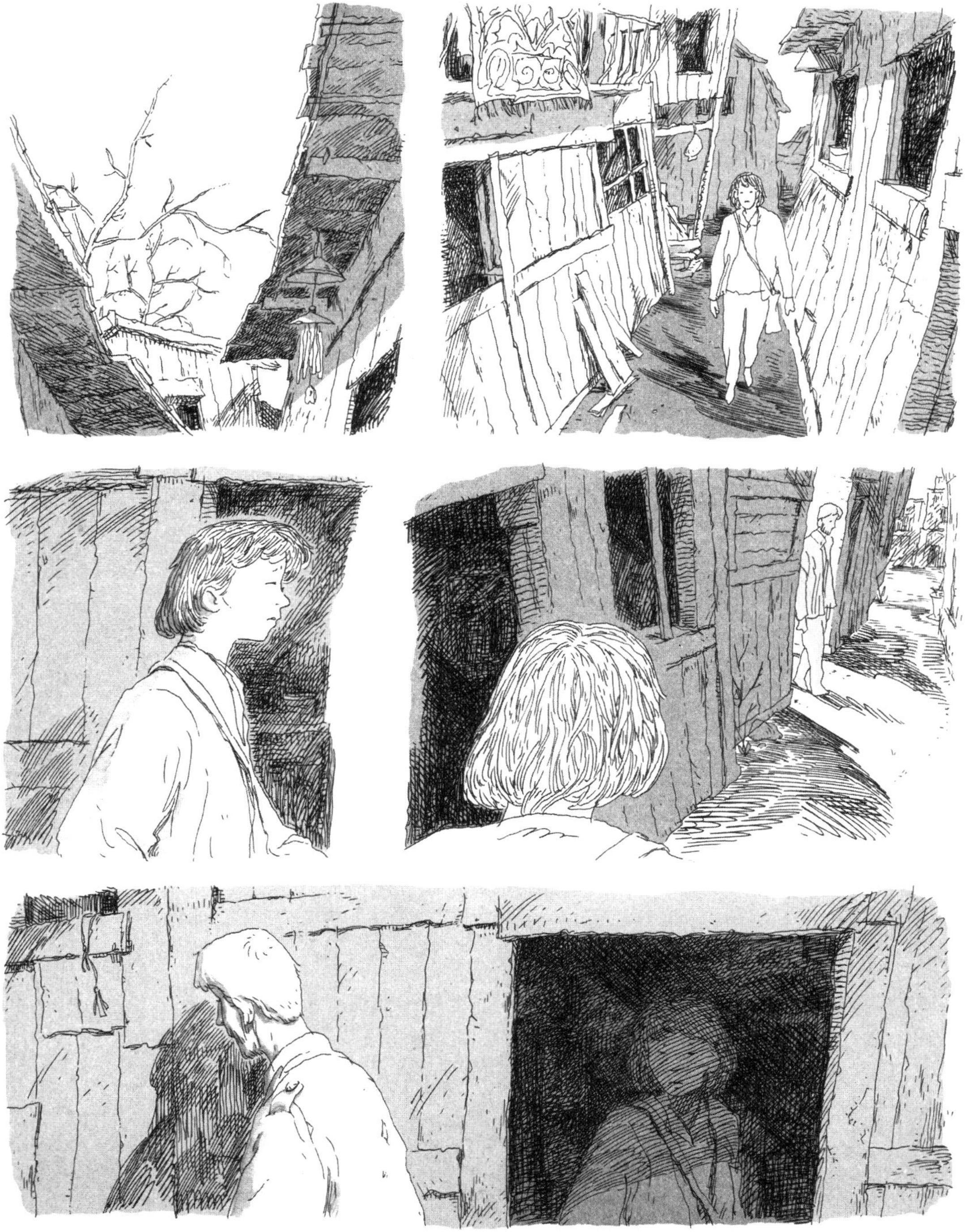

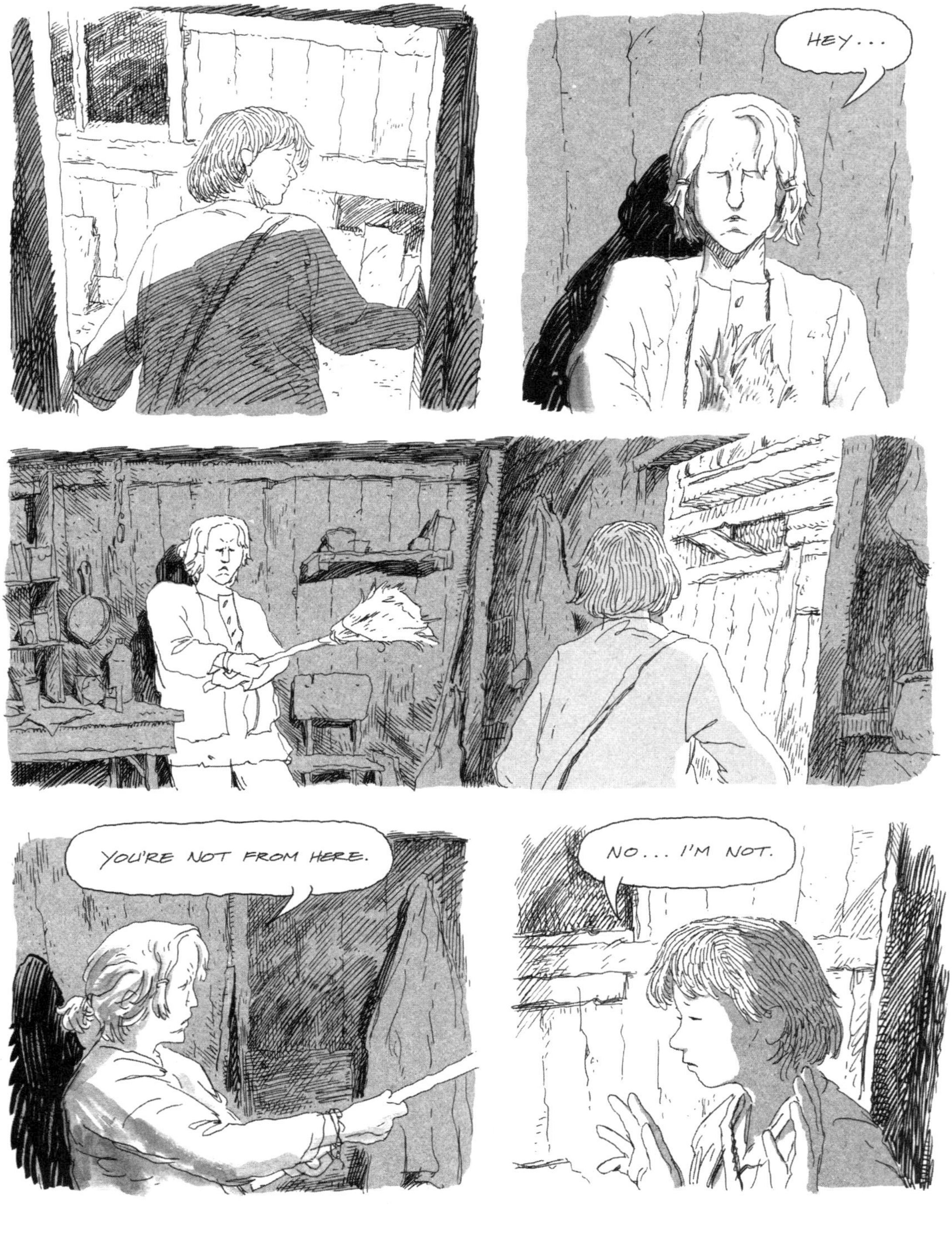
HEY...
YOU'RE NOT FROM HERE.
NO... I'M NOT.

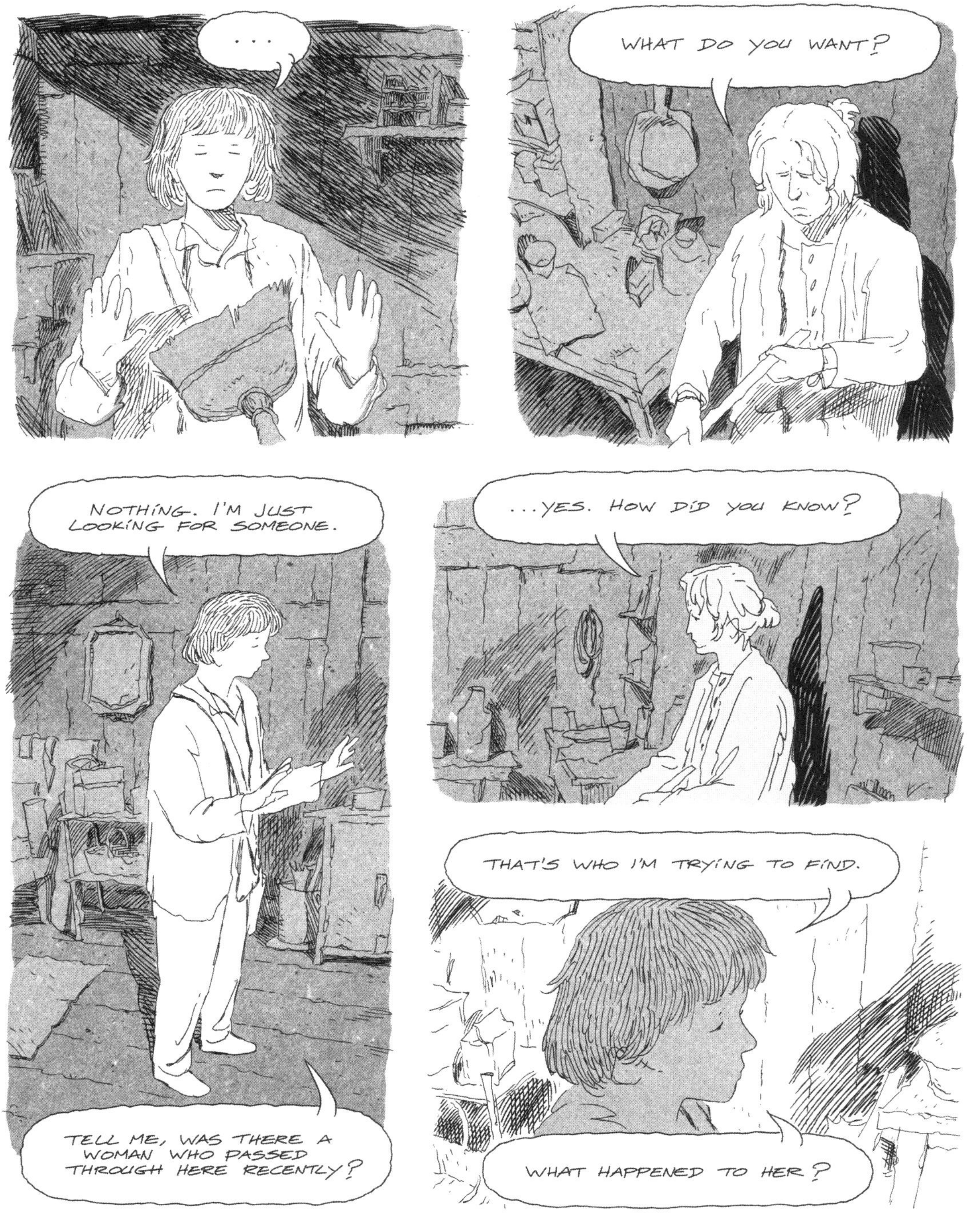
...
WHAT DO YOU WANT?
NOTHING. I'M JUST LOOKING FOR SOMEONE.
TELL ME, WAS THERE A WOMAN WHO PASSED THROUGH HERE RECENTLY?
...YES. HOW DID YOU KNOW?
THAT'S WHO I'M TRYING TO FIND.
WHAT HAPPENED TO HER?

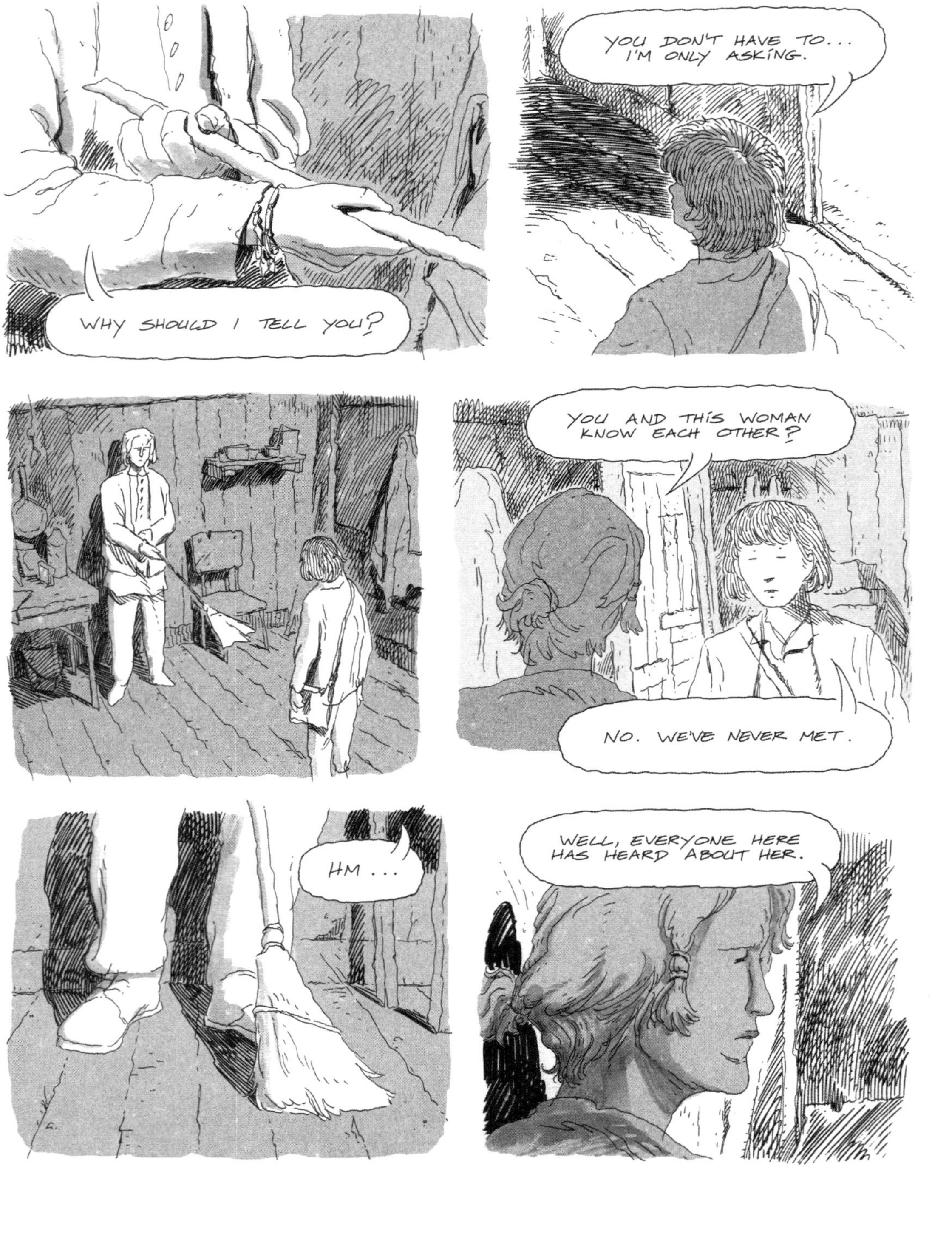
WHY SHOULD I TELL YOU?
YOU DON'T HAVE TO... I'M ONLY ASKING.
YOU AND THIS WOMAN KNOW EACH OTHER?
NO. WE'VE NEVER MET.
HM ...
WELL, EVERYONE HERE HAS HEARD ABOUT HER.

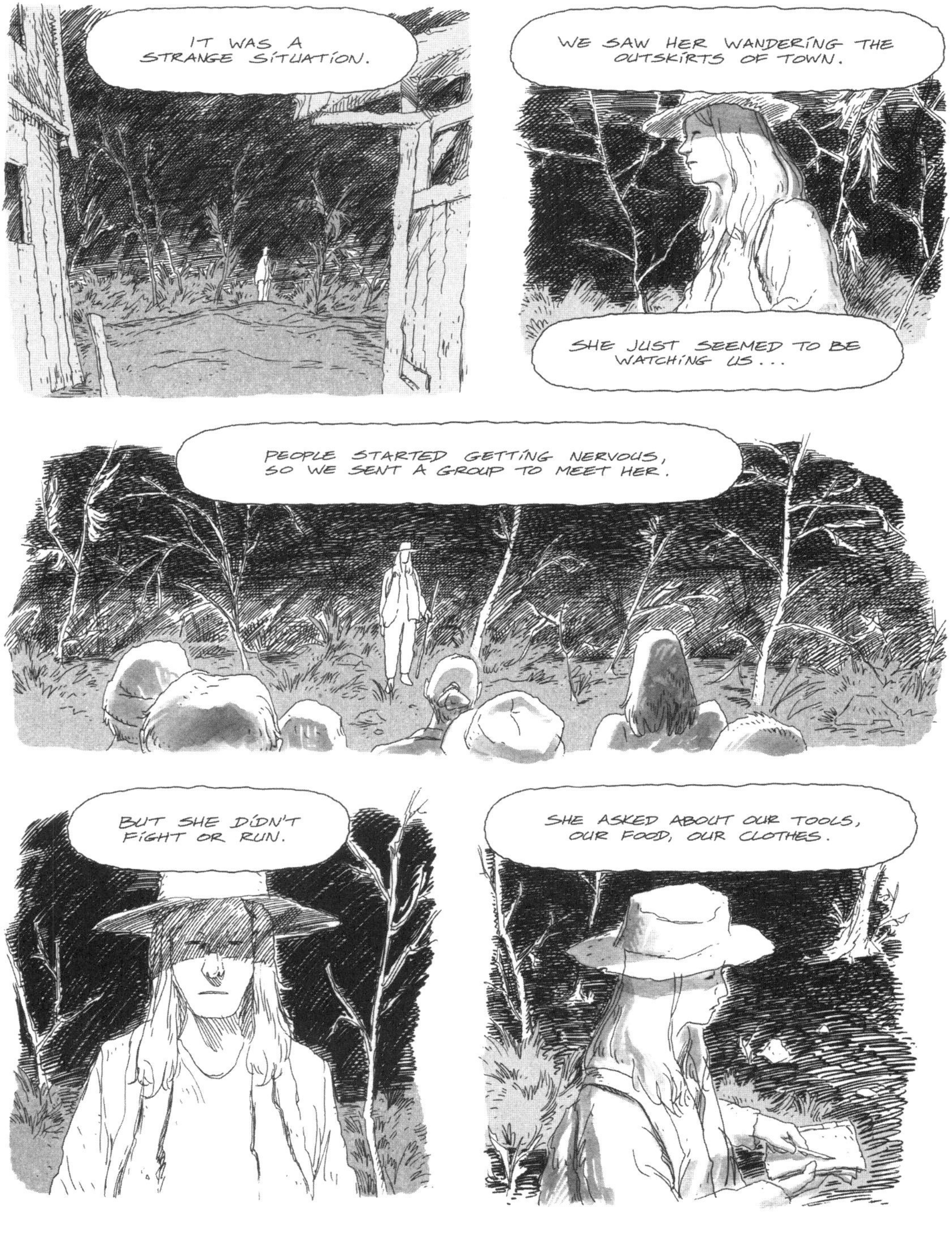
IT WAS A STRANGE SITUATION.
WE SAW HER WANDERING THE OUTSKIRTS OF TOWN.
SHE JUST SEEMED TO BE WATCHING US...
PEOPLE STARTED GETTING NERVOUS, SO WE SENT A GROUP TO MEET HER.
BUT SHE DIDN'T FIGHT OR RUN.
SHE ASKED ABOUT OUR TOOLS, OUR FOOD, OUR CLOTHES.

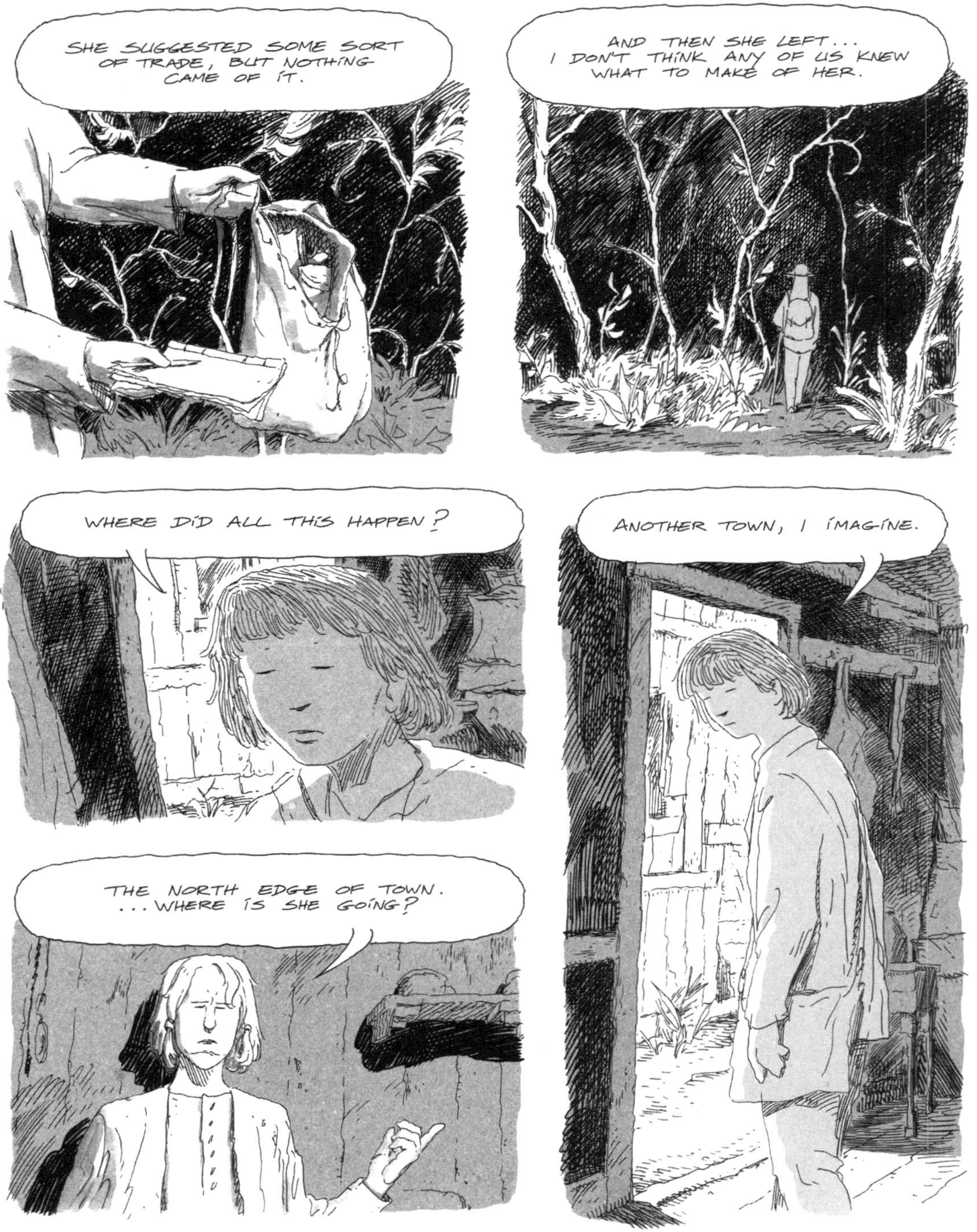
SHE SUGGESTED SOME SORT OF TRADE, BUT NOTHING CAME OF IT.
AND THEN SHE LEFT... I DON'T THINK ANY OF US KNEW WHAT TO MAKE OF HER.
WHERE DID ALL THIS HAPPEN?
ANOTHER TOWN, I IMAGINE.
THE NORTH EDGE OF TOWN. ...WHERE IS SHE GOING?

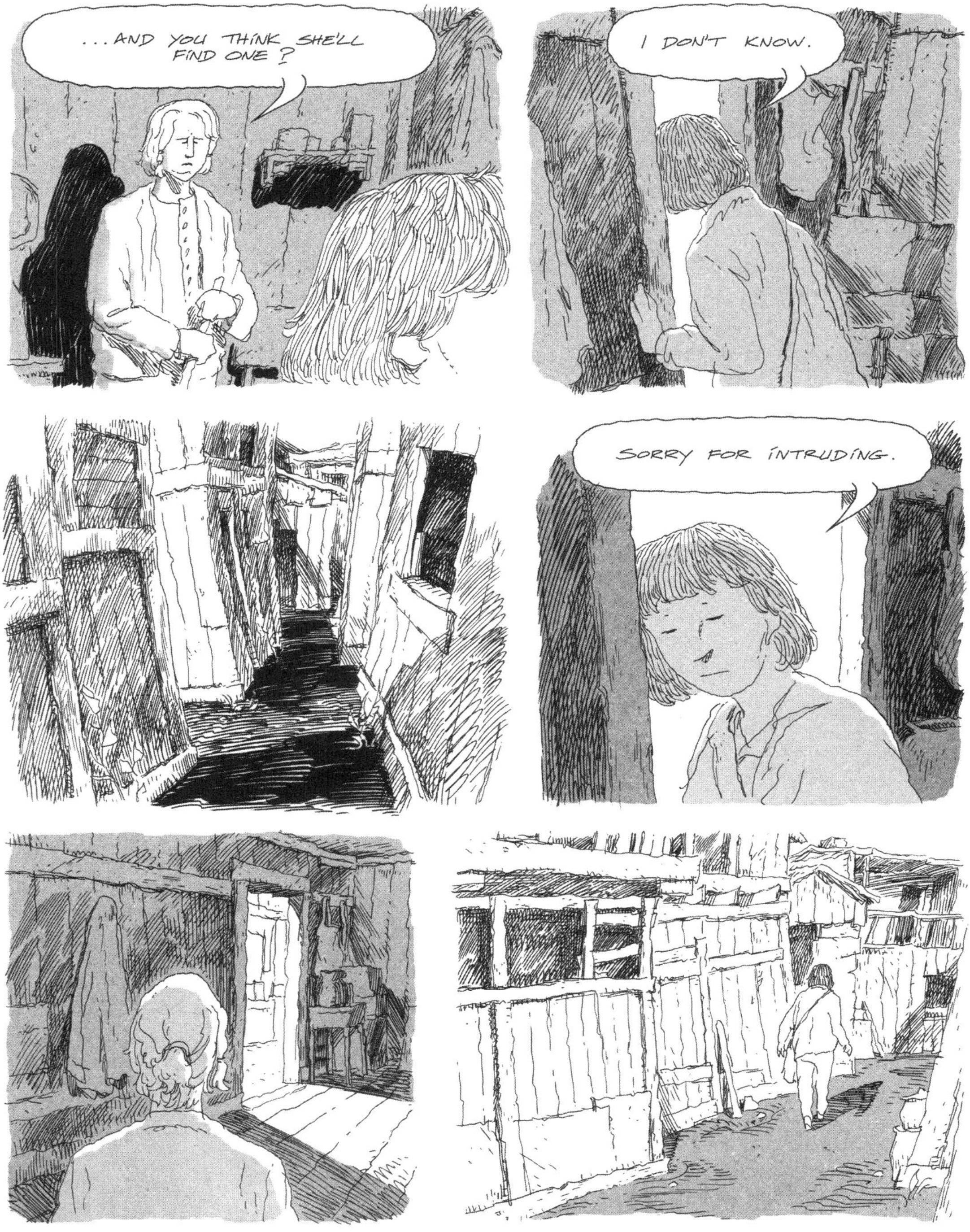
...AND YOU THINK SHE'LL FIND ONE?
I DON'T KNOW.
SORRY FOR INTRUDING.

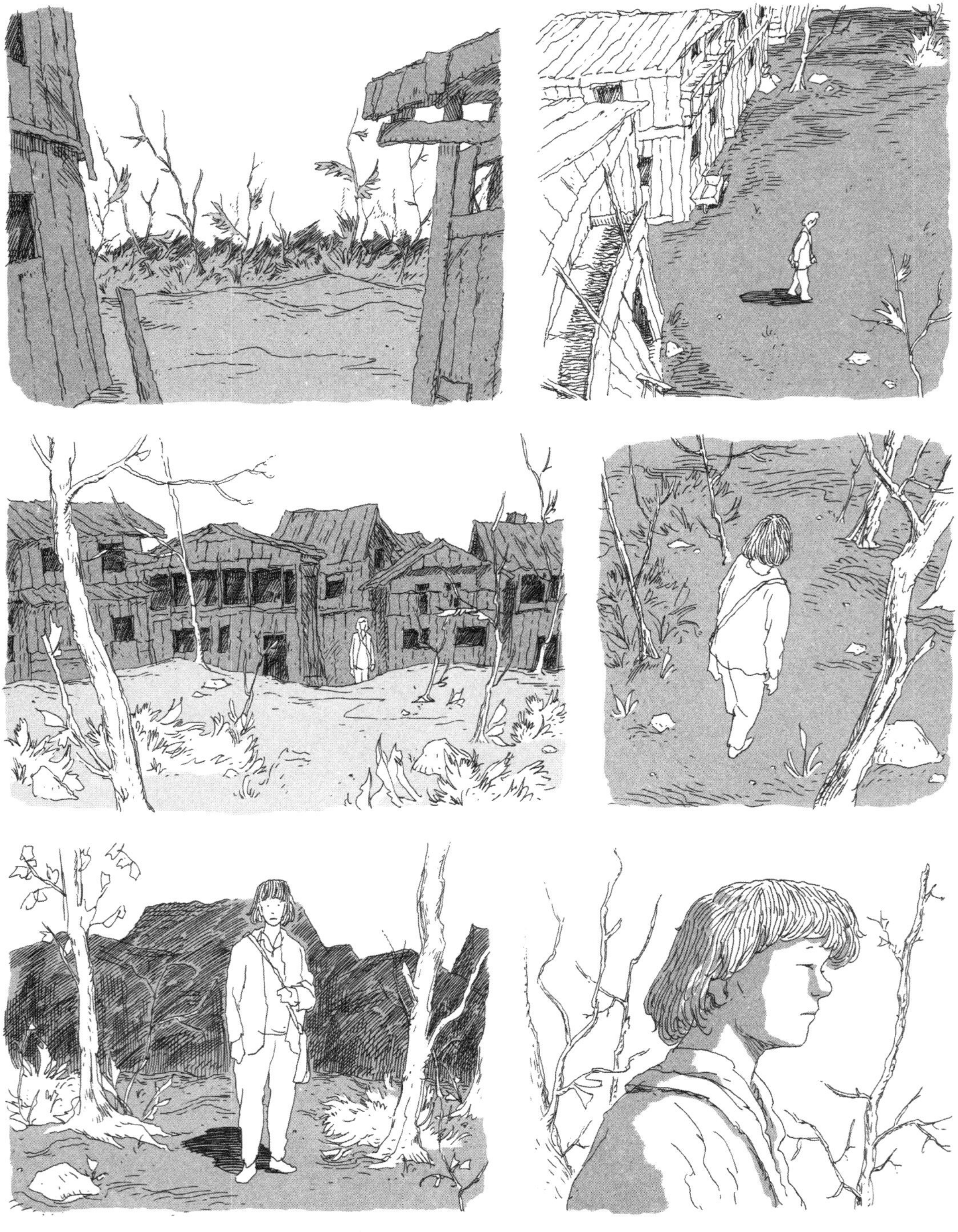

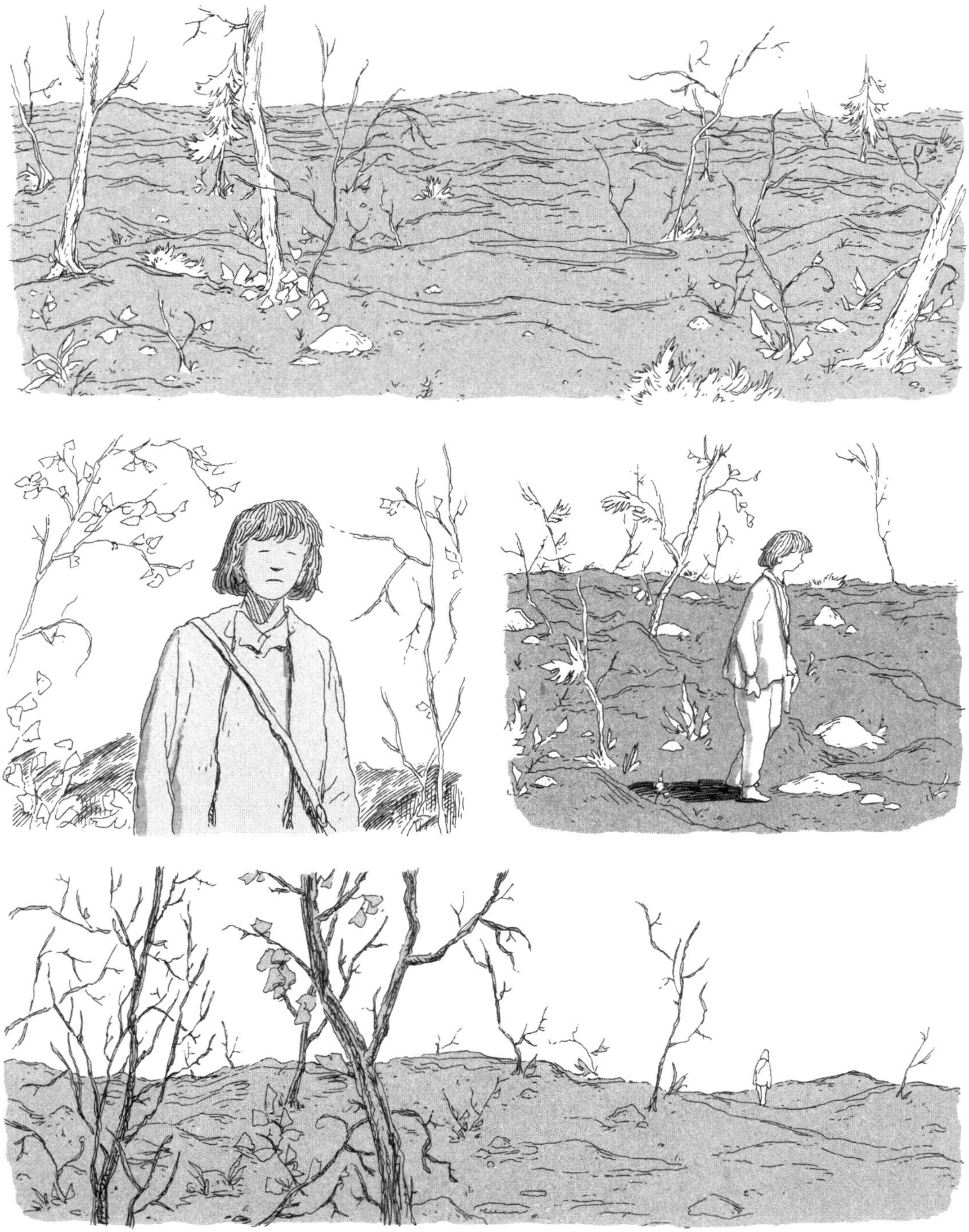

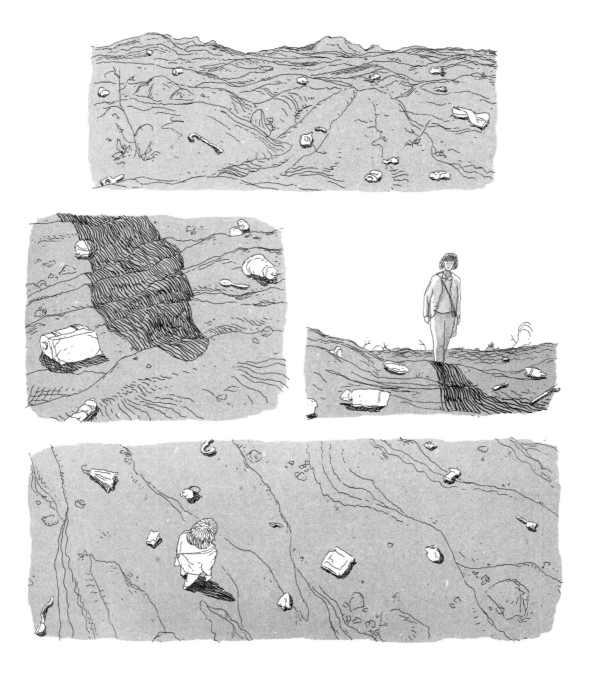

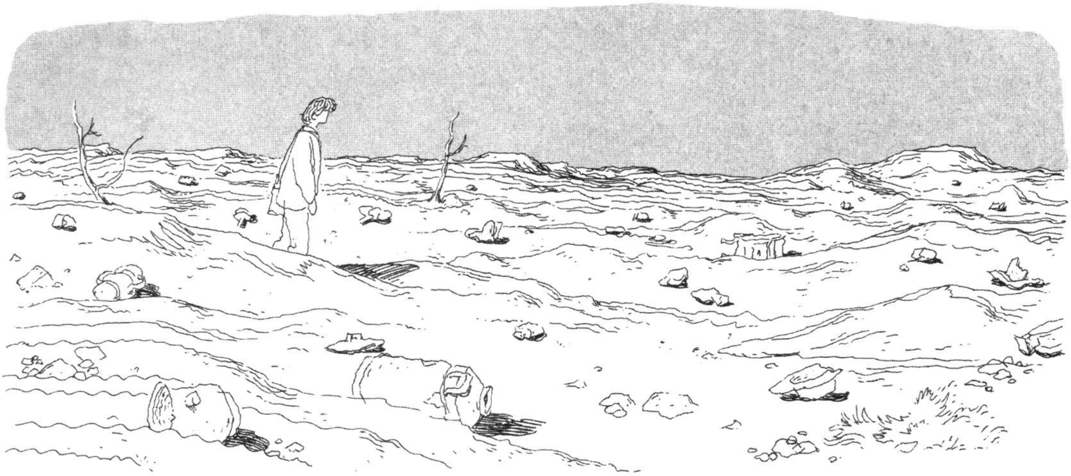
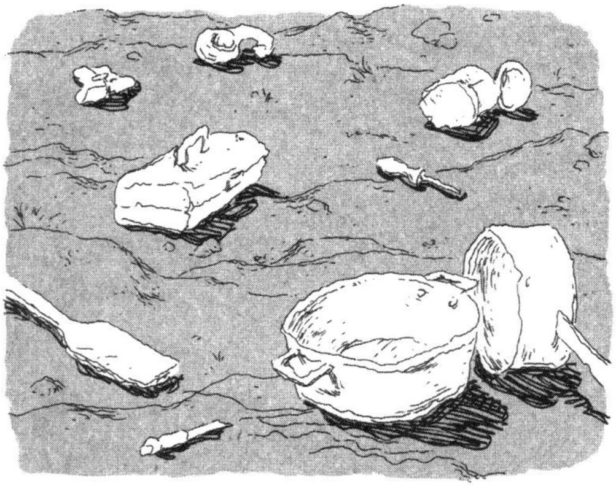
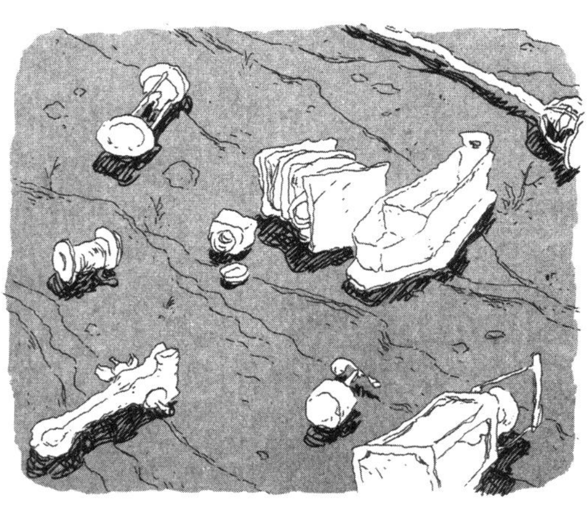
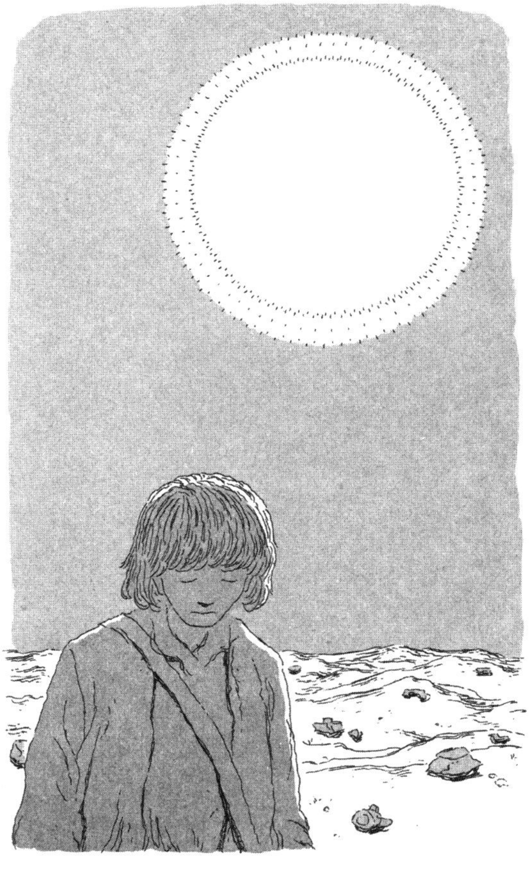

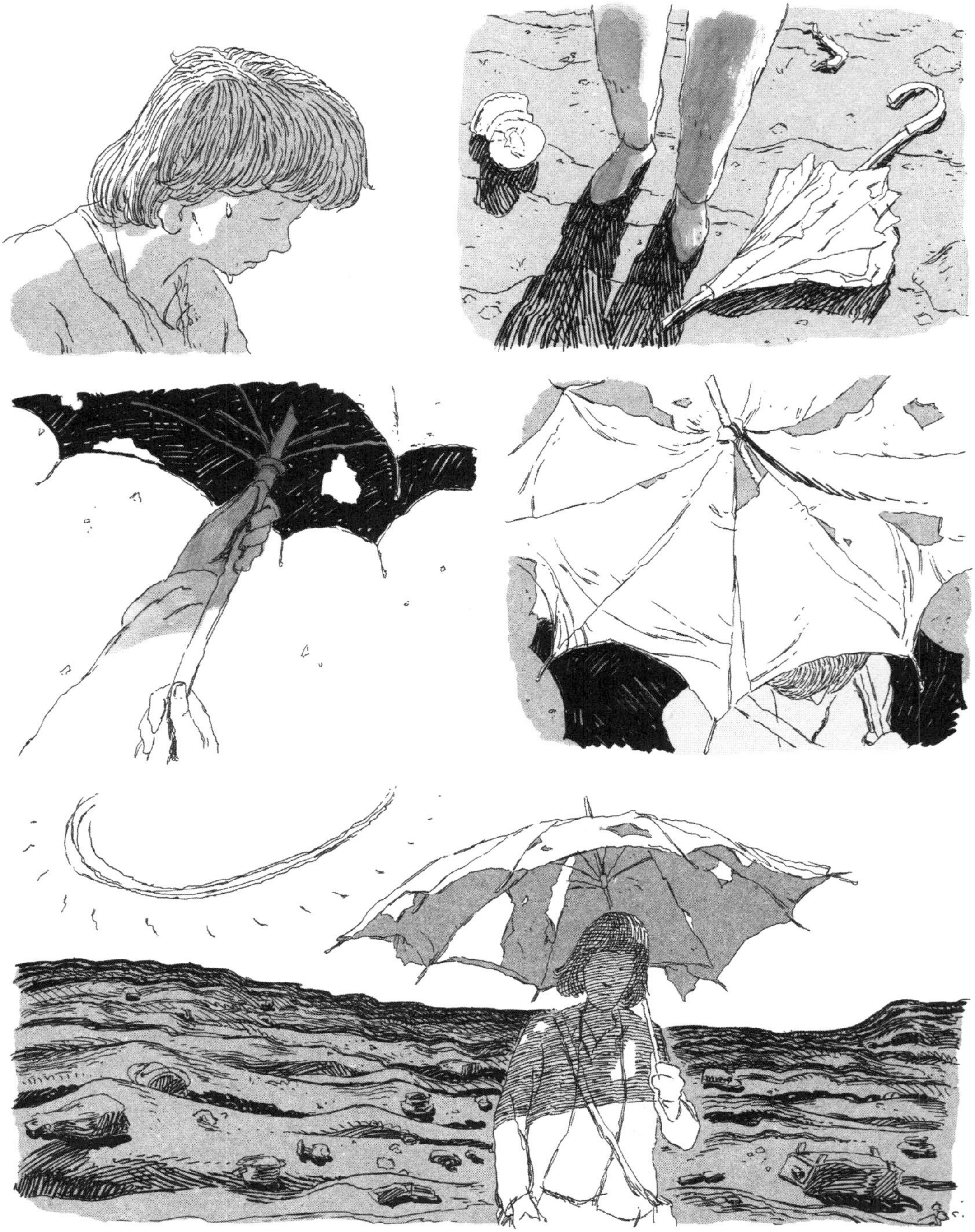

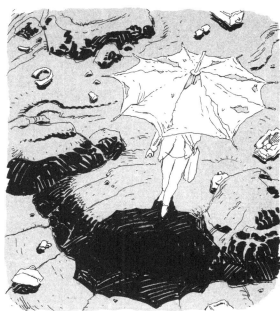

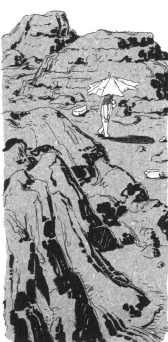

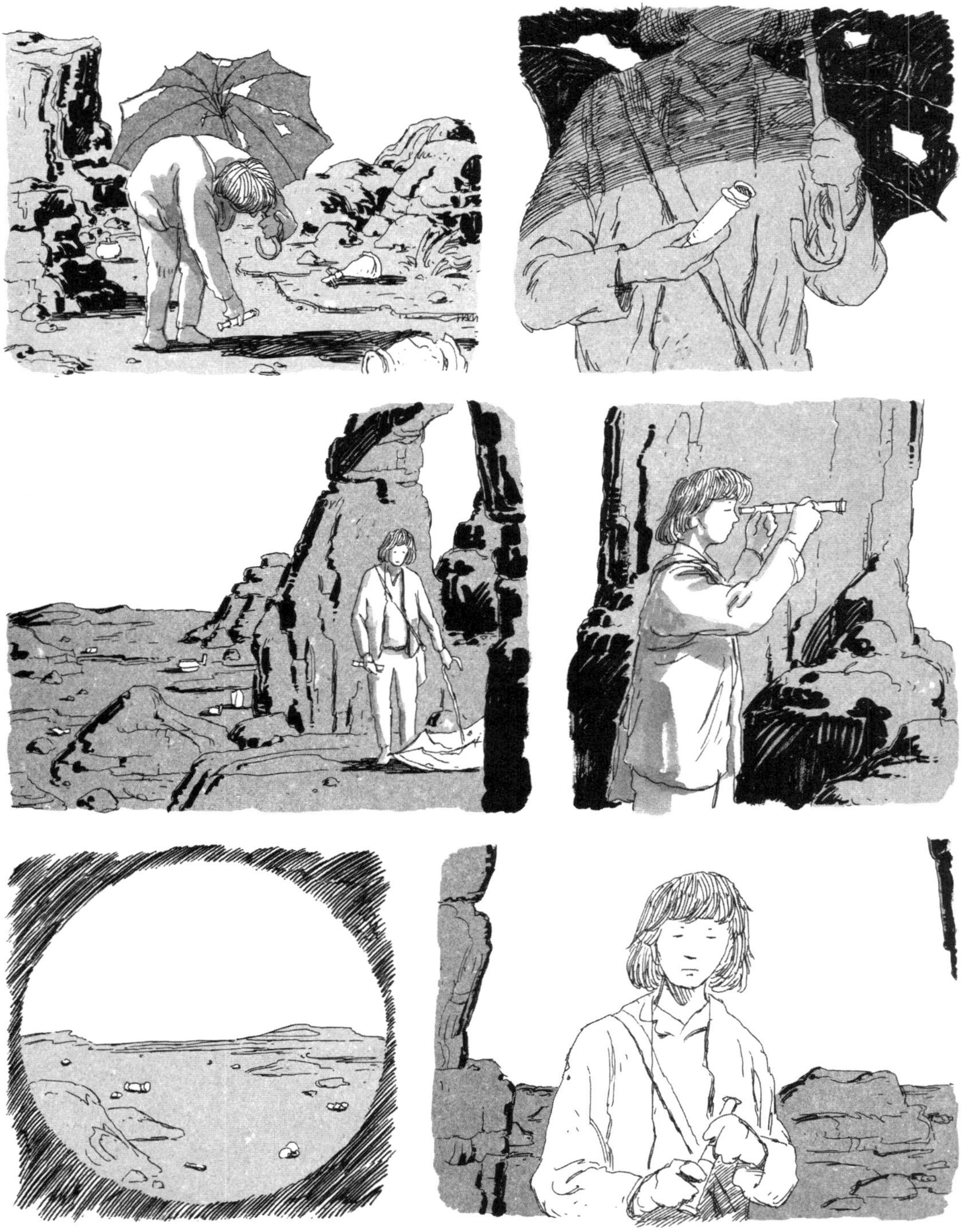

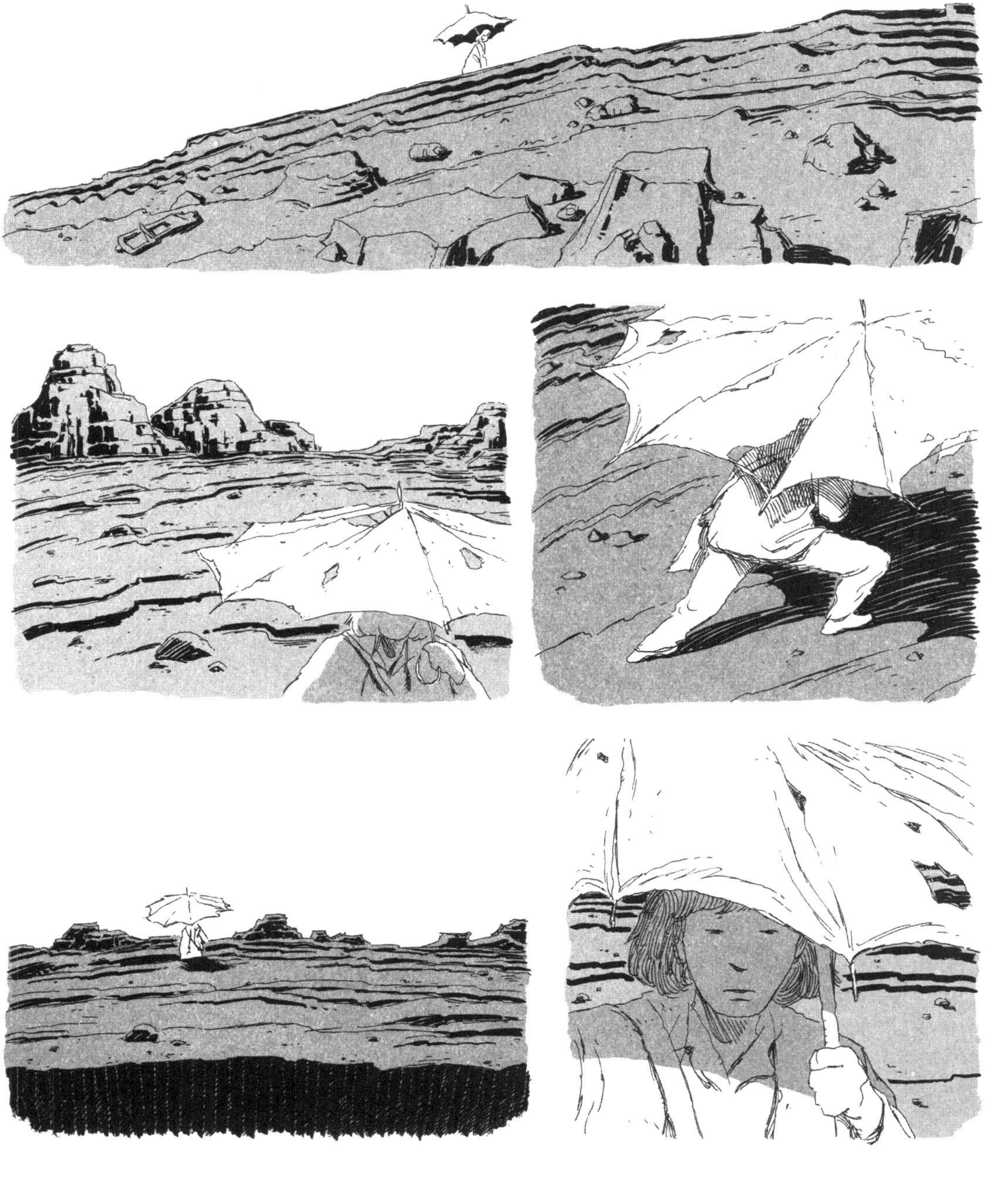

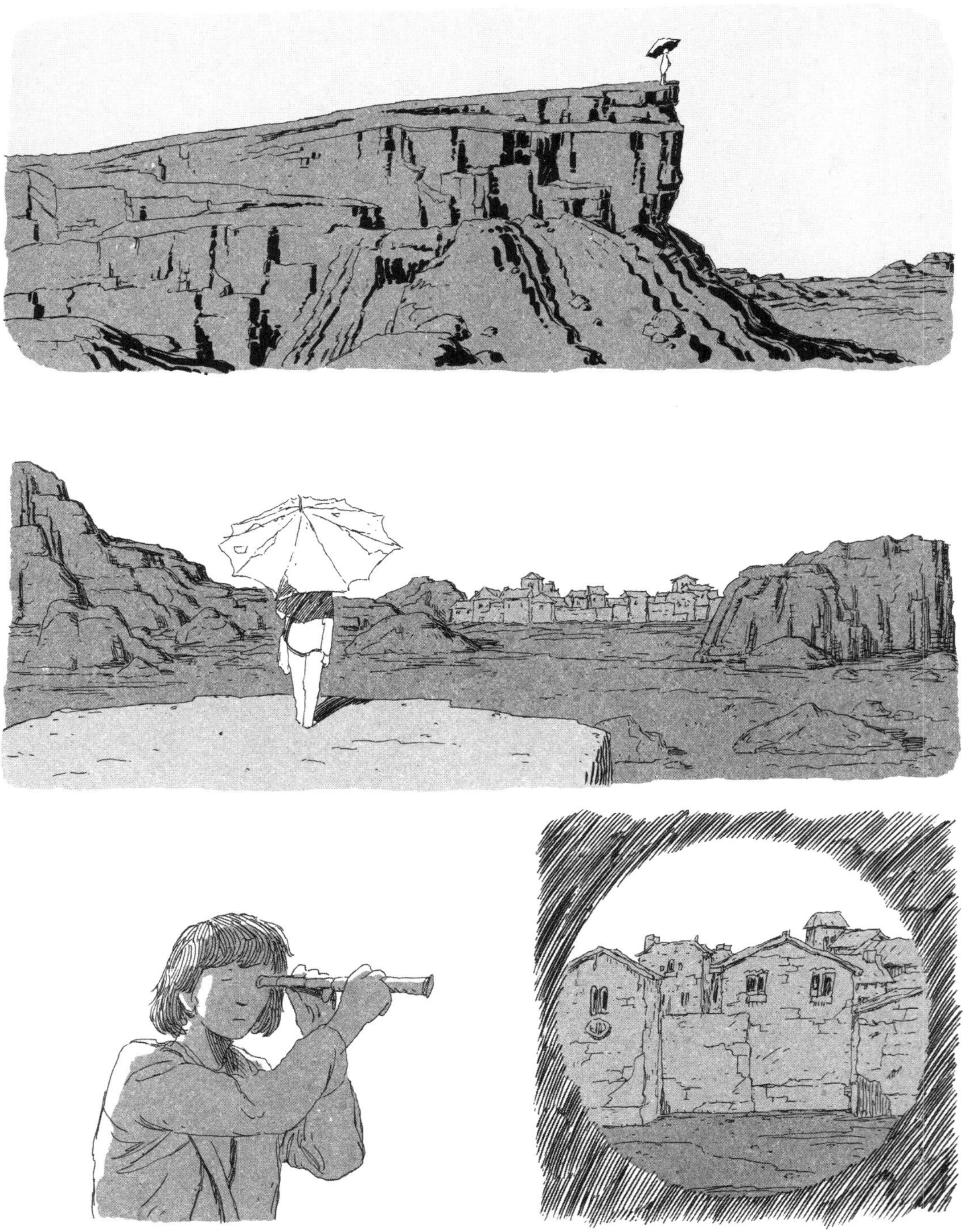

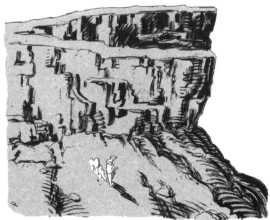

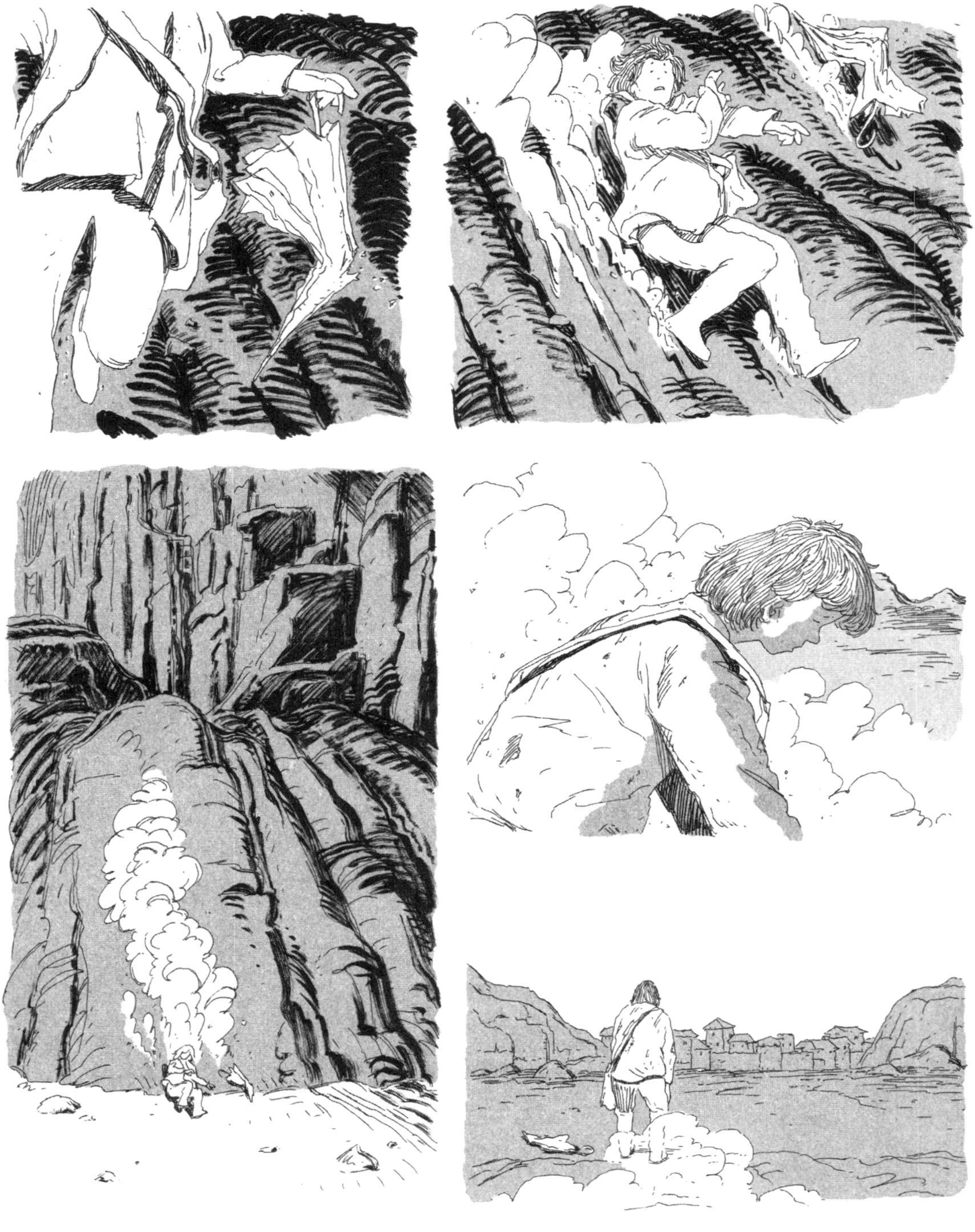

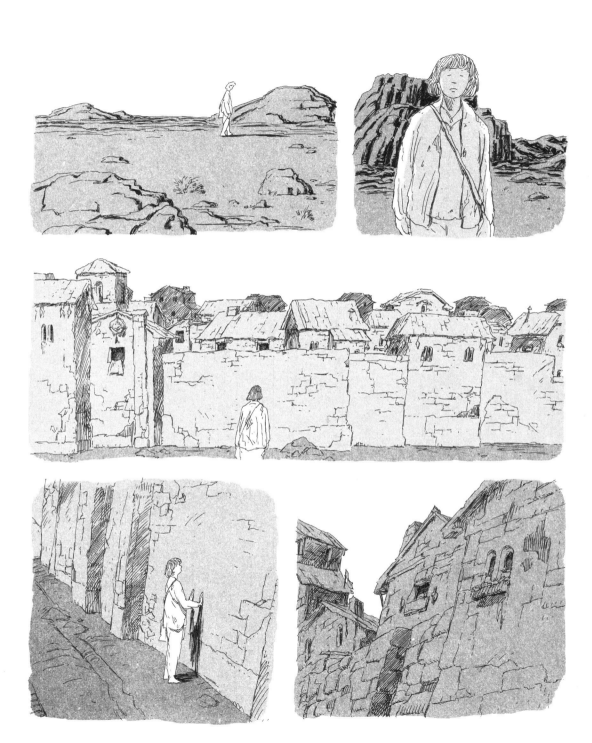

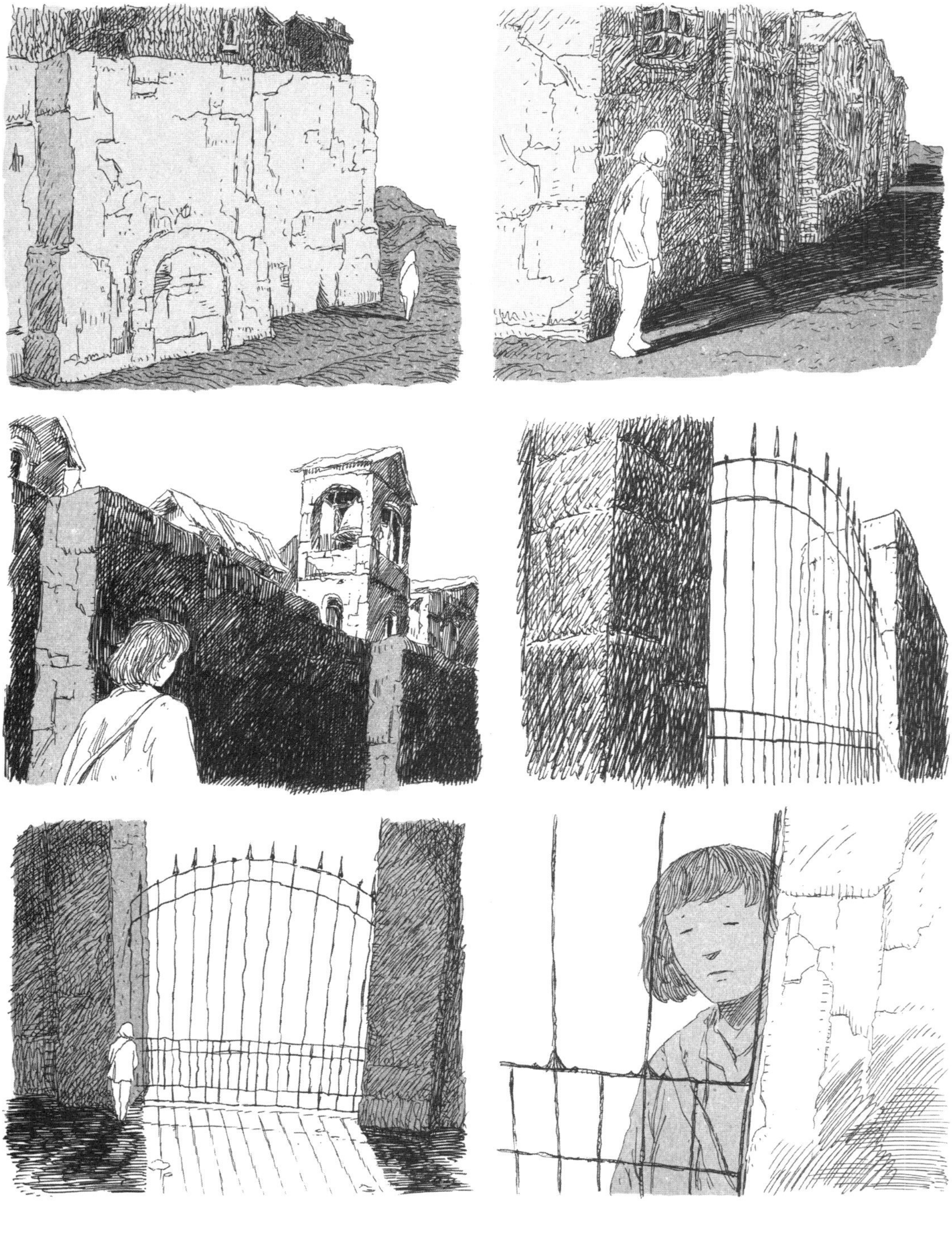

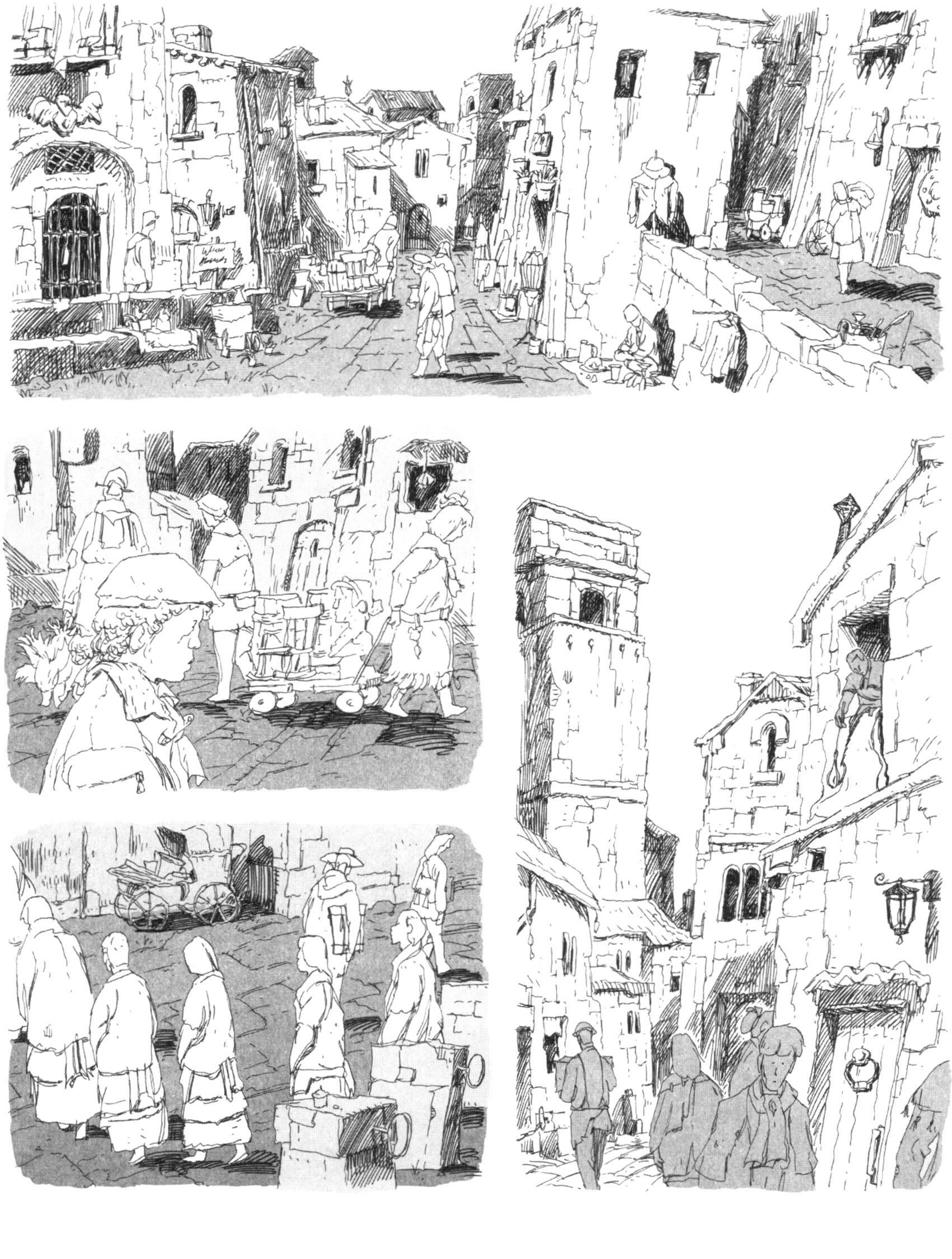

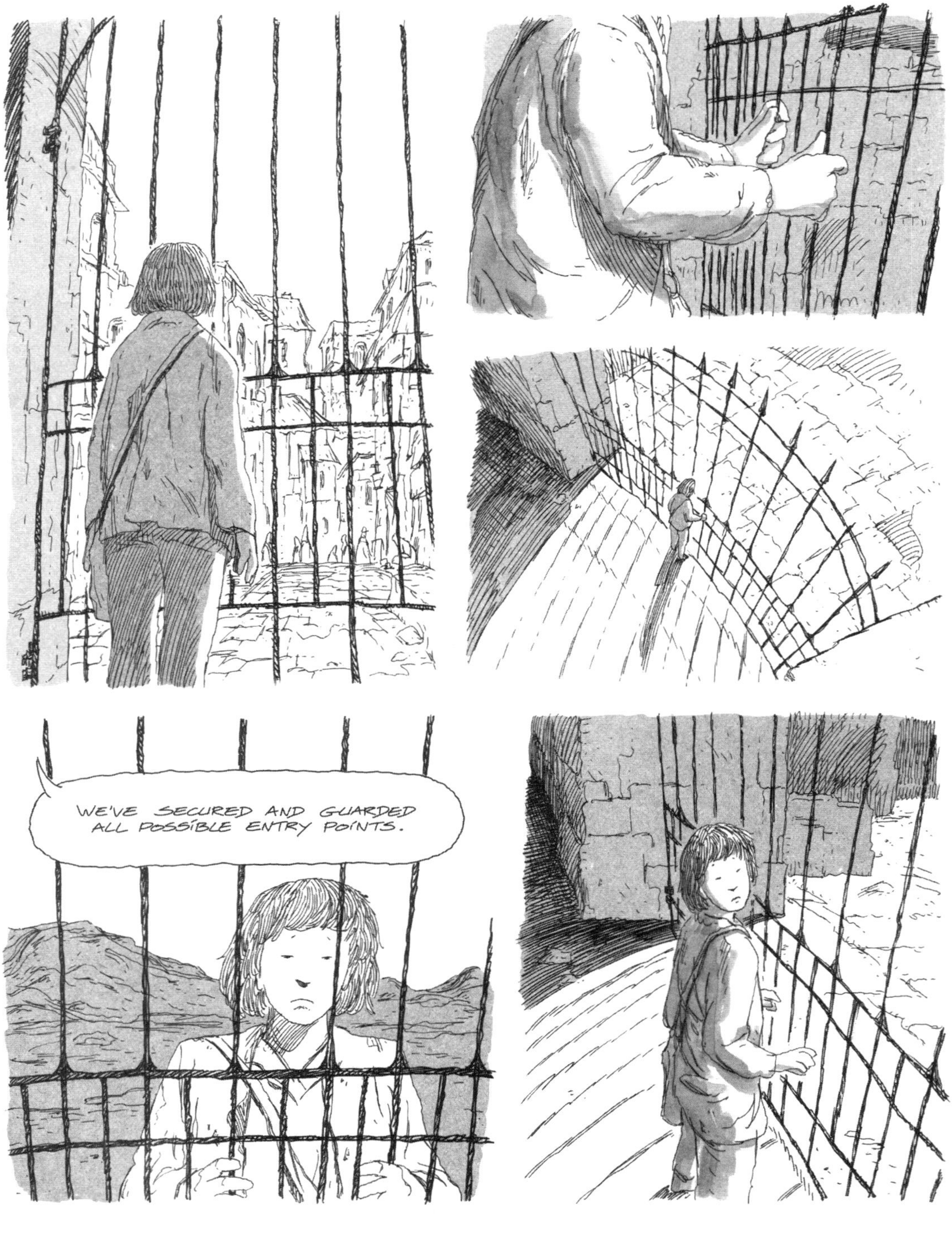
WE'VE SECURED AND GUARDED ALL POSSIBLE ENTRY POINTS.

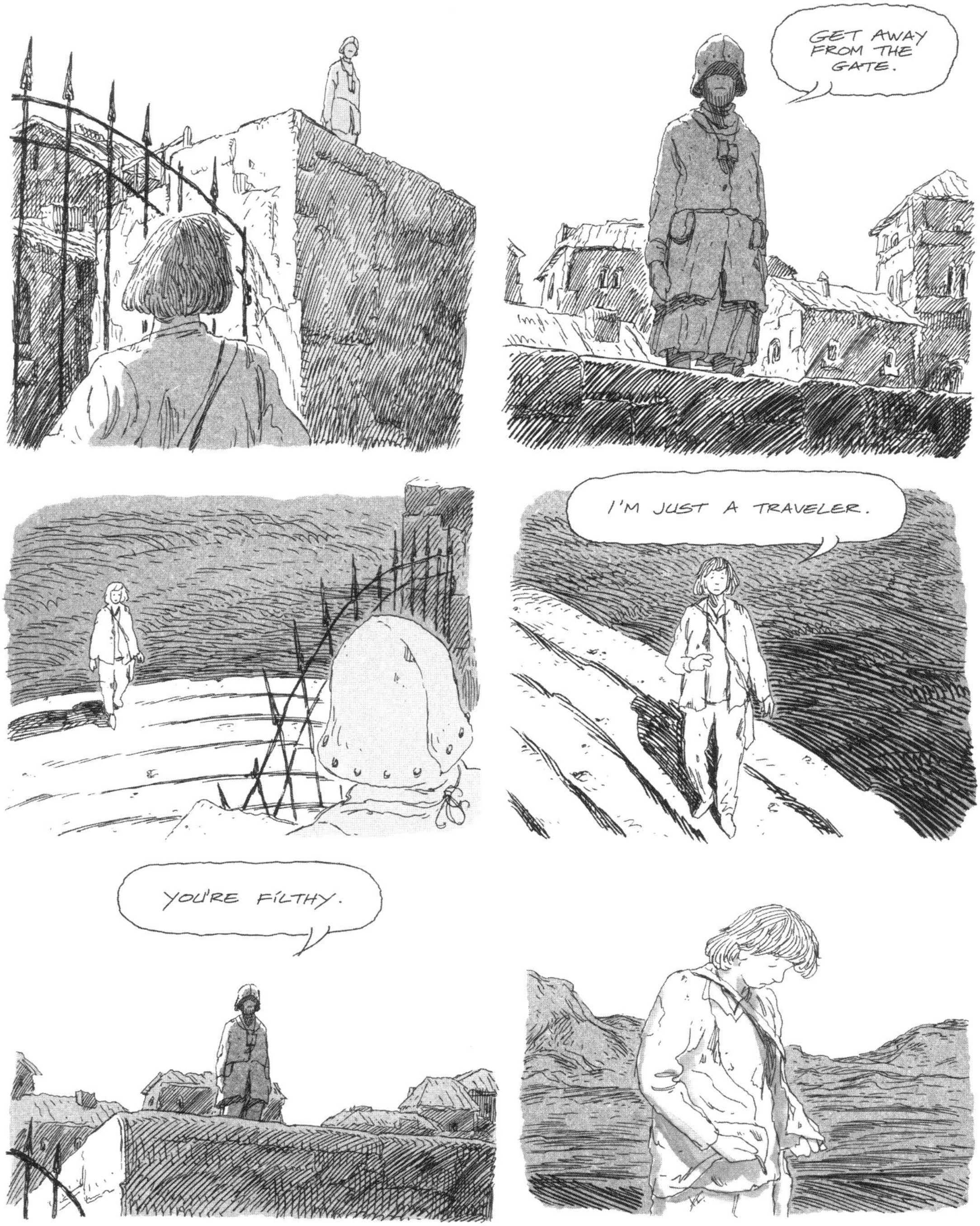
GET AWAY FROM THE GATE.
I'M JUST A TRAVELER.
YOU'RE FILTHY.

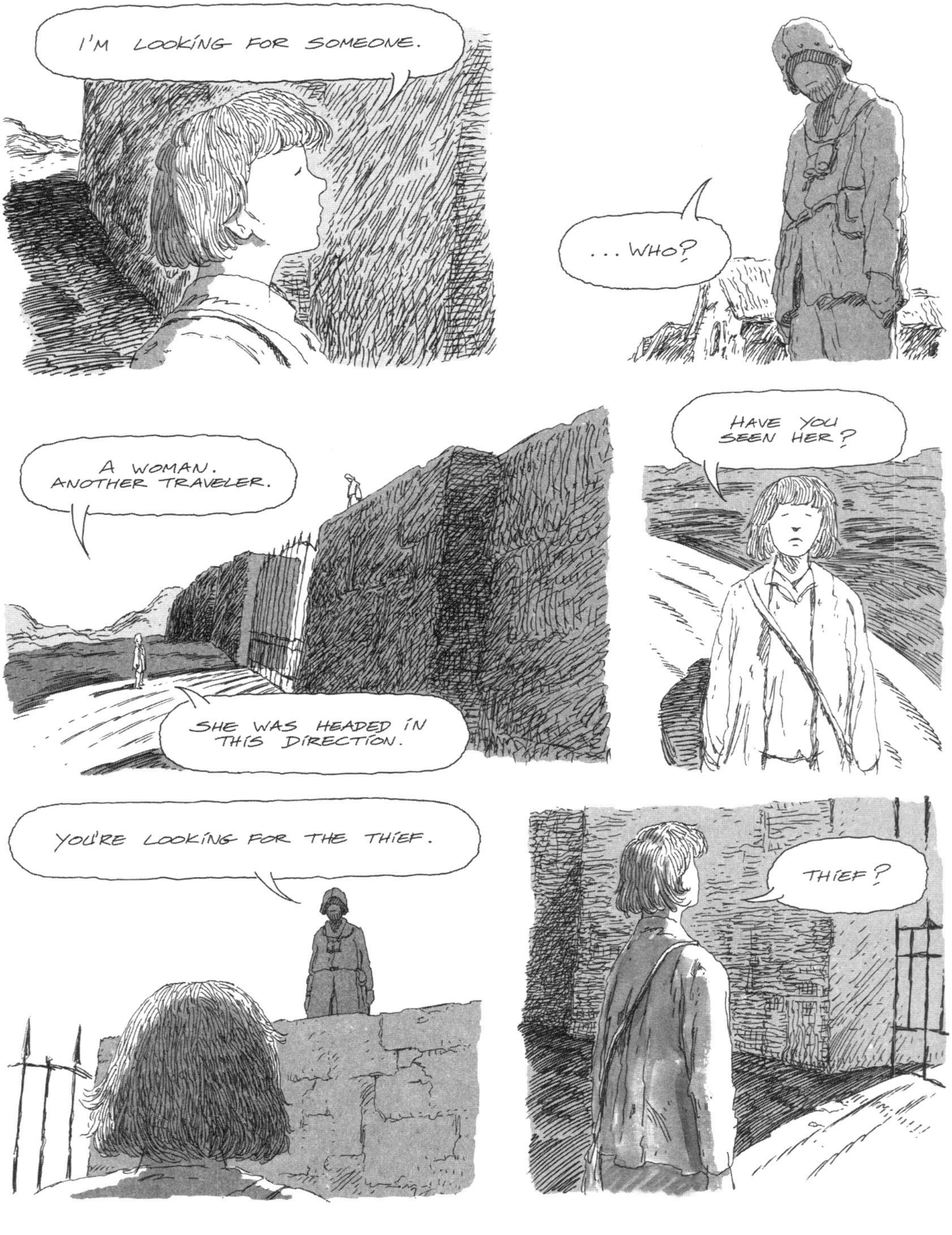
I'M LOOKING FOR SOMEONE.
...WHO?
A WOMAN. ANOTHER TRAVELER.
SHE WAS HEADED IN THIS DIRECTION.
HAVE YOU SEEN HER?
YOU'RE LOOKING FOR THE THIEF.
THIEF?

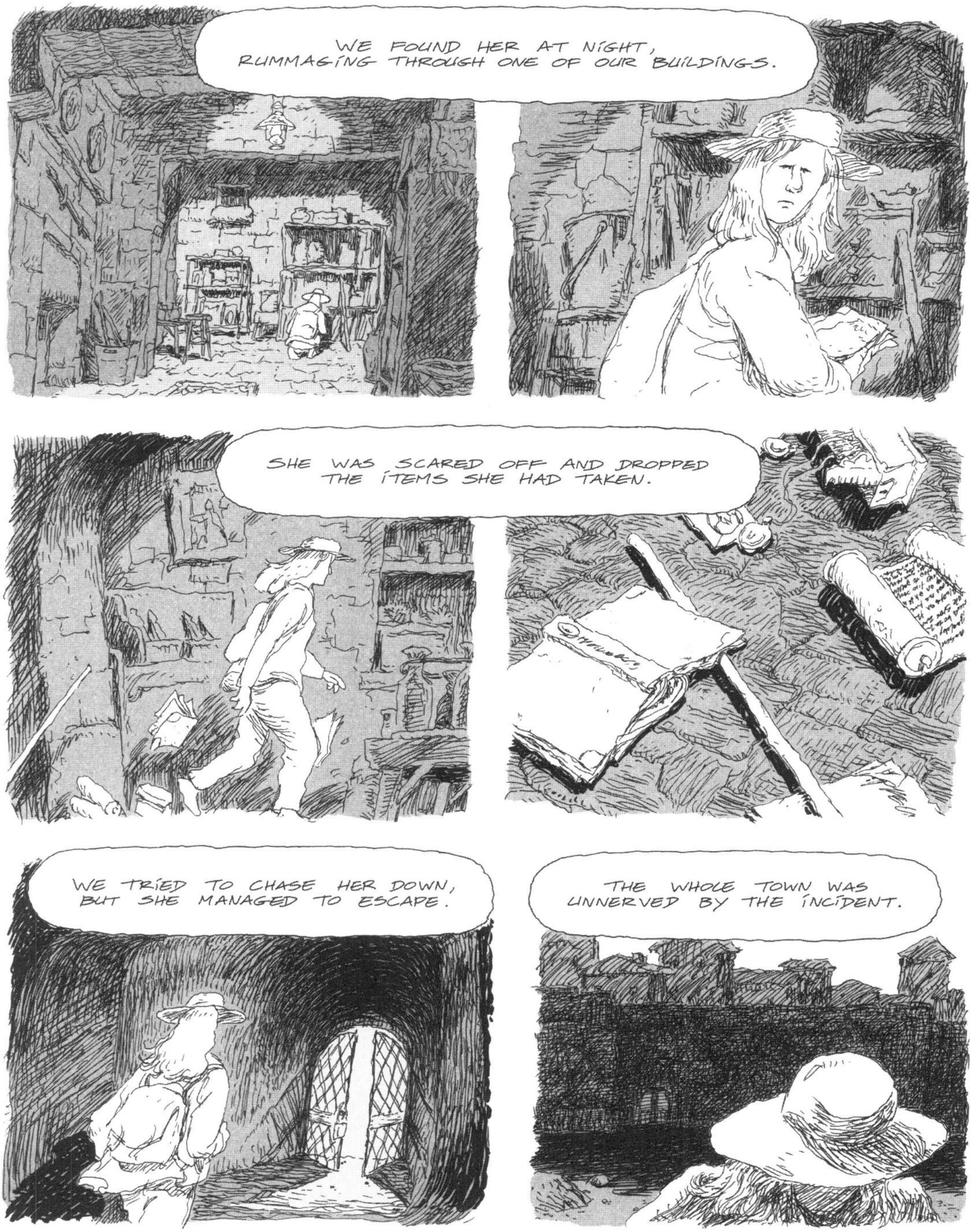
WE FOUND HER AT NIGHT, RUMMAGING THROUGH ONE OF OUR BUILDINGS.
SHE WAS SCARED OFF AND DROPPED THE ITEMS SHE HAD TAKEN.
WE TRIED TO CHASE HER DOWN, BUT SHE MANAGED TO ESCAPE.
THE WHOLE TOWN WAS UNNERVED BY THE INCIDENT.

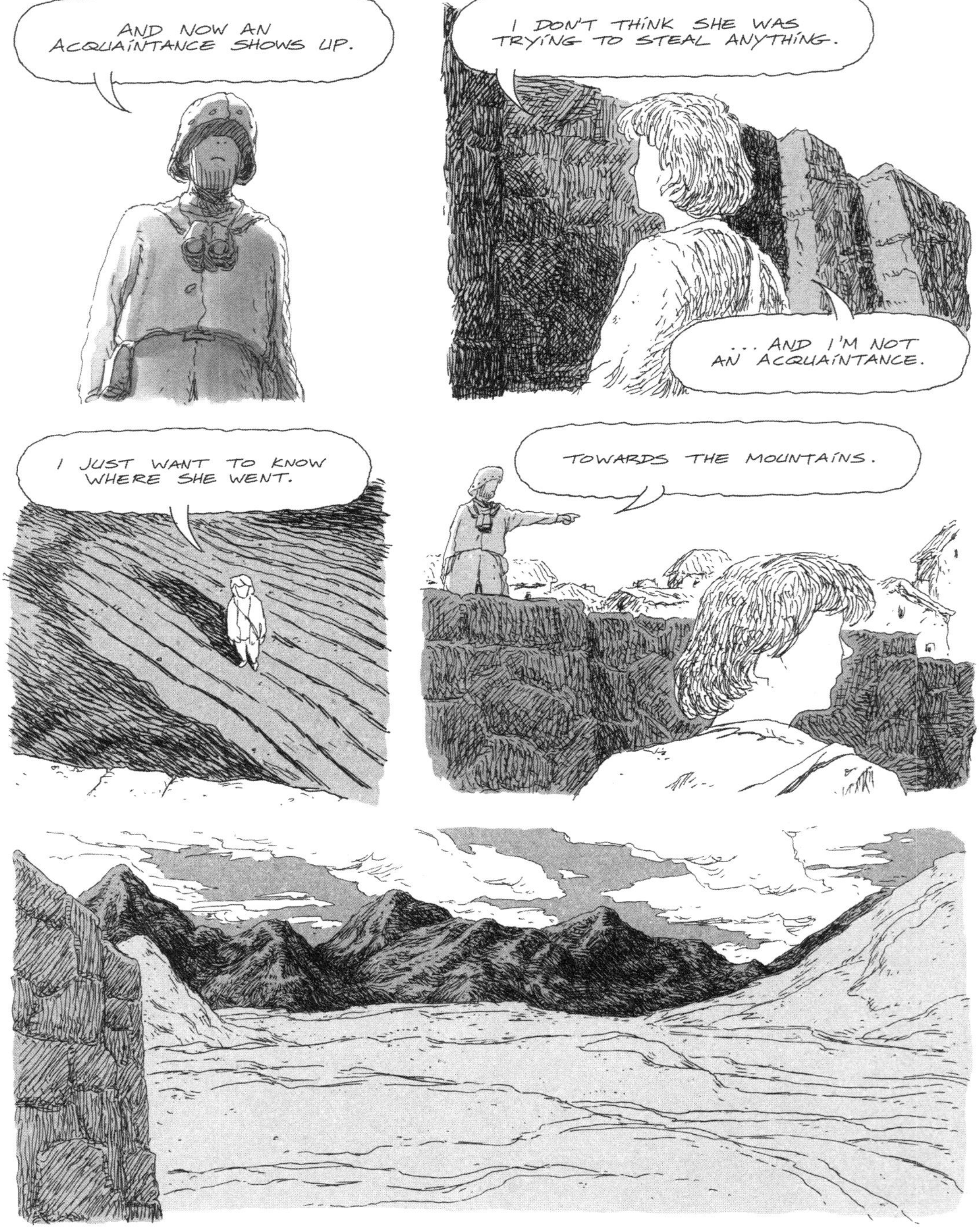
AND NOW AN ACQUAINTANCE SHOWS UP.
I DON'T THINK SHE WAS TRYING TO STEAL ANYTHING.
...AND I'M NOT AN ACQUAINTANCE.
I JUST WANT TO KNOW WHERE SHE WENT.
TOWARDS THE MOUNTAINS.

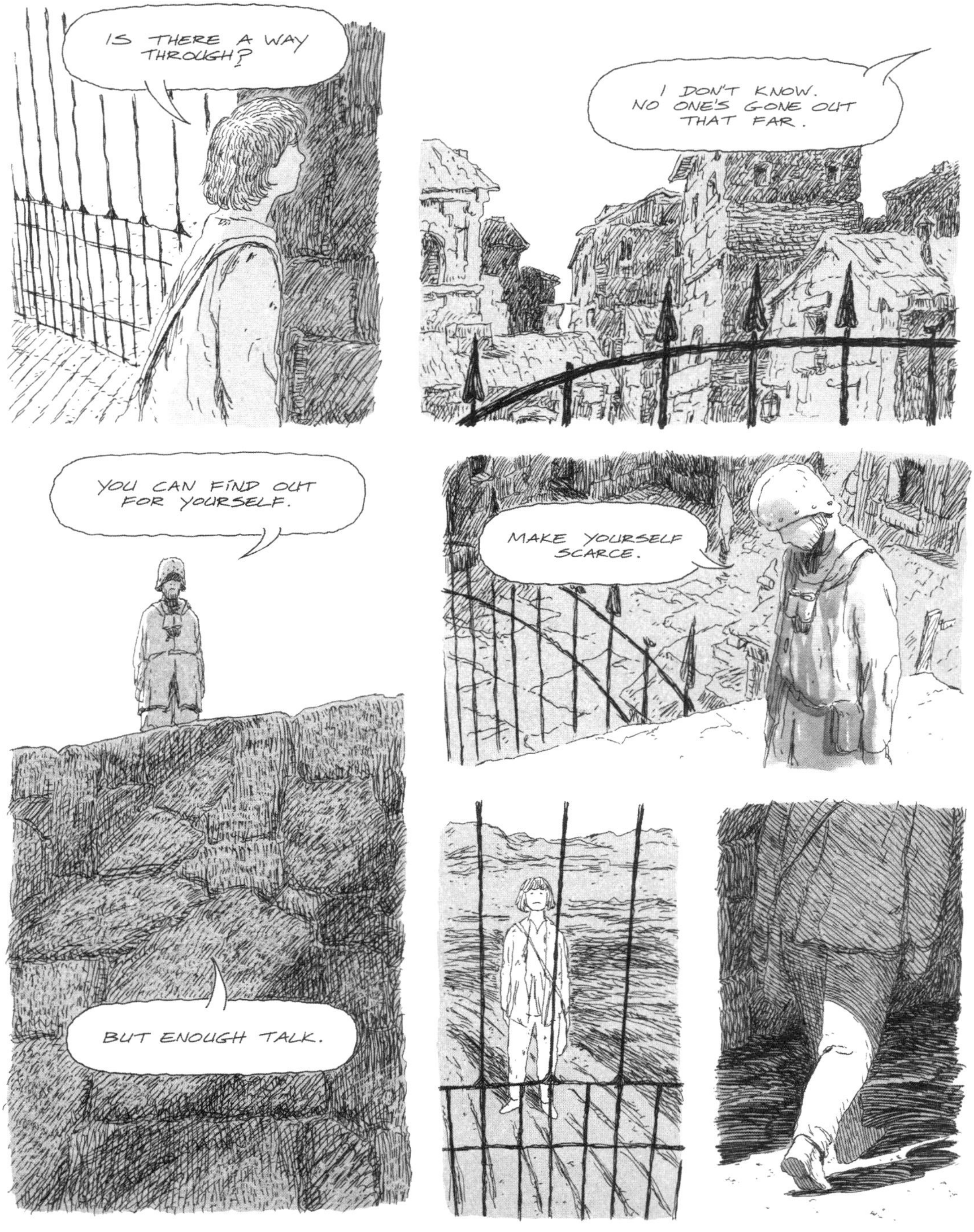
IS THERE A WAY THROUGH?
I DON'T KNOW. NO ONE'S GONE OUT THAT FAR.
YOU CAN FIND OUT FOR YOURSELF.
MAKE YOURSELF SCARCE.
BUT ENOUGH TALK.

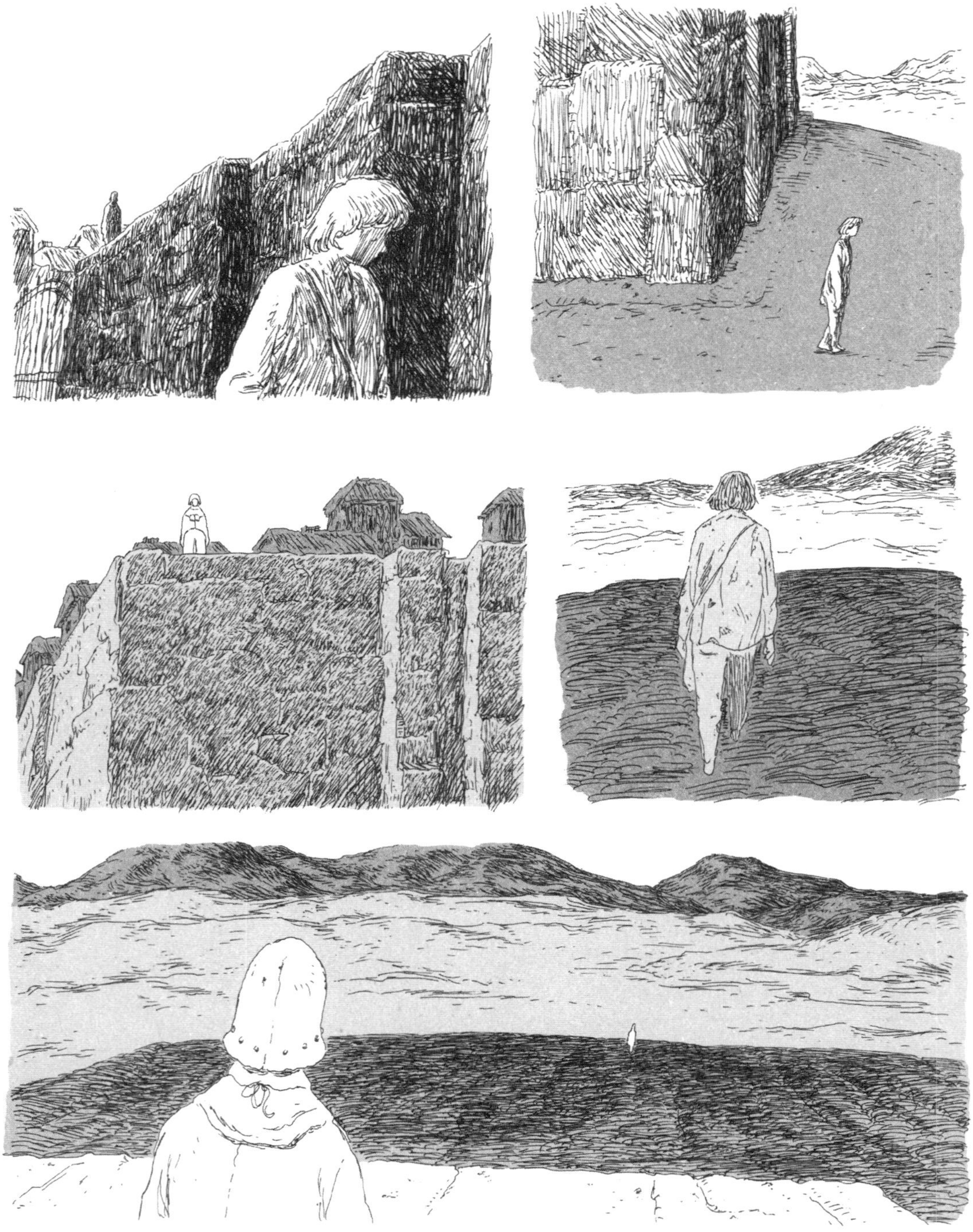

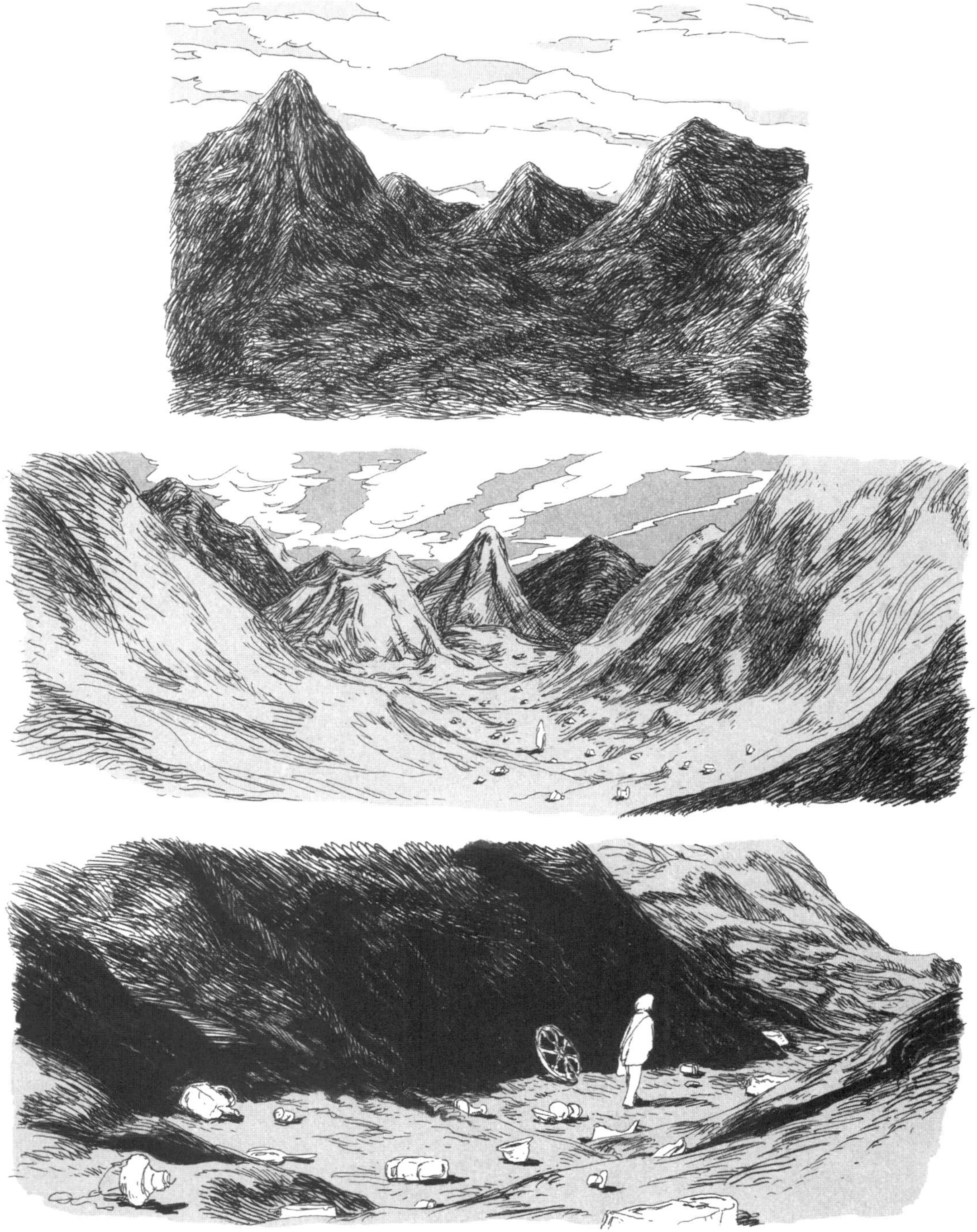

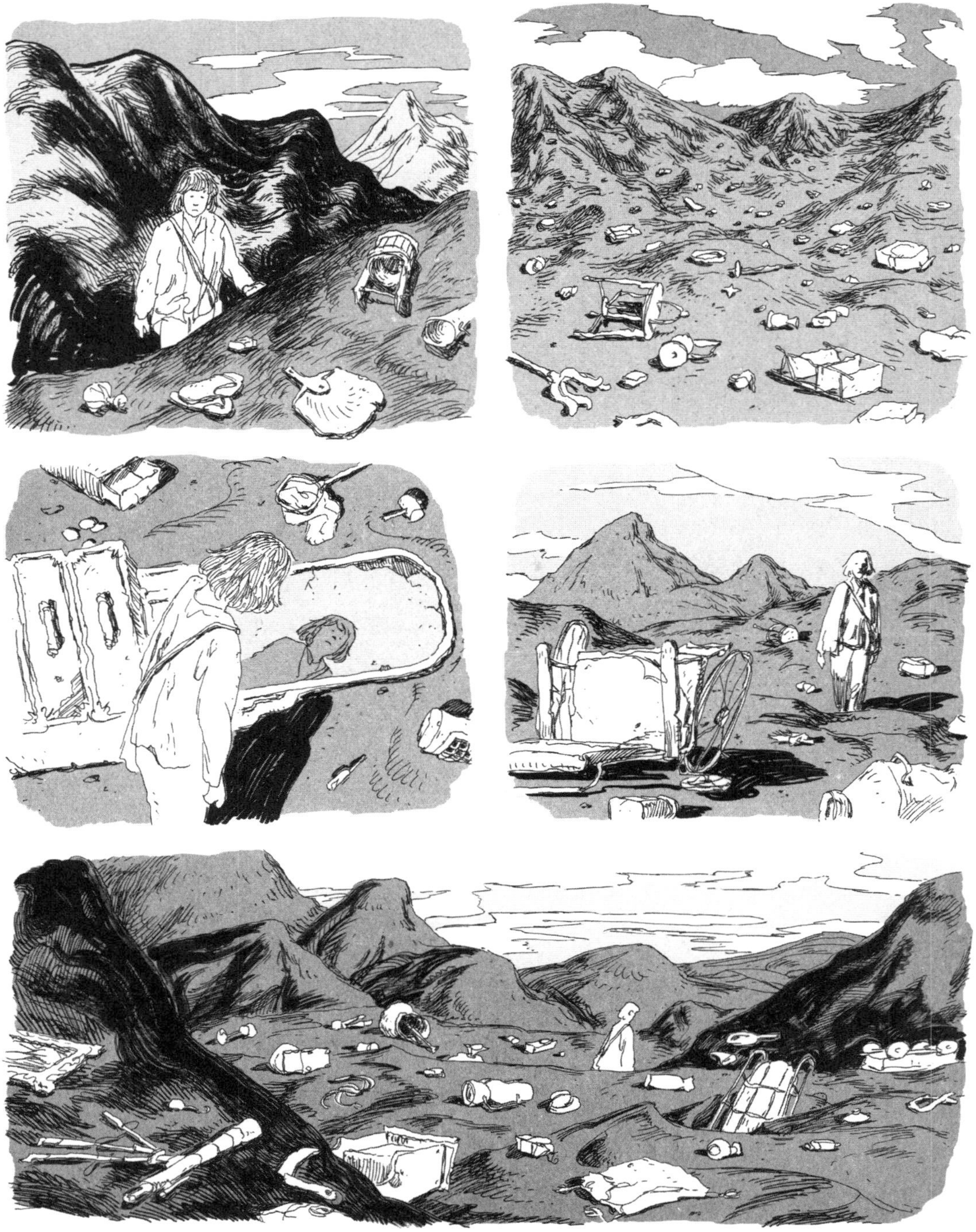

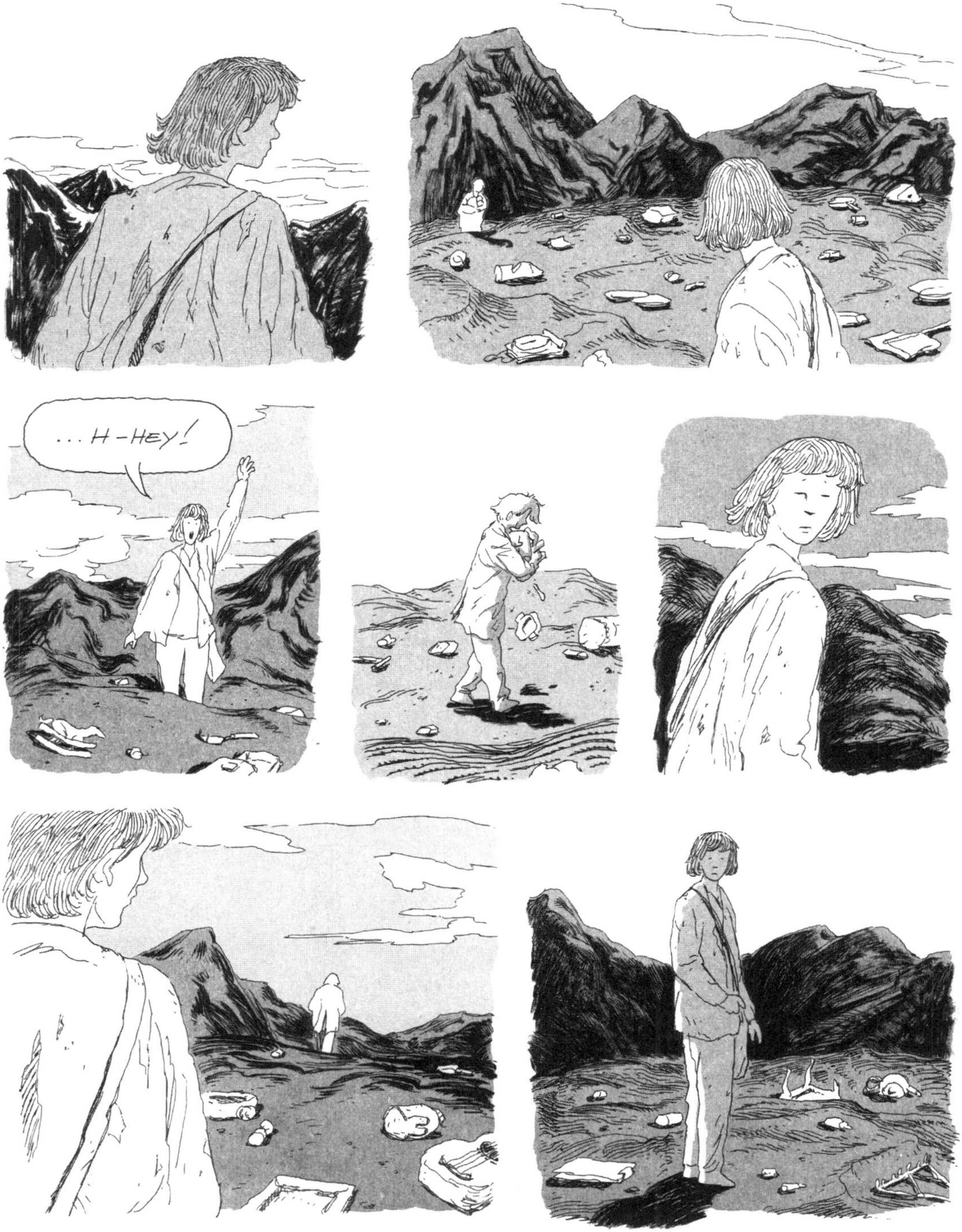
...H-HEY!

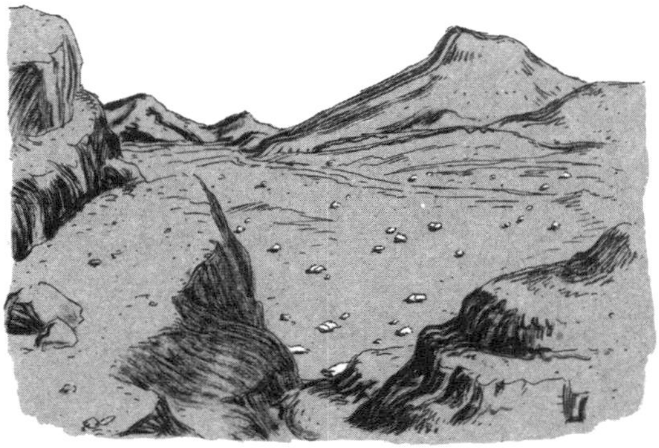
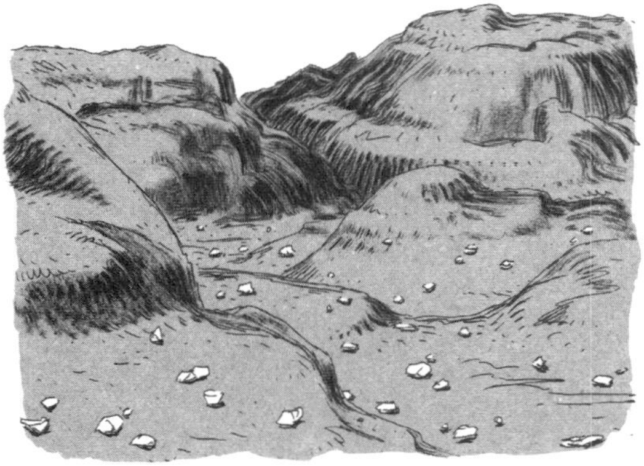
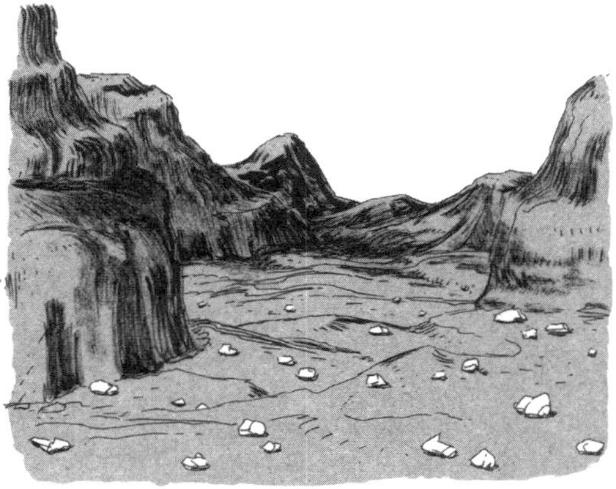
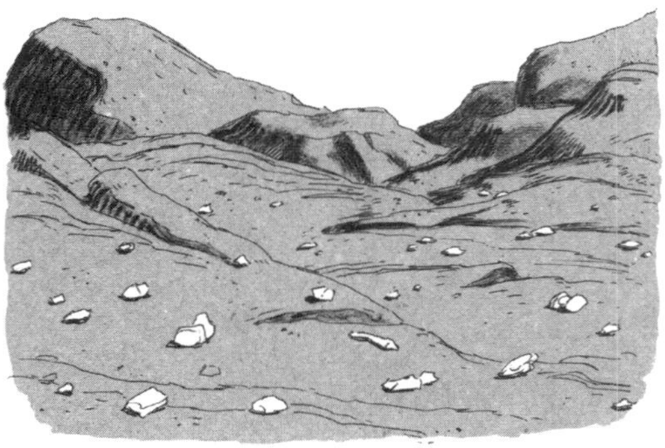
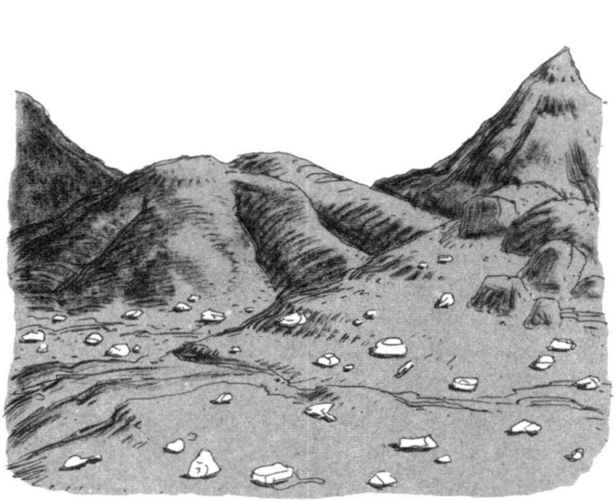
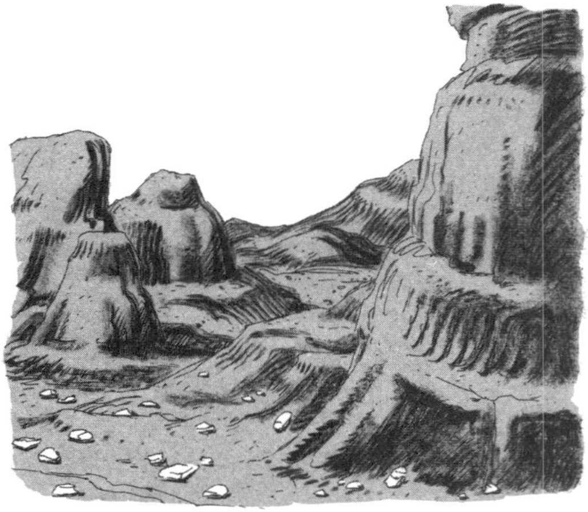

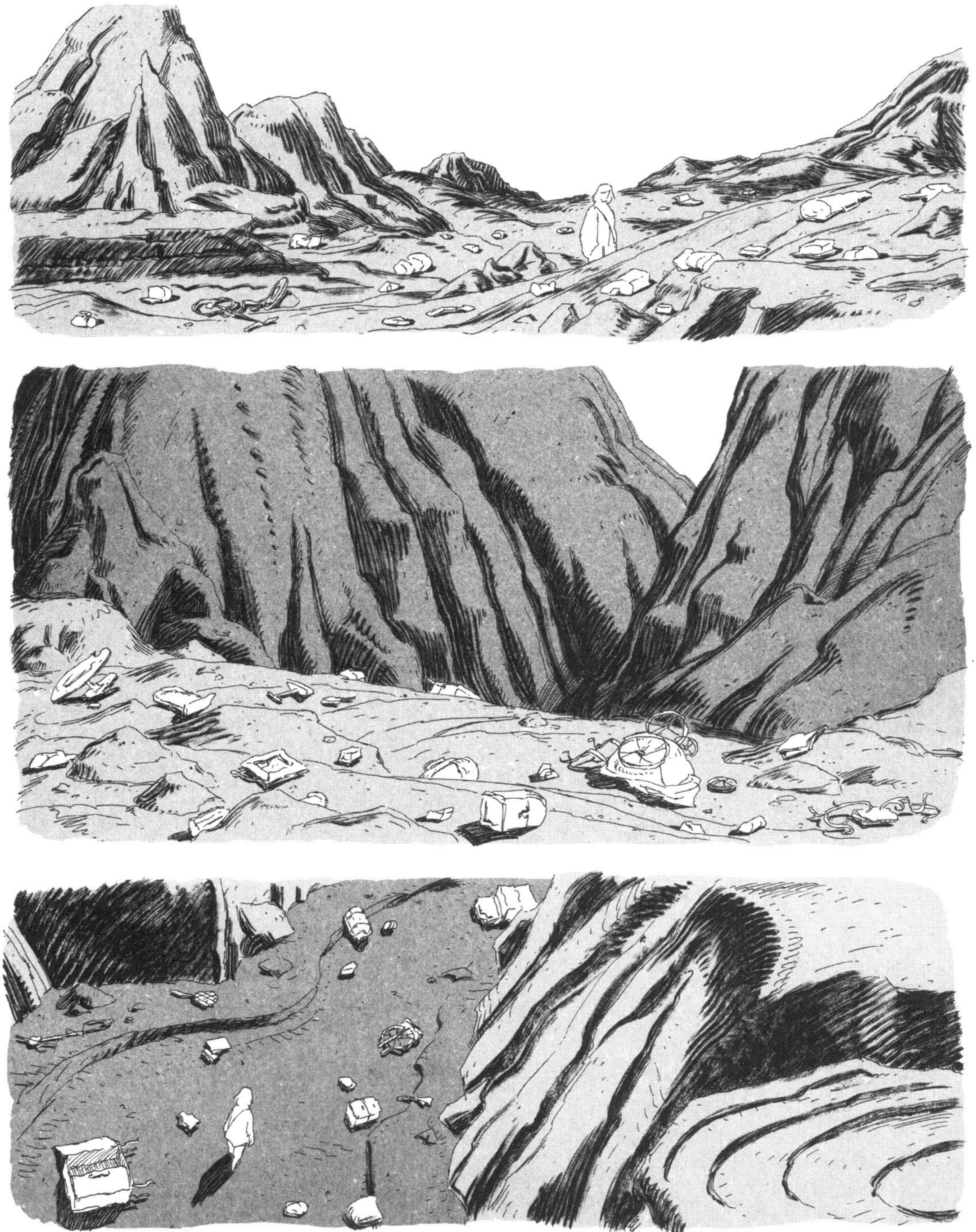

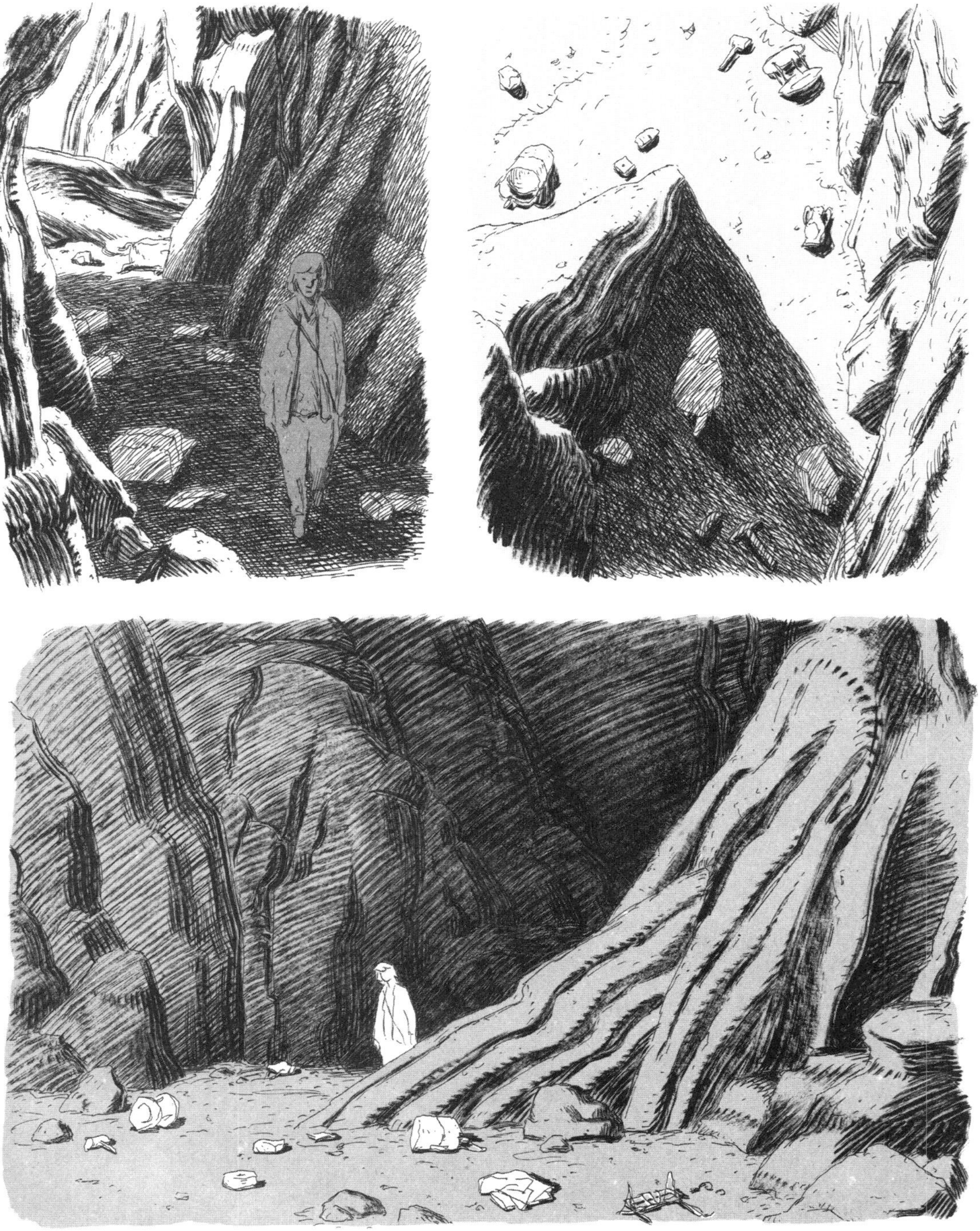

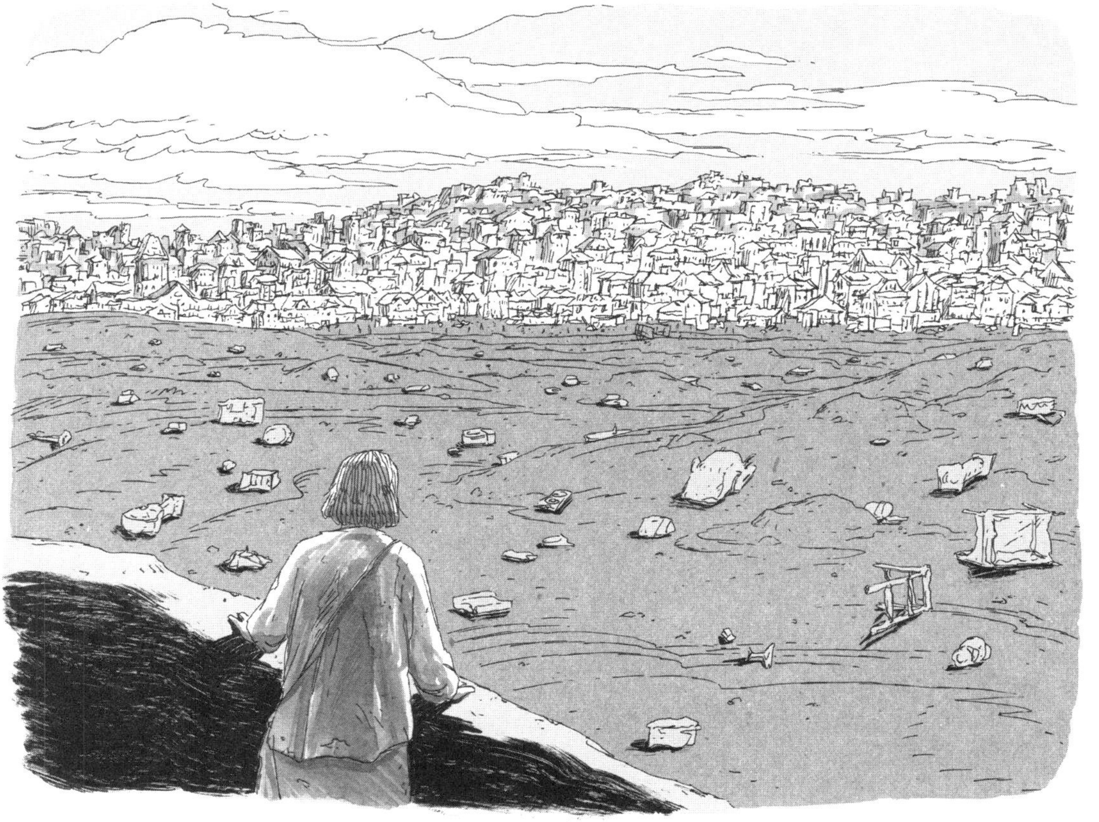

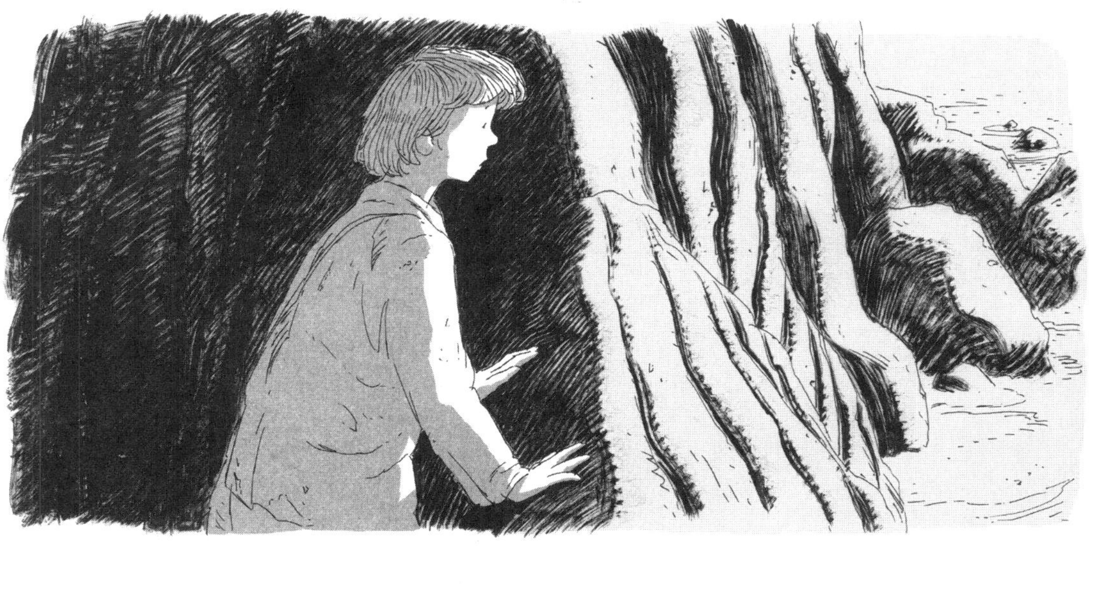

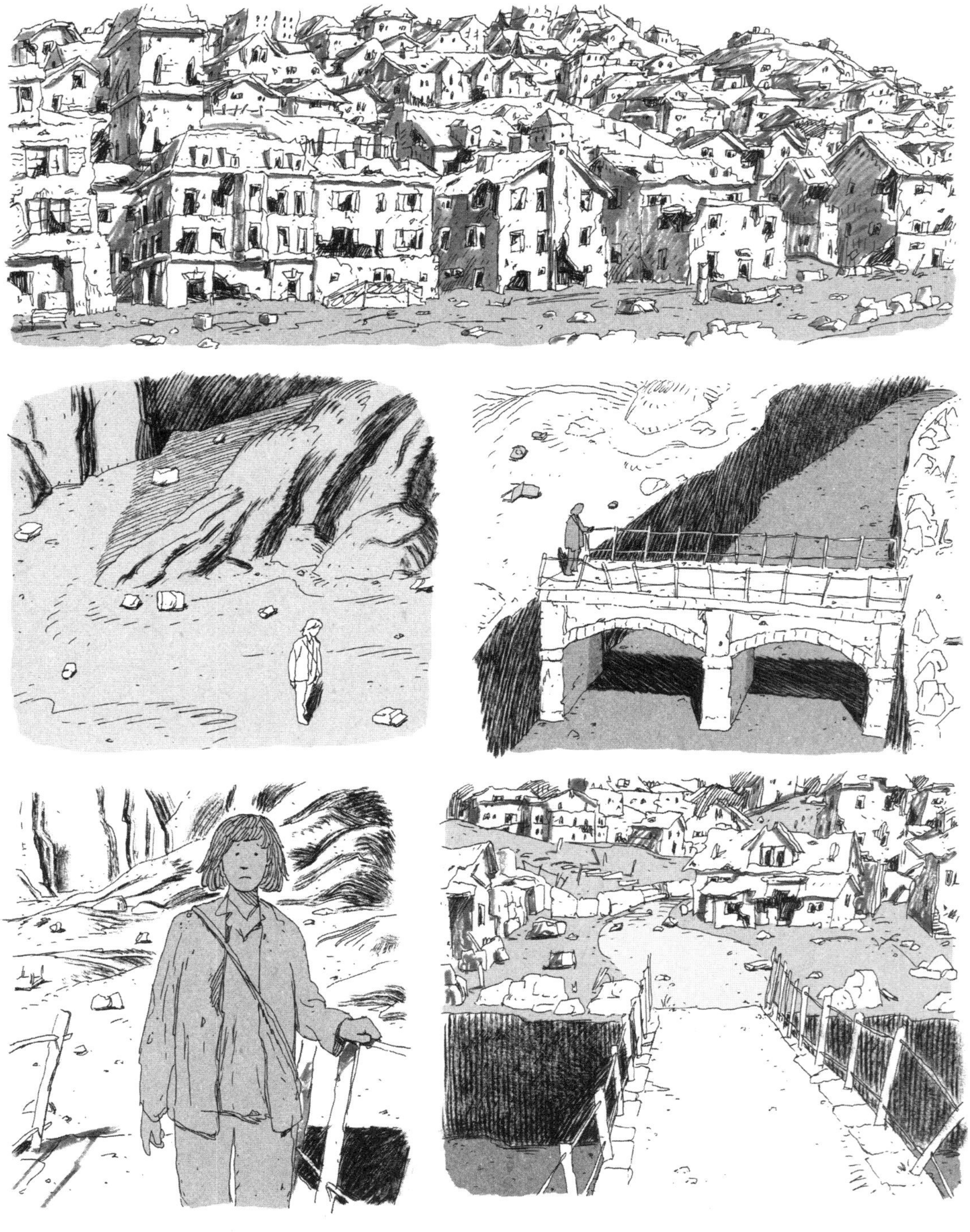

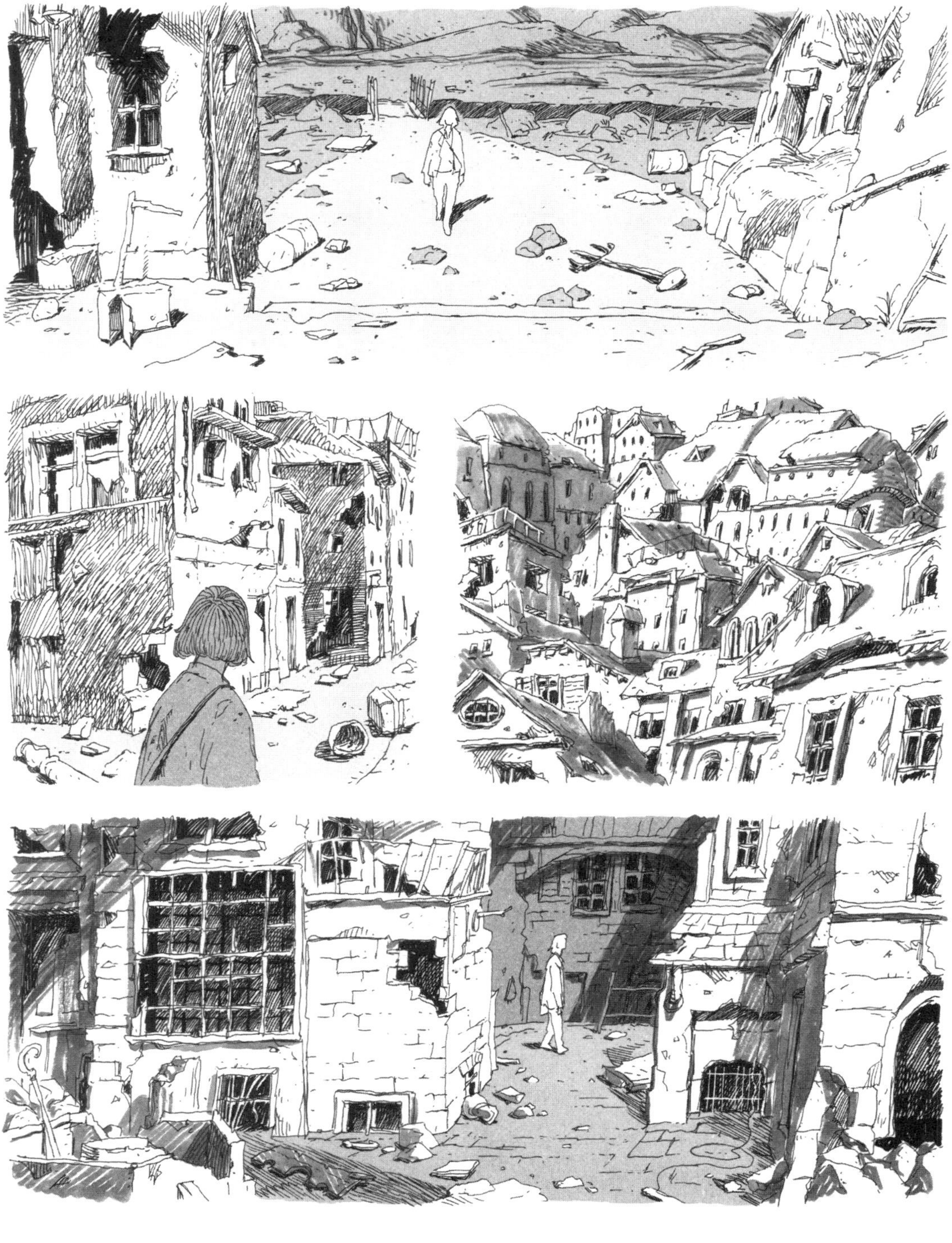

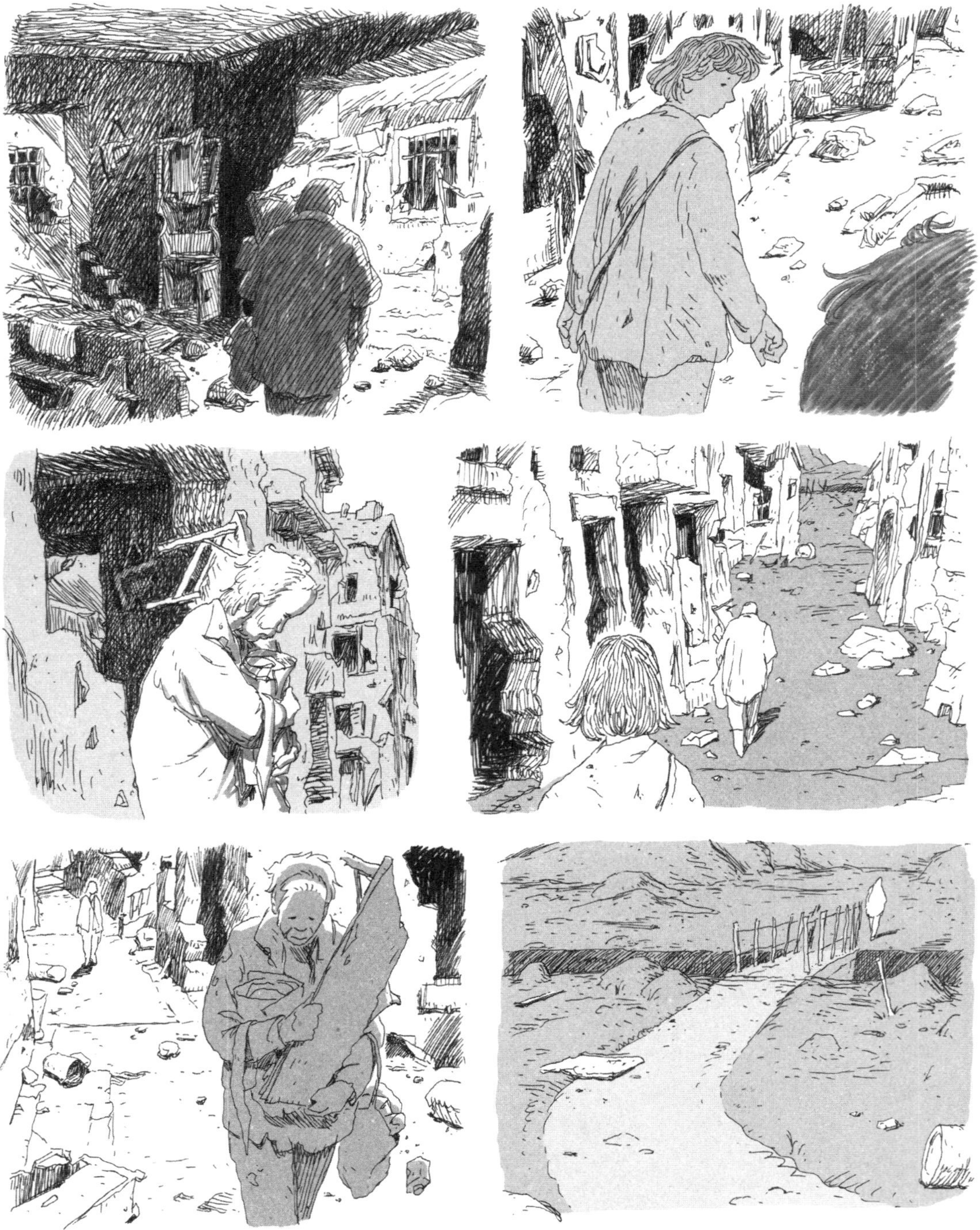

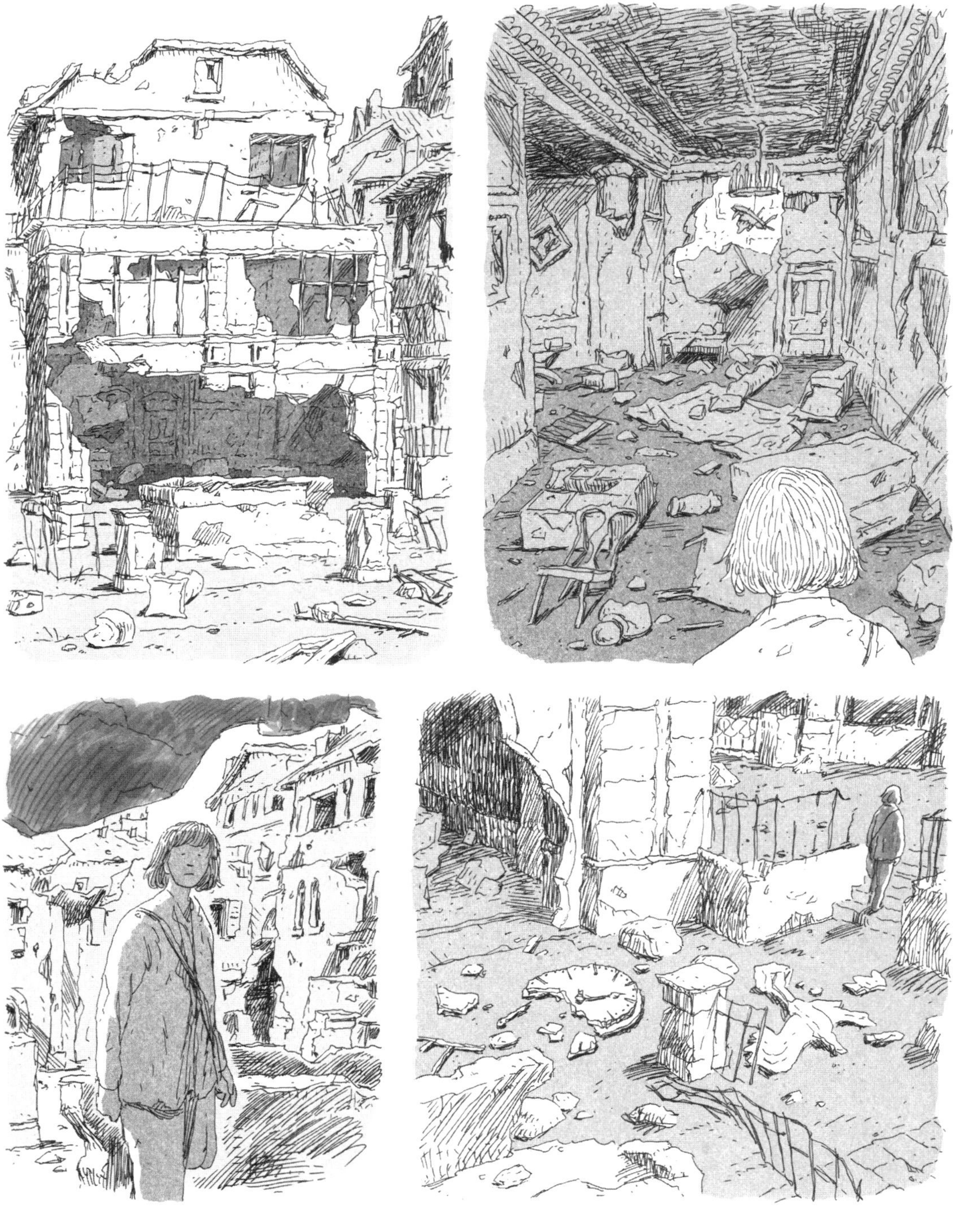

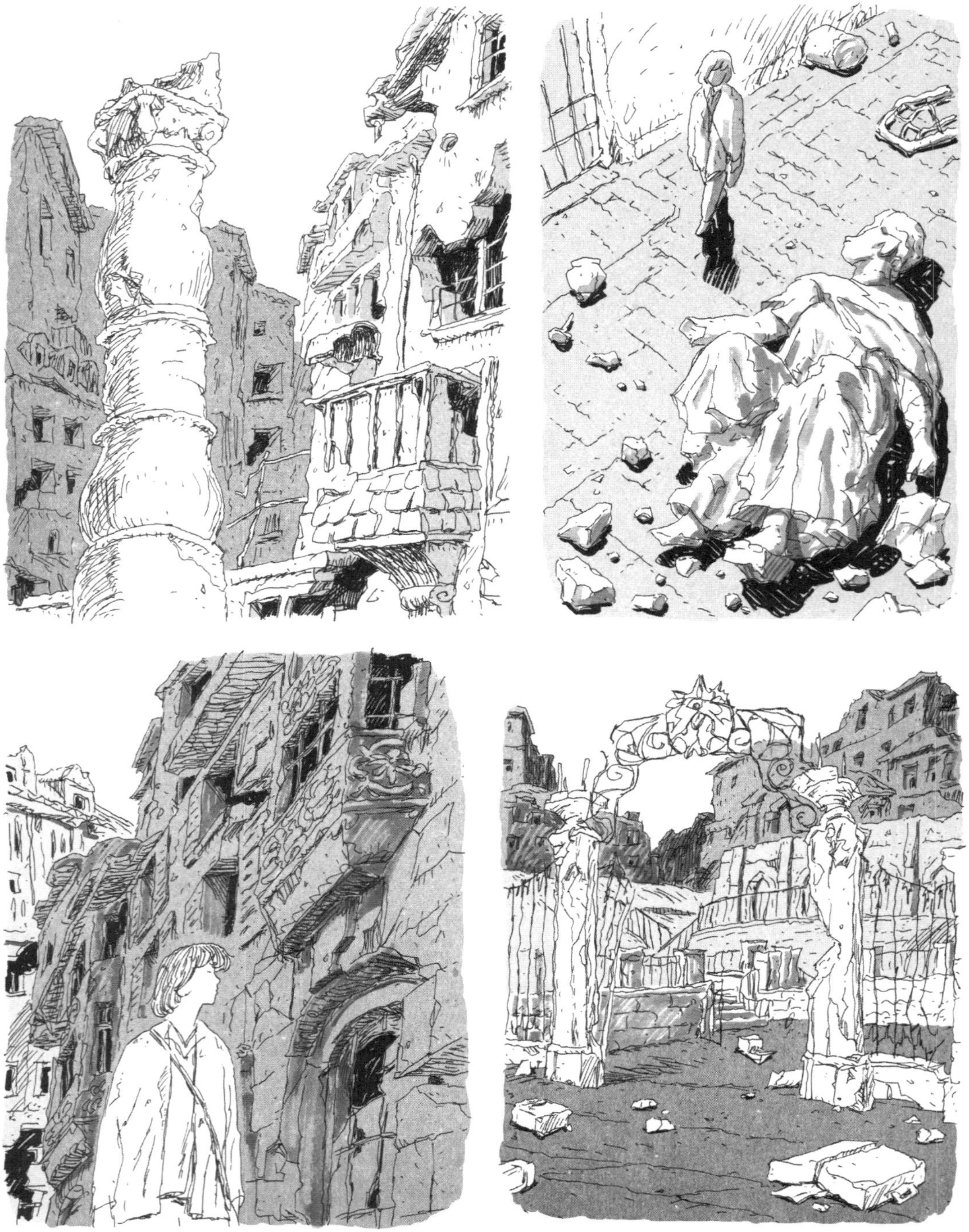

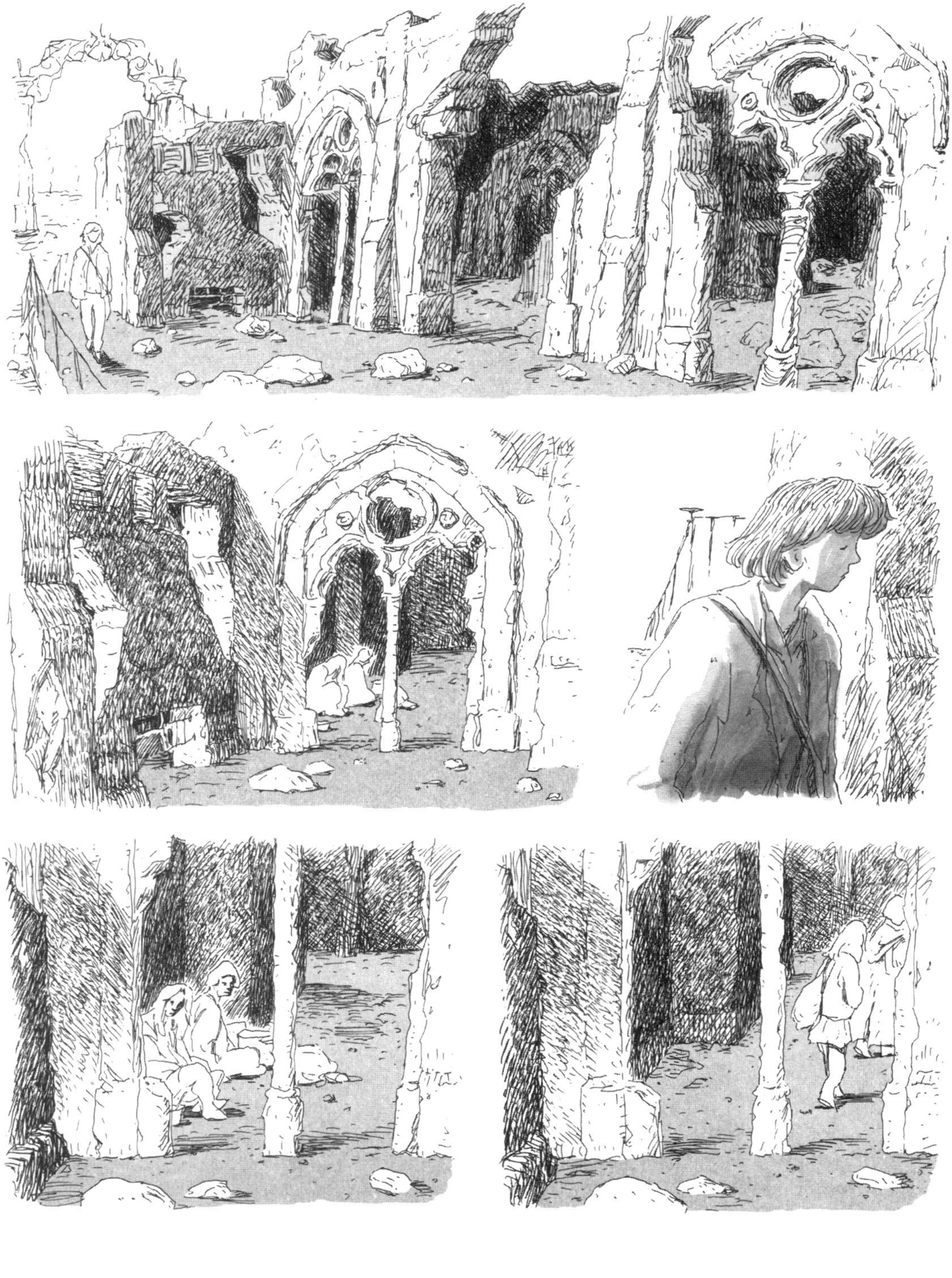

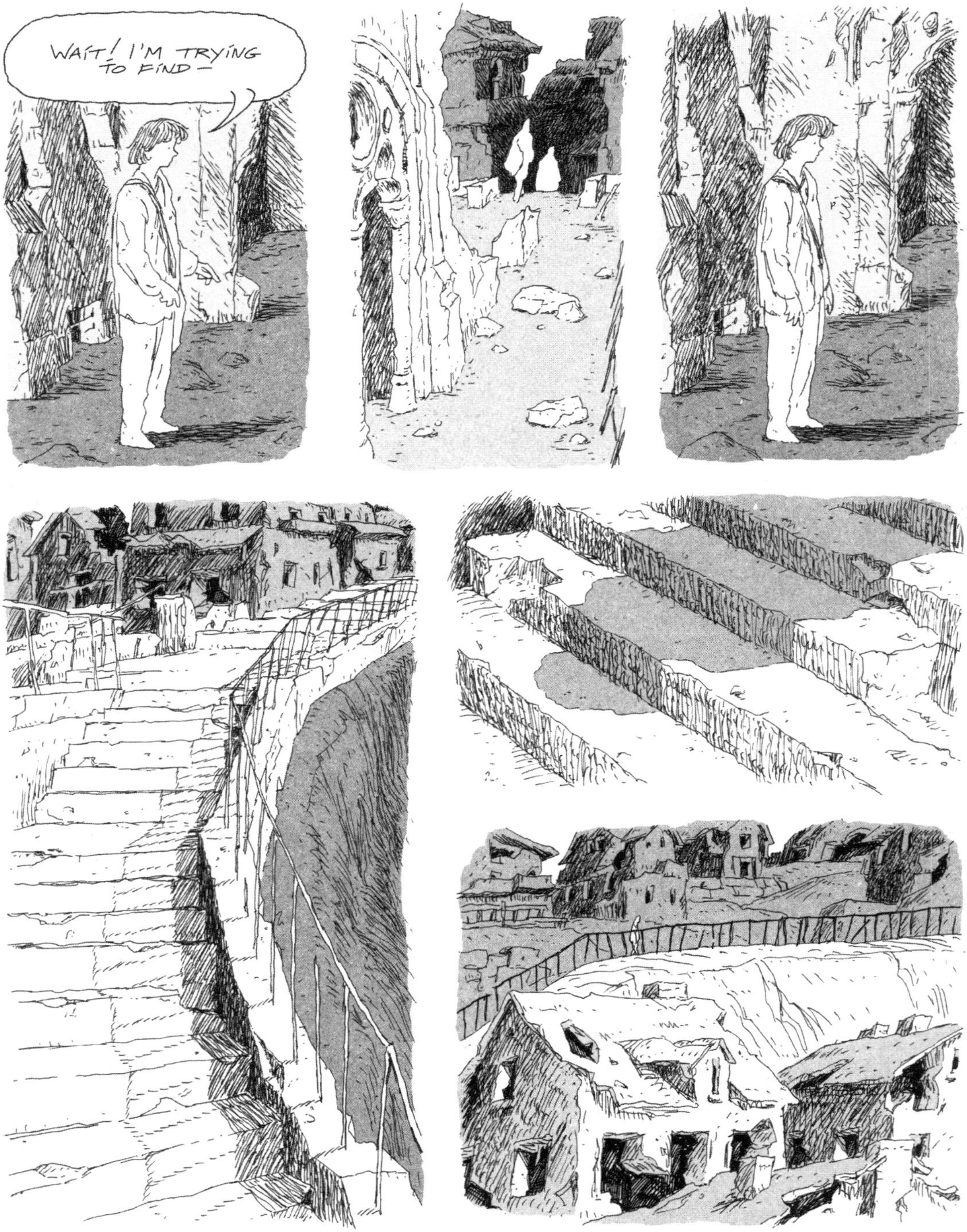
WAIT! I'M TRYING TO FIND—

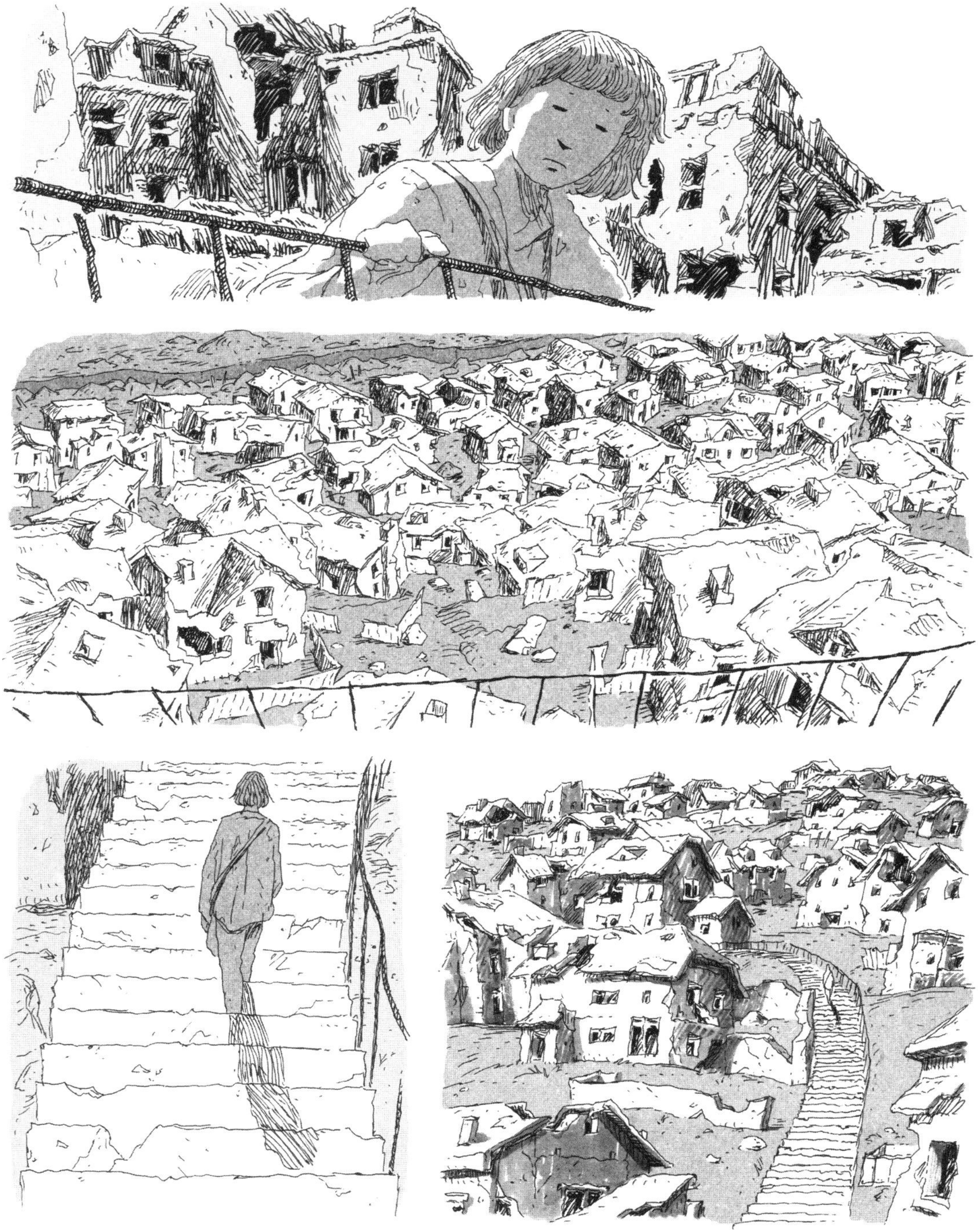

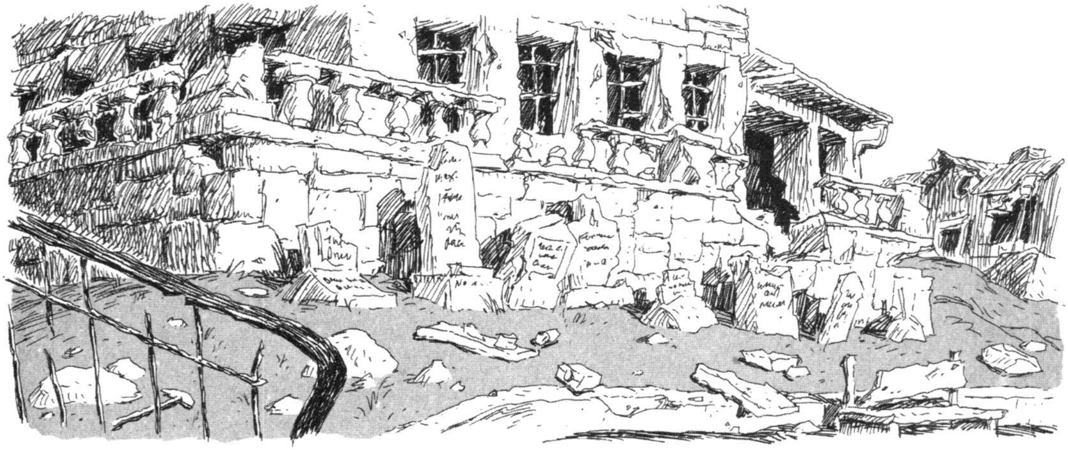

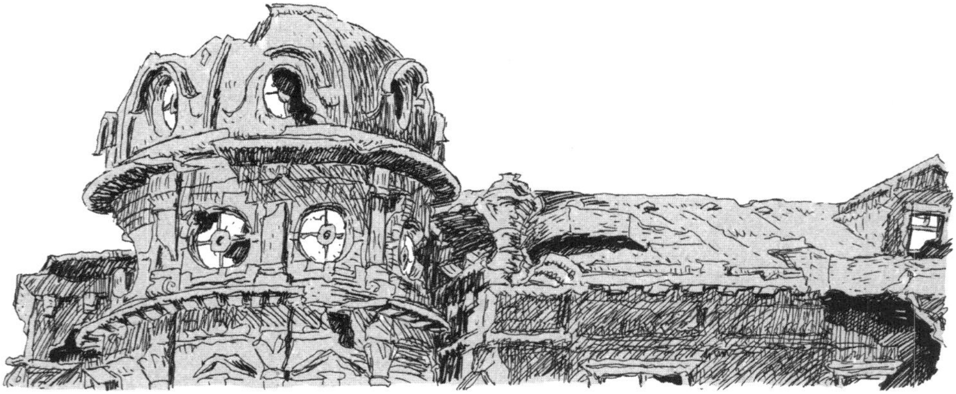

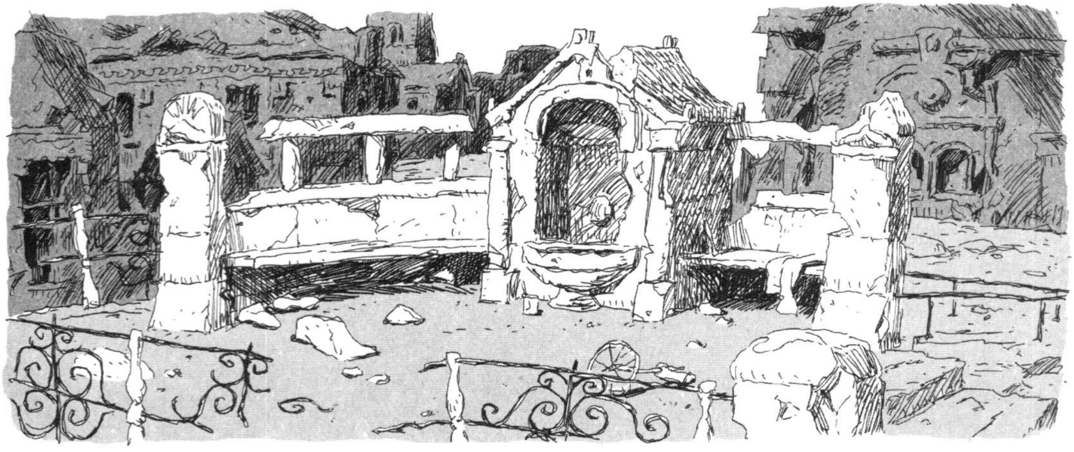

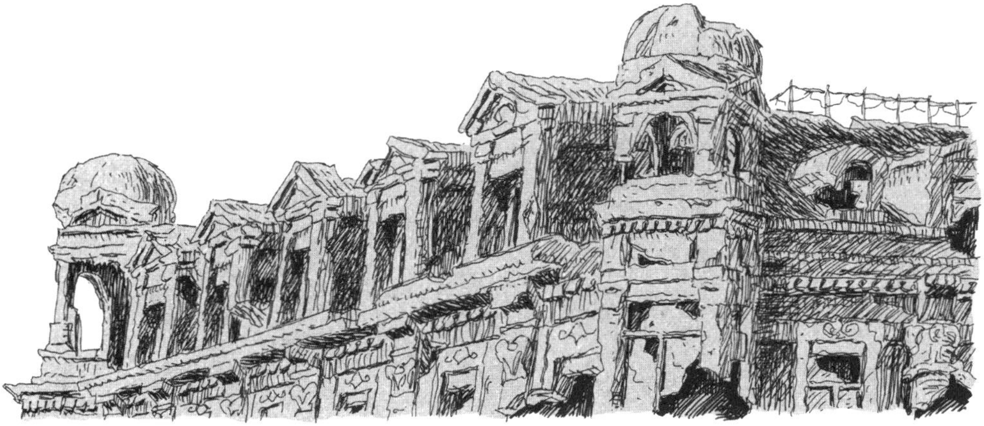
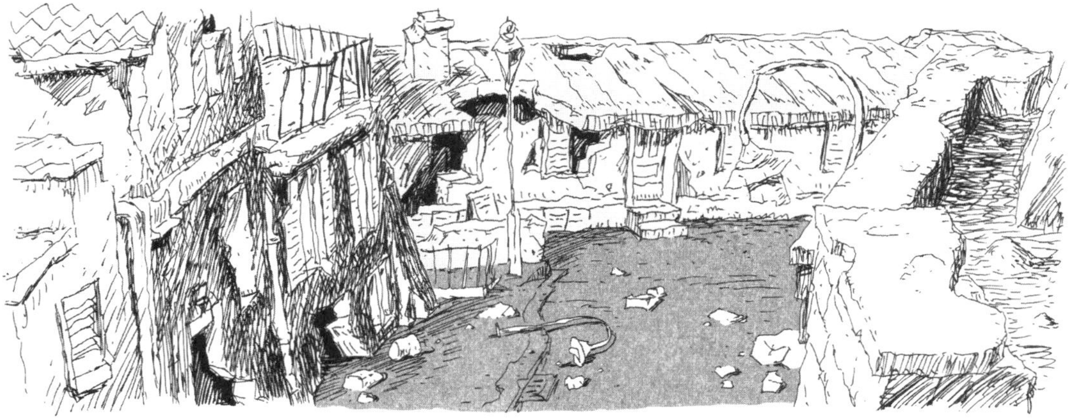
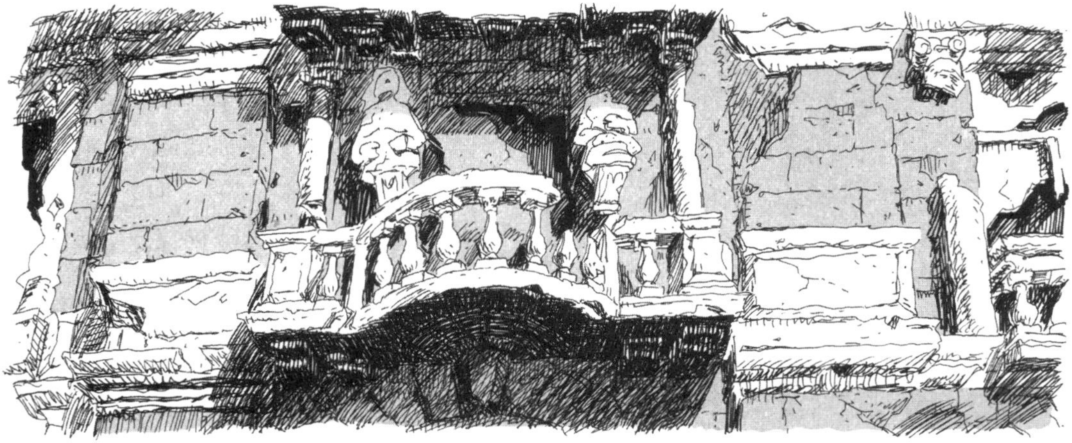

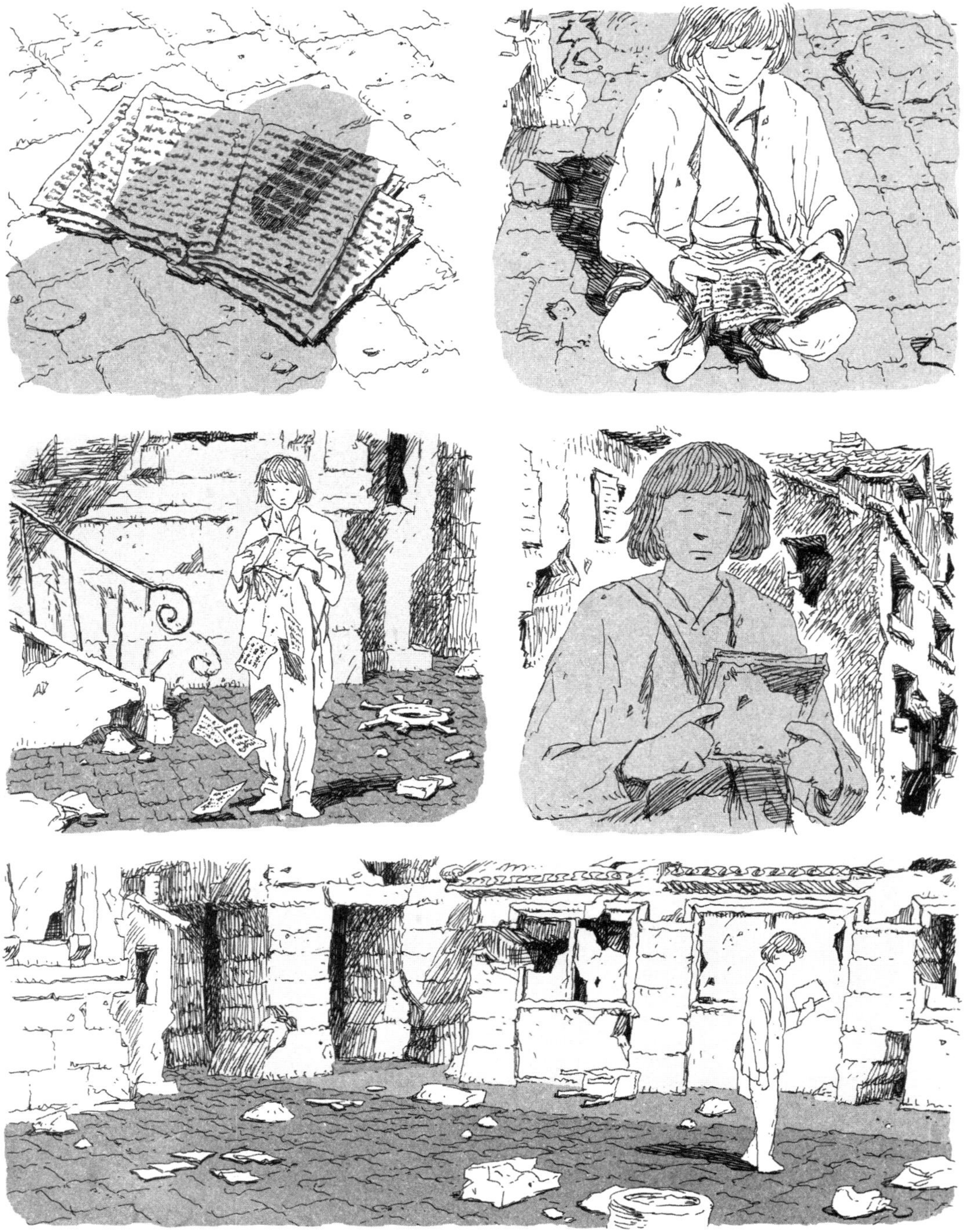

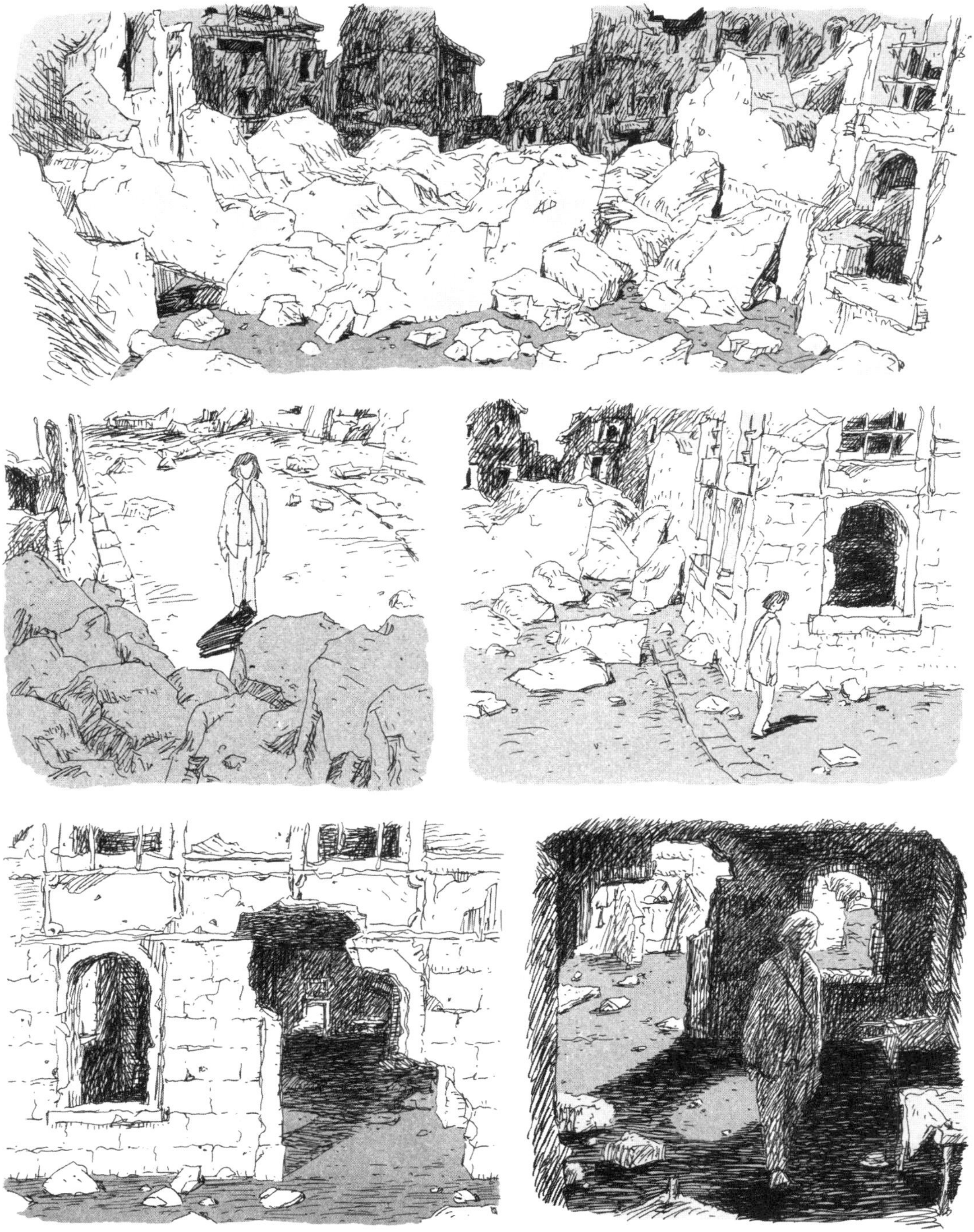

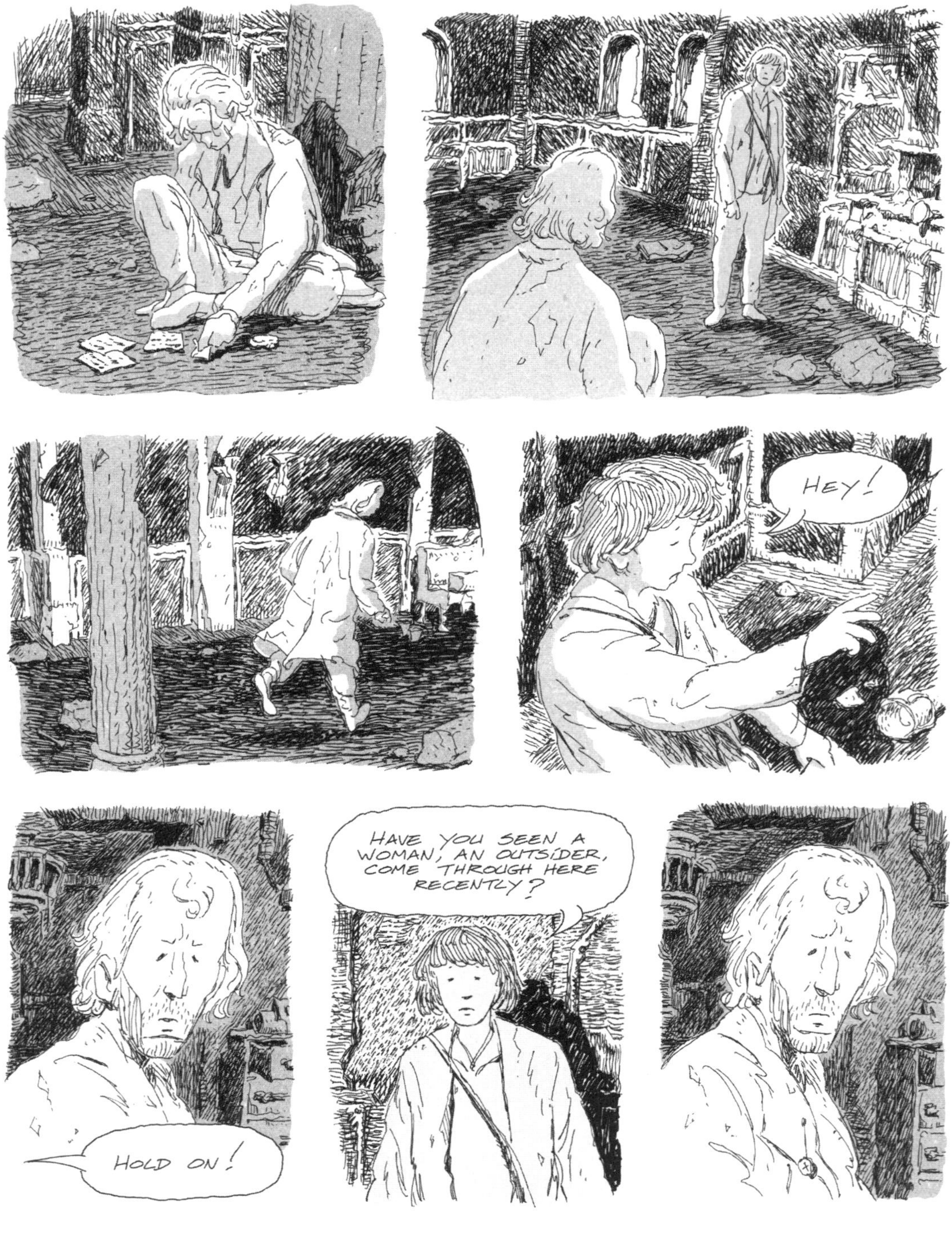
HEY!
HOLD ON!
HAVE YOU SEEN A WOMAN, AN OUTSIDER, COME THROUGH HERE RECENTLY?

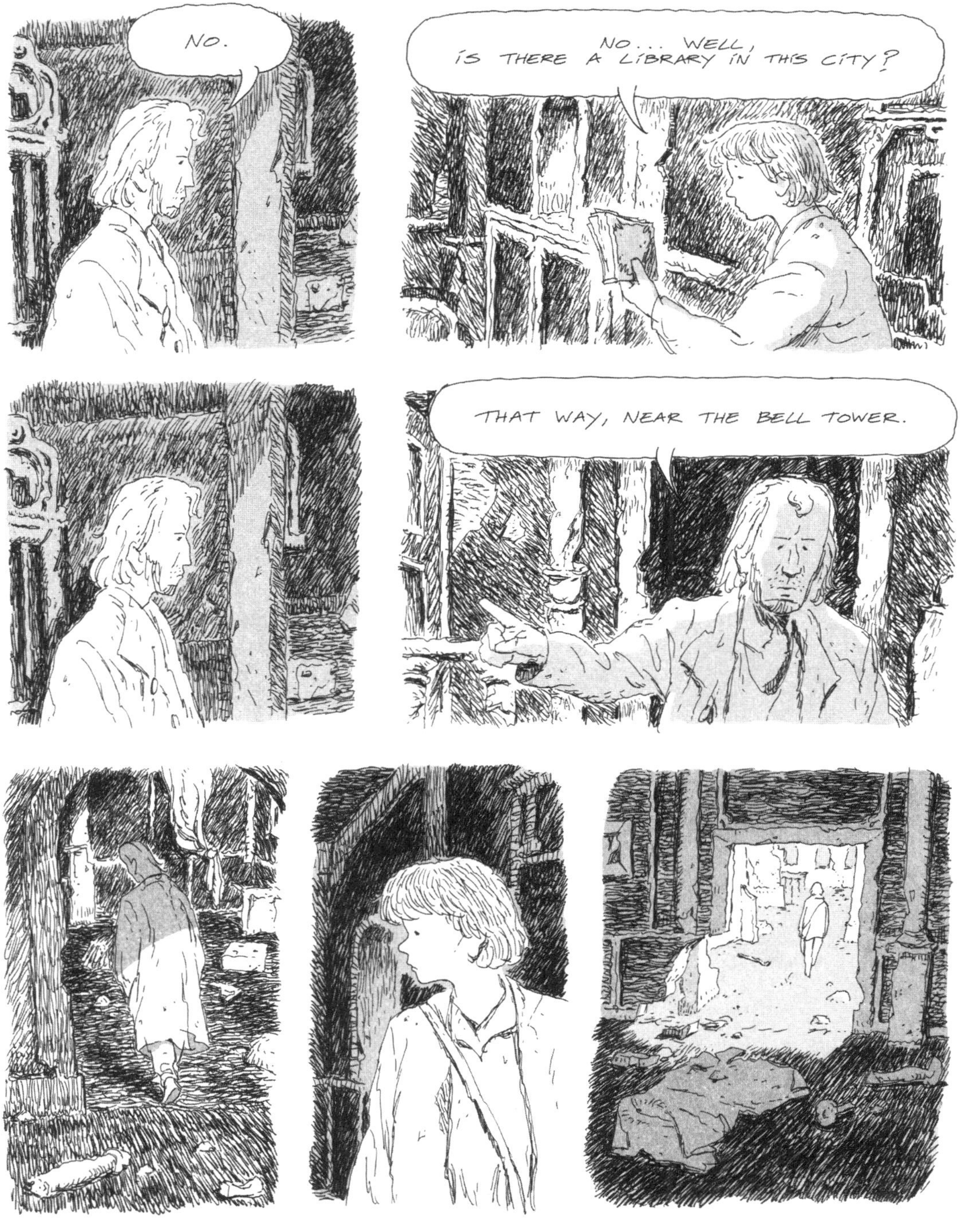
NO.
NO... WELL, IS THERE A LIBRARY IN THIS CITY?
THAT WAY, NEAR THE BELL TOWER.

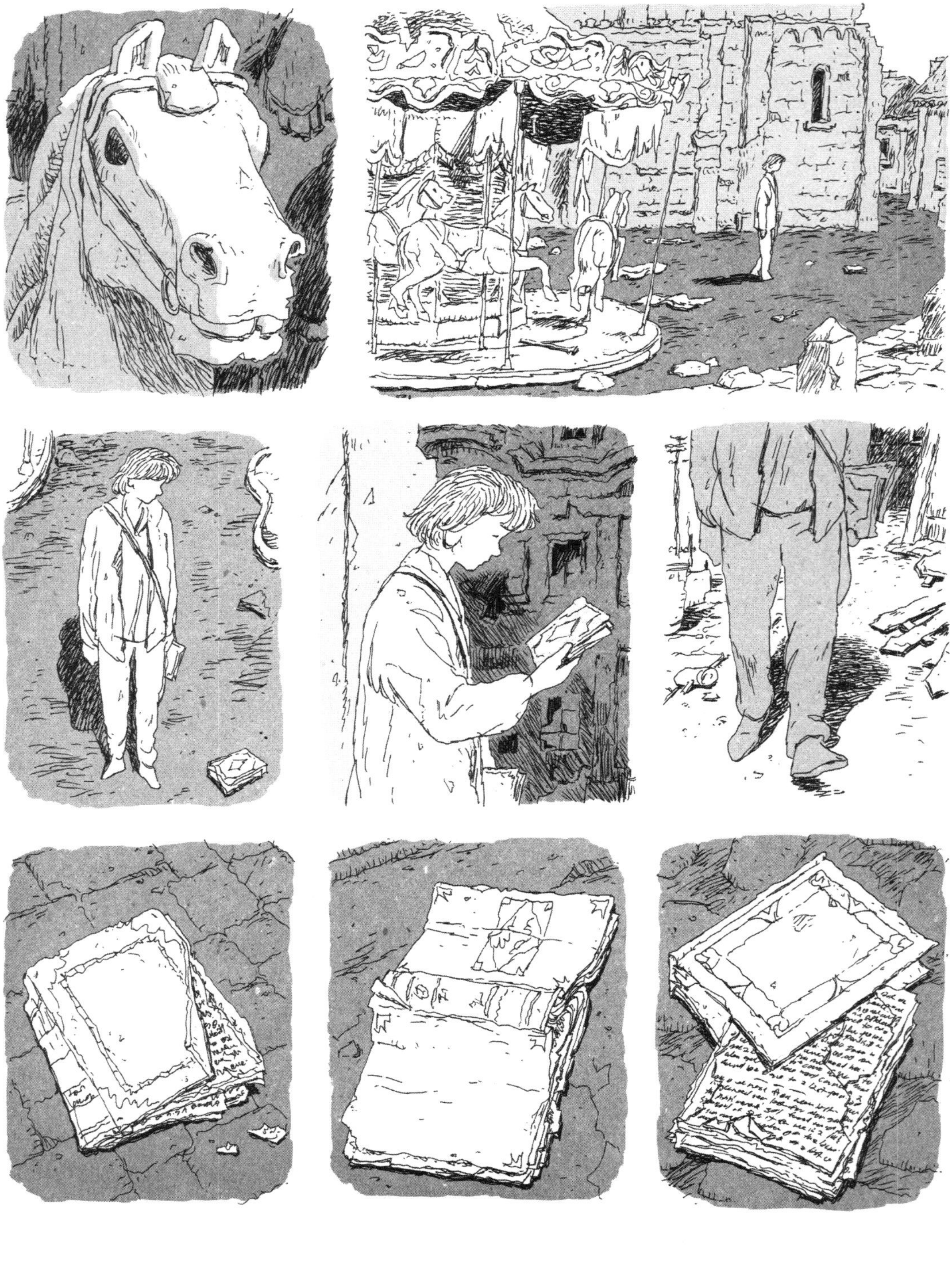

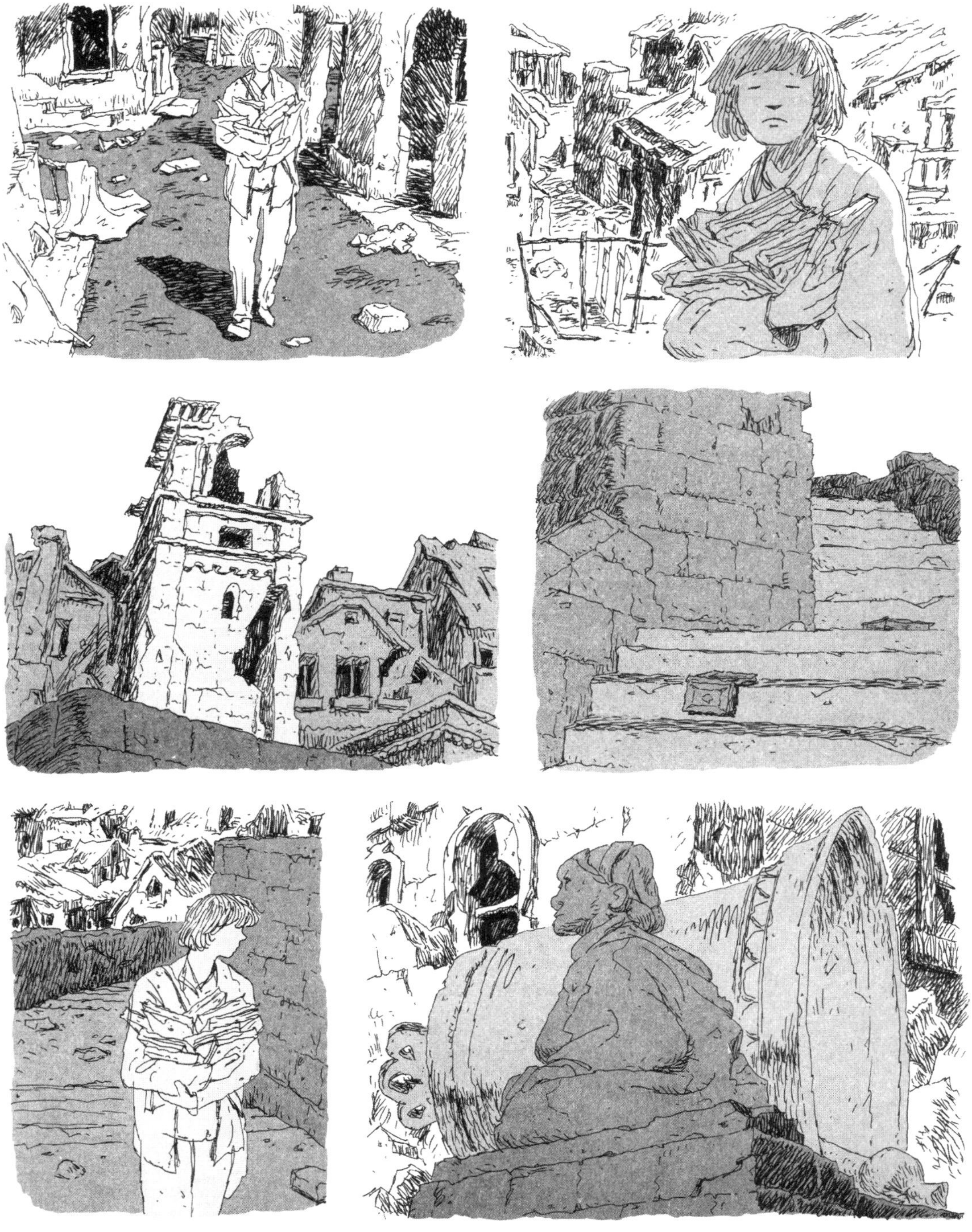

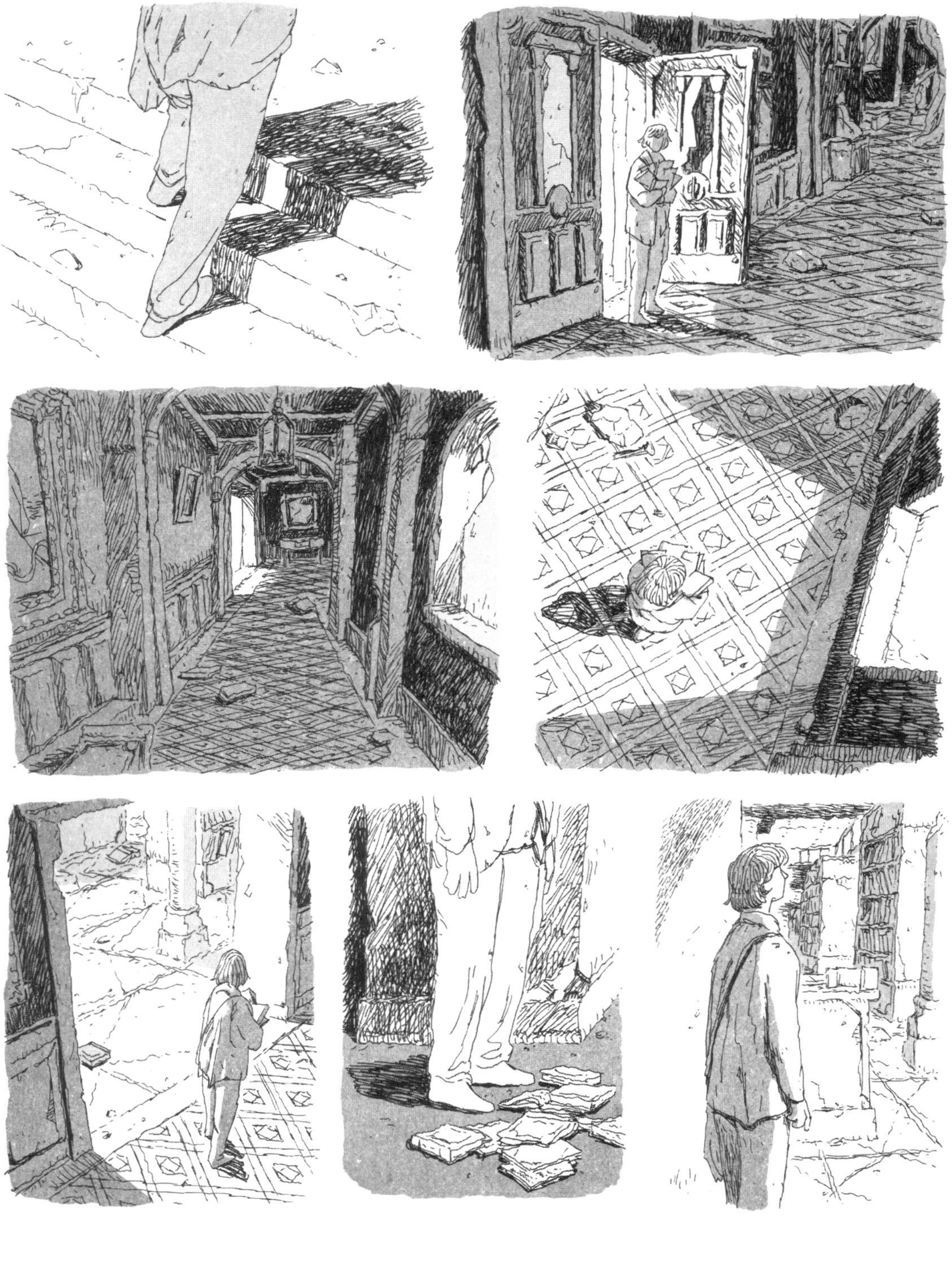

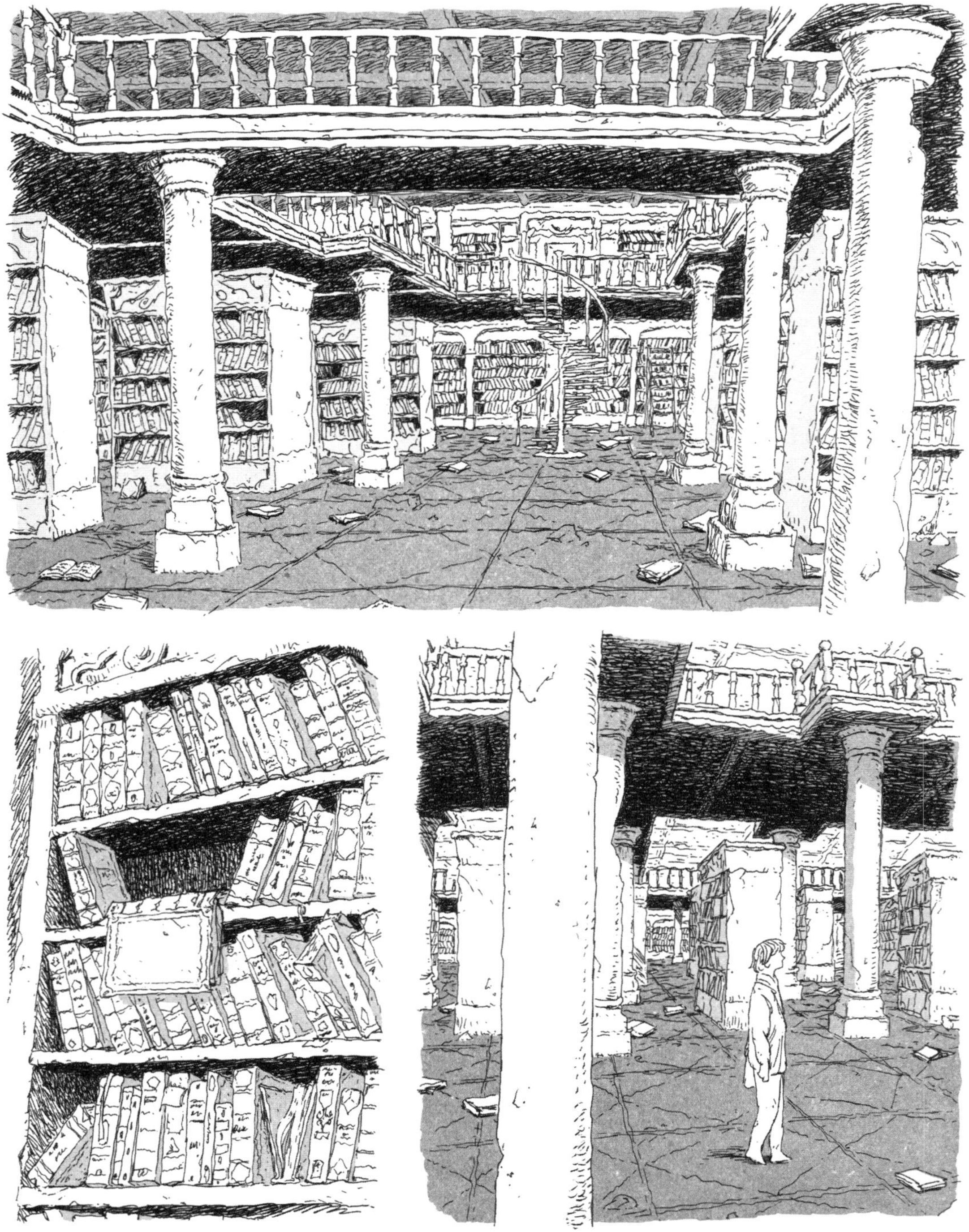

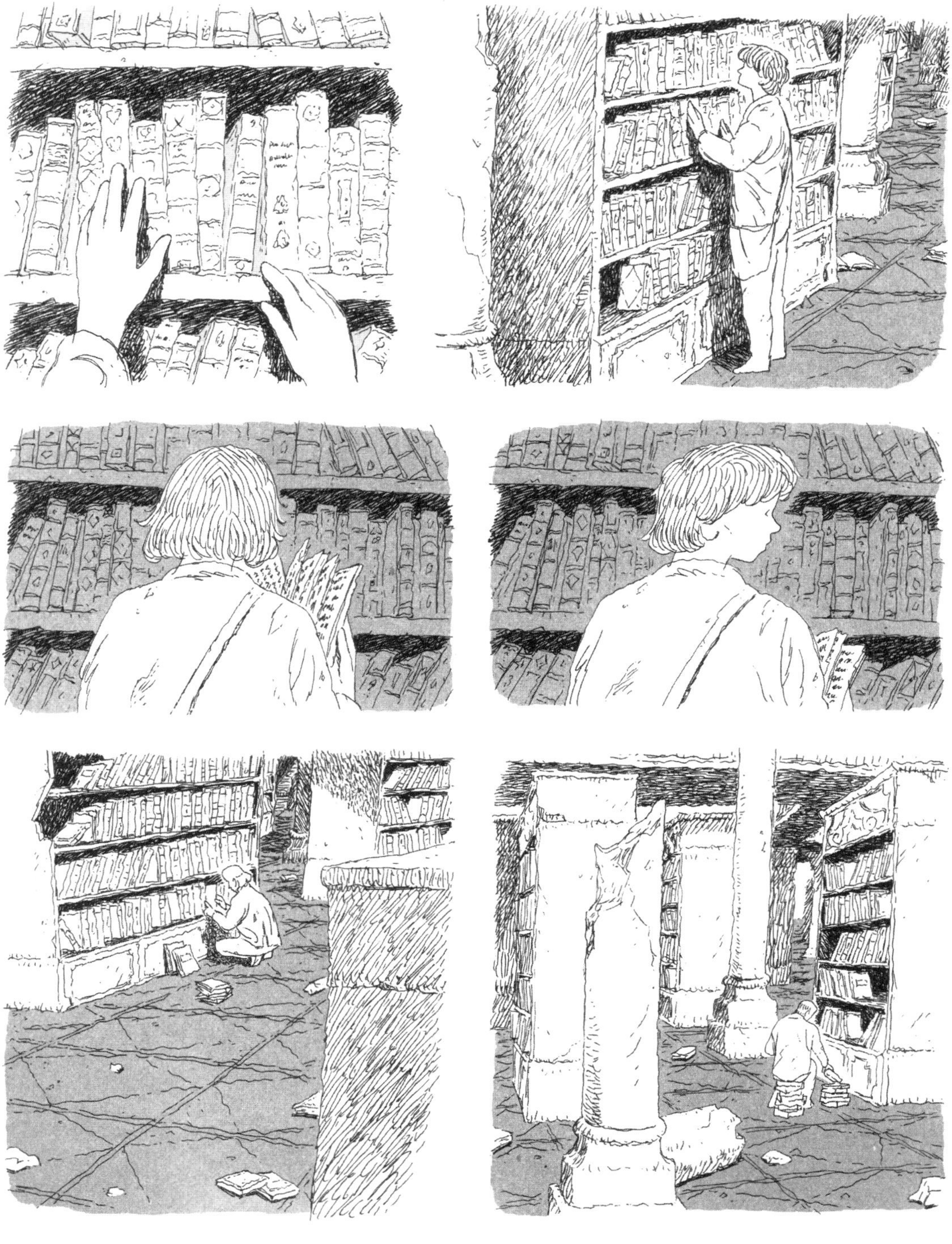

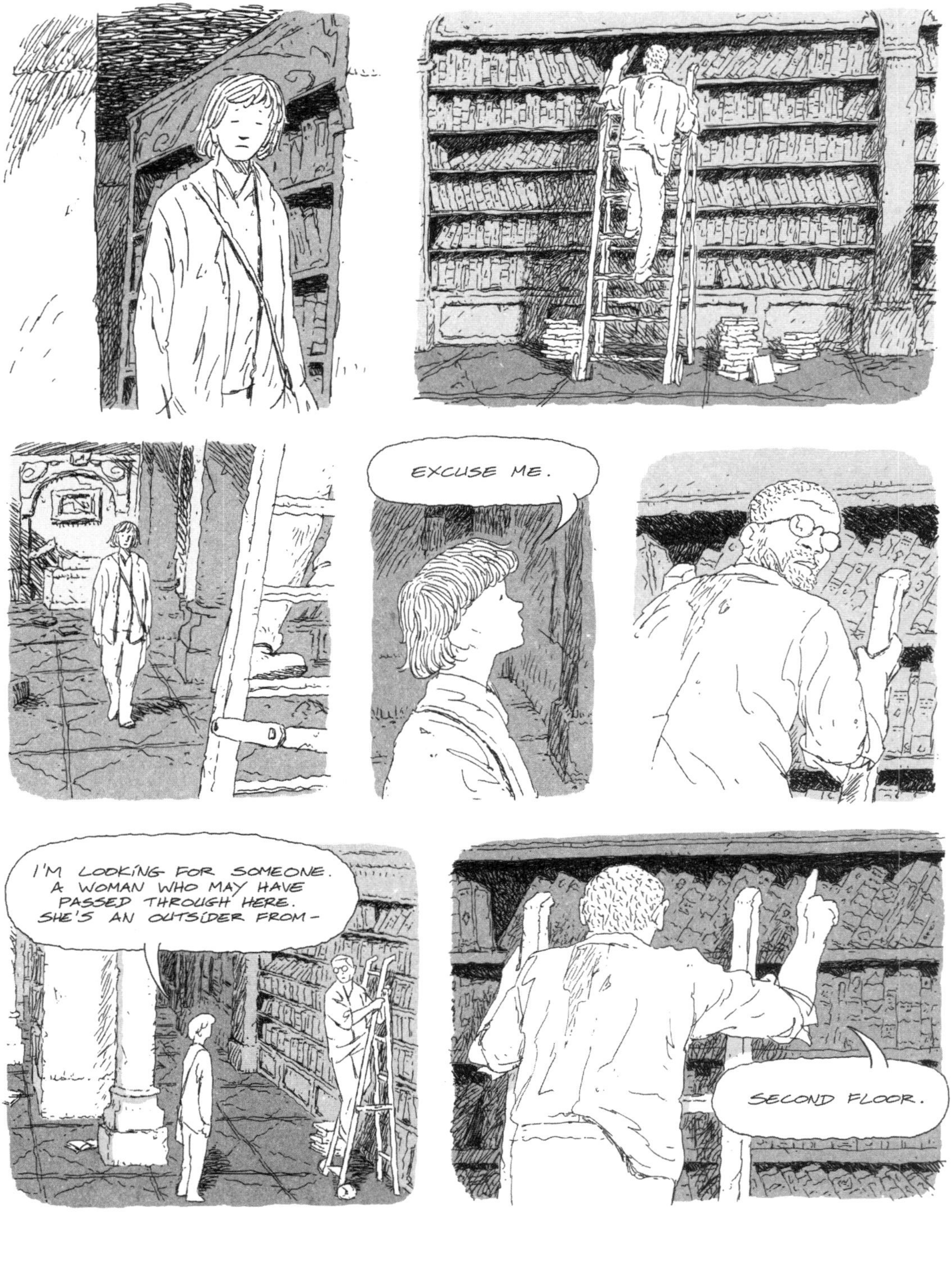
EXCUSE ME.
I'M LOOKING FOR SOMEONE. A WOMAN WHO MAY HAVE PASSED THROUGH HERE. SHE'S AN OUTSIDER FROM-
SECOND FLOOR.

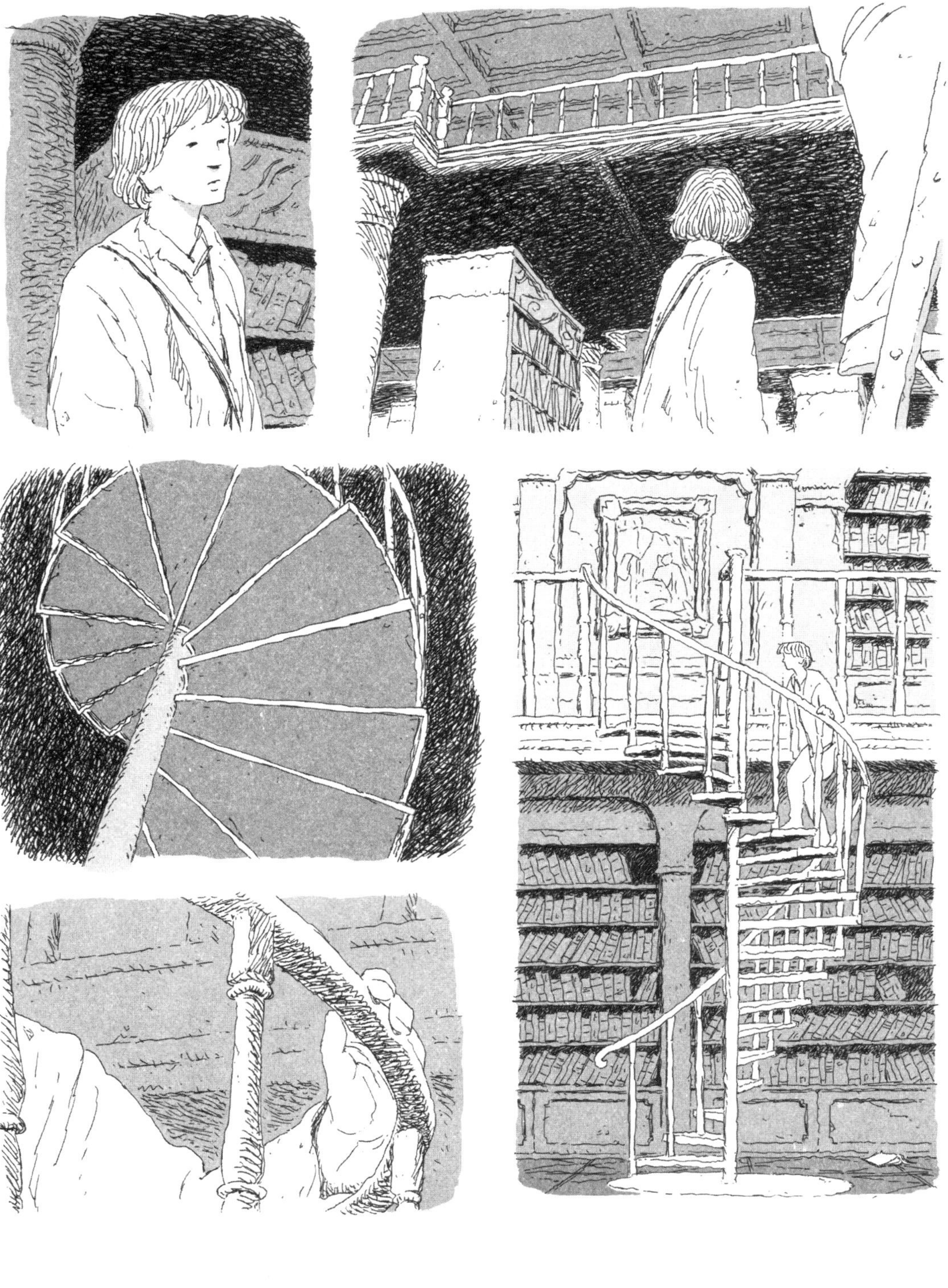

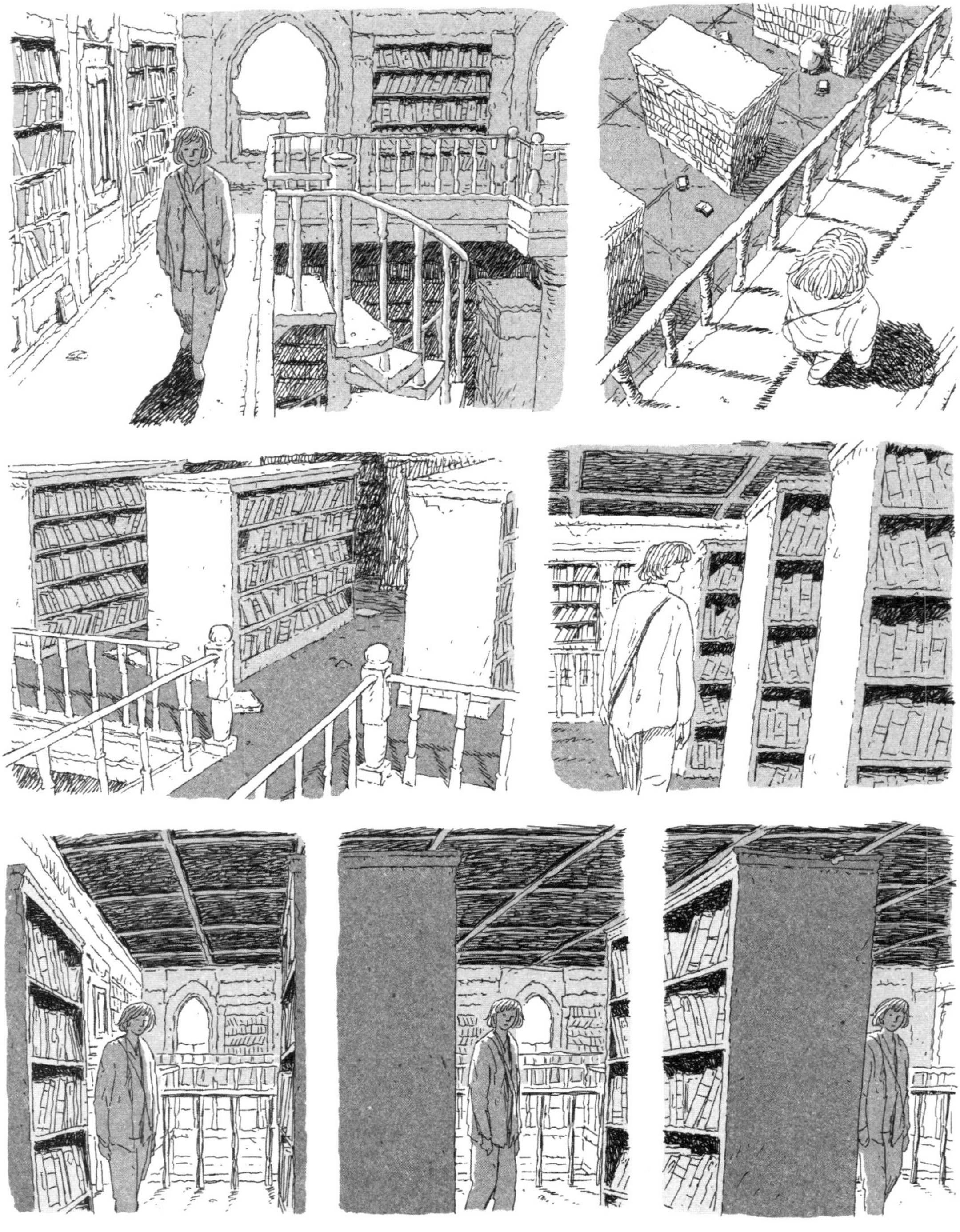

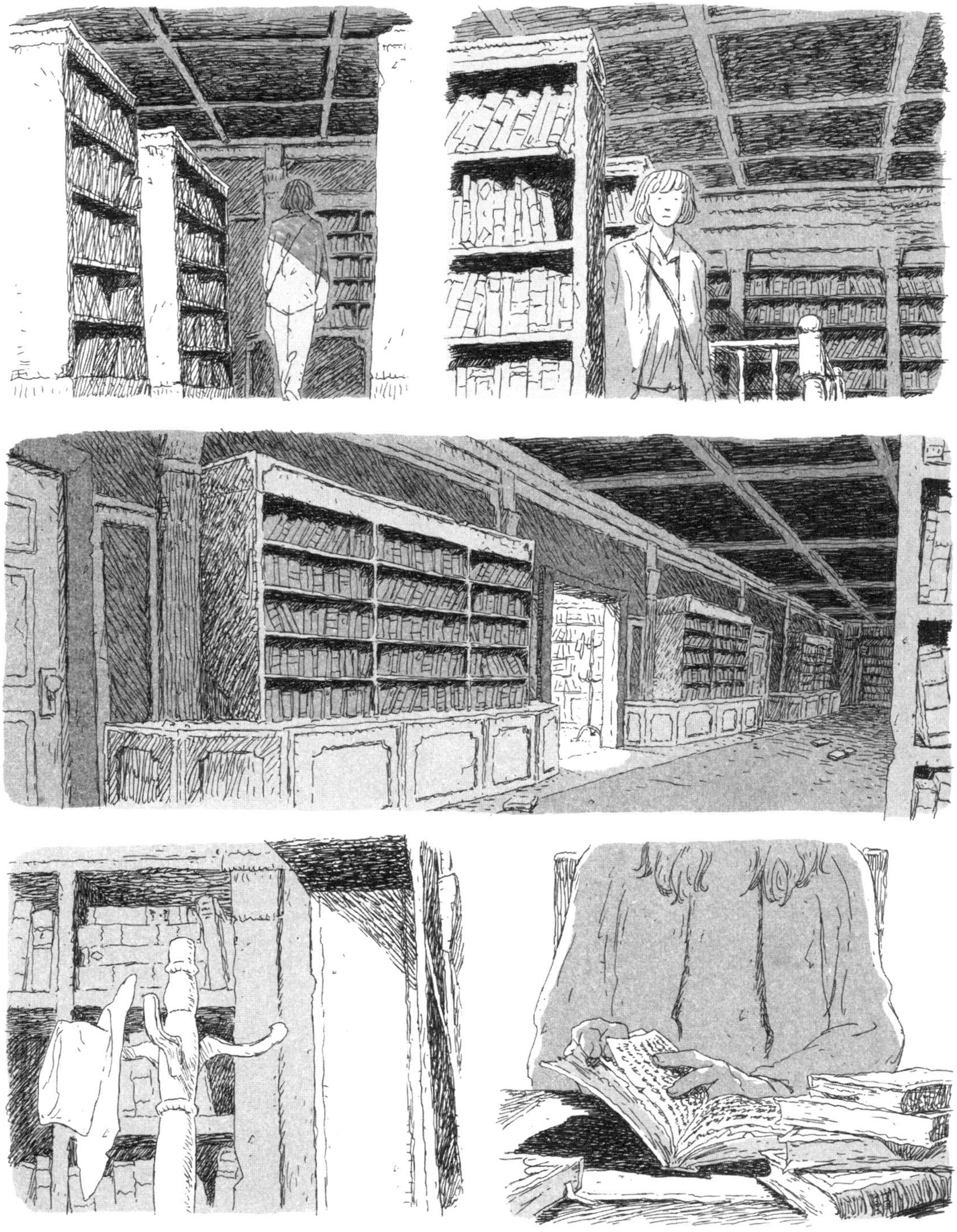

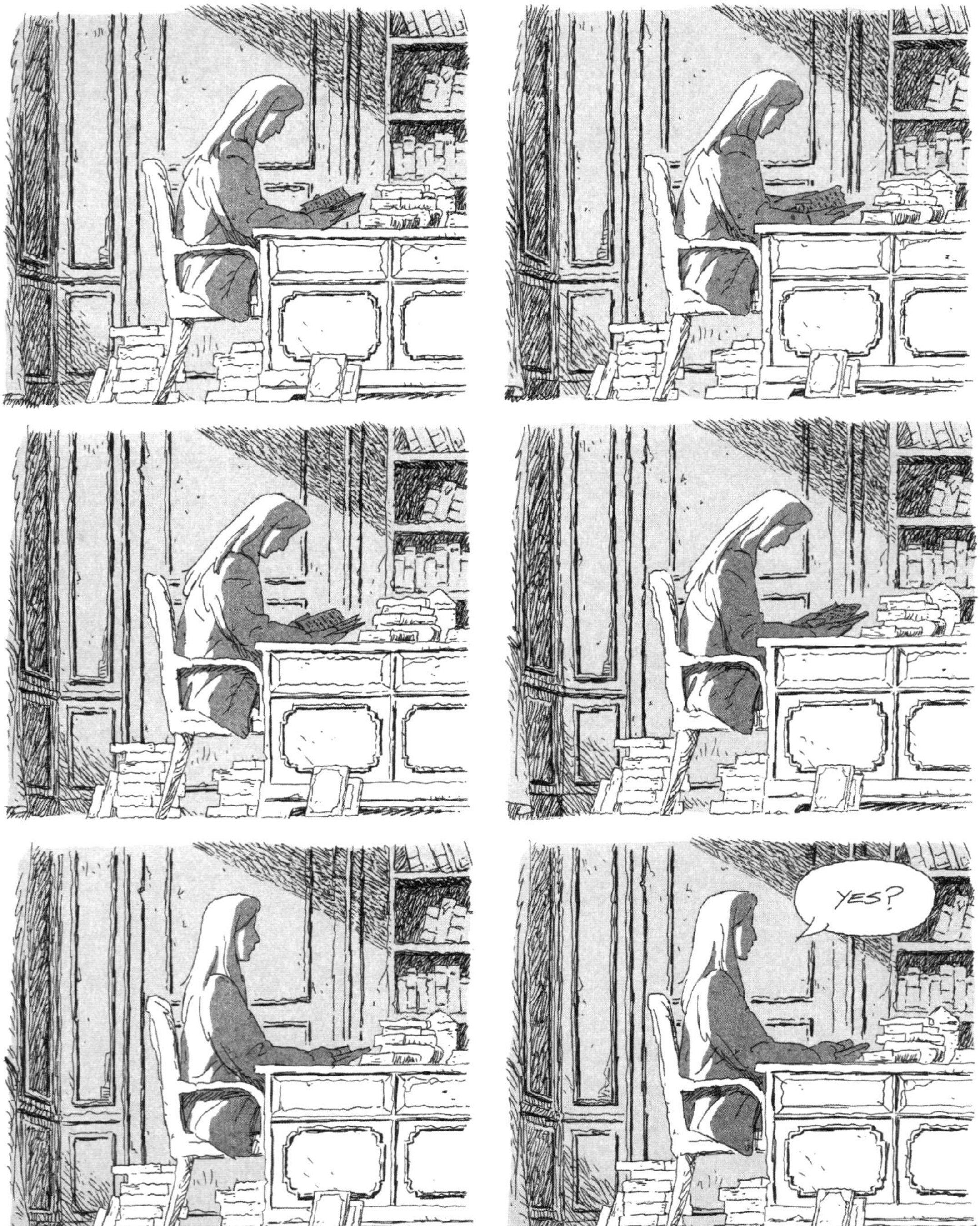
YES?

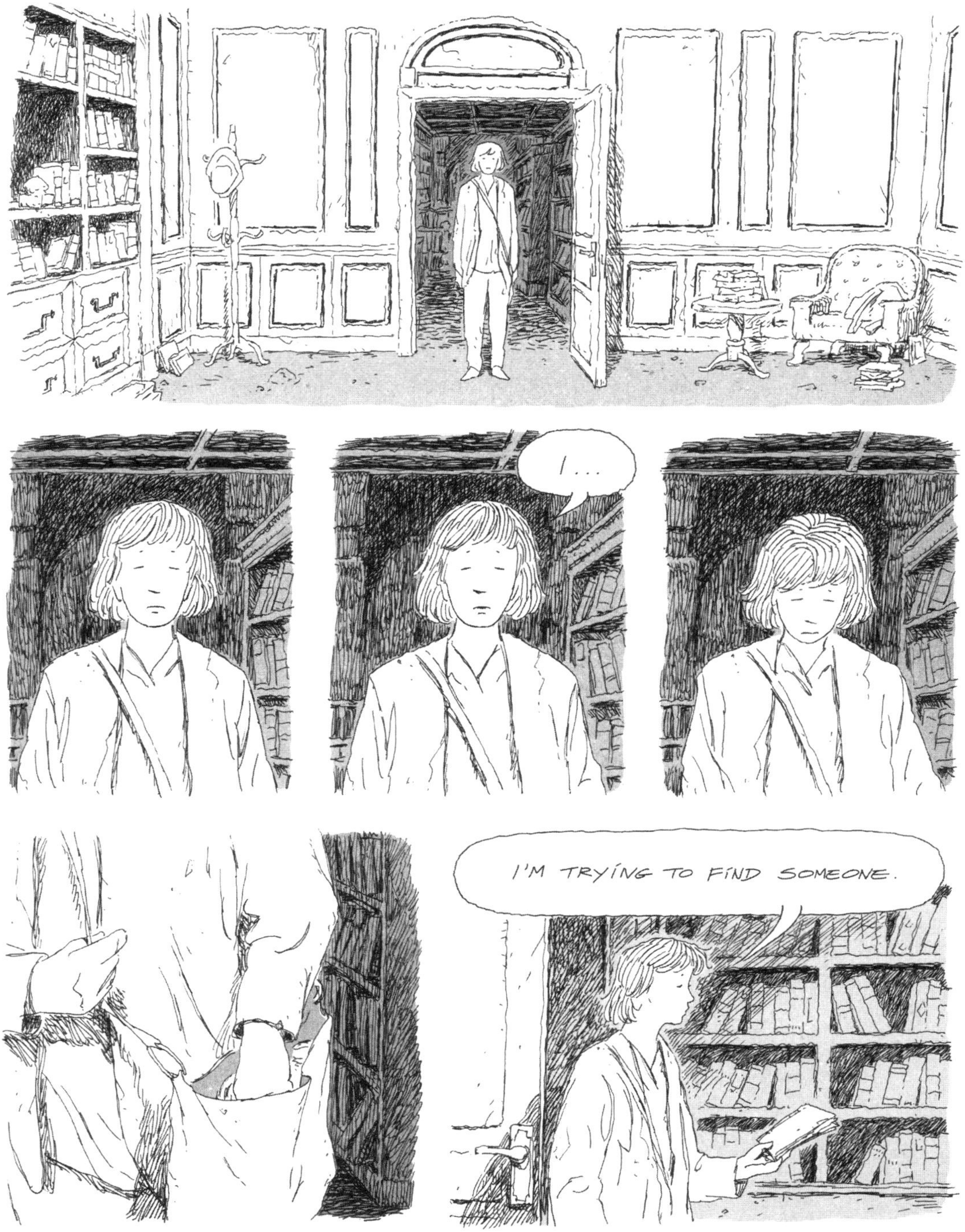
I...
I'M TRYING TO FIND SOMEONE.

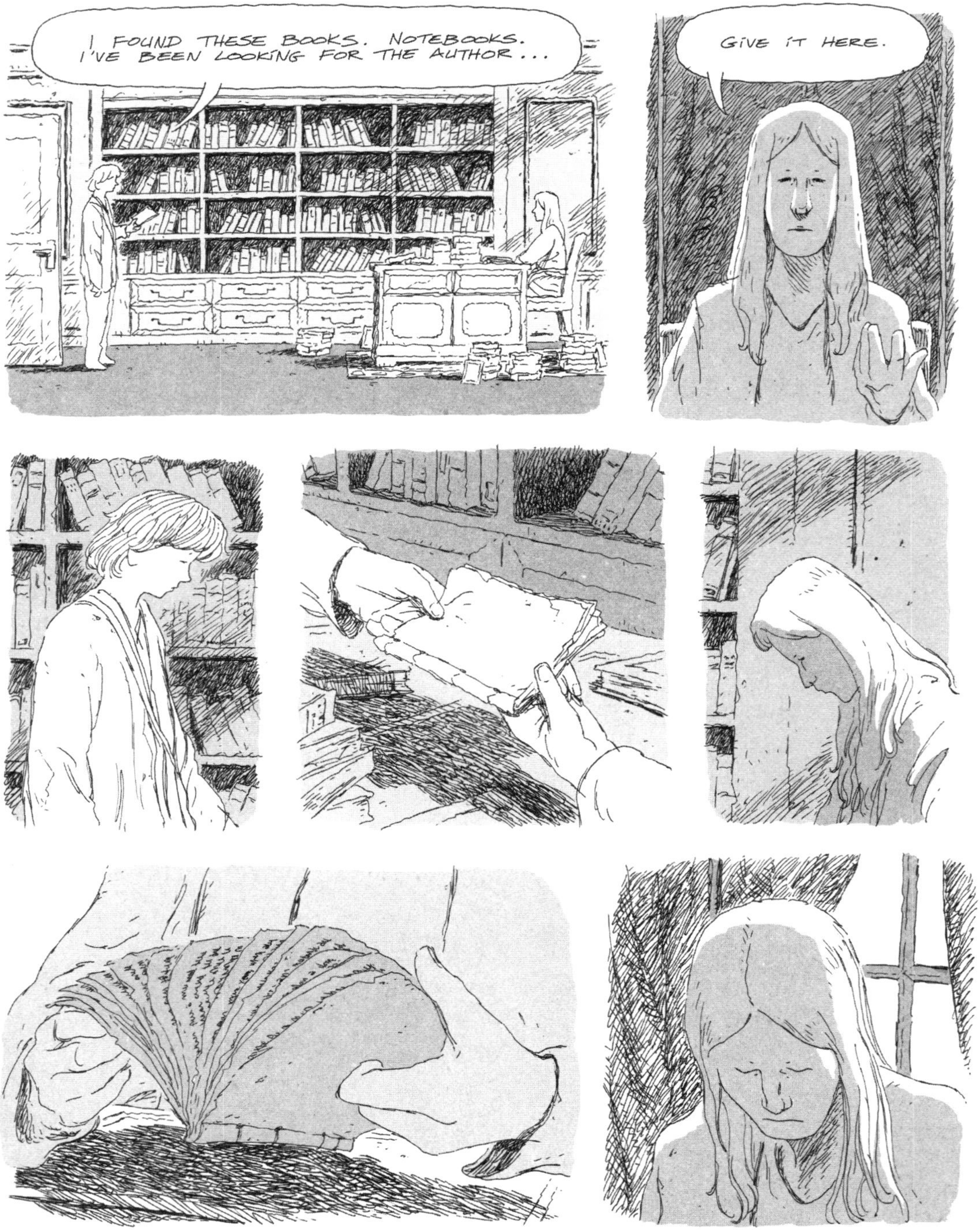
I FOUND THESE BOOKS. NOTEBOOKS. I'VE BEEN LOOKING FOR THE AUTHOR...
GIVE IT HERE.

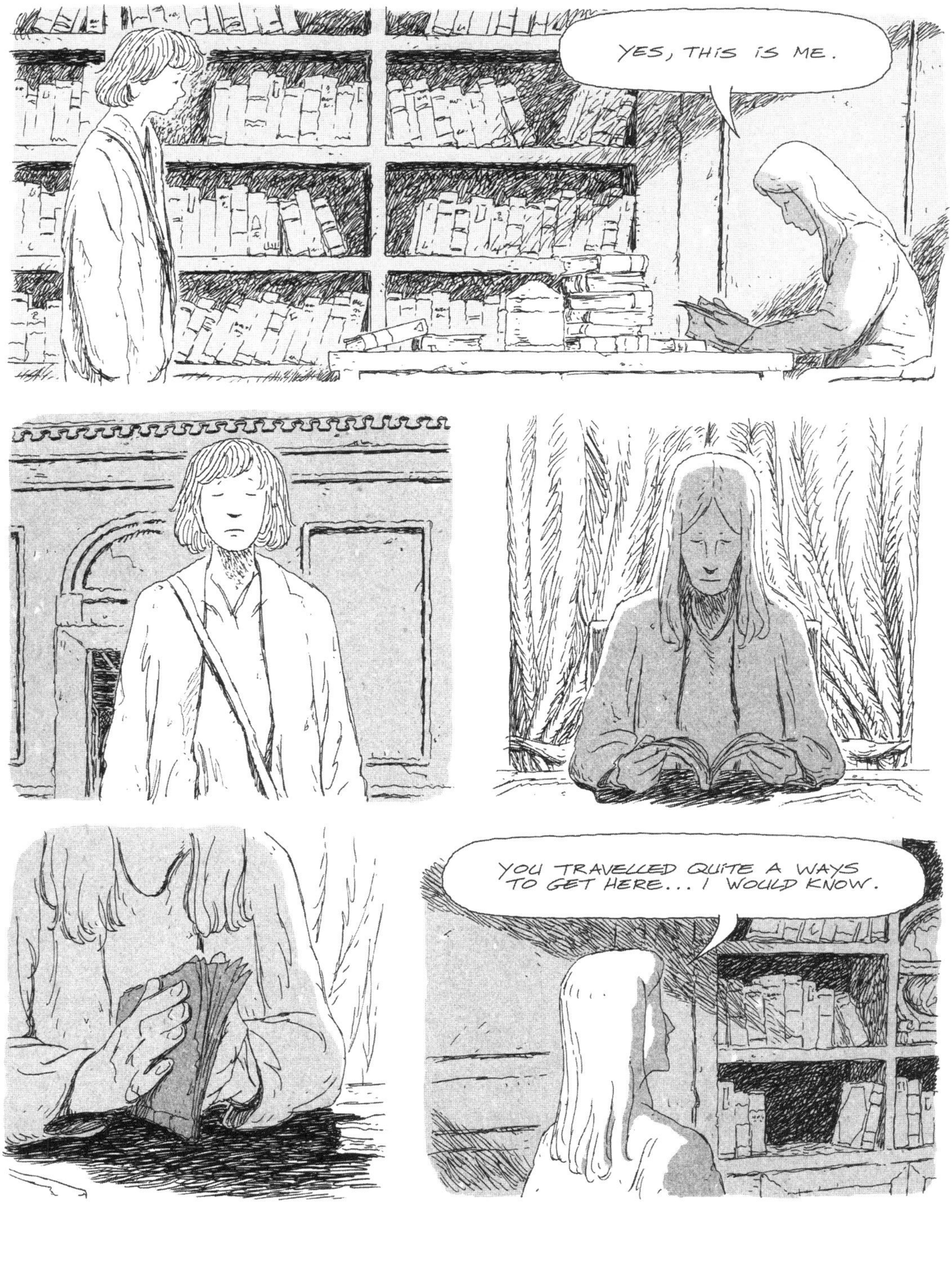
YES, THIS IS ME.
YOU TRAVELLED QUITE A WAYS TO GET HERE... I WOULD KNOW.

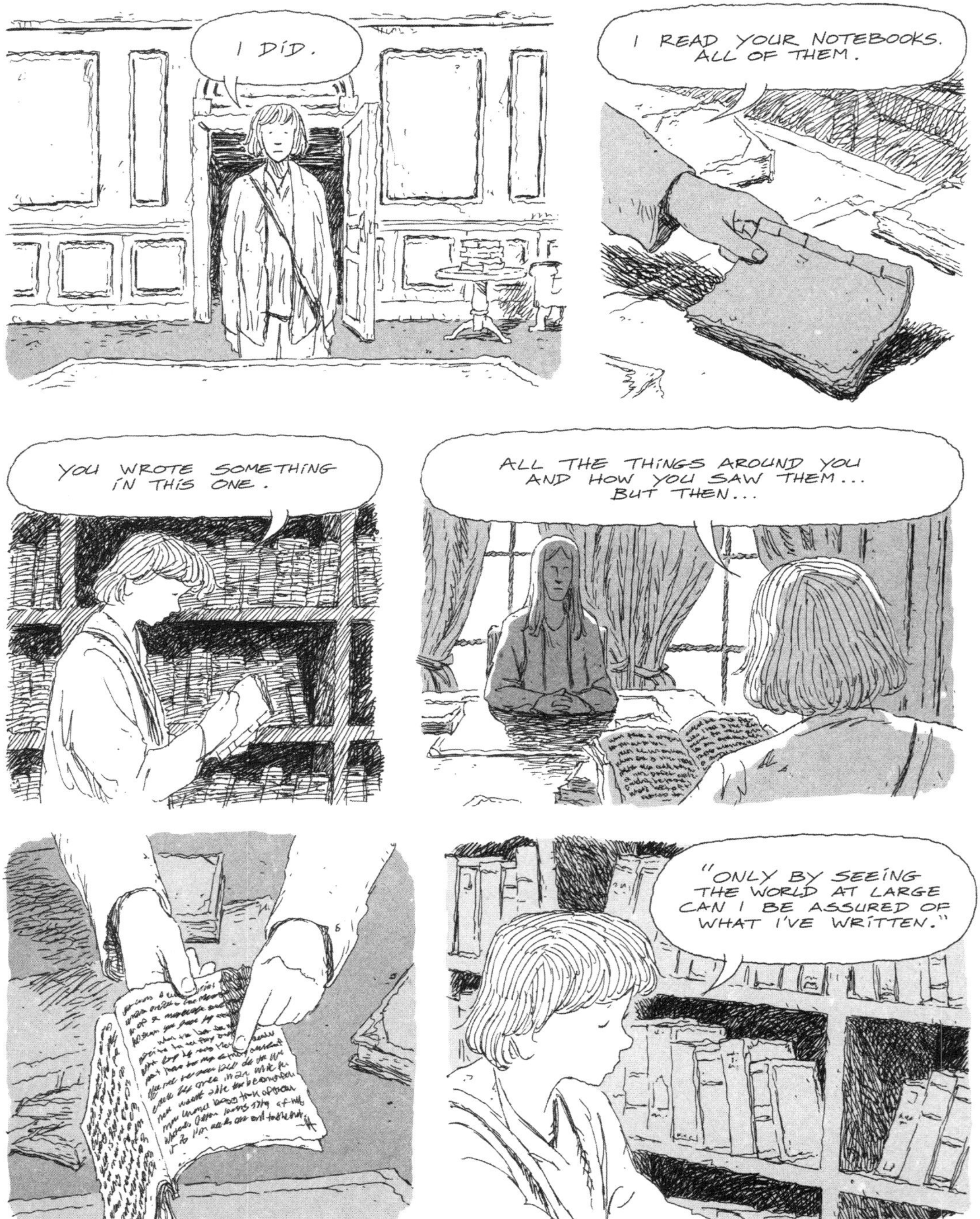

I DID.
I READ YOUR NOTEBOOKS. ALL OF THEM.
YOU WROTE SOMETHING IN THIS ONE.
ALL THE THINGS AROUND YOU AND HOW YOU SAW THEM... BUT THEN...
"ONLY BY SEEING THE WORLD AT LARGE CAN I BE ASSURED OF WHAT I'VE WRITTEN."

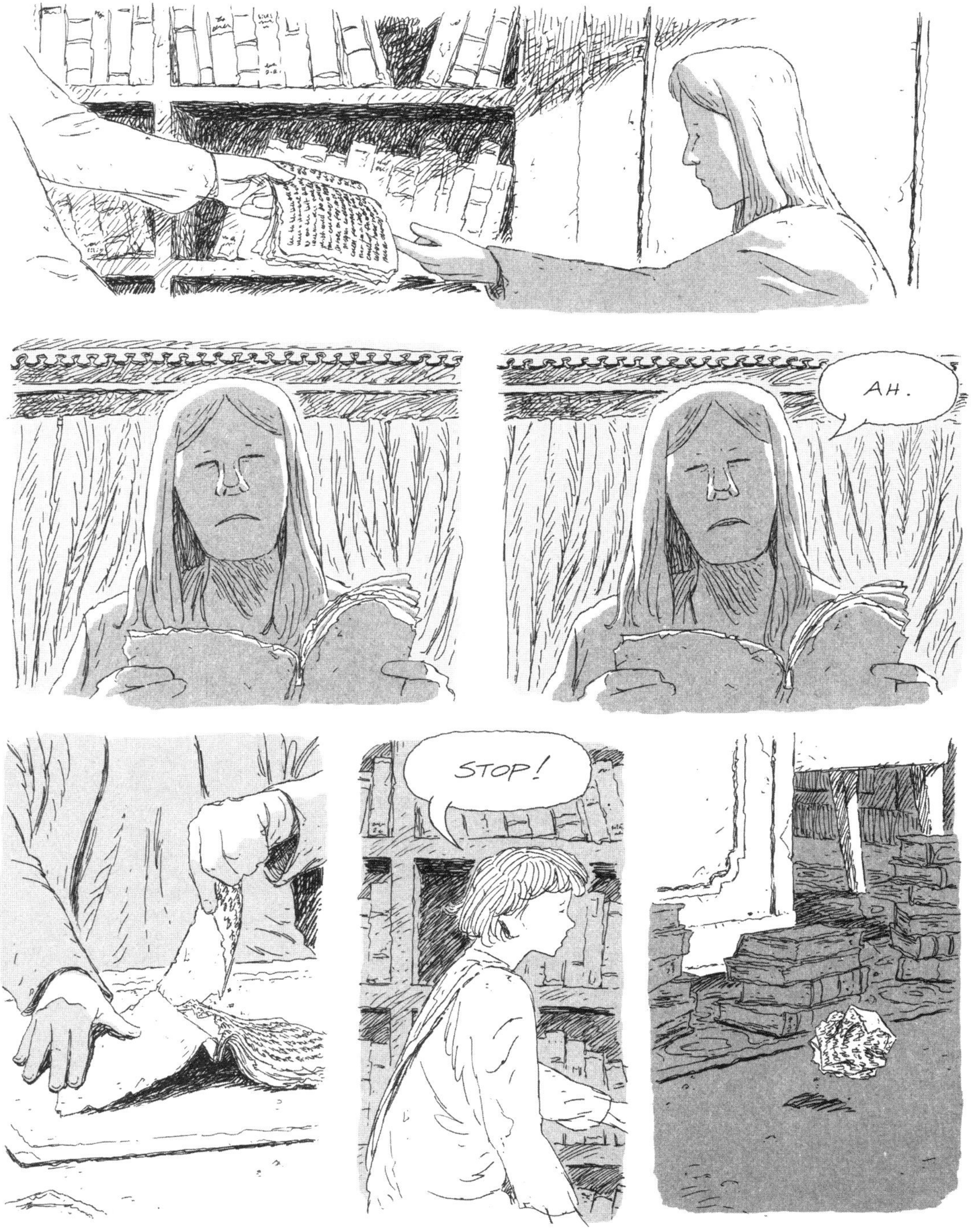
AH.
STOP!

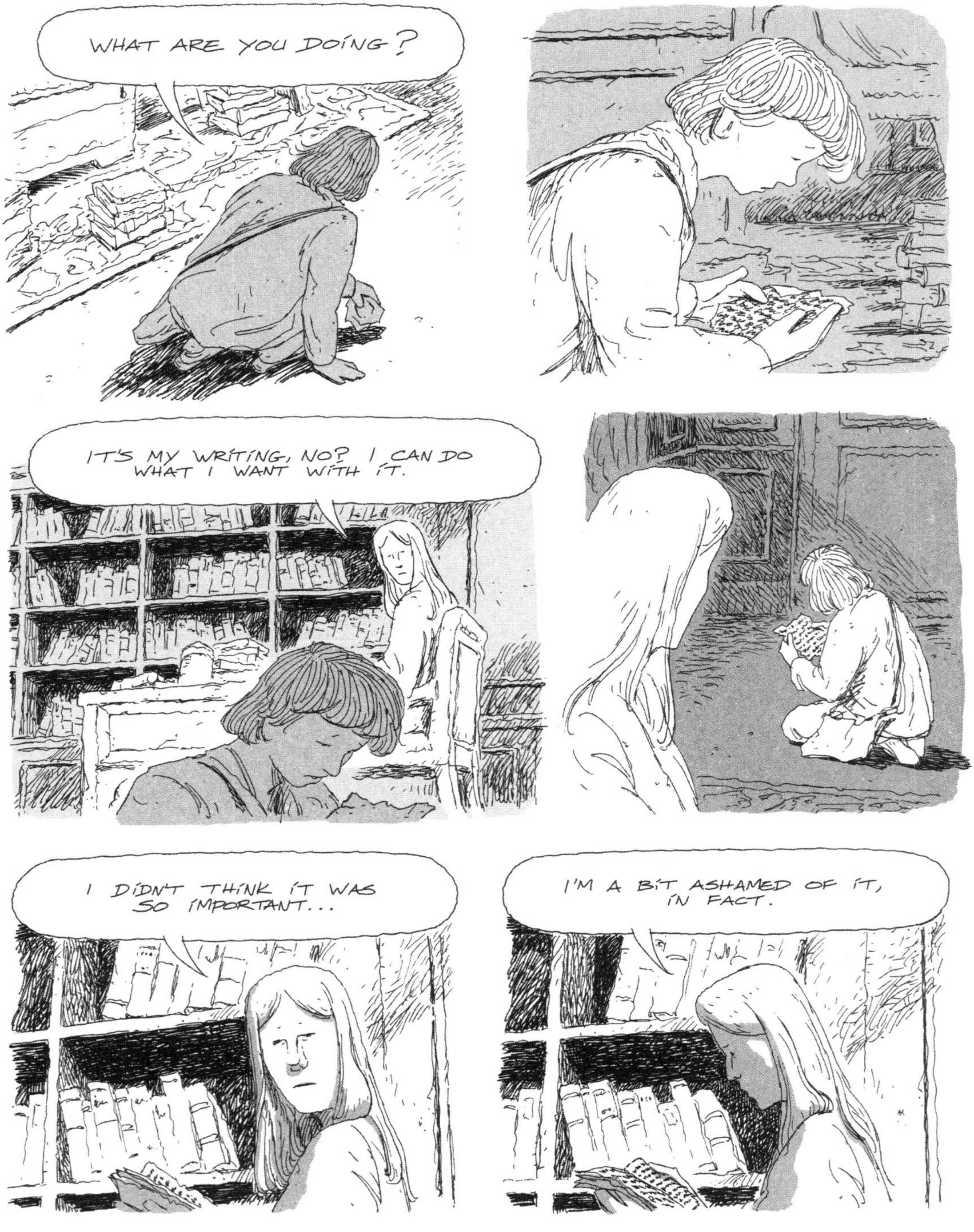
WHAT ARE YOU DOING?
IT'S MY WRITING, NO? I CAN DO WHAT I WANT WITH IT.
I DIDN'T THINK IT WAS SO IMPORTANT...
I'M A BIT ASHAMED OF IT, IN FACT.

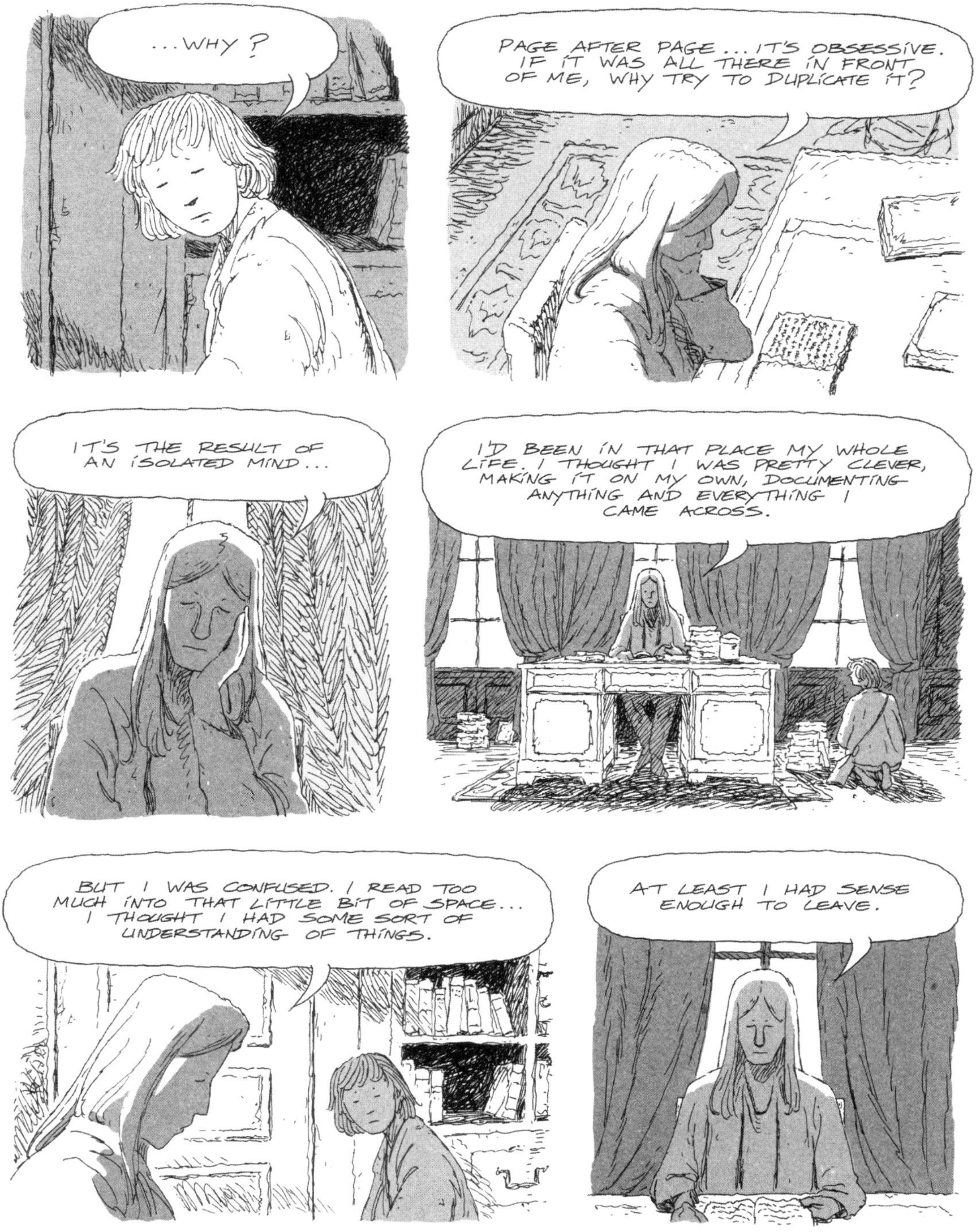
...WHY?
PAGE AFTER PAGE... IT'S OBSESSIVE. IF IT WAS ALL THERE IN FRONT OF ME, WHY TRY TO DUPLICATE IT?
IT'S THE RESULT OF AN ISOLATED MIND...
I'D BEEN IN THAT PLACE MY WHOLE LIFE. I THOUGHT I WAS PRETTY CLEVER, MAKING IT ON MY OWN, DOCUMENTING ANYTHING AND EVERYTHING I CAME ACROSS.
BUT I WAS CONFUSED. I READ TOO MUCH INTO THAT LITTLE BIT OF SPACE... I THOUGHT I HAD SOME SORT OF UNDERSTANDING OF THINGS.
AT LEAST I HAD SENSE ENOUGH TO LEAVE.

BUT YOUR WRITING... THERE'S NOTHING YOU TAKE FOR GRANTED. YOU'RE SENSITIVE TO EVERY PART OF —

PLEASE... DON'T GET TAKEN IN BY ALL THAT. YOU MADE YOUR WAY HERE, SAME AS ME. WHAT WAS YOUR IMPRESSION OF THE WORLD AT LARGE?

IT CERTAINLY DIDN'T LEAVE ME MUCH TO BE ASSURED OF.

MAYBE NOT... I DON'T KNOW WHAT TO MAKE OF IT JUST YET. THIS CITY ALONE... IT'S TOO MUCH TO TAKE IN.

THAT'S EXACTLY RIGHT. HOW COULD YOU KNOW? FORGET ANY ASSURANCE.

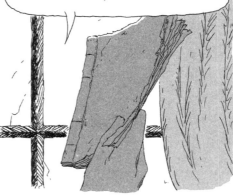

ANY ATTEMPT TO WRITE DOWN EVERY LITTLE DETAIL.

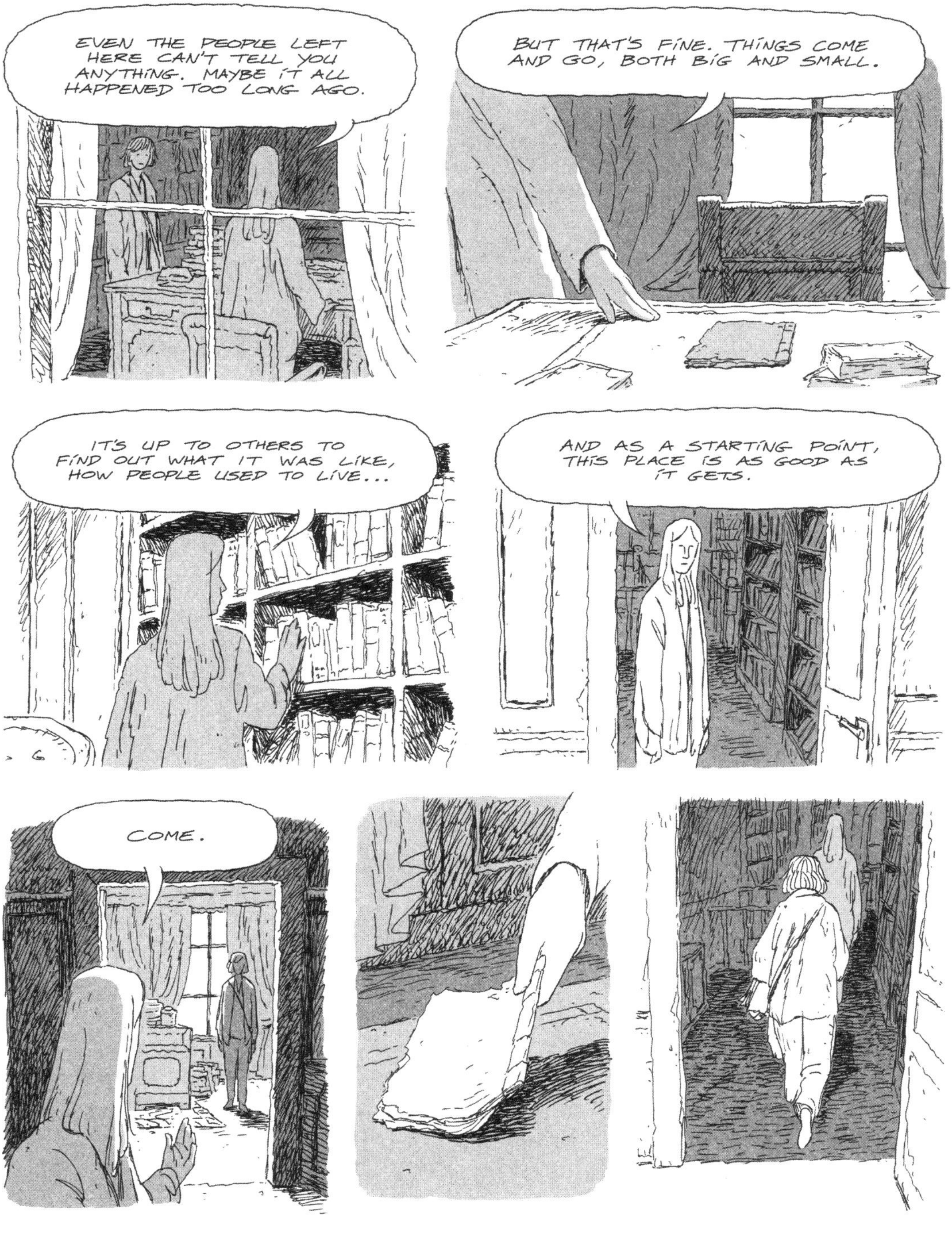
EVEN THE PEOPLE LEFT HERE CAN'T TELL YOU ANYTHING. MAYBE IT ALL HAPPENED TOO LONG AGO.
BUT THAT'S FINE. THINGS COME AND GO, BOTH BIG AND SMALL.
IT'S UP TO OTHERS TO FIND OUT WHAT IT WAS LIKE, HOW PEOPLE USED TO LIVE...
AND AS A STARTING POINT, THIS PLACE IS AS GOOD AS IT GETS.
COME.

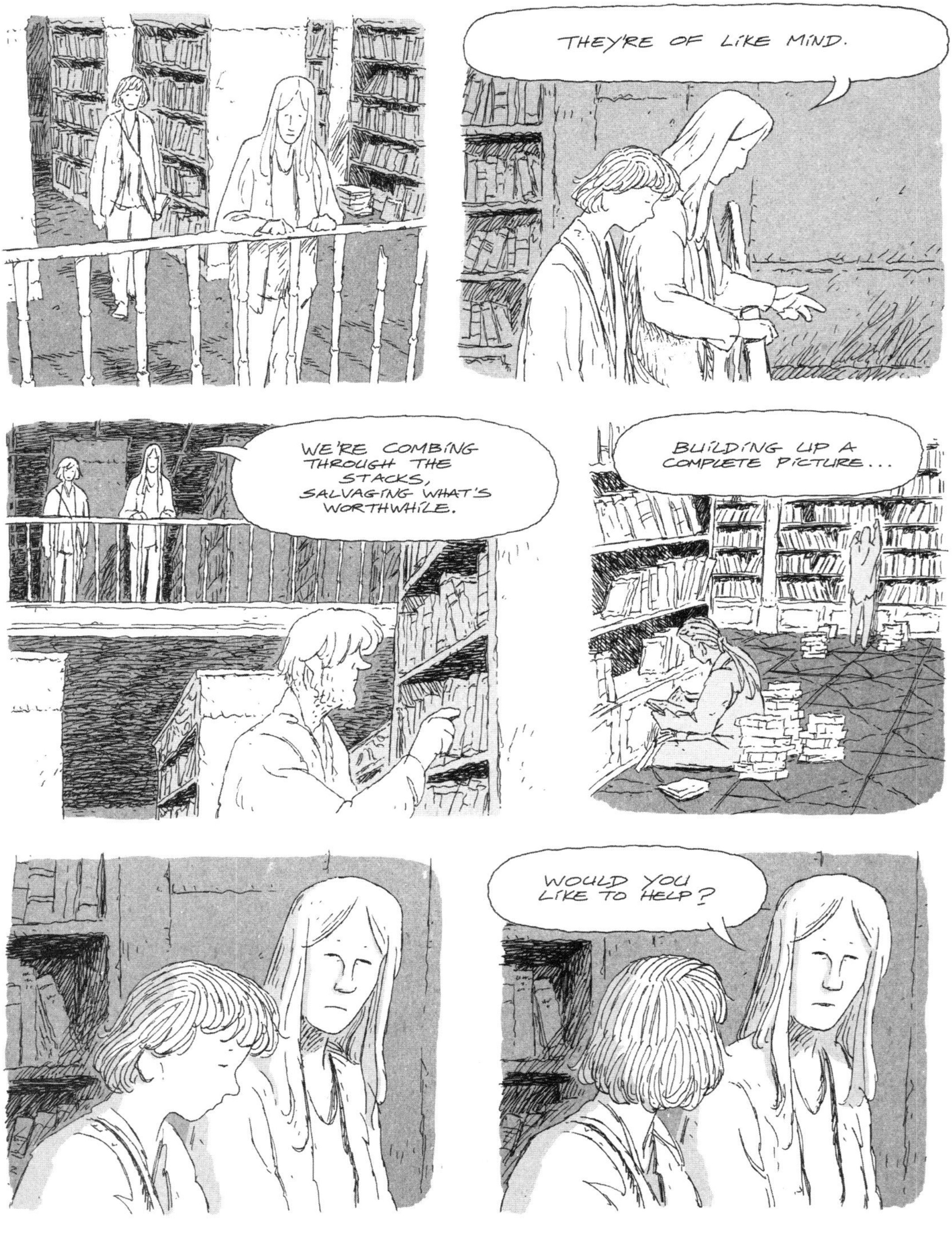
THEY'RE OF LIKE MIND.
WE'RE COMBING THROUGH THE STACKS, SALVAGING WHAT'S WORTHWHILE.
BUILDING UP A COMPLETE PICTURE...
WOULD YOU LIKE TO HELP?

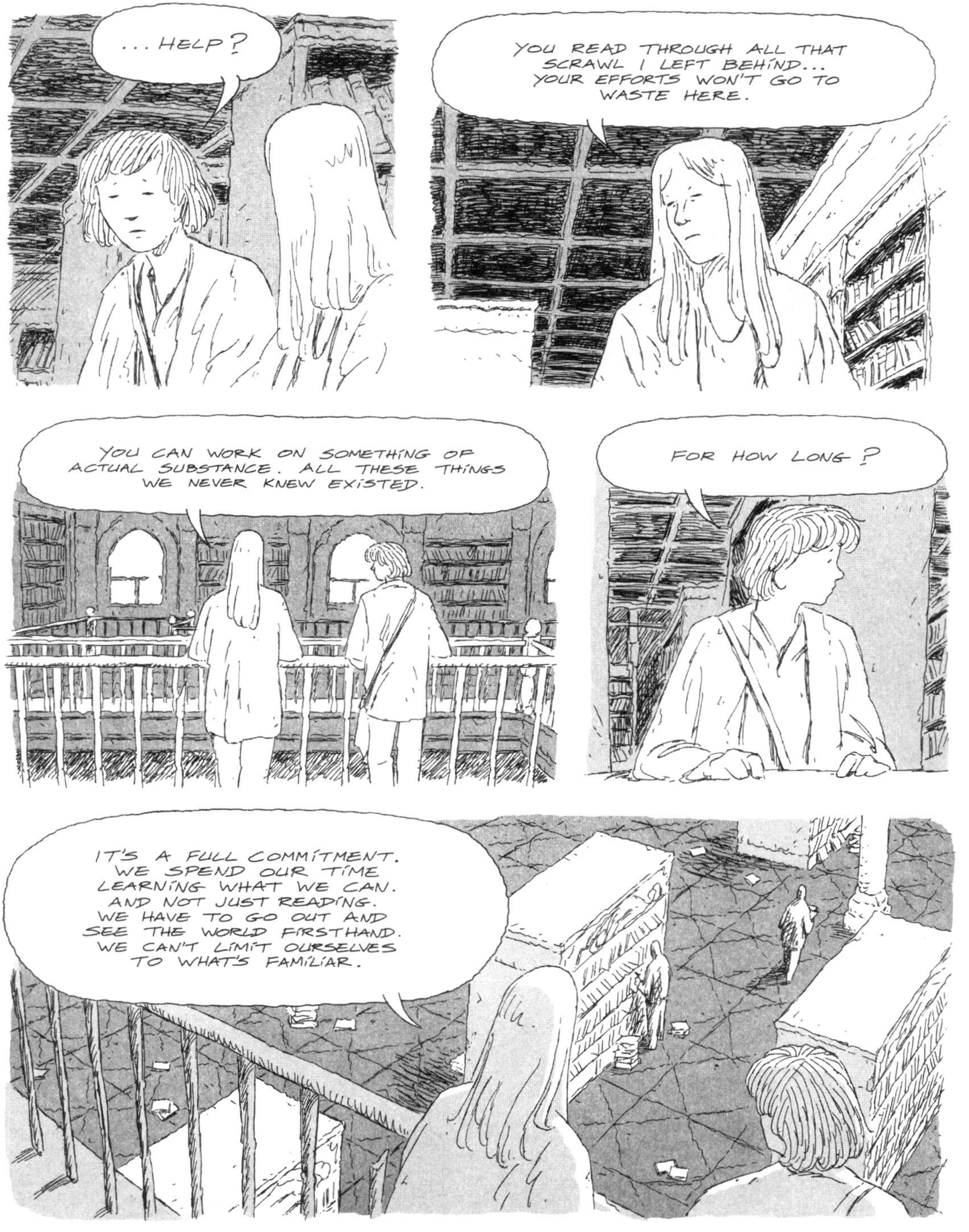
...HELP?
YOU READ THROUGH ALL THAT SCRAWL I LEFT BEHIND... YOUR EFFORTS WON'T GO TO WASTE HERE.
YOU CAN WORK ON SOMETHING OF ACTUAL SUBSTANCE. ALL THESE THINGS WE NEVER KNEW EXISTED.
FOR HOW LONG?
IT'S A FULL COMMITMENT. WE SPEND OUR TIME LEARNING WHAT WE CAN. AND NOT JUST READING. WE HAVE TO GO OUT AND SEE THE WORLD FIRSTHAND. WE CAN'T LIMIT OURSELVES TO WHAT'S FAMILIAR.

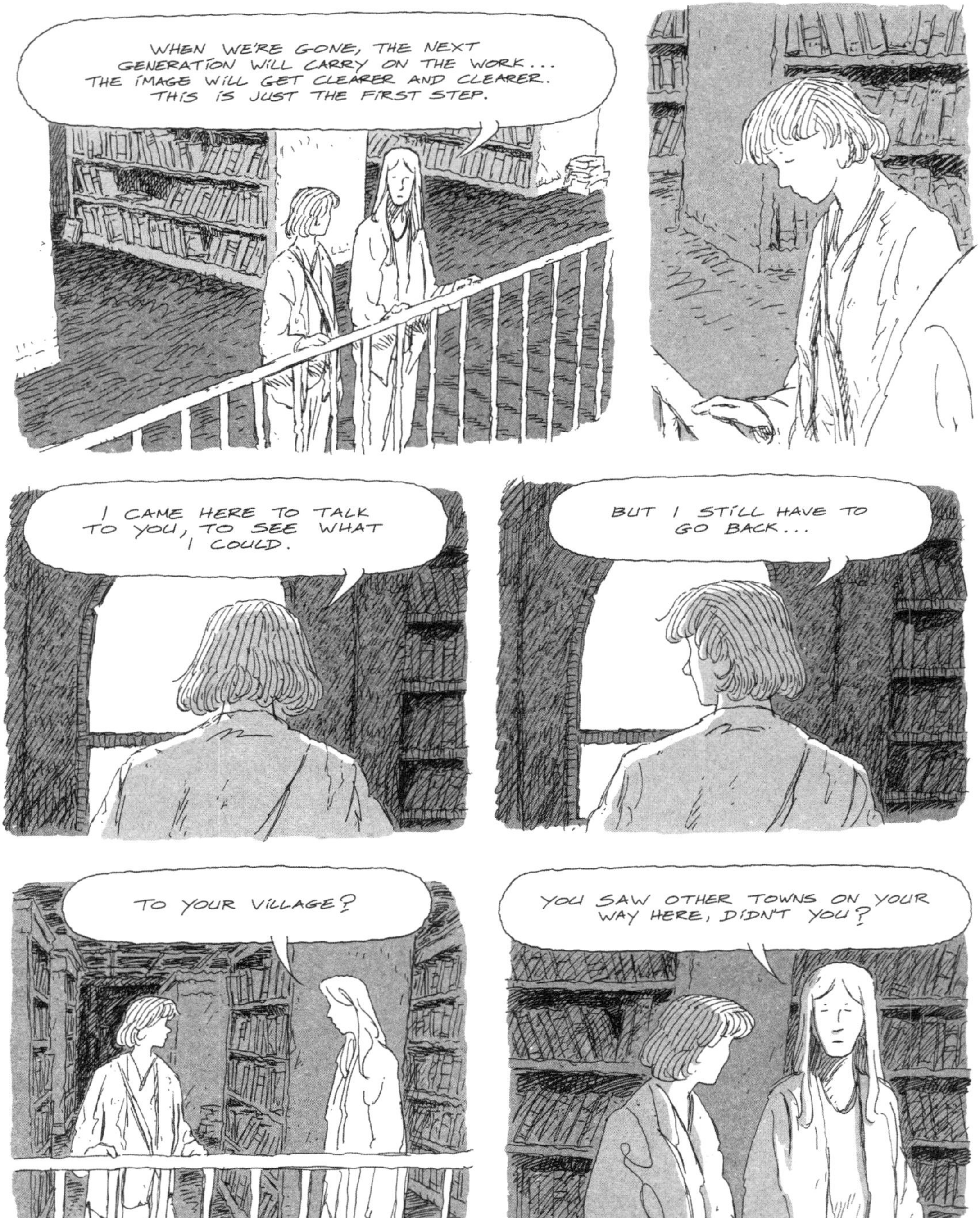
WHEN WE'RE GONE, THE NEXT GENERATION WILL CARRY ON THE WORK... THE IMAGE WILL GET CLEARER AND CLEARER. THIS IS JUST THE FIRST STEP.
I CAME HERE TO TALK TO YOU, TO SEE WHAT I COULD.
BUT I STILL HAVE TO GO BACK...
TO YOUR VILLAGE?
YOU SAW OTHER TOWNS ON YOUR WAY HERE, DIDN'T YOU?

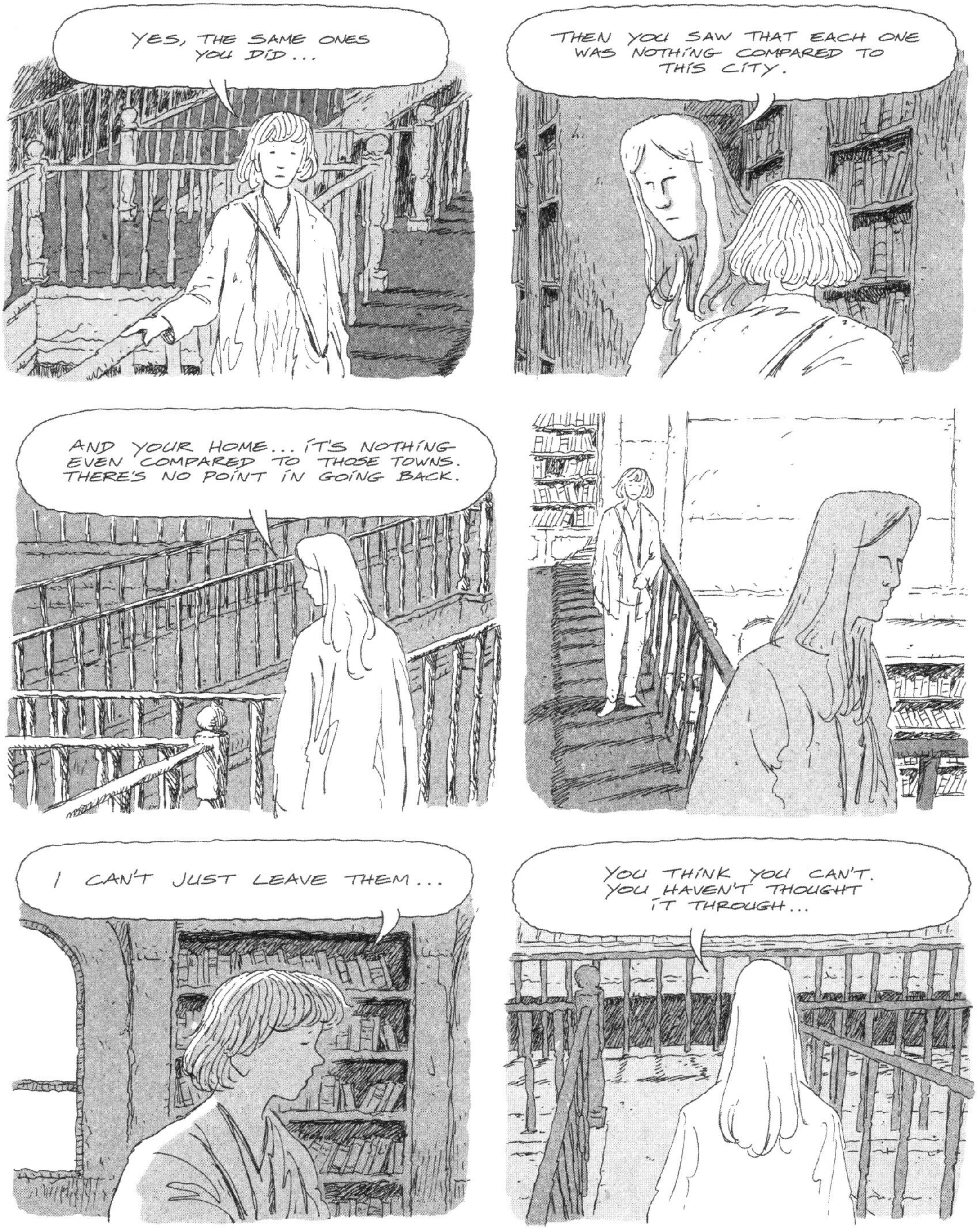
YES, THE SAME ONES YOU DID...
THEN YOU SAW THAT EACH ONE WAS NOTHING COMPARED TO THIS CITY.
AND YOUR HOME... IT'S NOTHING EVEN COMPARED TO THOSE TOWNS. THERE'S NO POINT IN GOING BACK.
I CAN'T JUST LEAVE THEM...
YOU THINK YOU CAN'T. YOU HAVEN'T THOUGHT IT THROUGH...

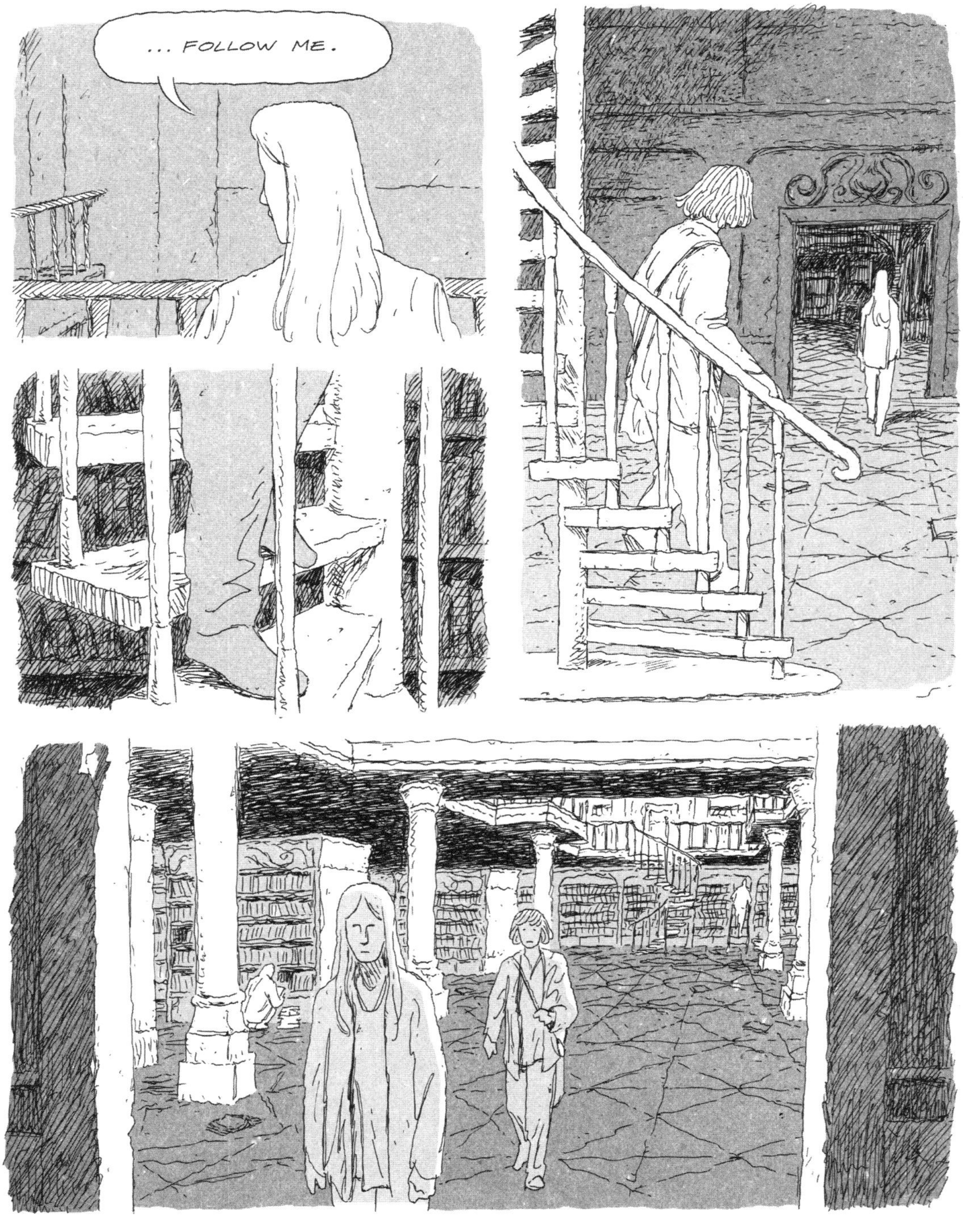
... FOLLOW ME.

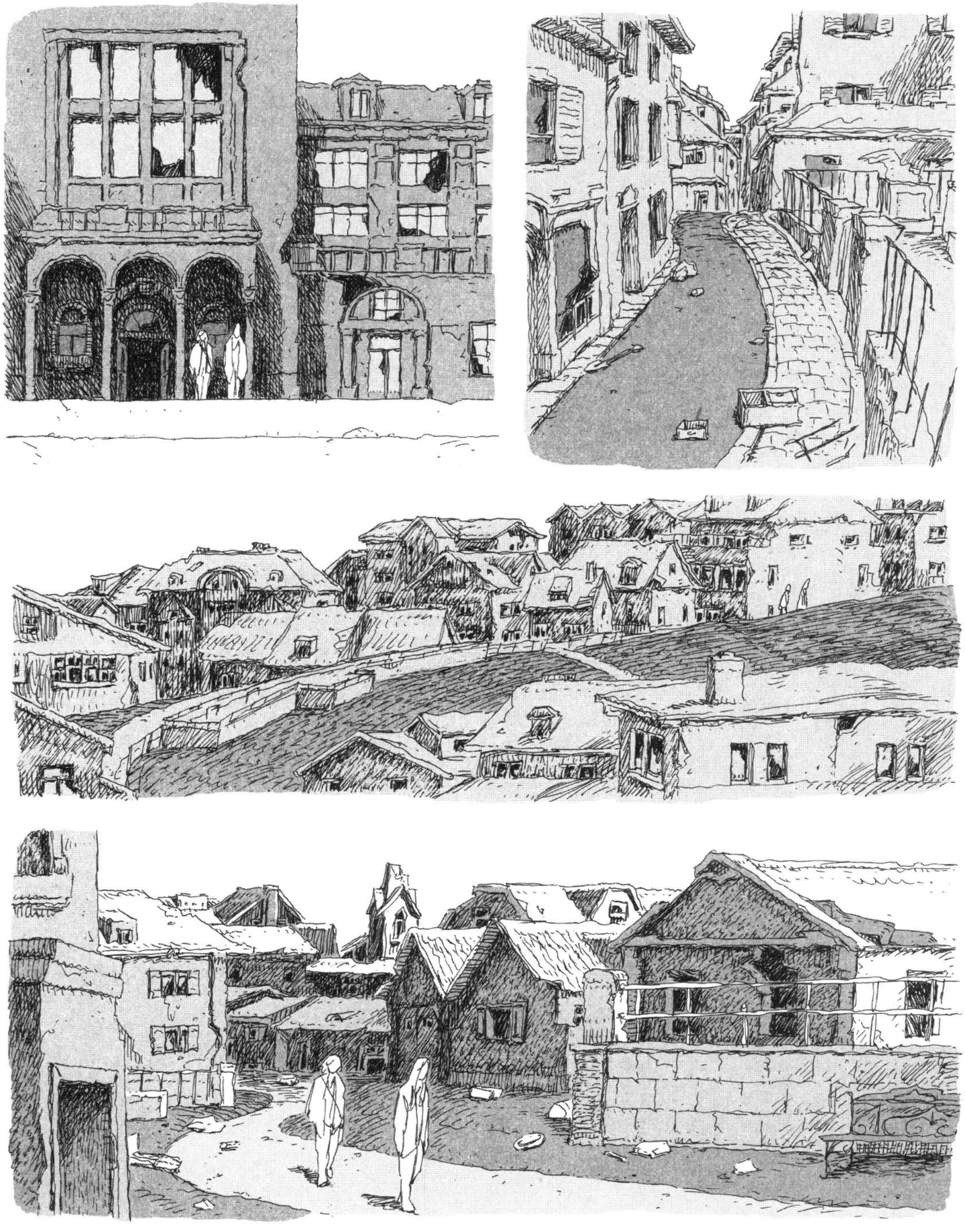

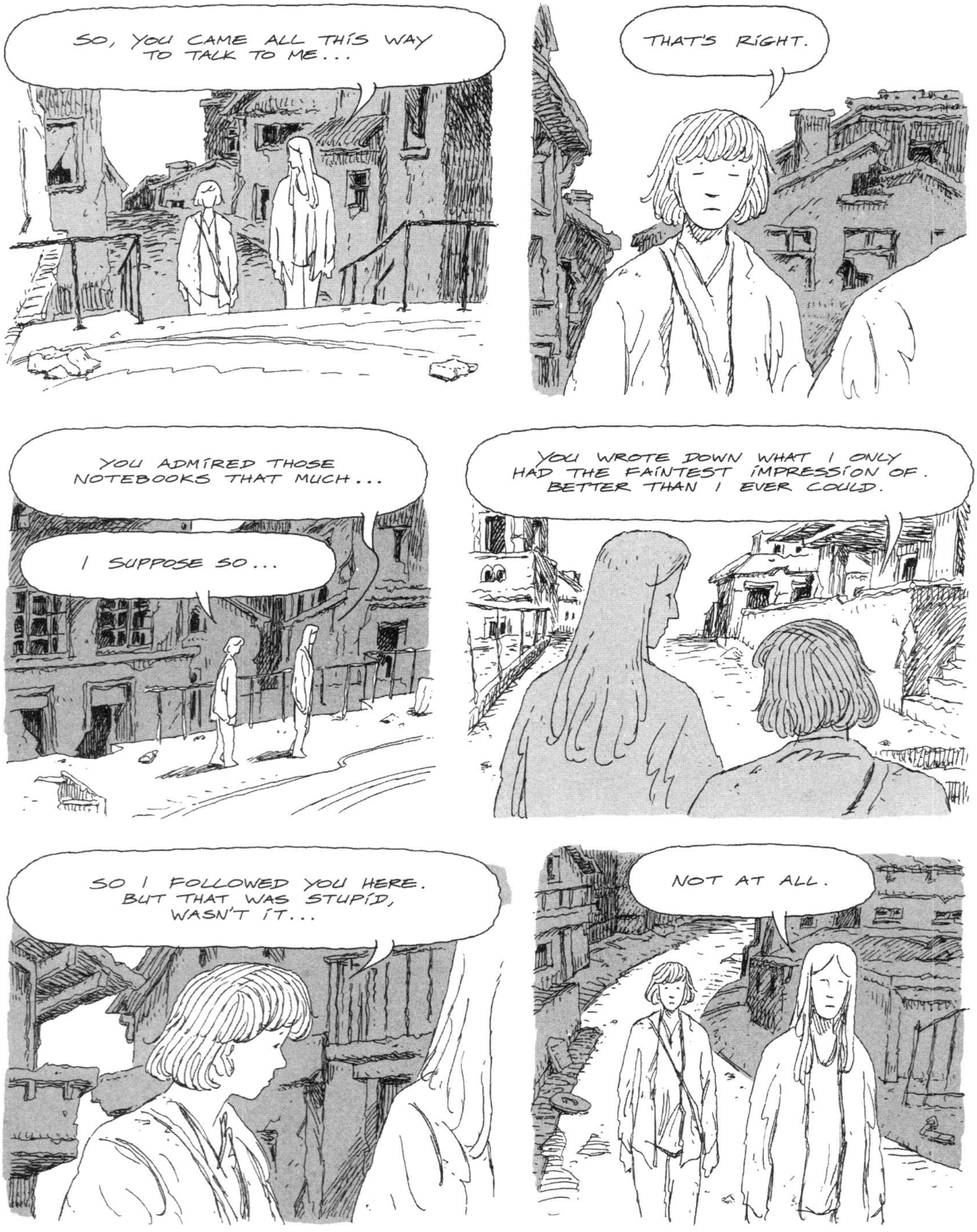
SO, YOU CAME ALL THIS WAY TO TALK TO ME...
THAT'S RIGHT.
YOU ADMIRED THOSE NOTEBOOKS THAT MUCH...
I SUPPOSE SO...
YOU WROTE DOWN WHAT I ONLY HAD THE FAINTEST IMPRESSION OF. BETTER THAN I EVER COULD.
SO I FOLLOWED YOU HERE. BUT THAT WAS STUPID, WASN'T IT...
NOT AT ALL.

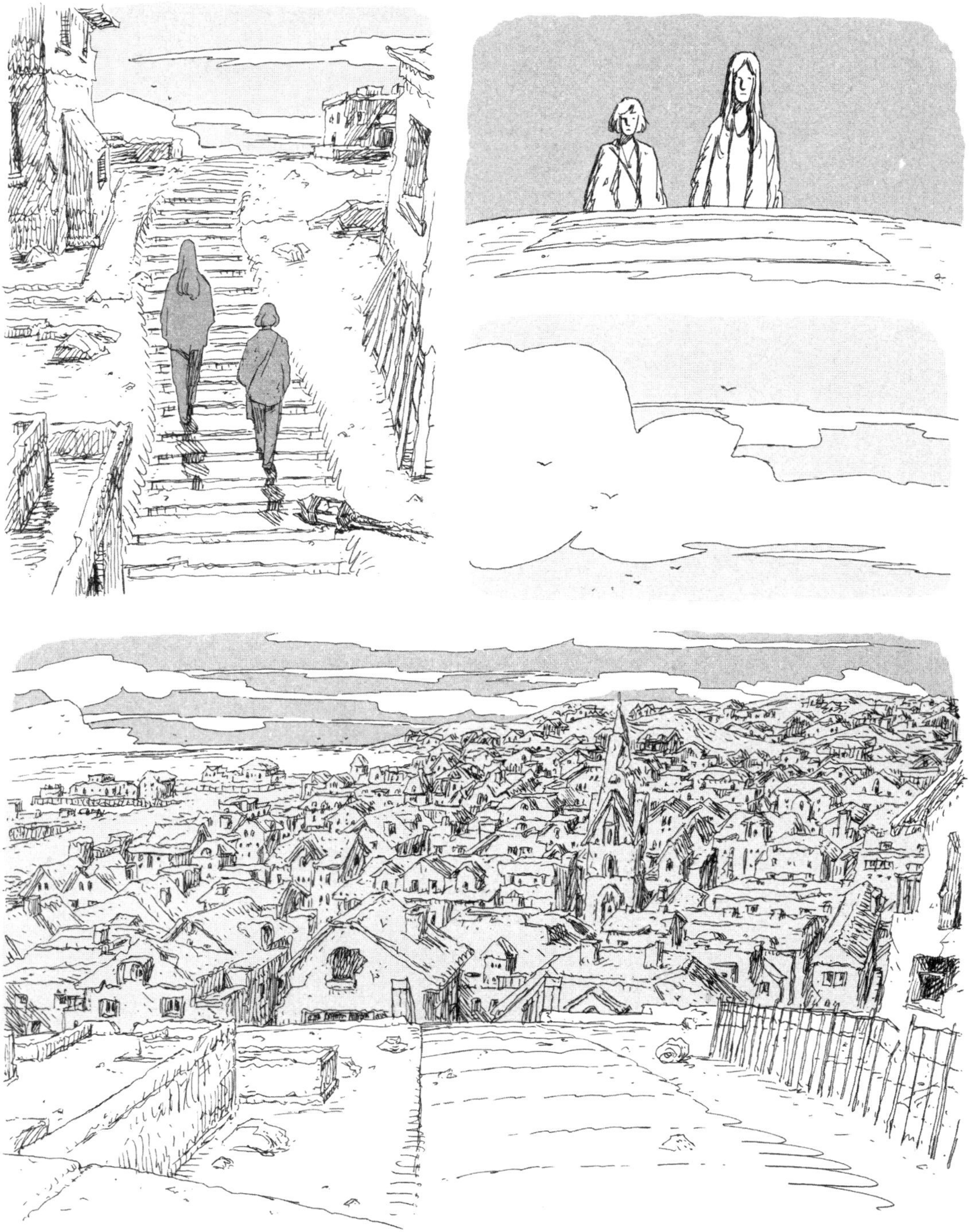

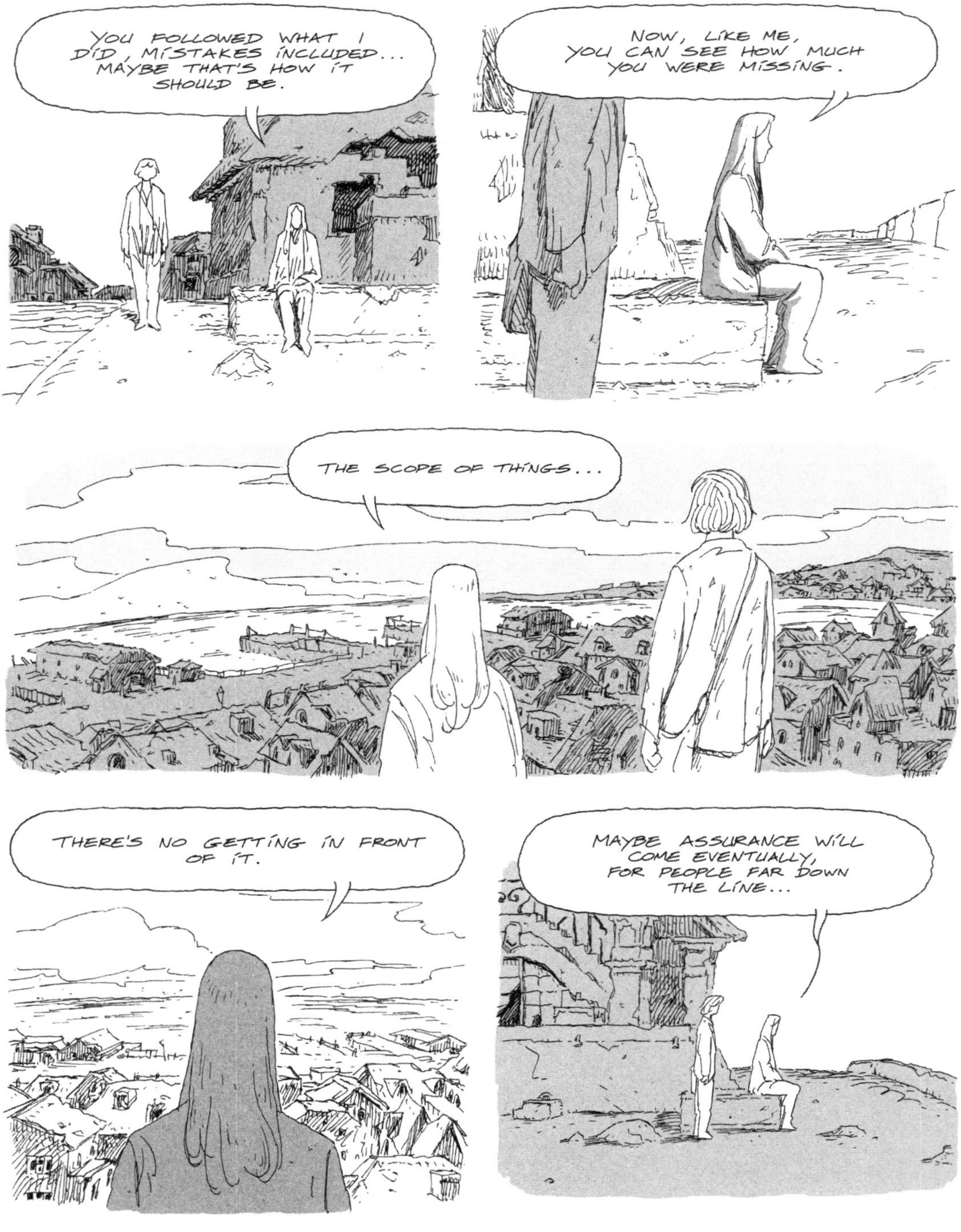
YOU FOLLOWED WHAT I DID, MISTAKES INCLUDED... MAYBE THAT'S HOW IT SHOULD BE.
NOW, LIKE ME, YOU CAN SEE HOW MUCH YOU WERE MISSING.
THE SCOPE OF THINGS...
THERE'S NO GETTING IN FRONT OF IT.
MAYBE ASSURANCE WILL COME EVENTUALLY, FOR PEOPLE FAR DOWN THE LINE...

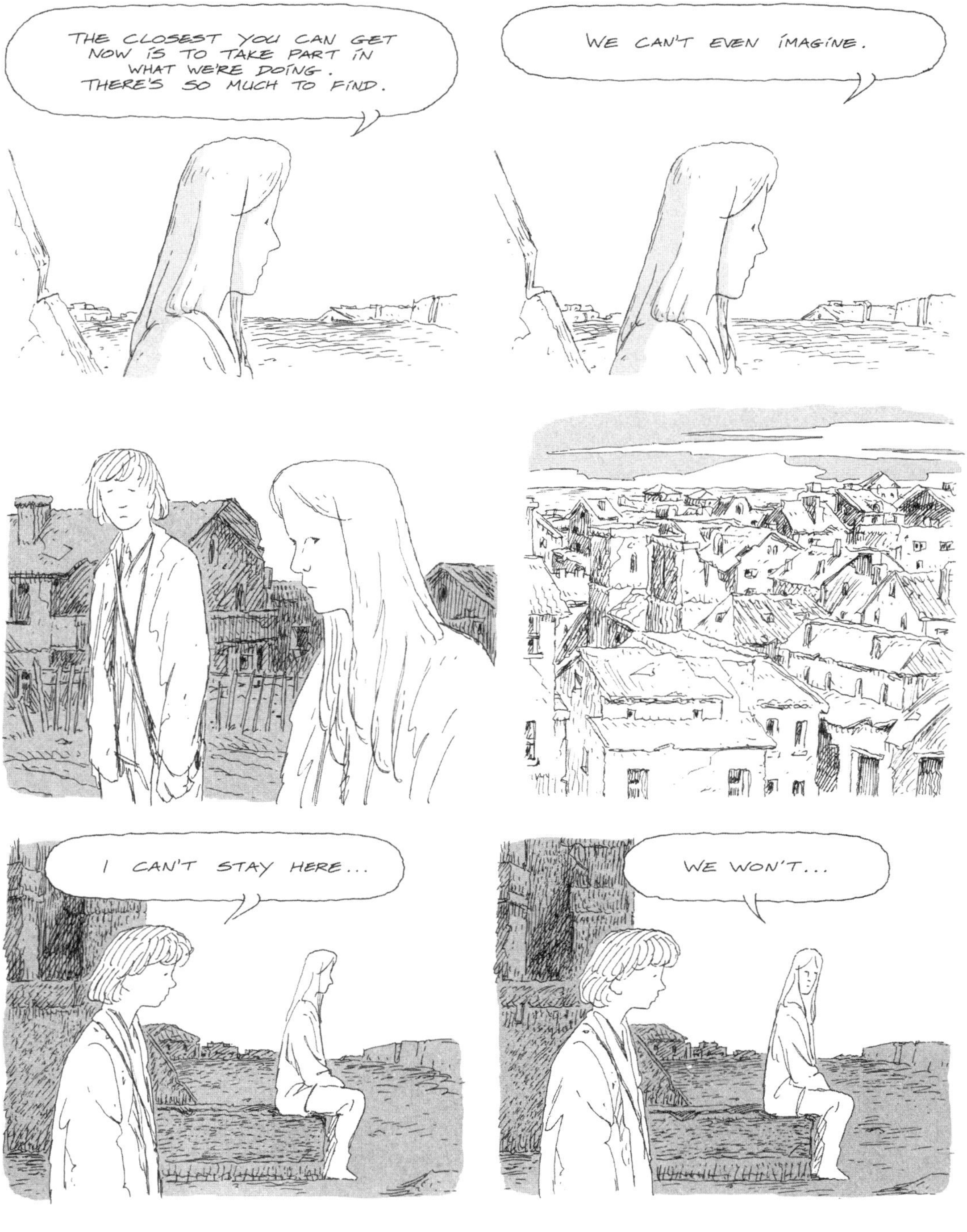
THE CLOSEST YOU CAN GET NOW IS TO TAKE PART IN WHAT WE'RE DOING. THERE'S SO MUCH TO FIND.
WE CAN'T EVEN IMAGINE.
I CAN'T STAY HERE...
WE WON'T...

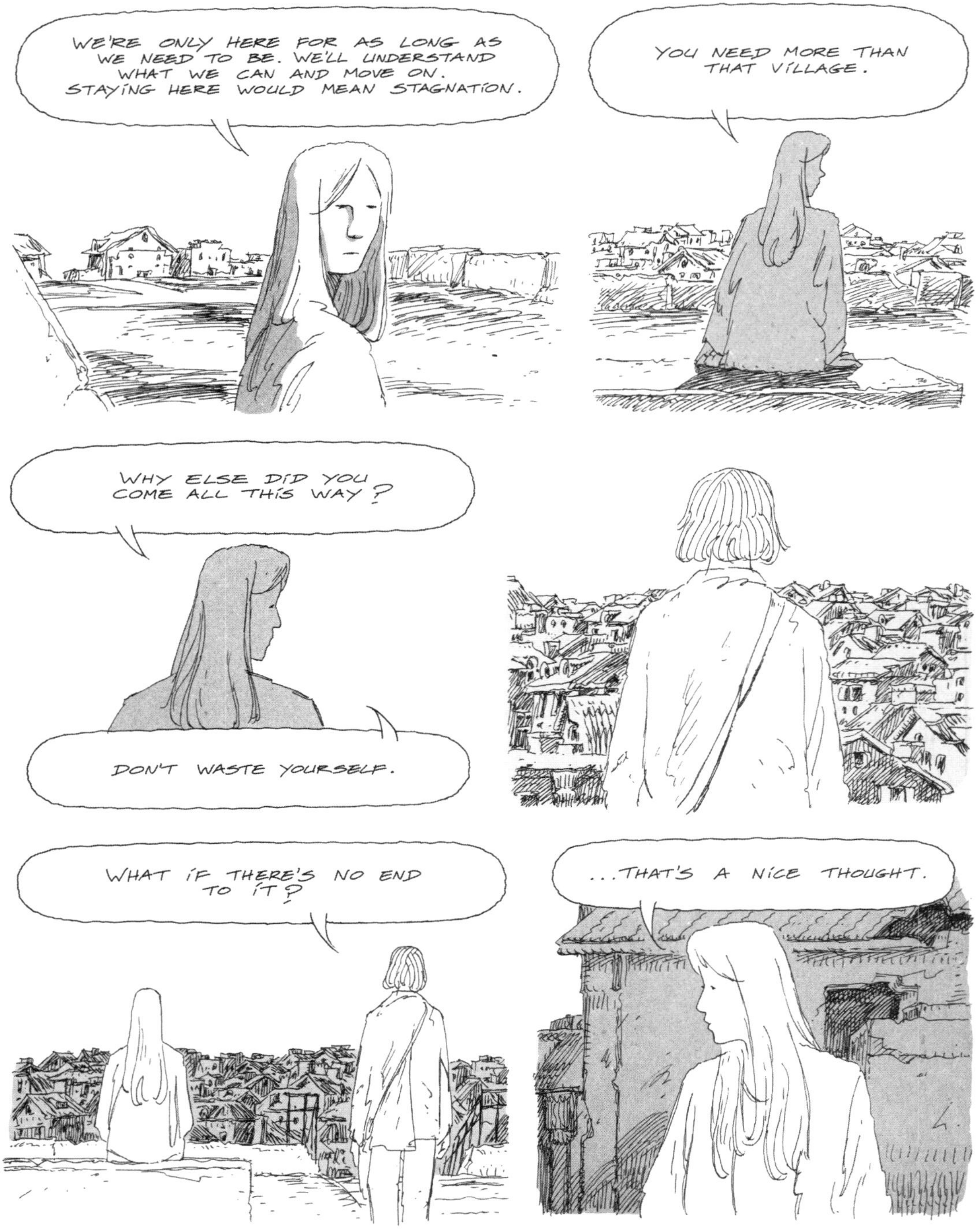
WE'RE ONLY HERE FOR AS LONG AS WE NEED TO BE. WE'LL UNDERSTAND WHAT WE CAN AND MOVE ON. STAYING HERE WOULD MEAN STAGNATION.
YOU NEED MORE THAN THAT VILLAGE.
WHY ELSE DID YOU COME ALL THIS WAY?
DON'T WASTE YOURSELF.
WHAT IF THERE'S NO END TO IT?
...THAT'S A NICE THOUGHT.

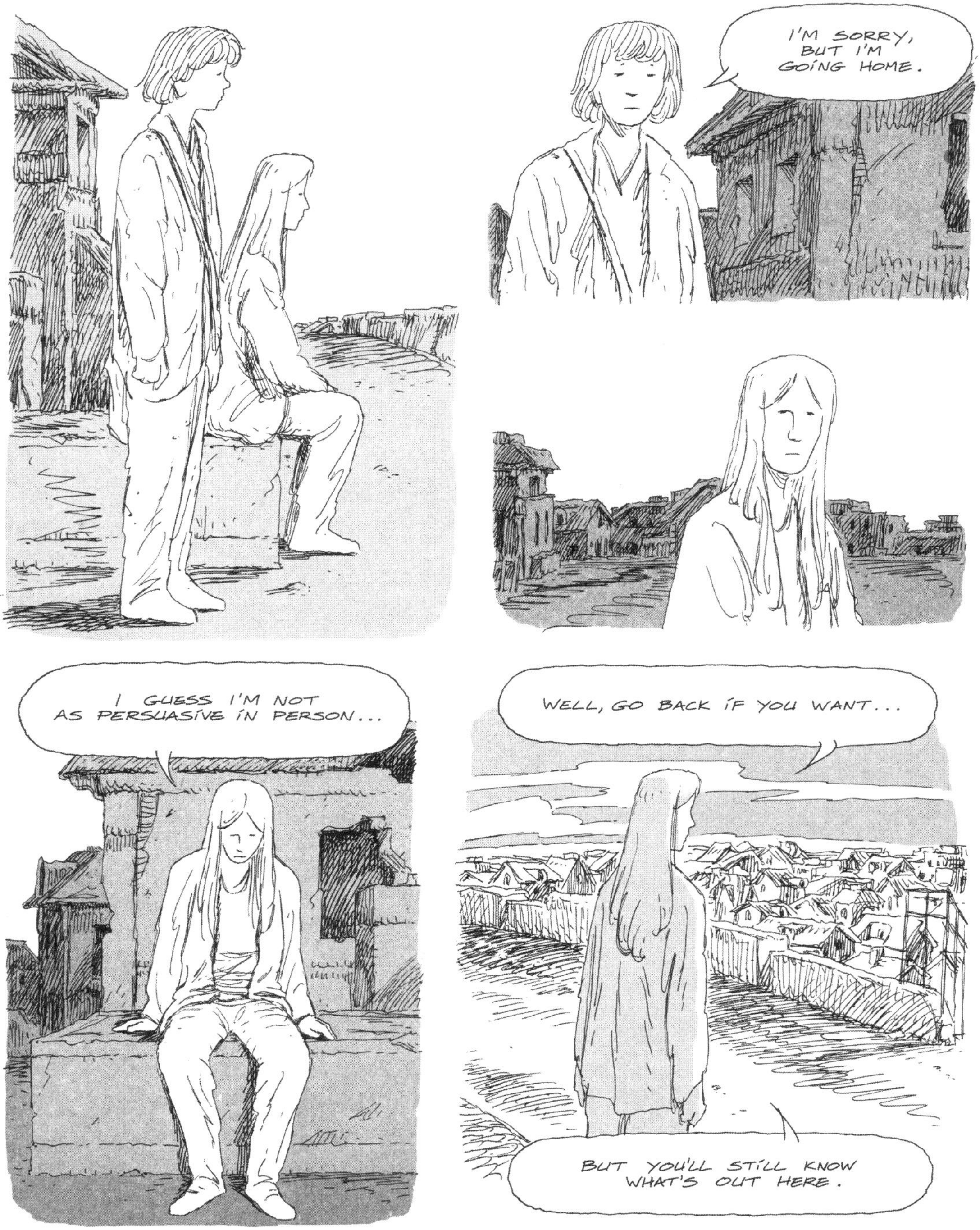
I'M SORRY, BUT I'M GOING HOME.
I GUESS I'M NOT AS PERSUASIVE IN PERSON...
WELL, GO BACK IF YOU WANT...
BUT YOU'LL STILL KNOW WHAT'S OUT HERE.

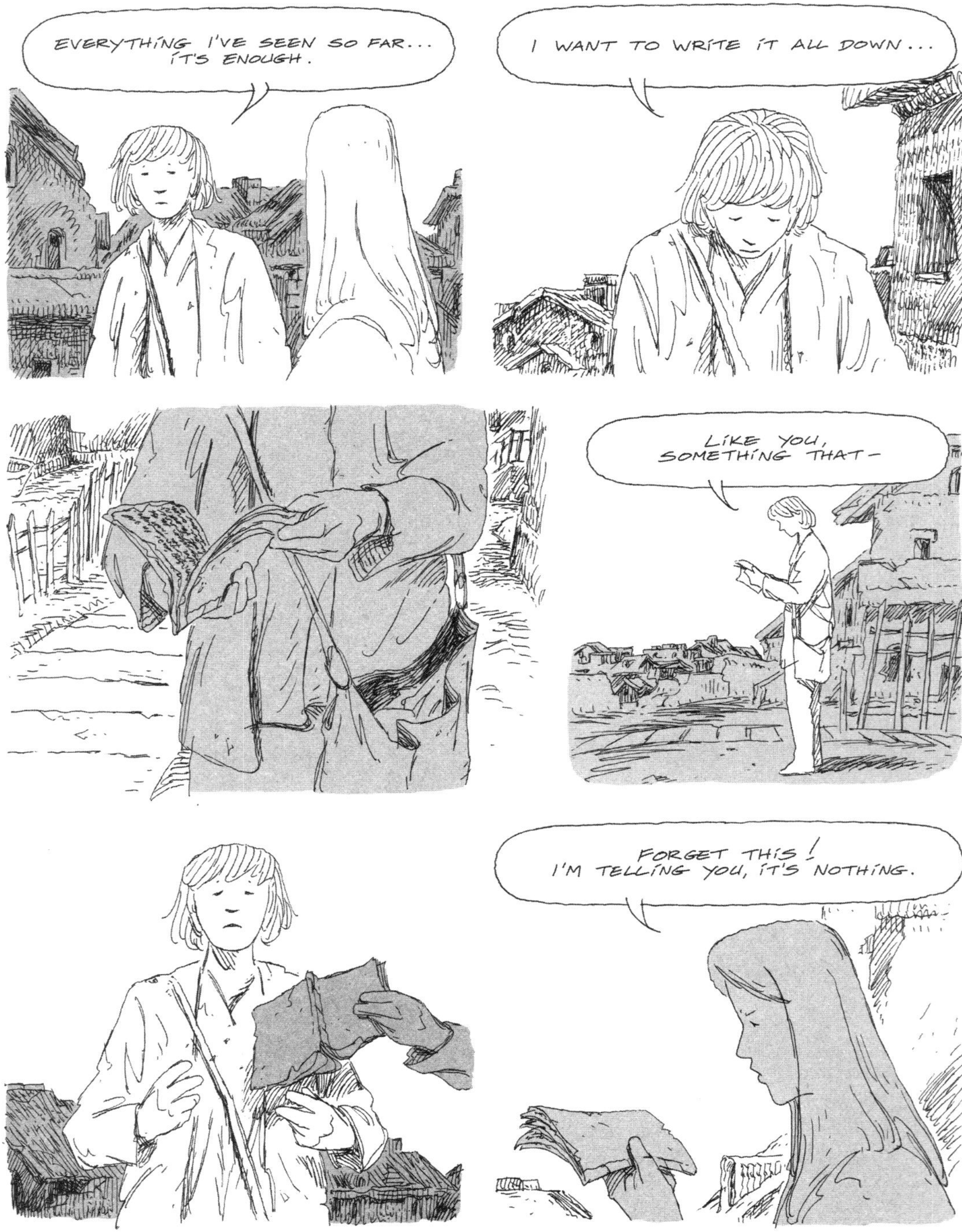
EVERYTHING I'VE SEEN SO FAR... IT'S ENOUGH.
I WANT TO WRITE IT ALL DOWN...
LIKE YOU, SOMETHING THAT-
FORGET THIS! I'M TELLING YOU, IT'S NOTHING.

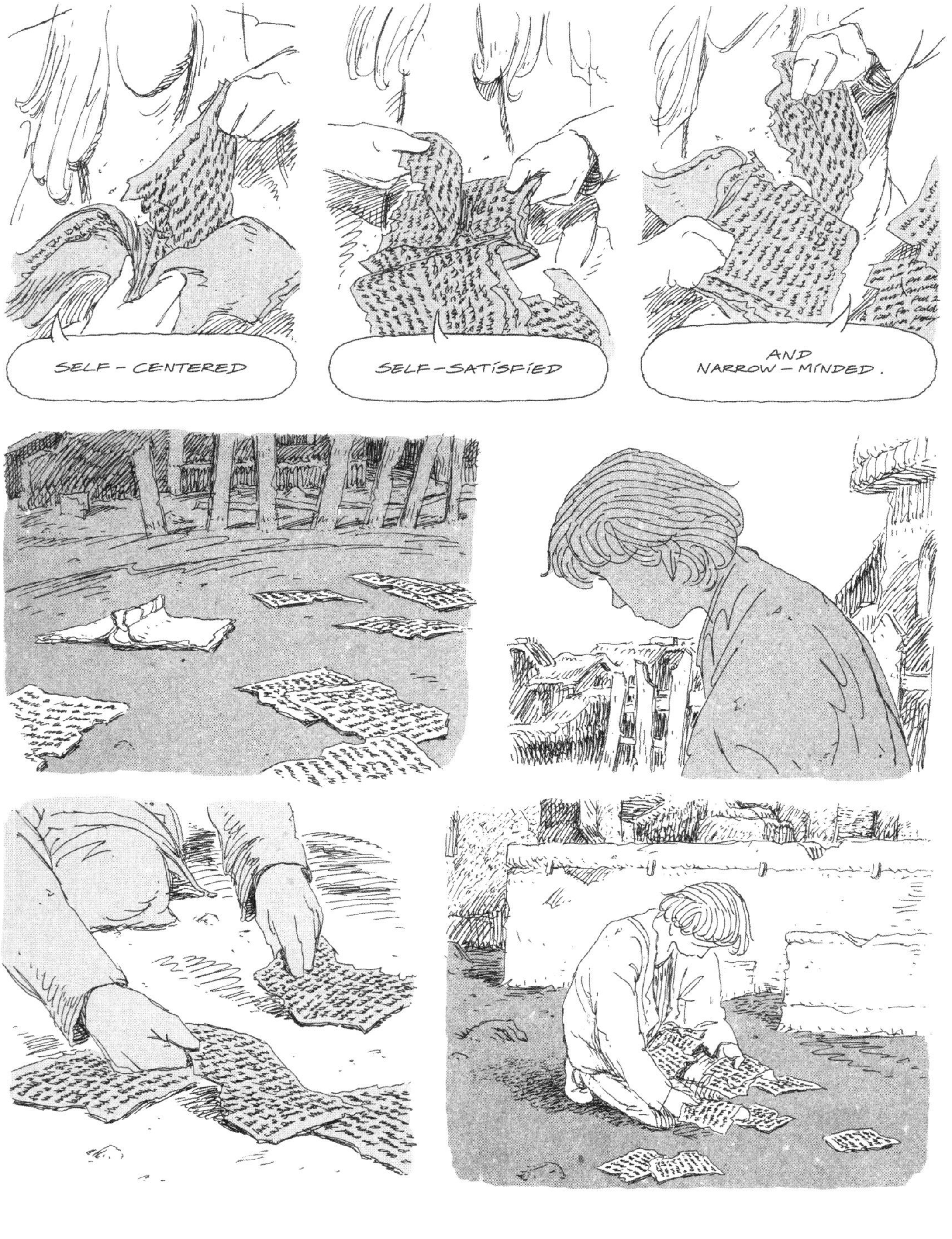
SELF-CENTERED
SELF-SATISFIED
AND NARROW-MINDED.

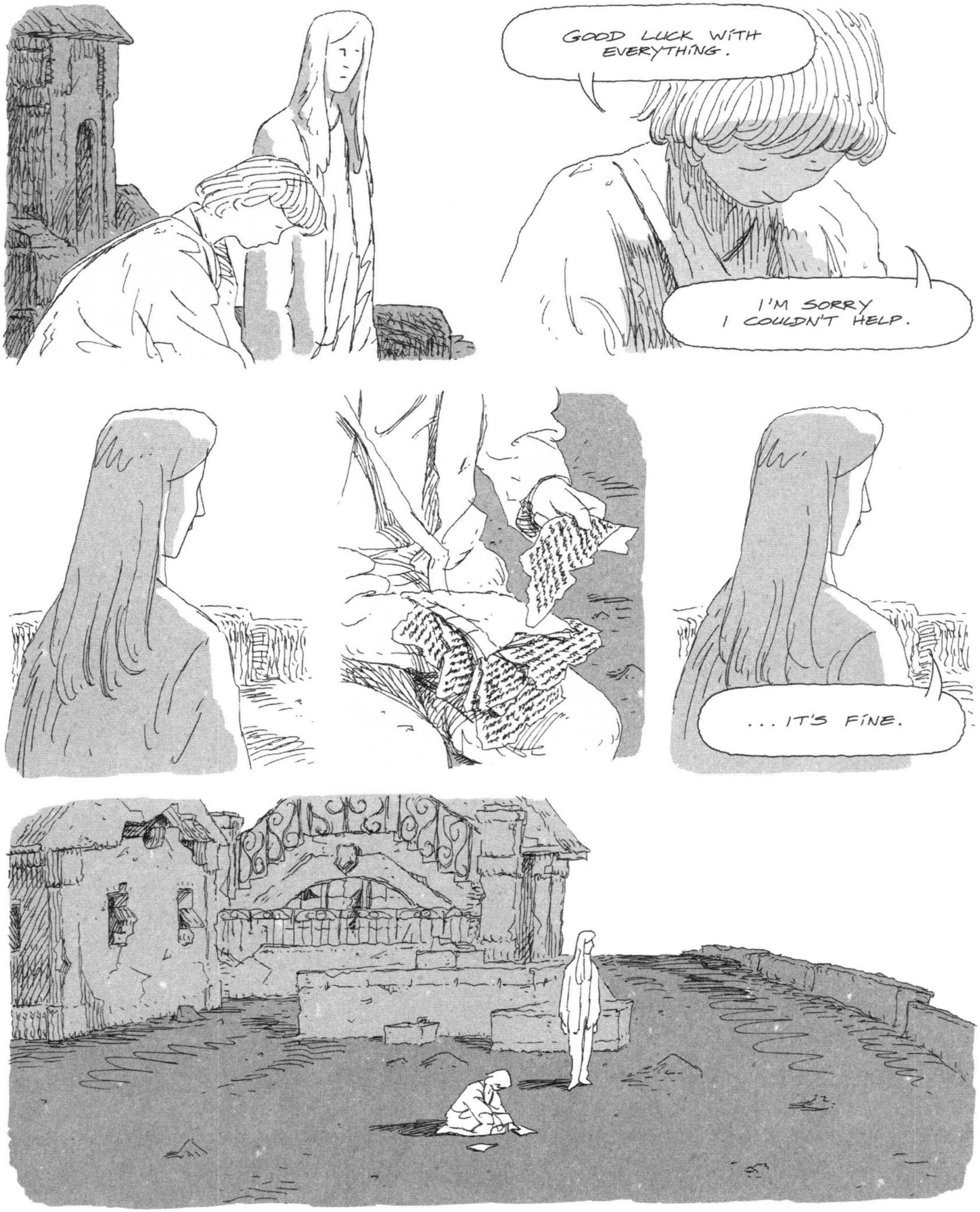
GOOD LUCK WITH EVERYTHING.
I'M SORRY I COULDN'T HELP.
...IT'S FINE.

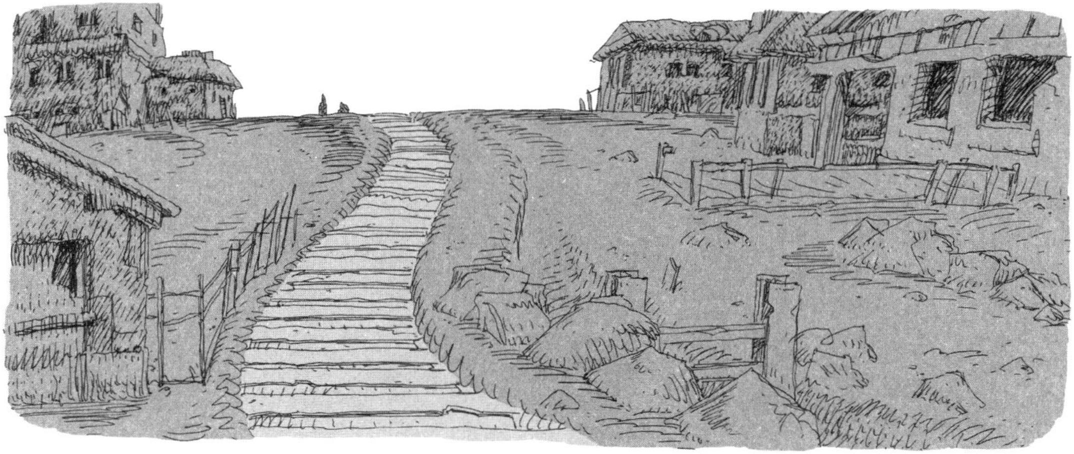

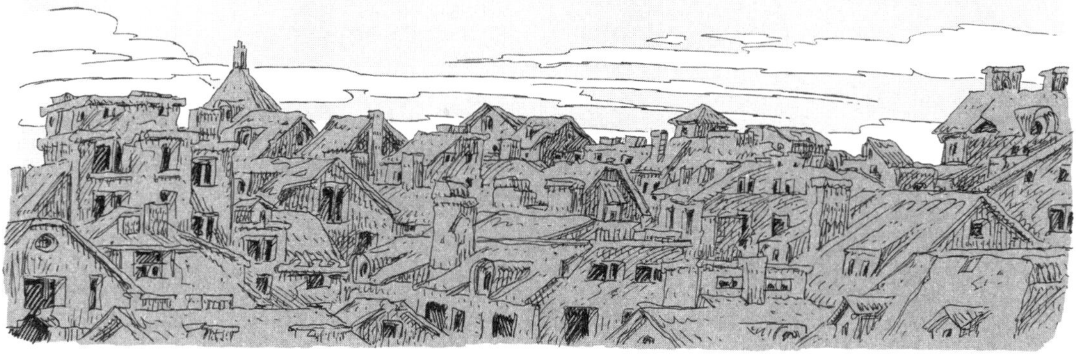

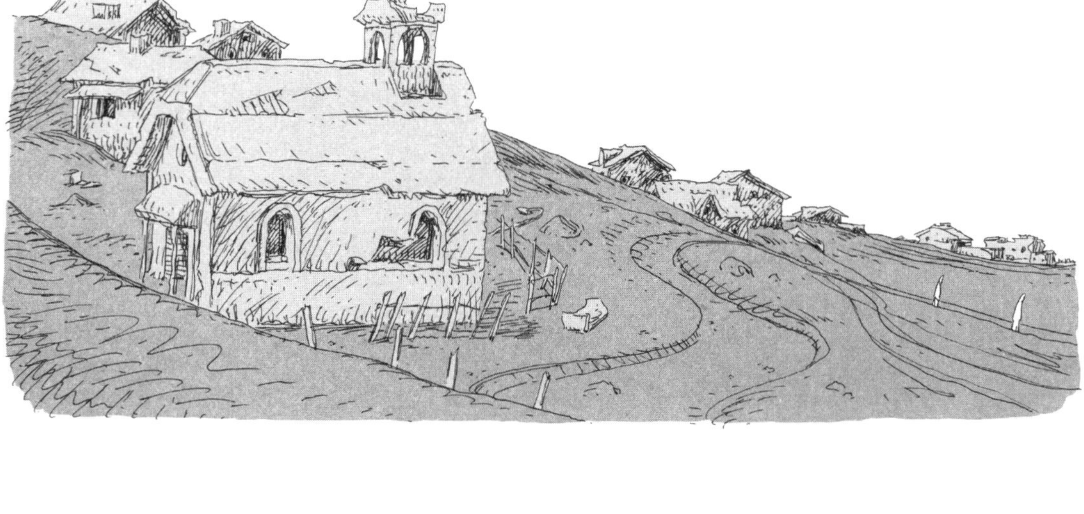

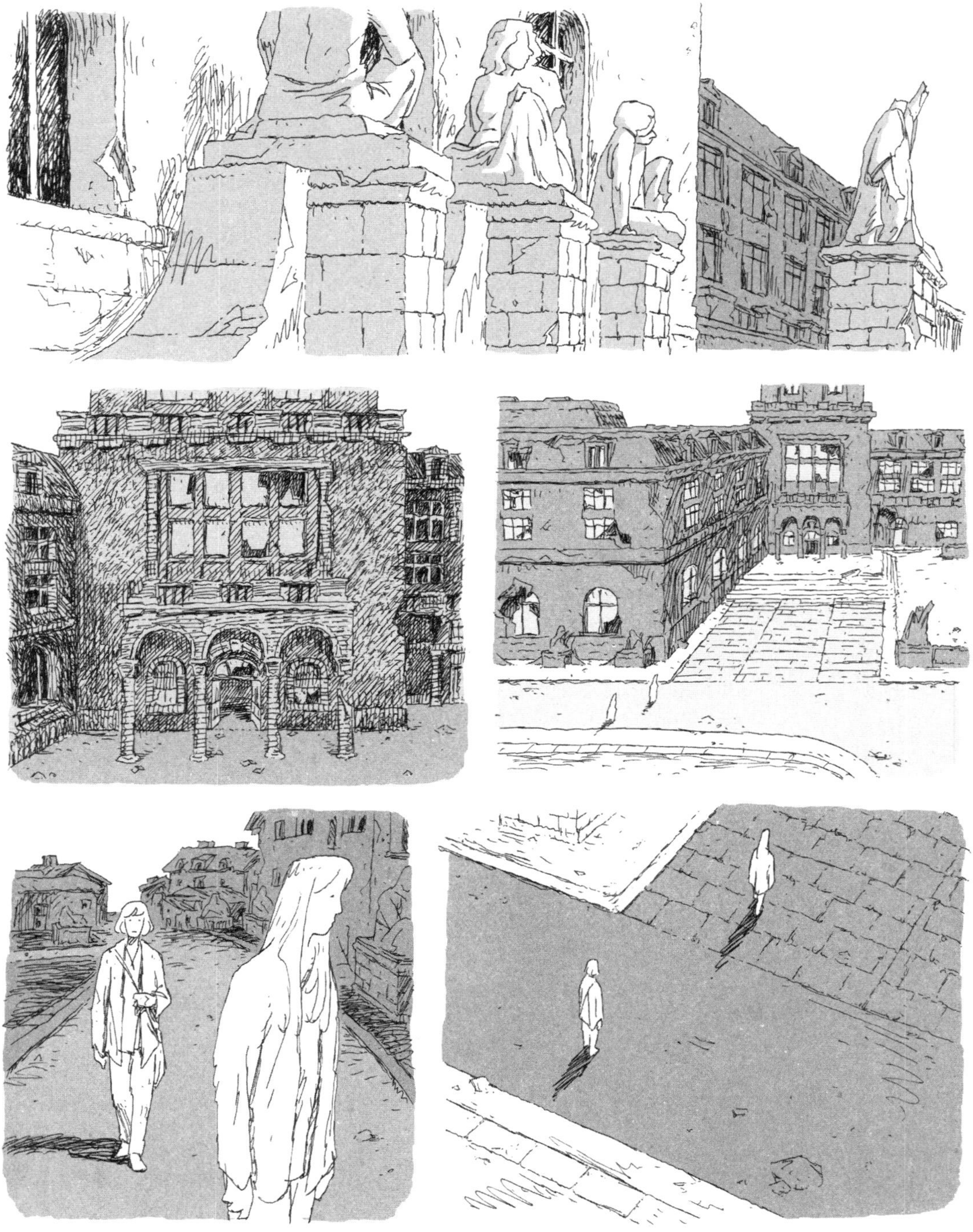

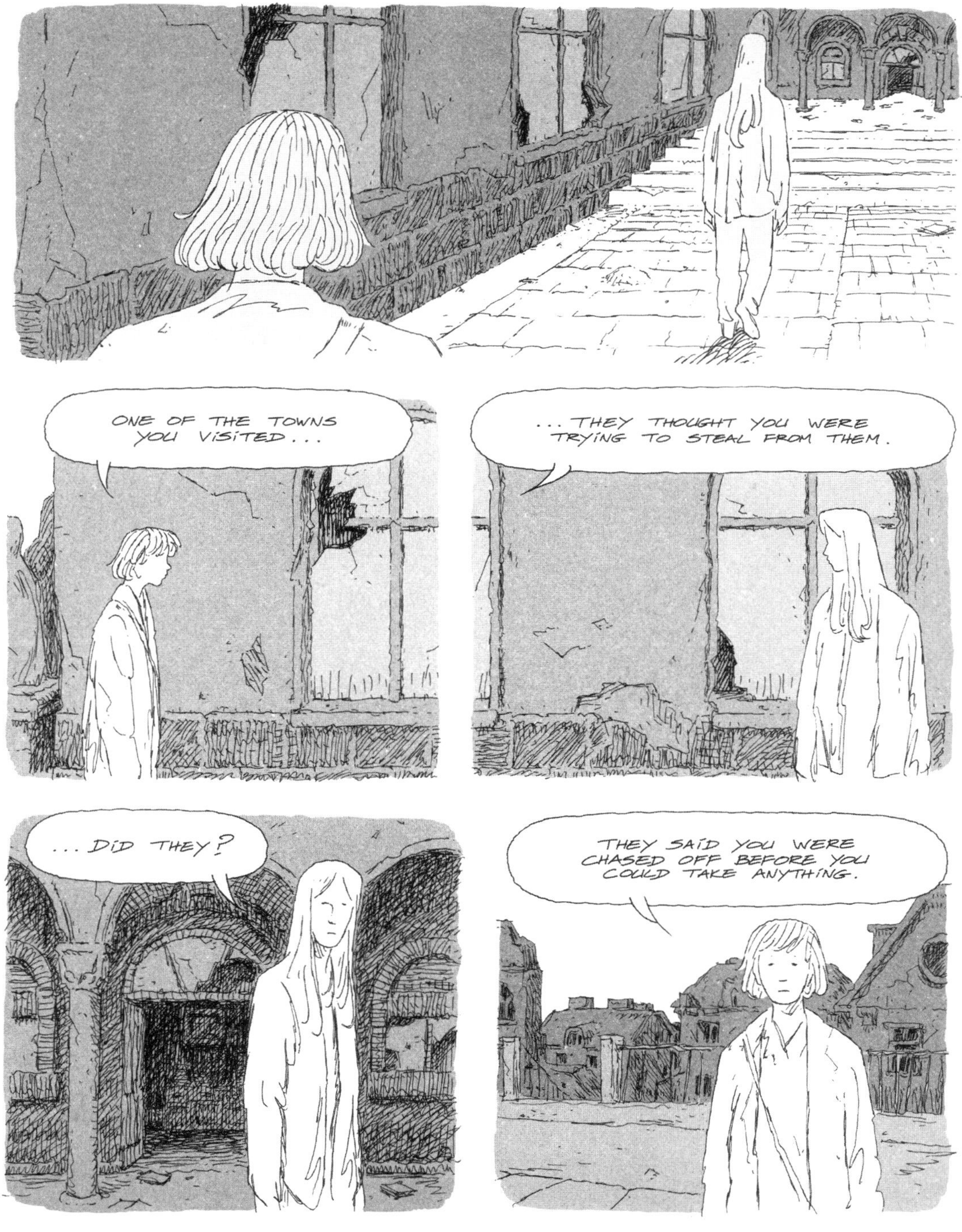
ONE OF THE TOWNS YOU VISITED...
...THEY THOUGHT YOU WERE TRYING TO STEAL FROM THEM.
...DID THEY?
THEY SAID YOU WERE CHASED OFF BEFORE YOU COULD TAKE ANYTHING.

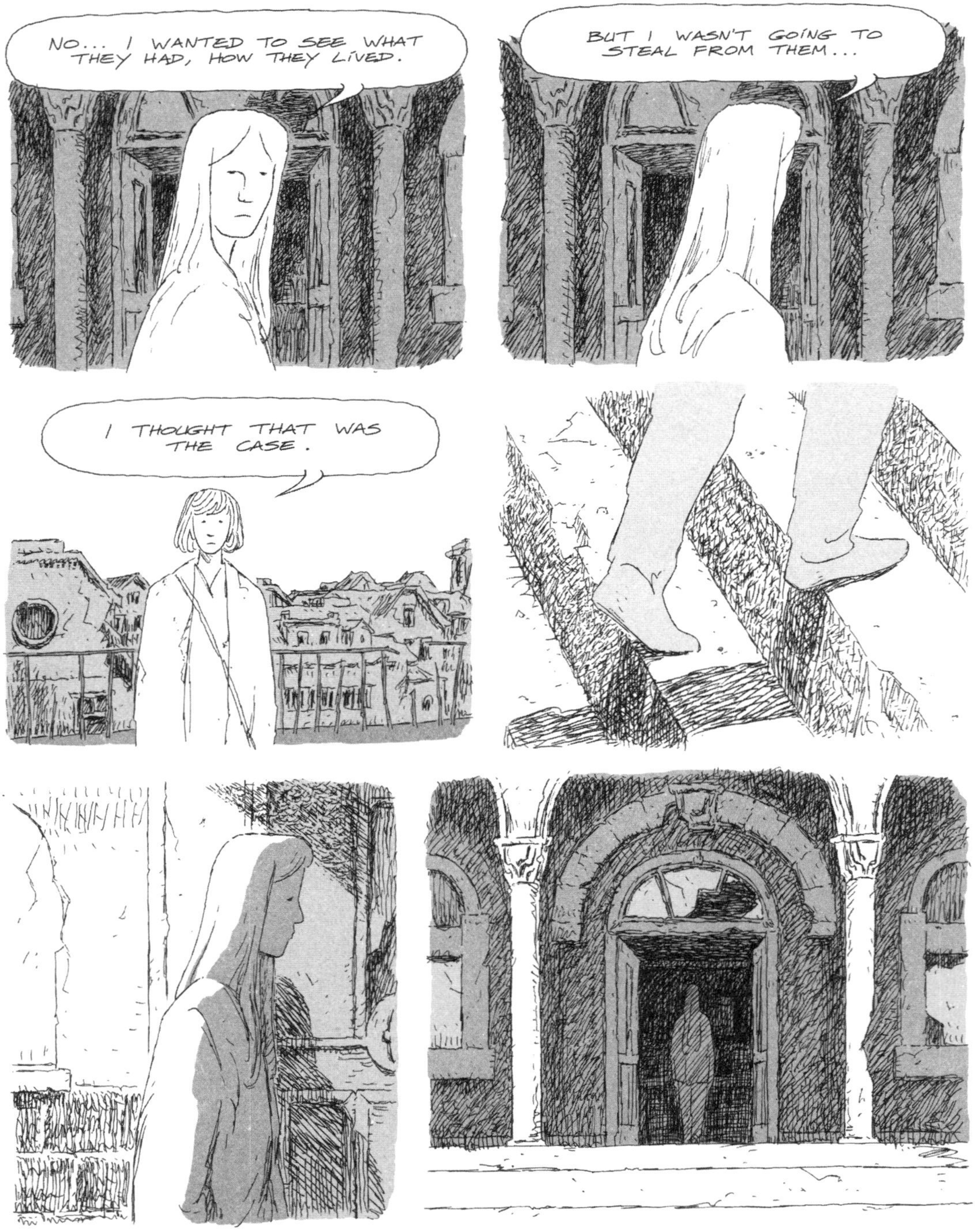
NO... I WANTED TO SEE WHAT THEY HAD, HOW THEY LIVED.
BUT I WASN'T GOING TO STEAL FROM THEM...
I THOUGHT THAT WAS THE CASE.

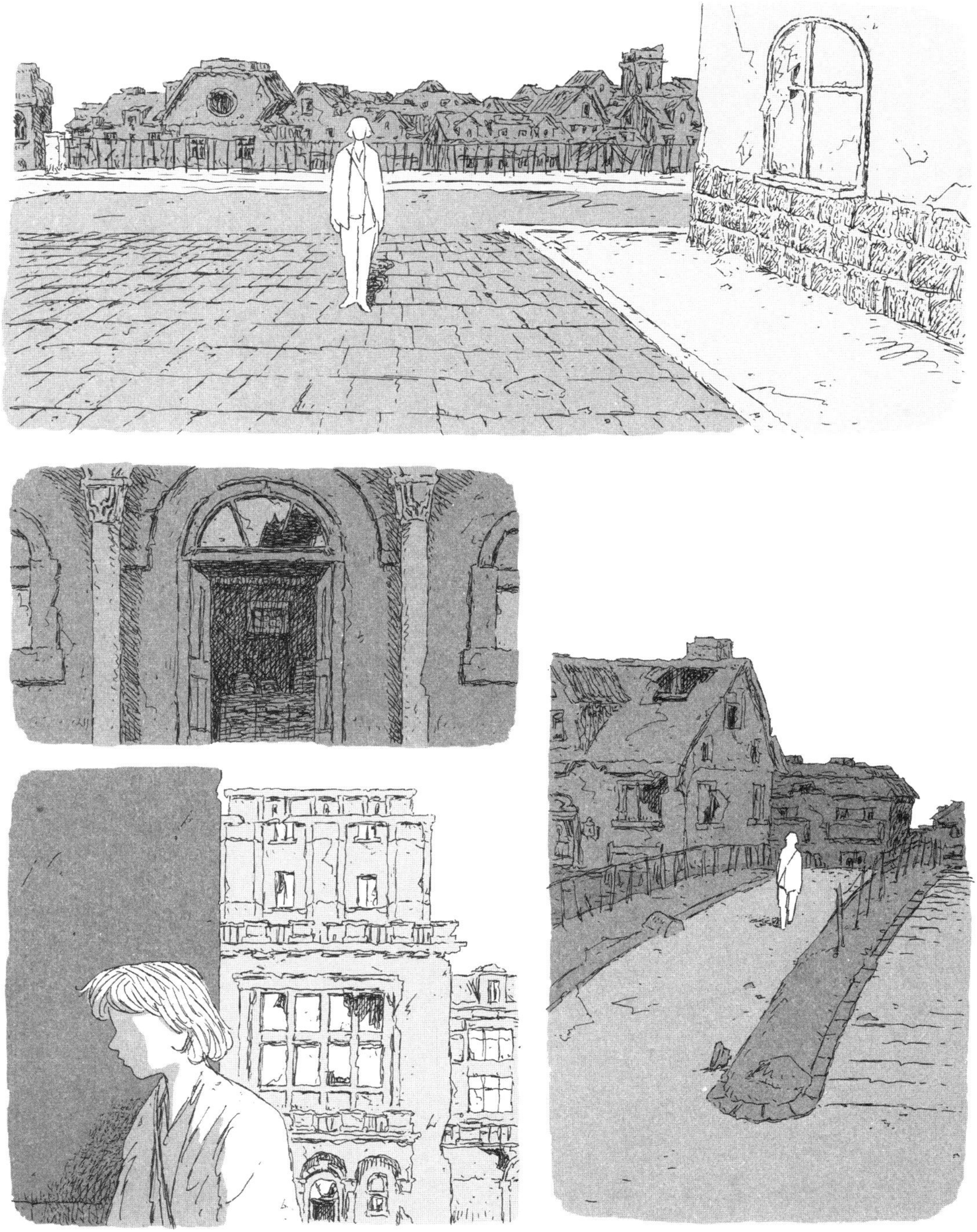

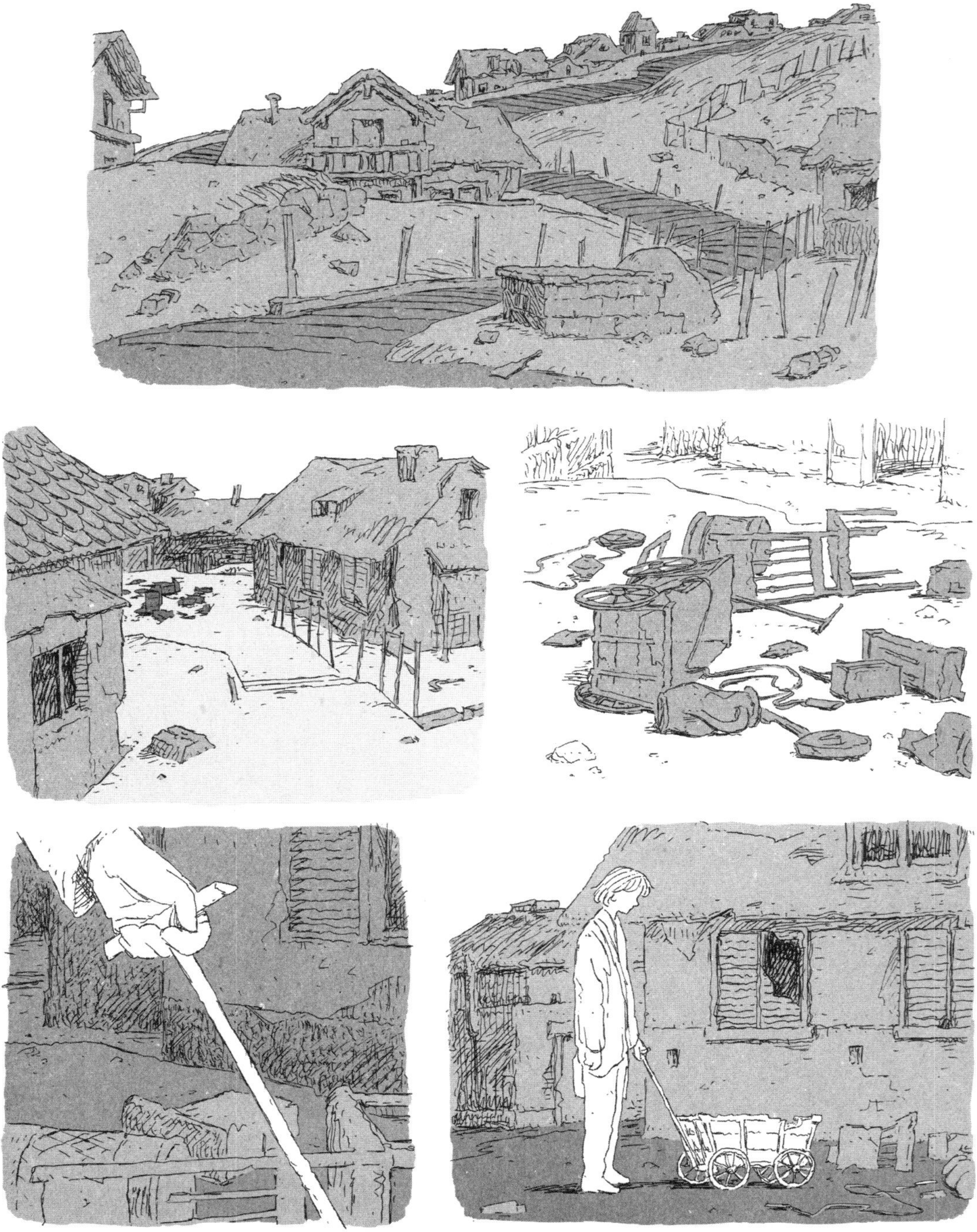

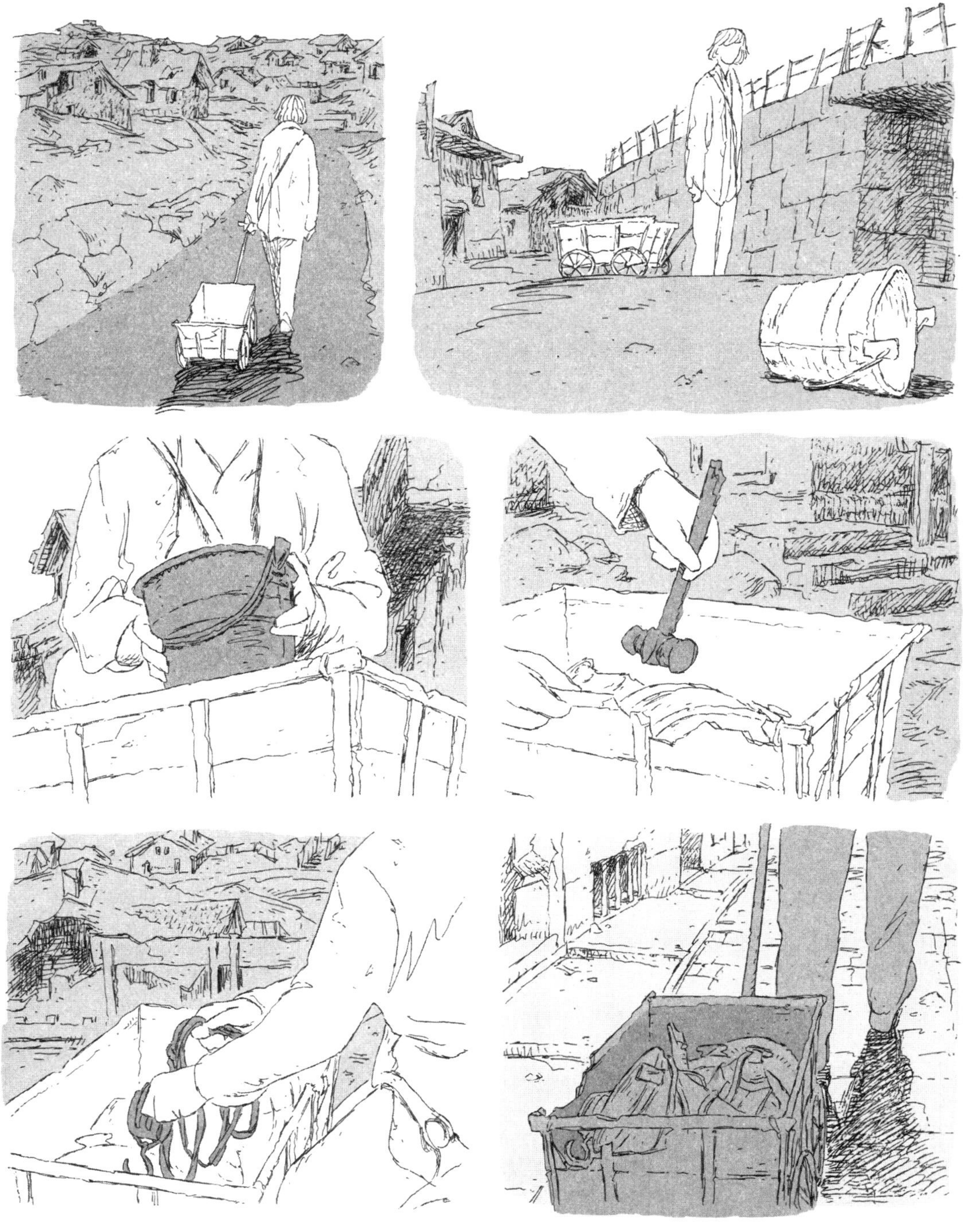

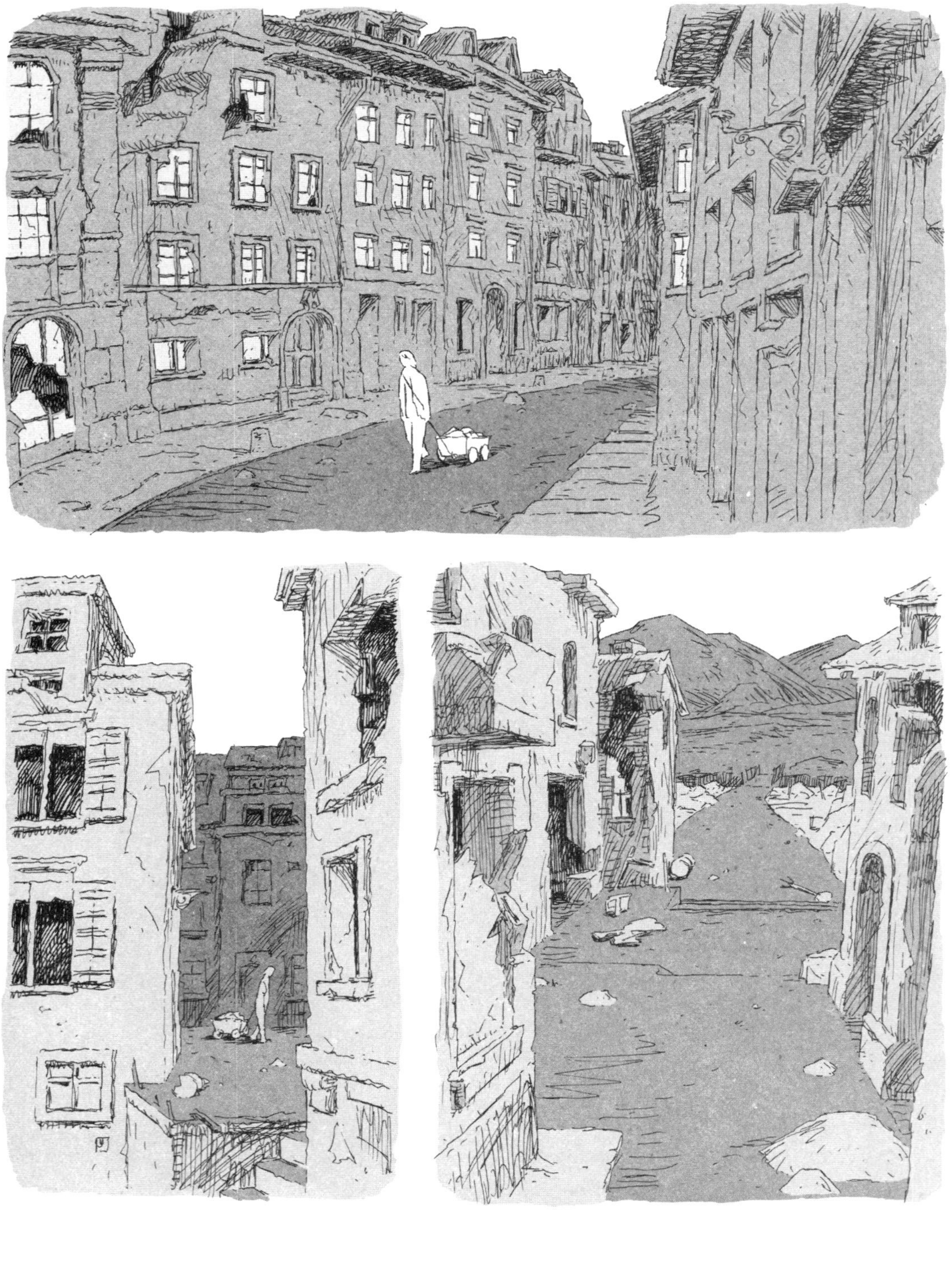

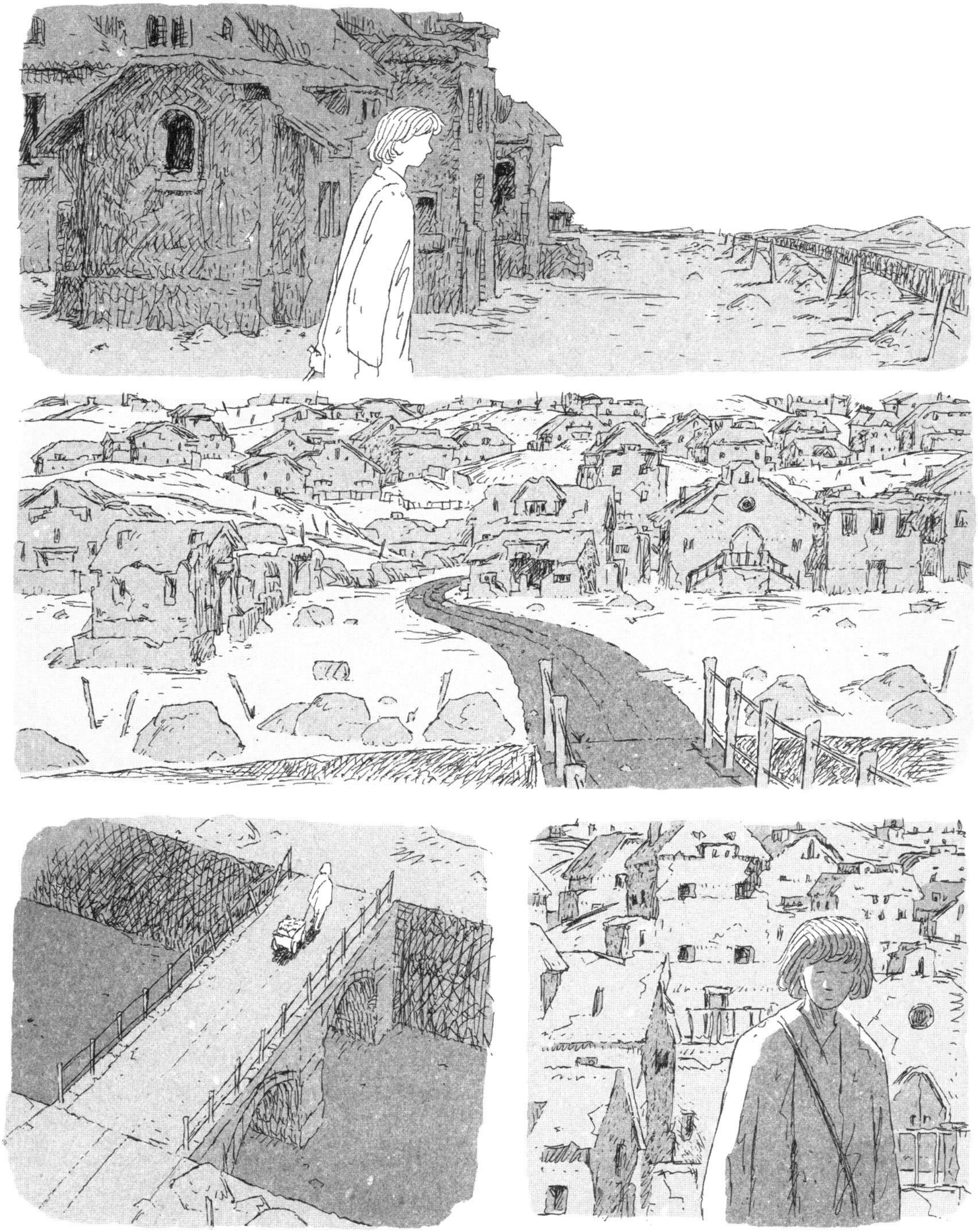

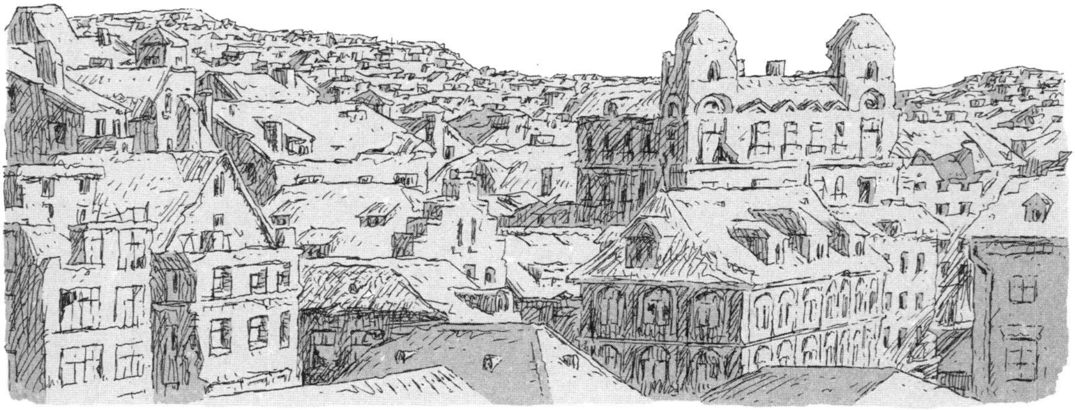

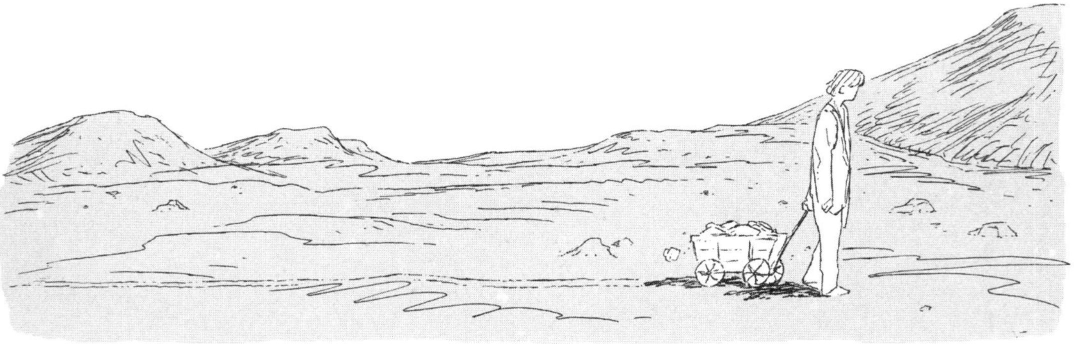

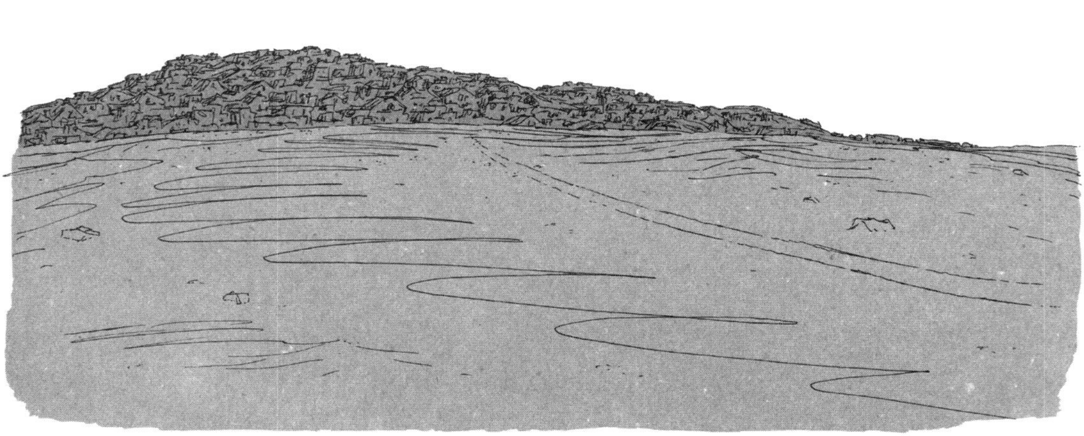

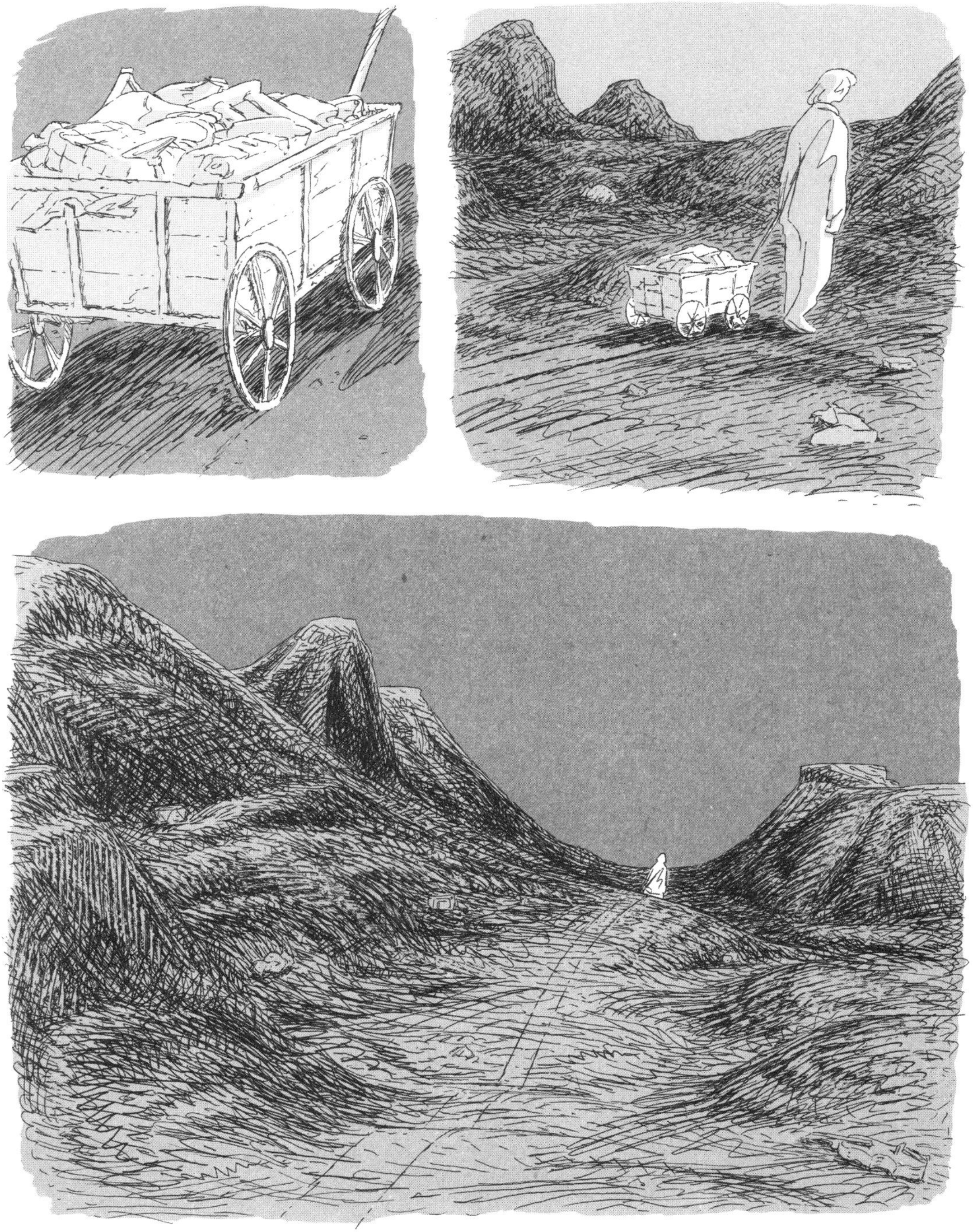

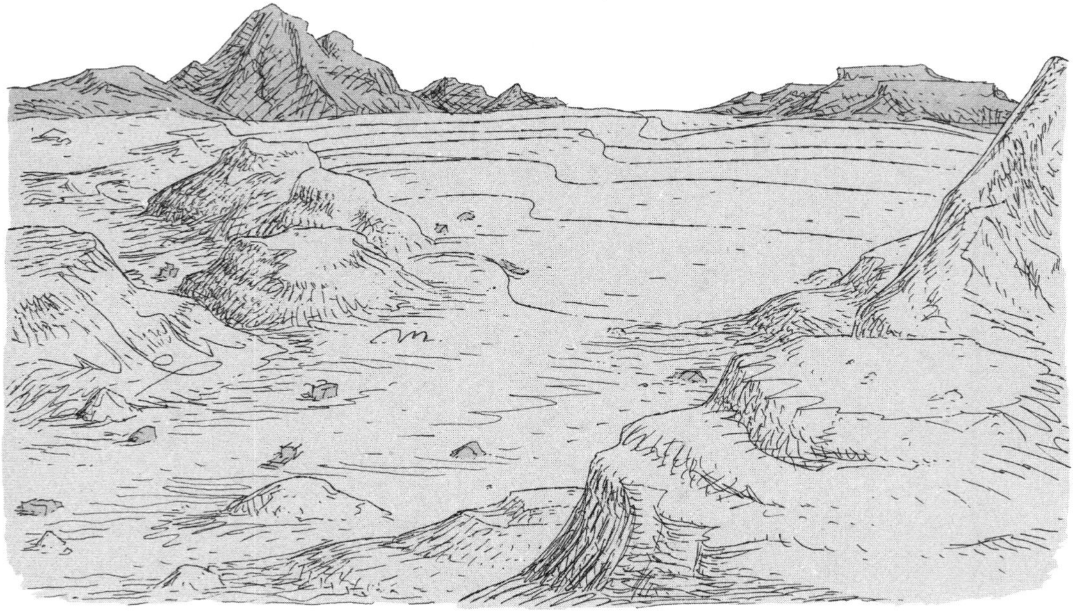

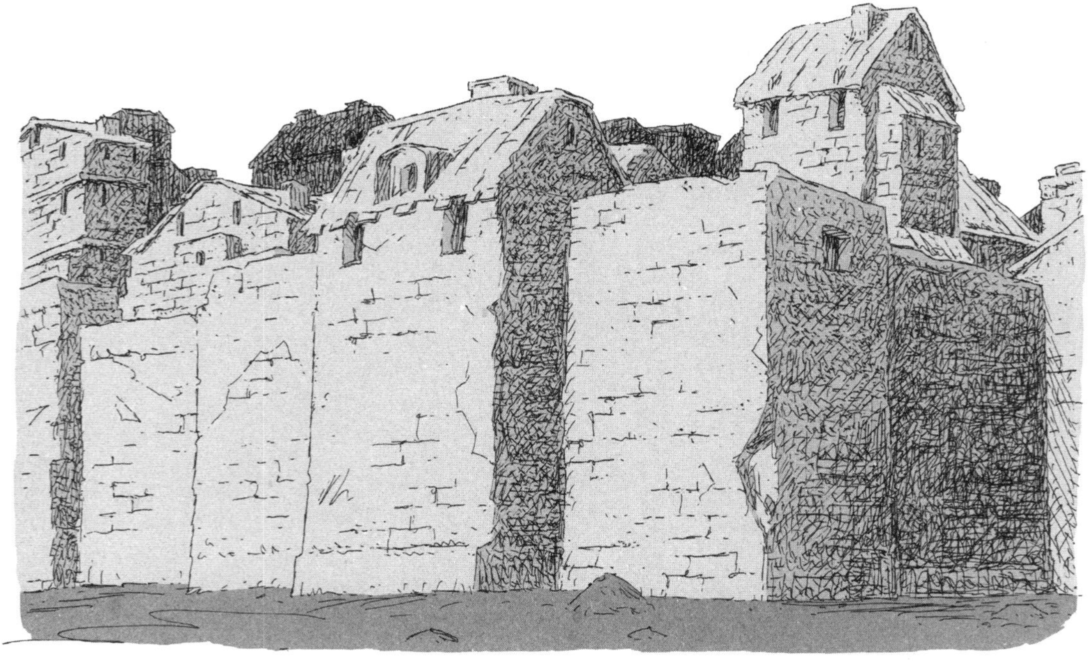

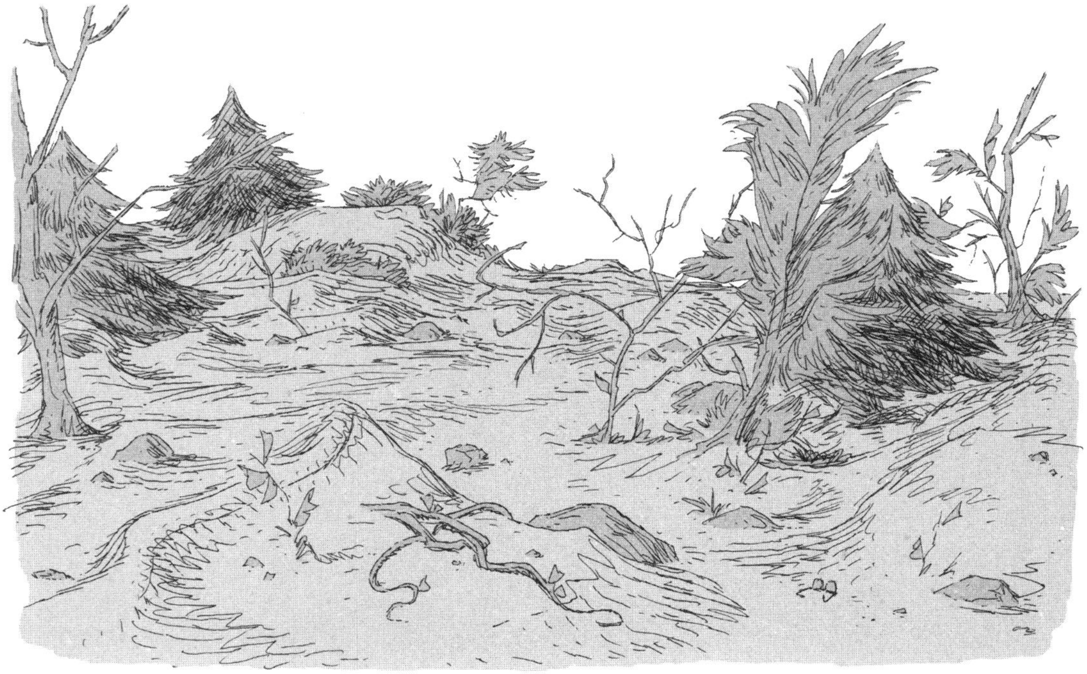

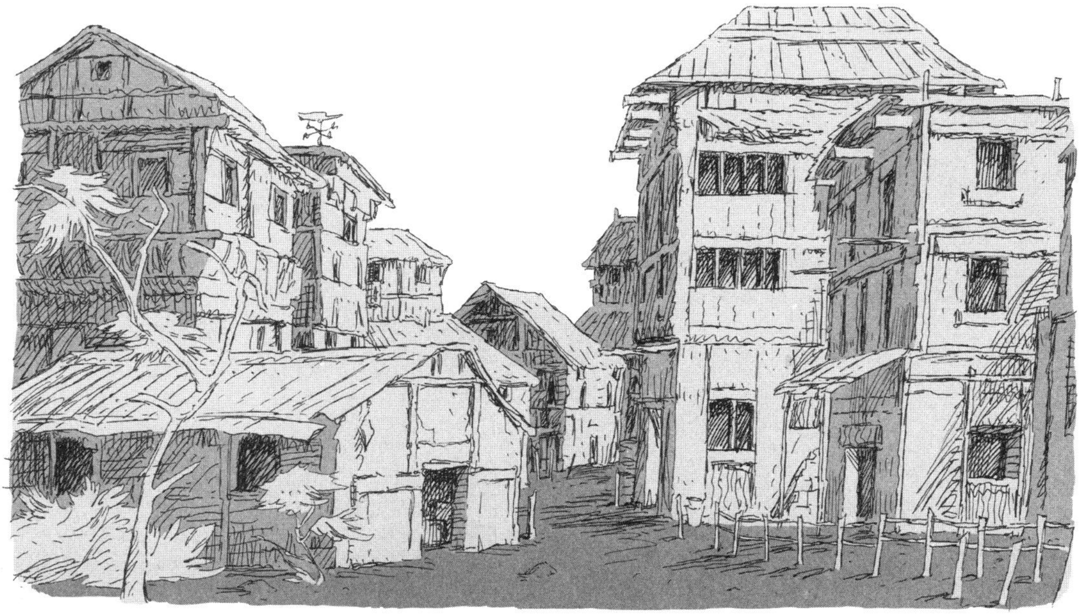

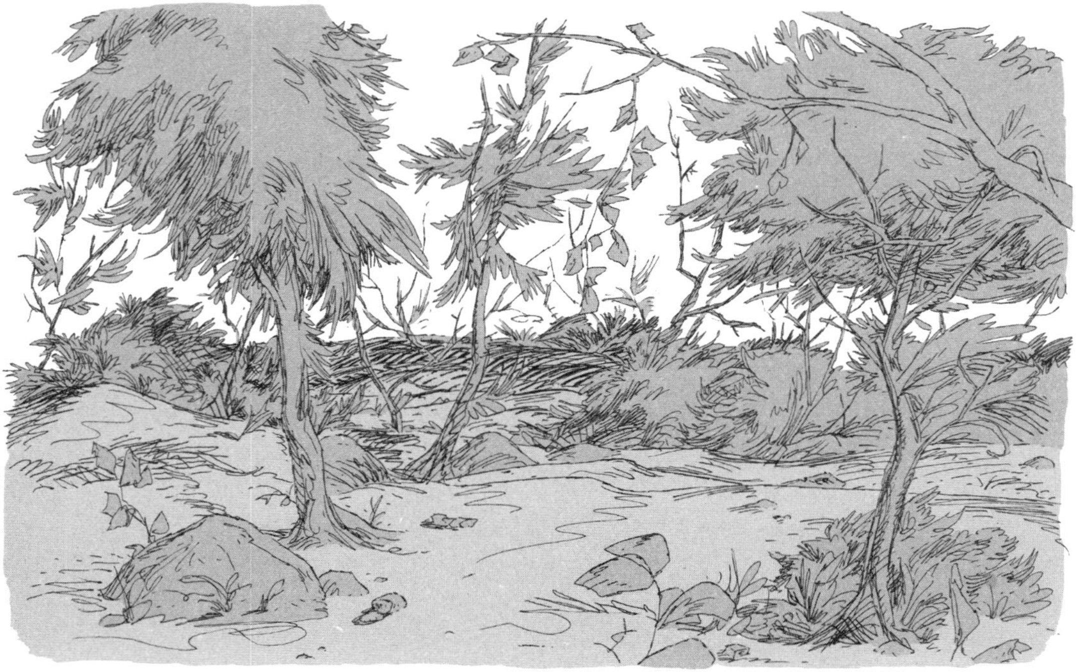

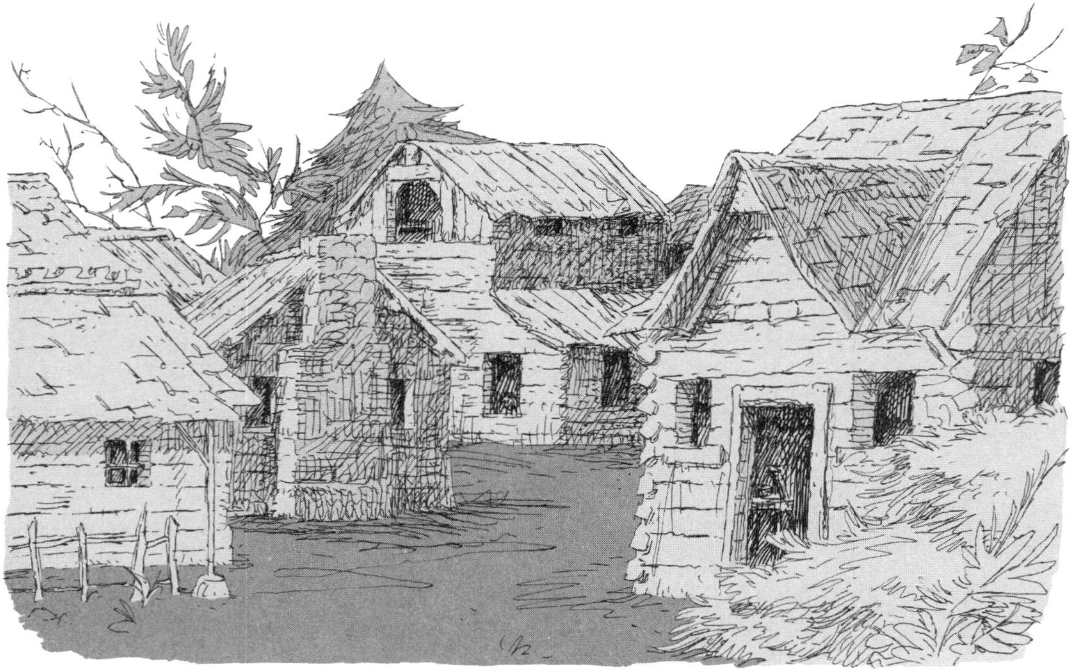

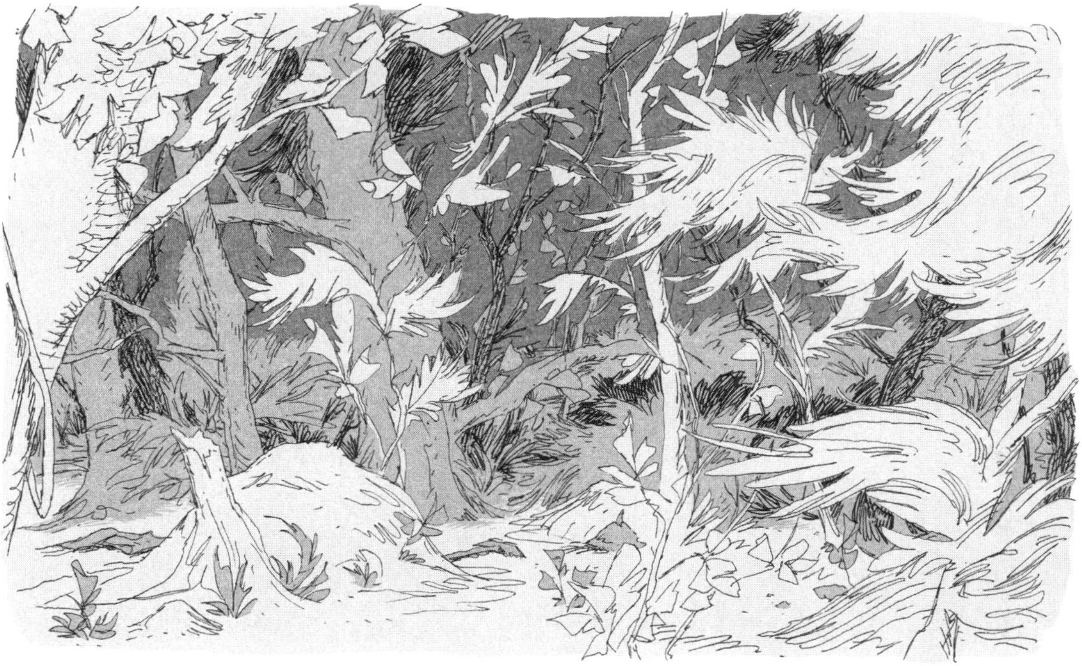

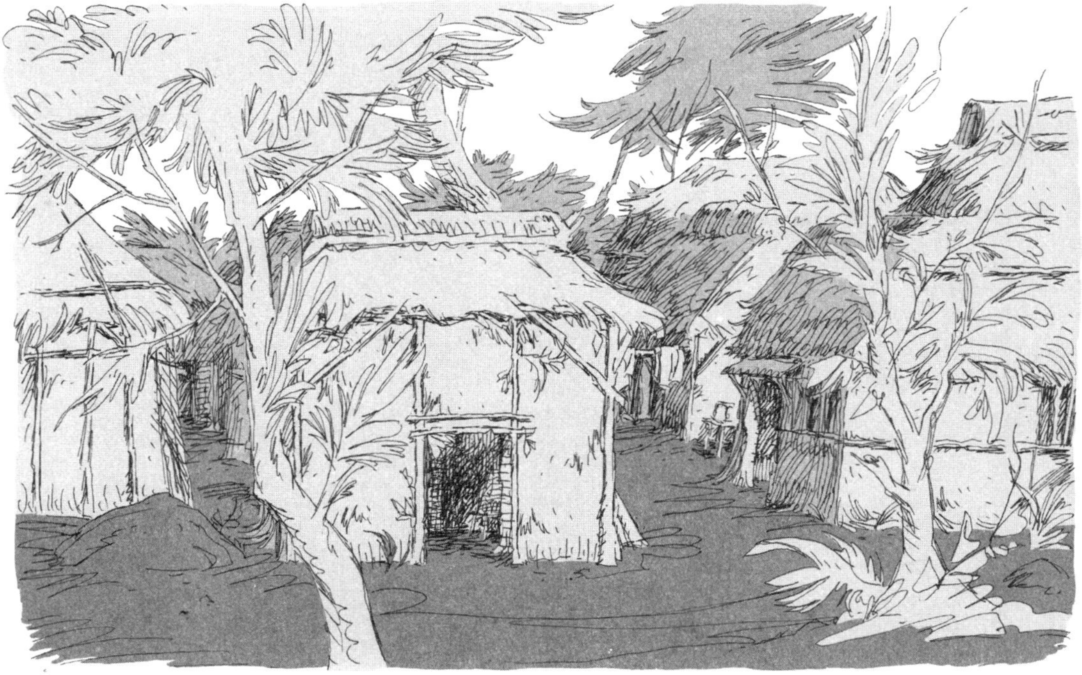

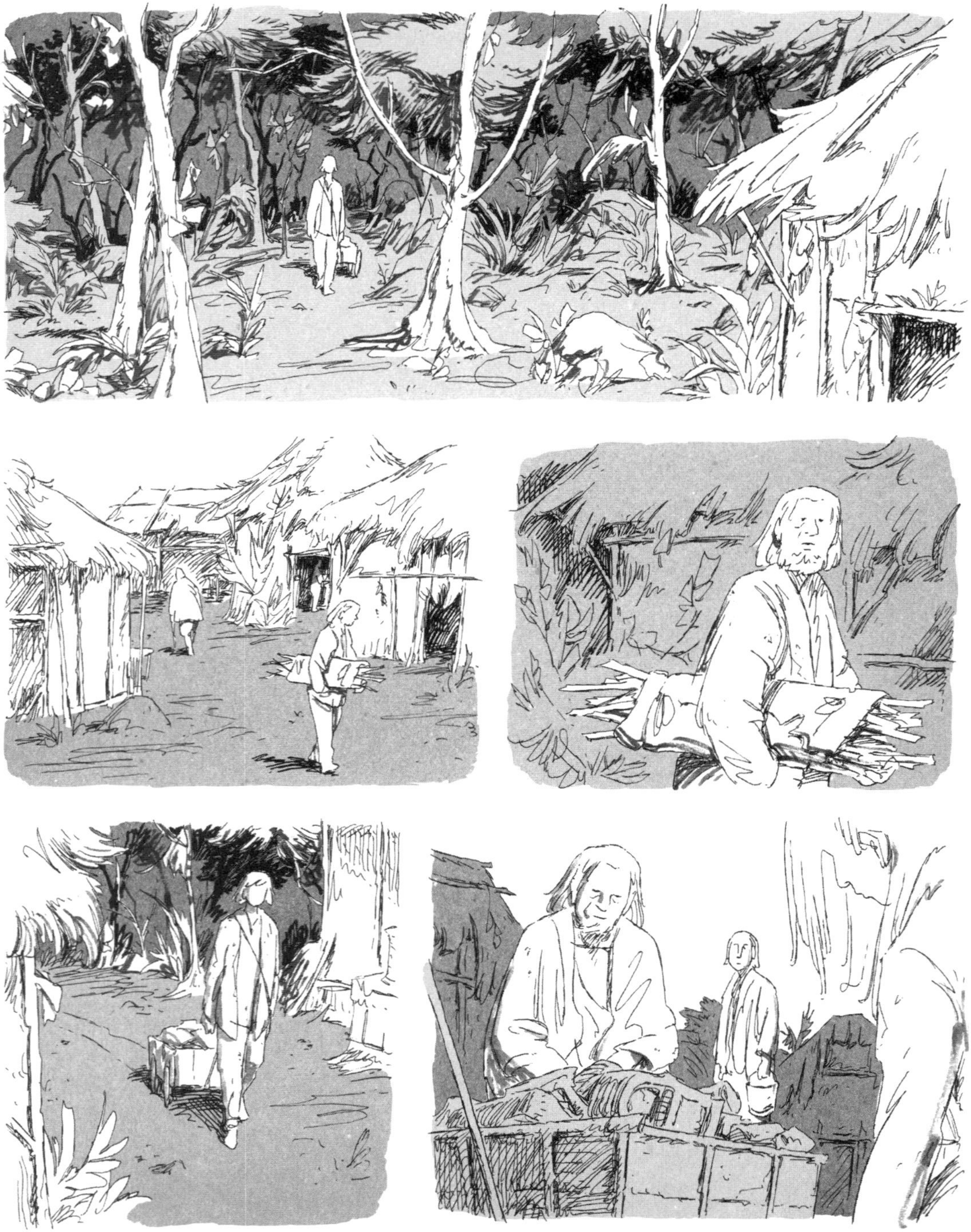

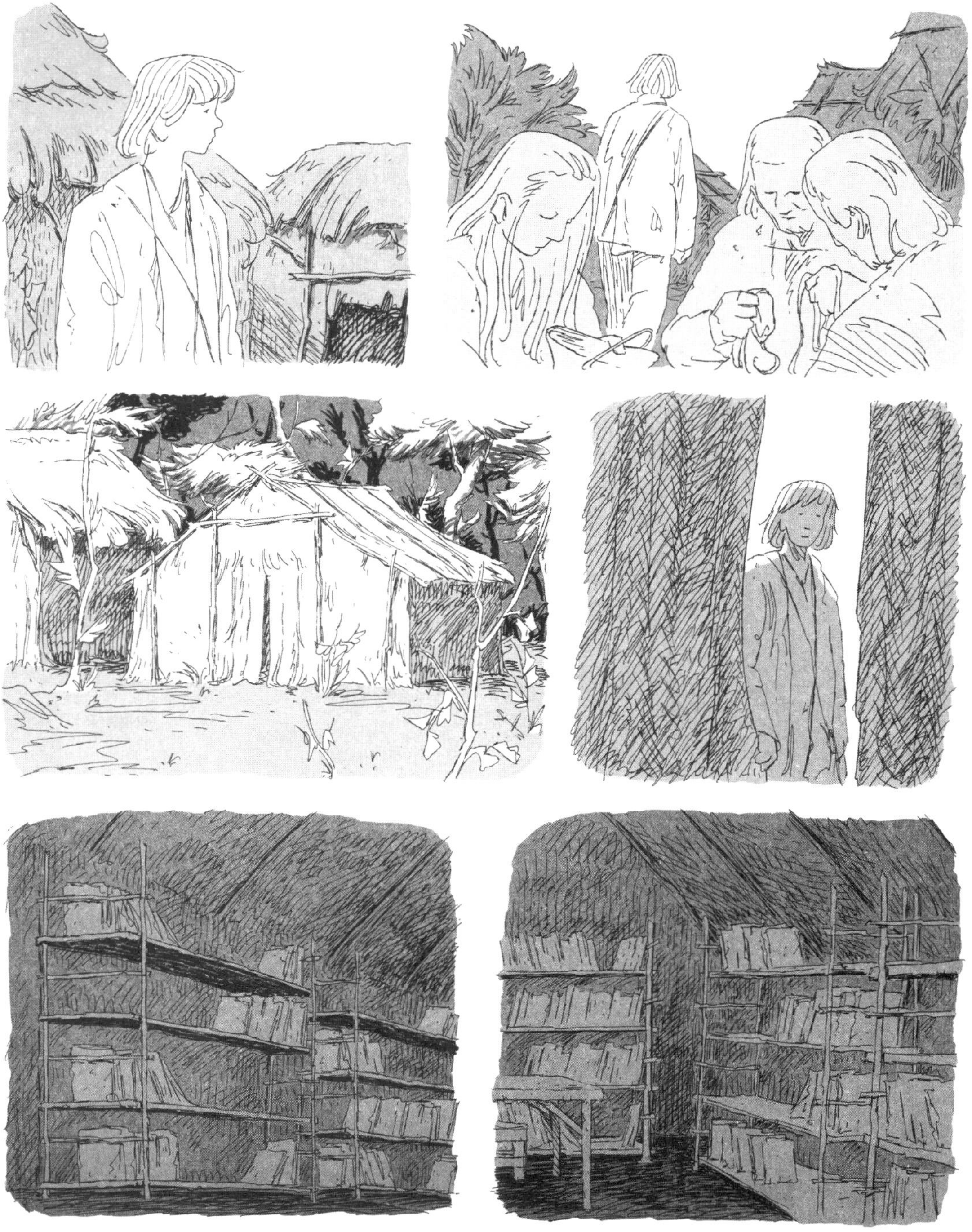

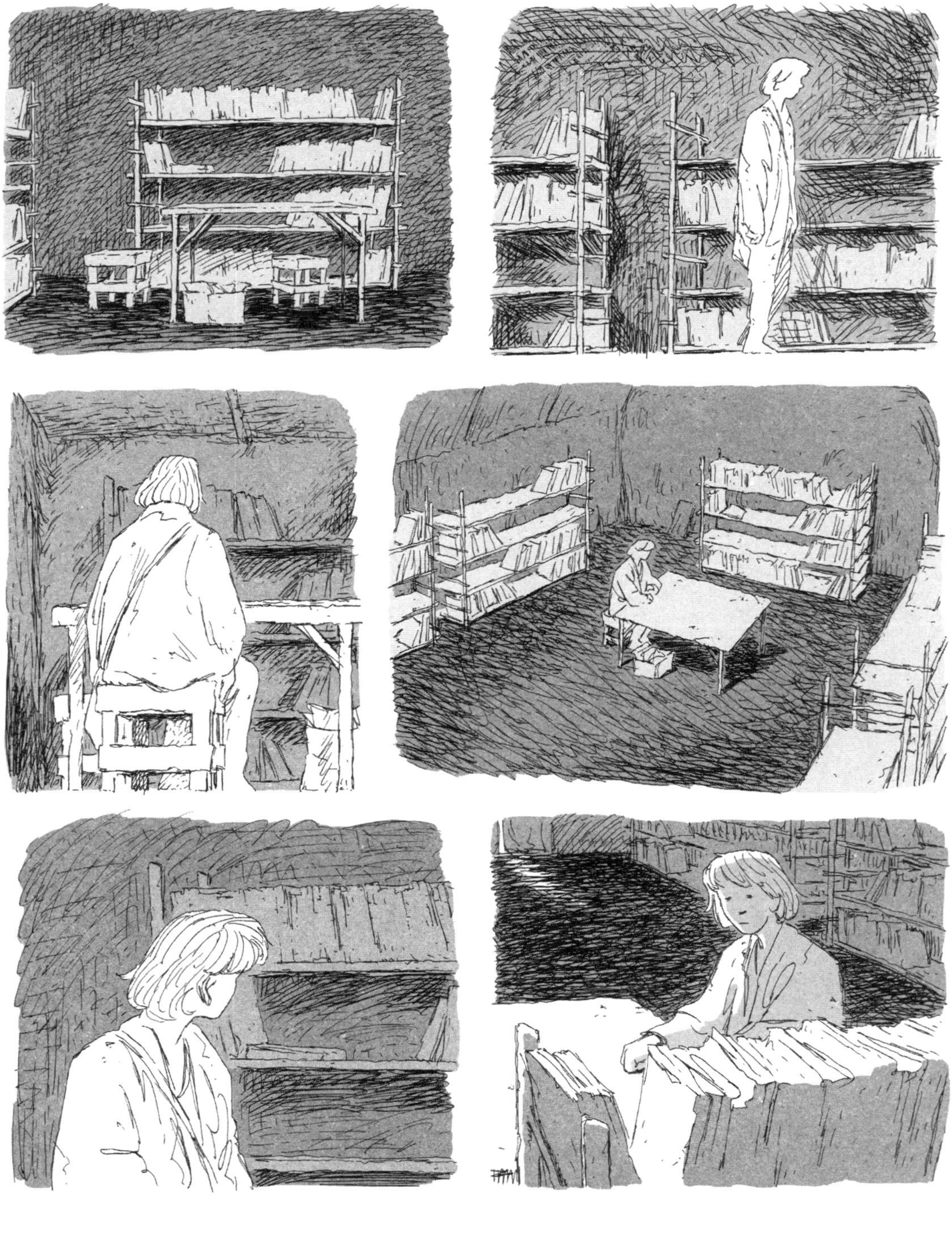

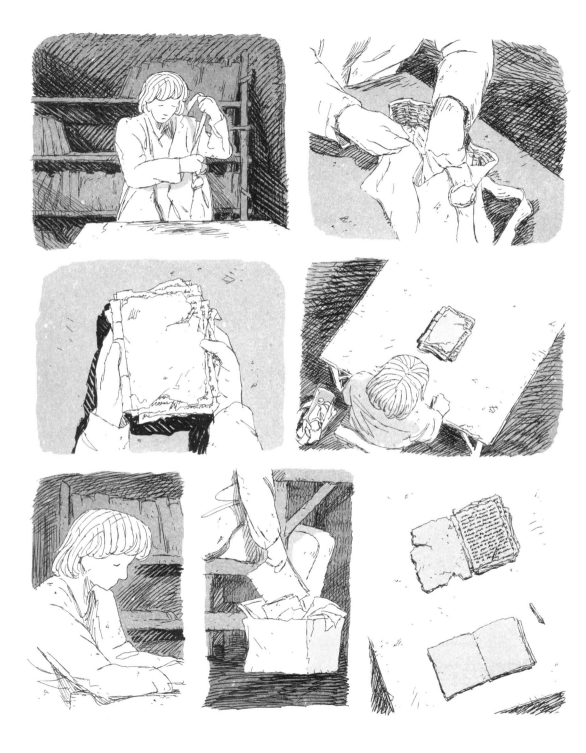

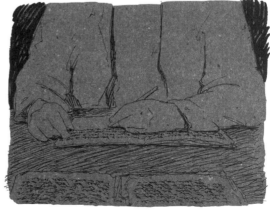

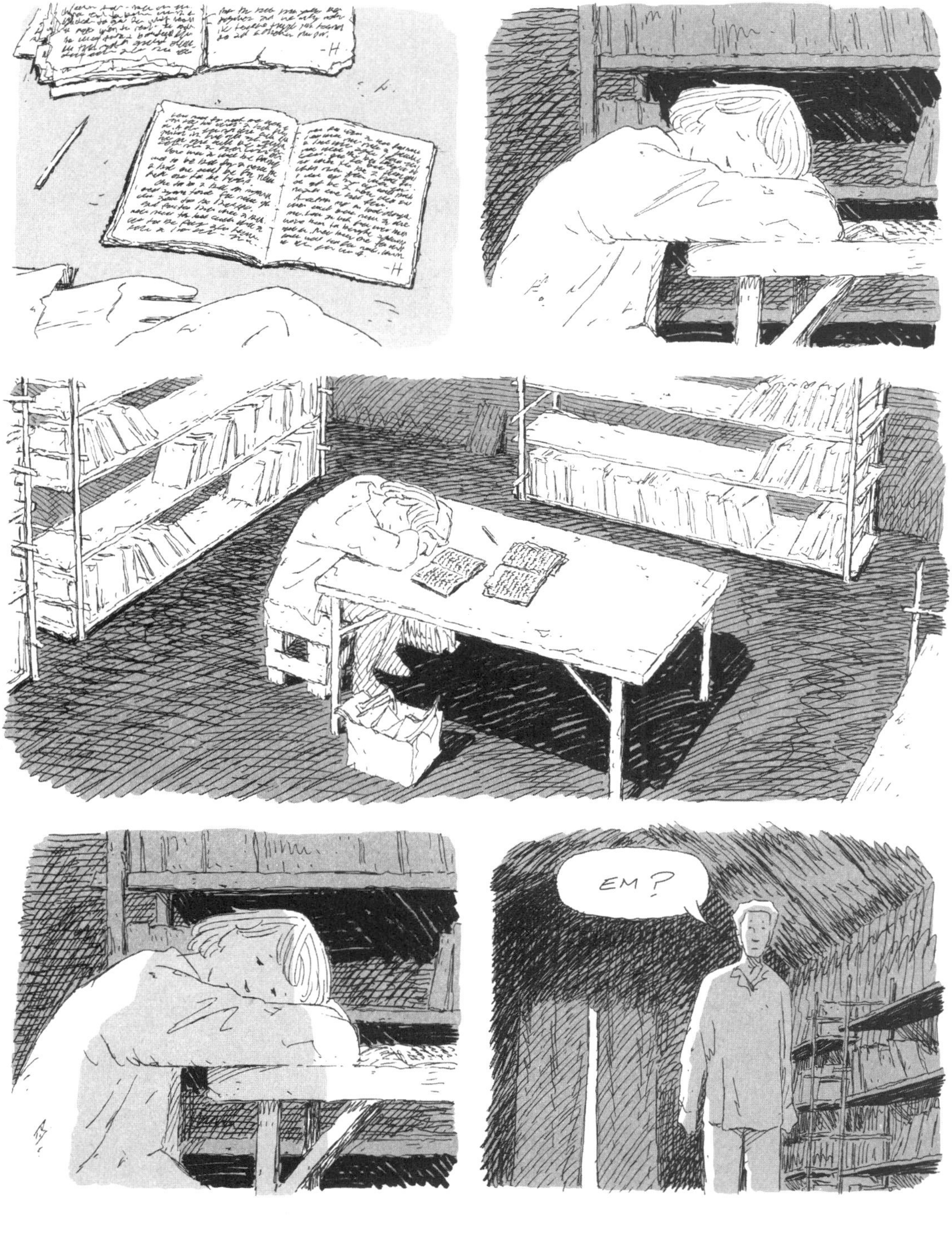
EM?

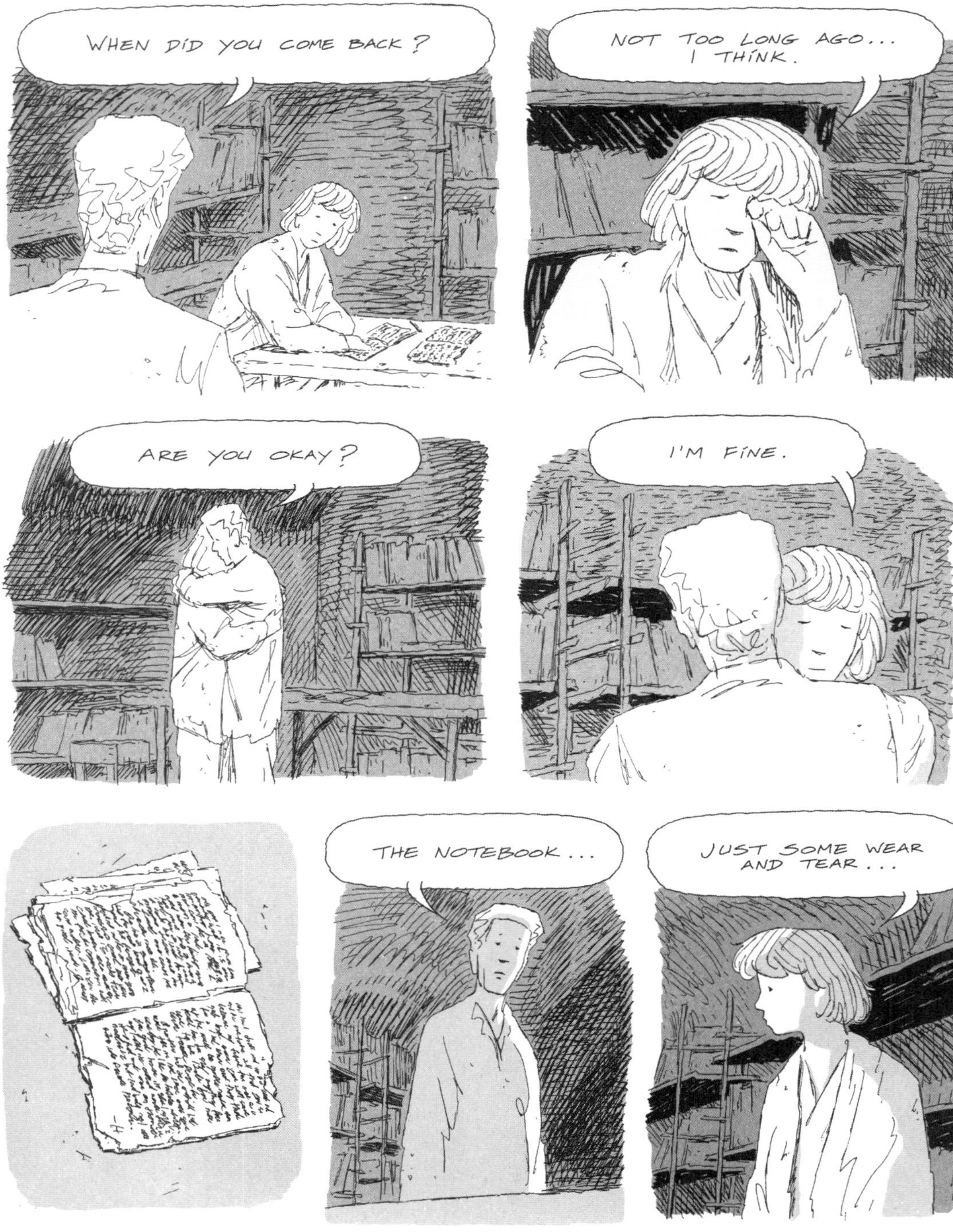
WHEN DID YOU COME BACK?
NOT TOO LONG AGO... I THINK.
ARE YOU OKAY?
I'M FINE.
THE NOTEBOOK...
JUST SOME WEAR AND TEAR...

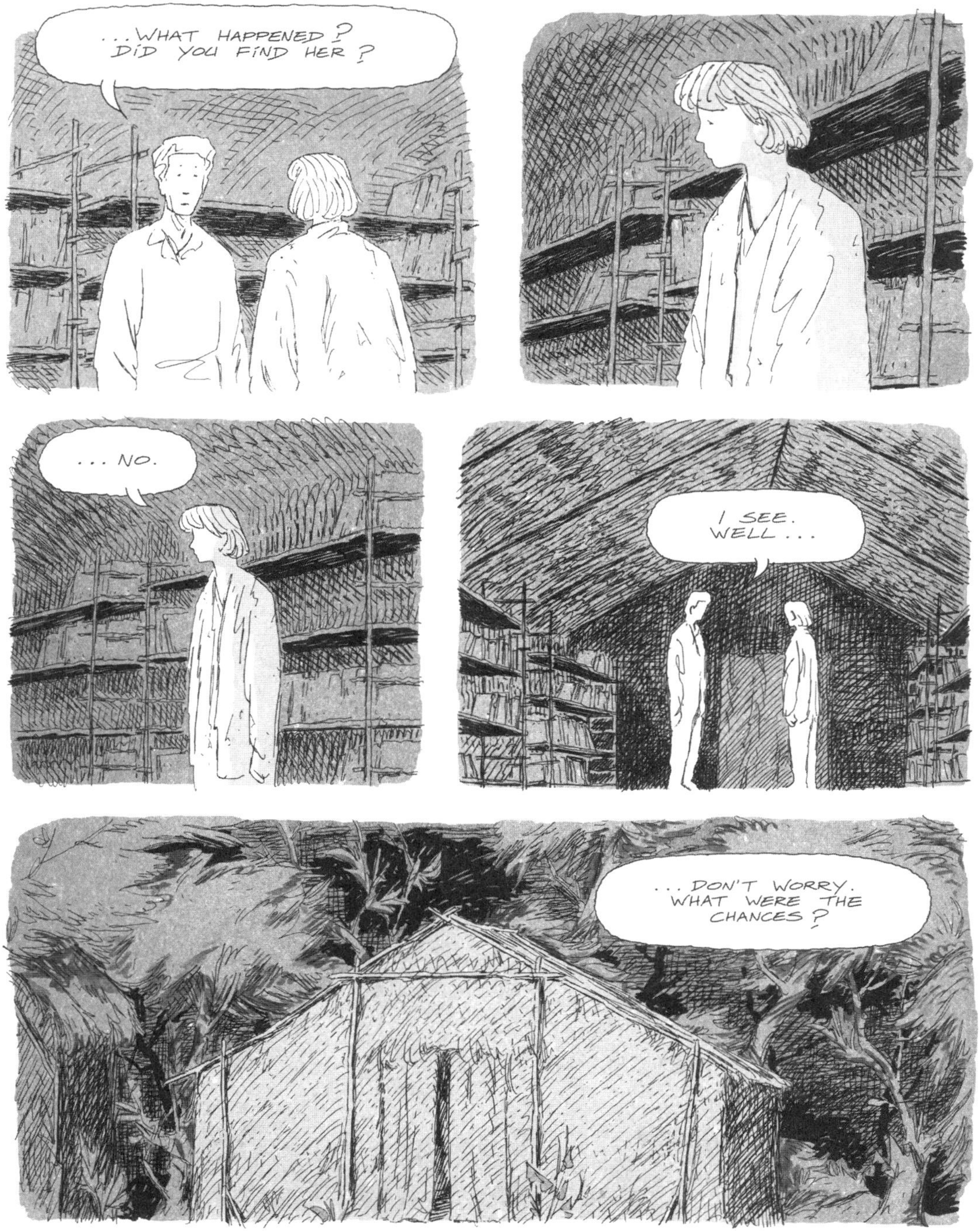
...WHAT HAPPENED? DID YOU FIND HER?
... NO.
I SEE. WELL ...
... DON'T WORRY. WHAT WERE THE CHANCES?

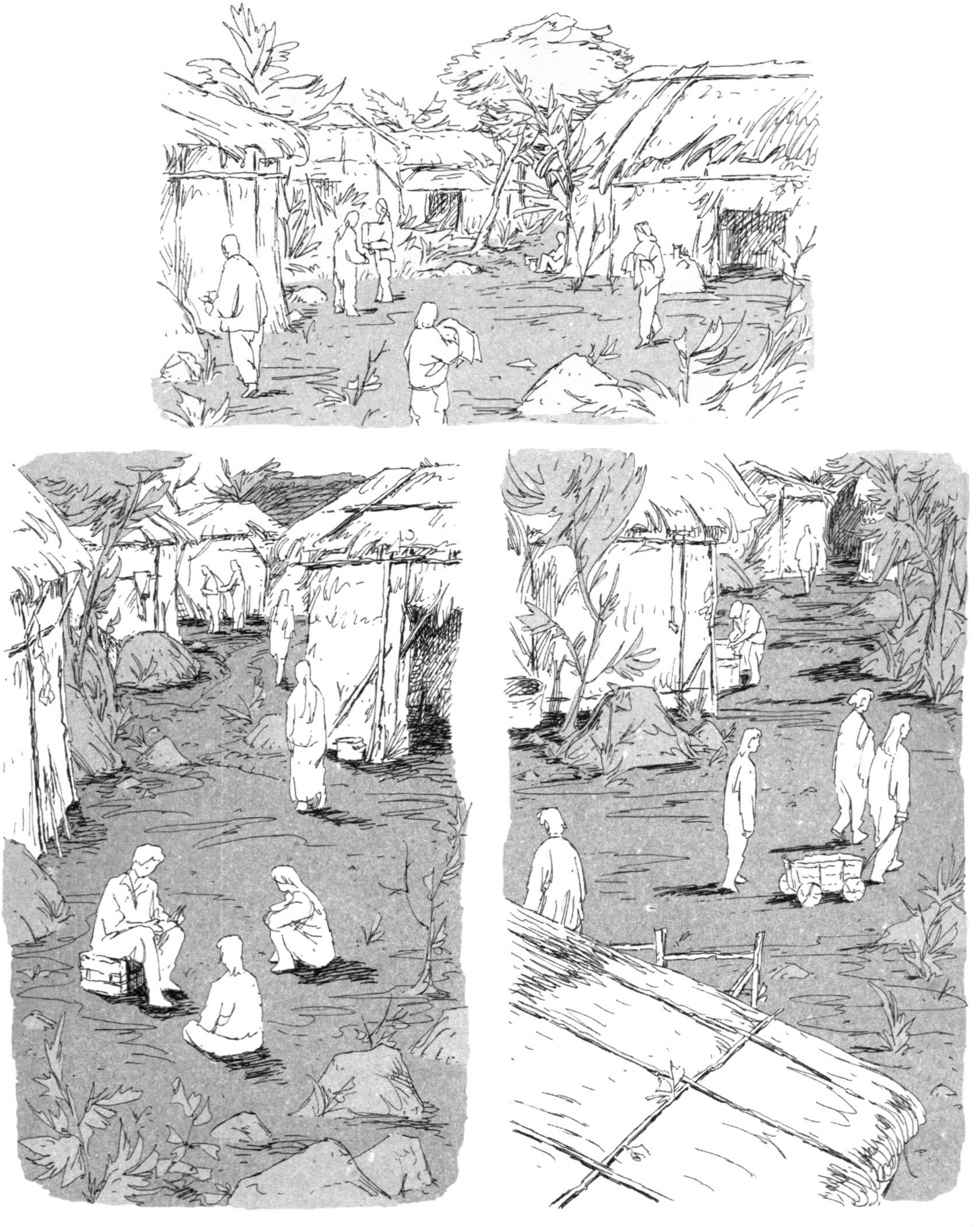

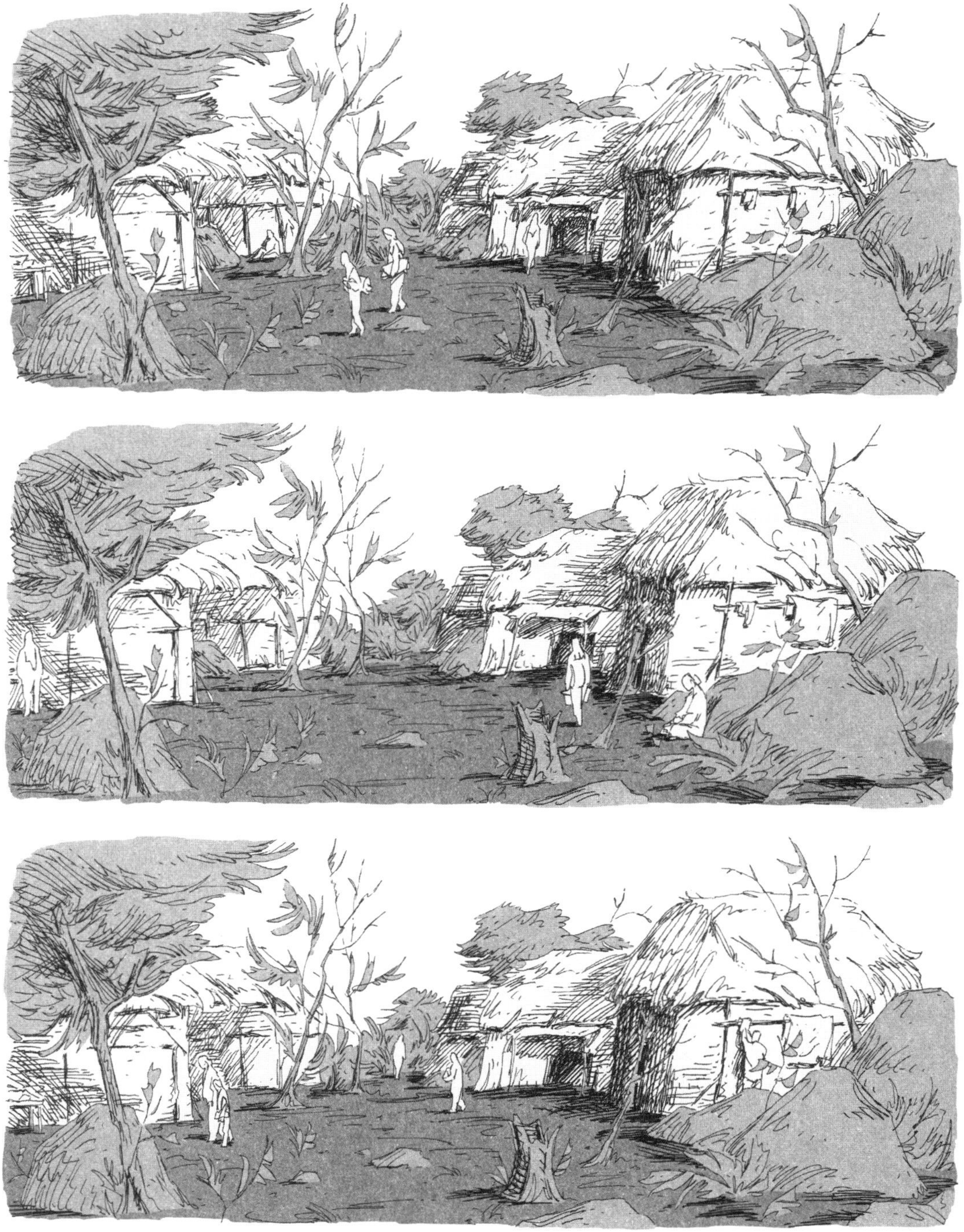

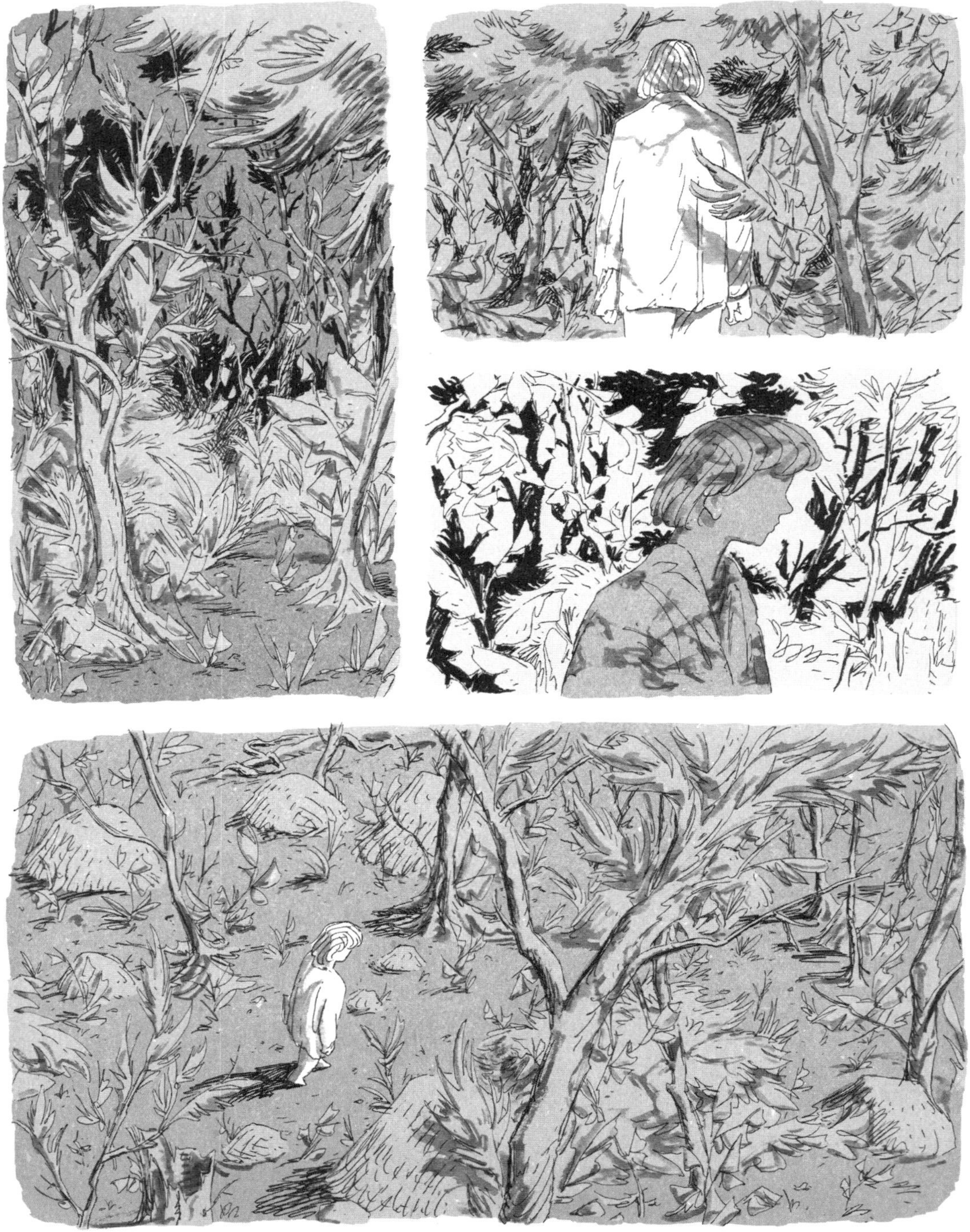

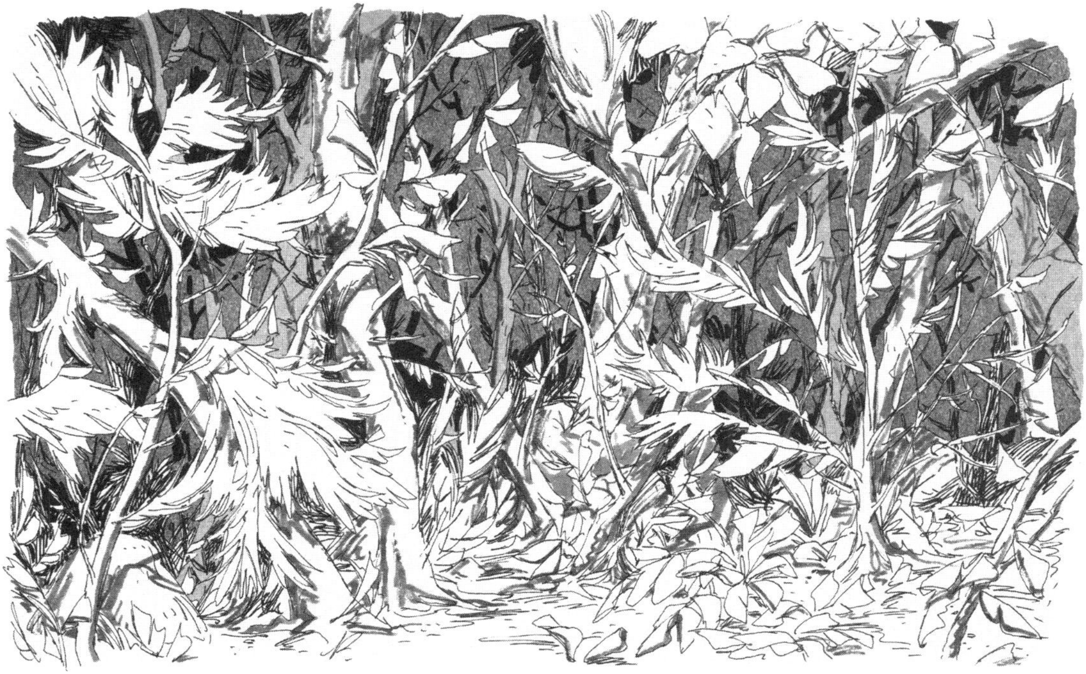

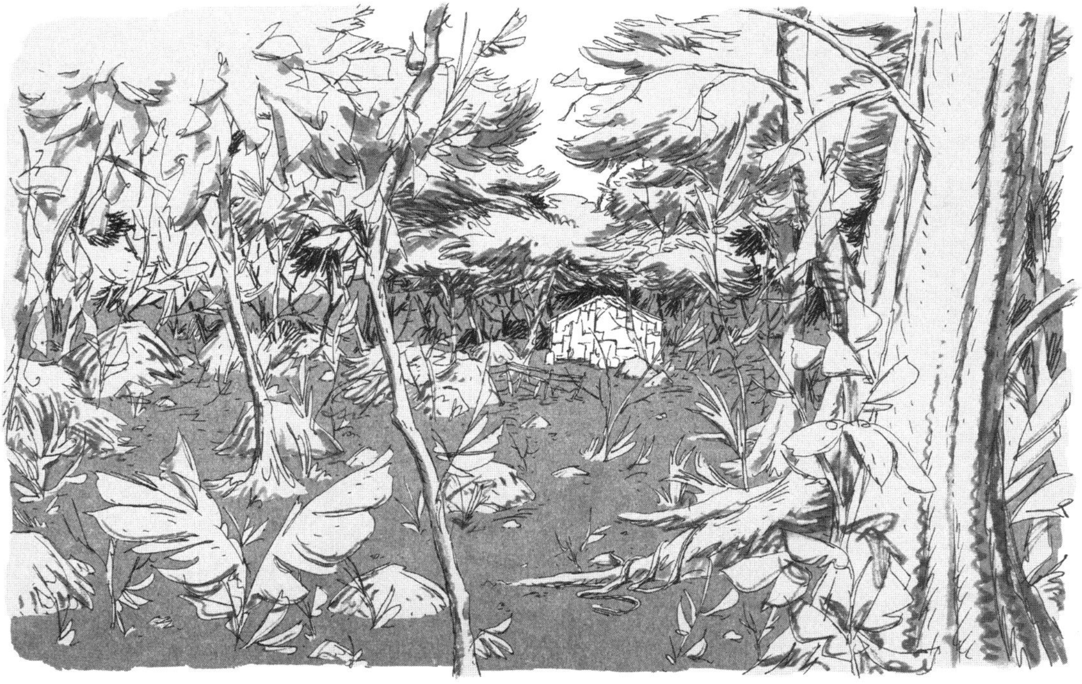

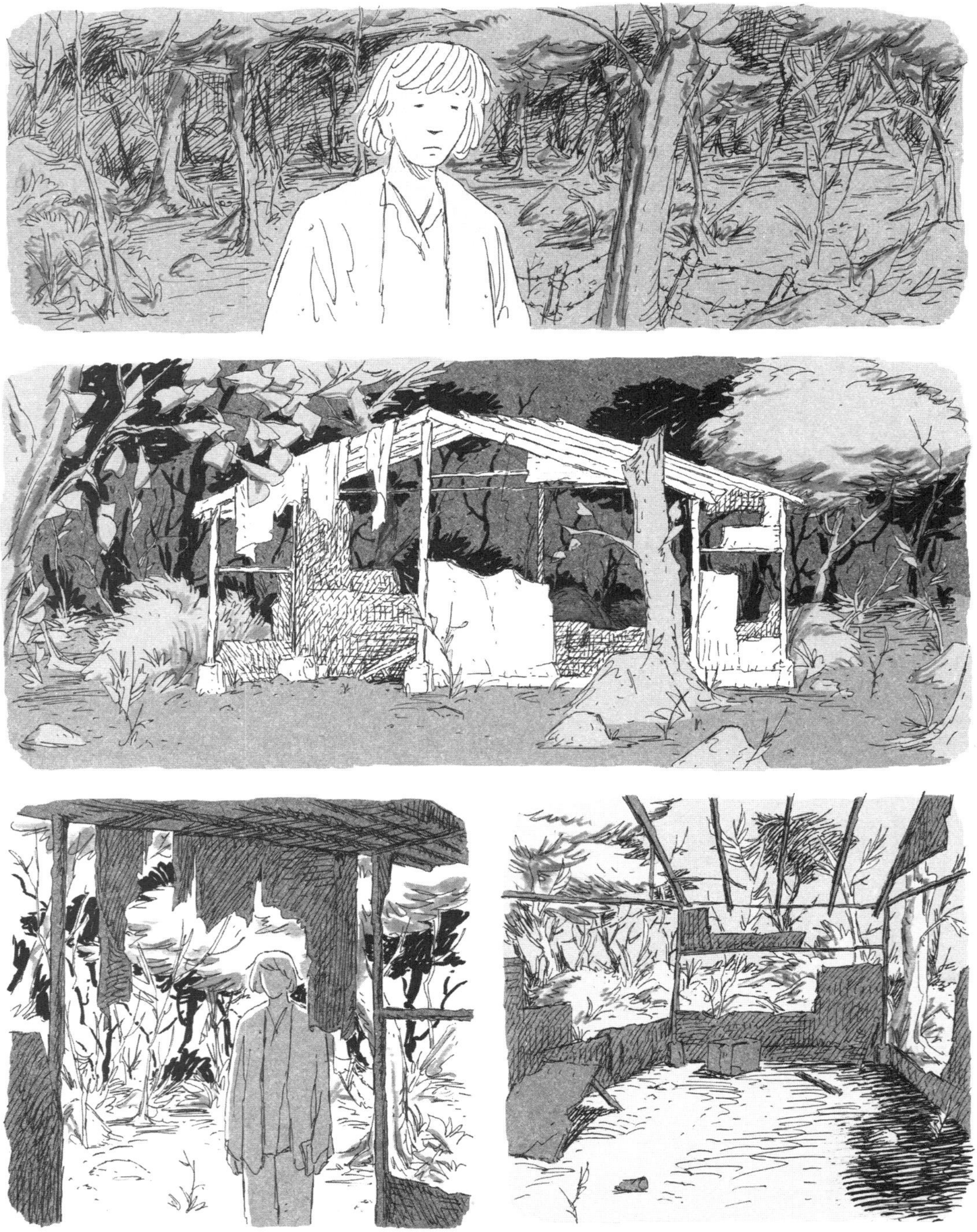

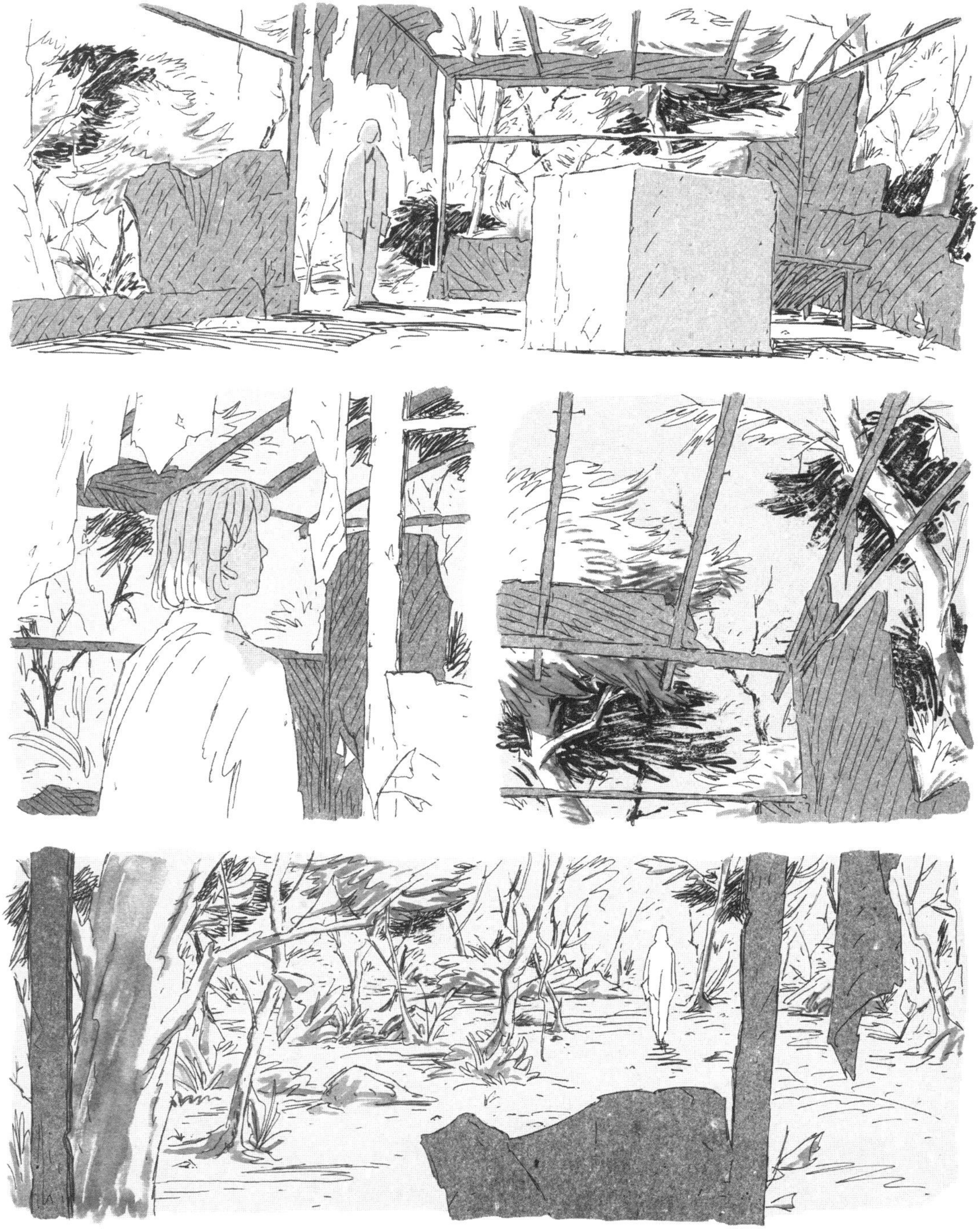

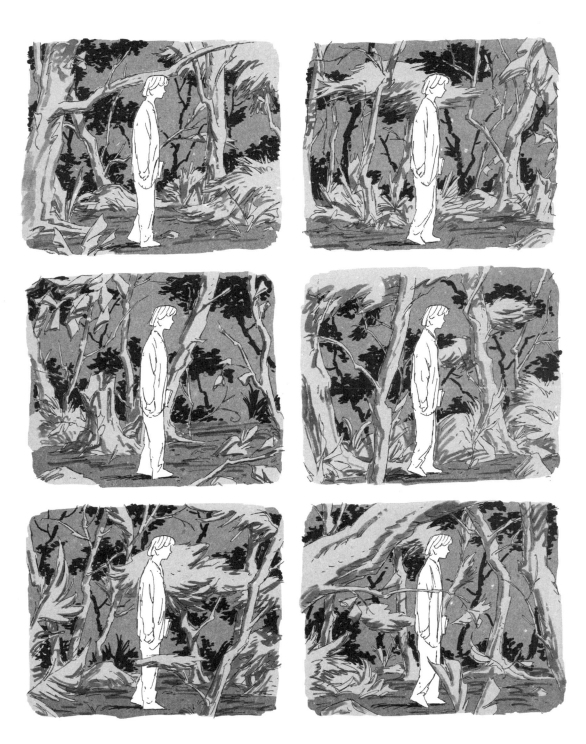

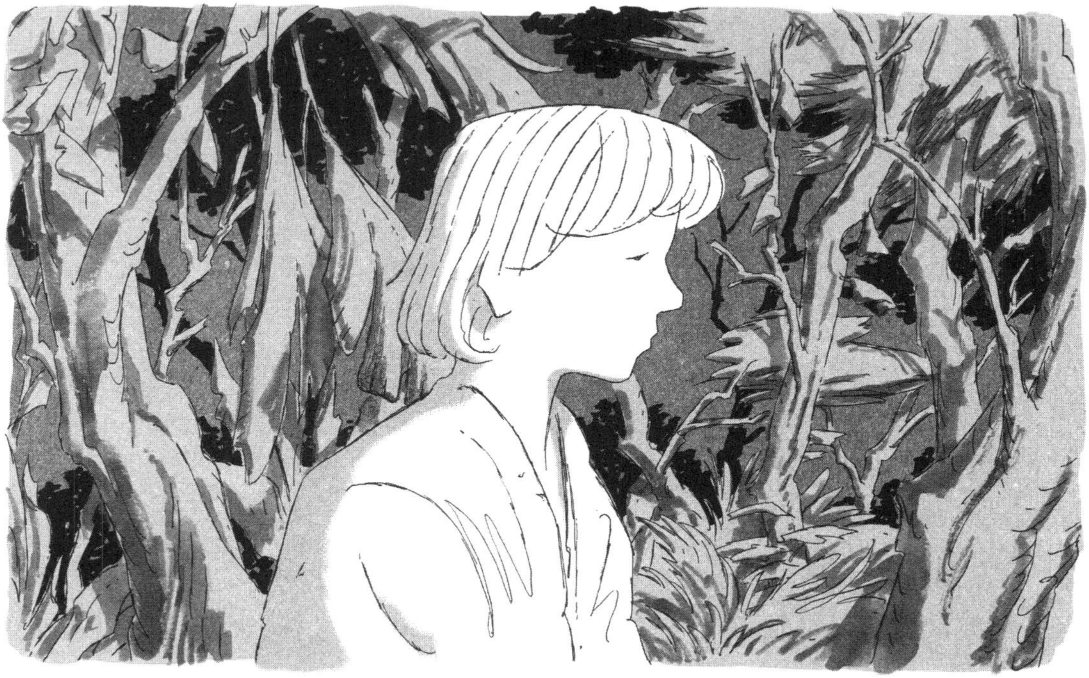
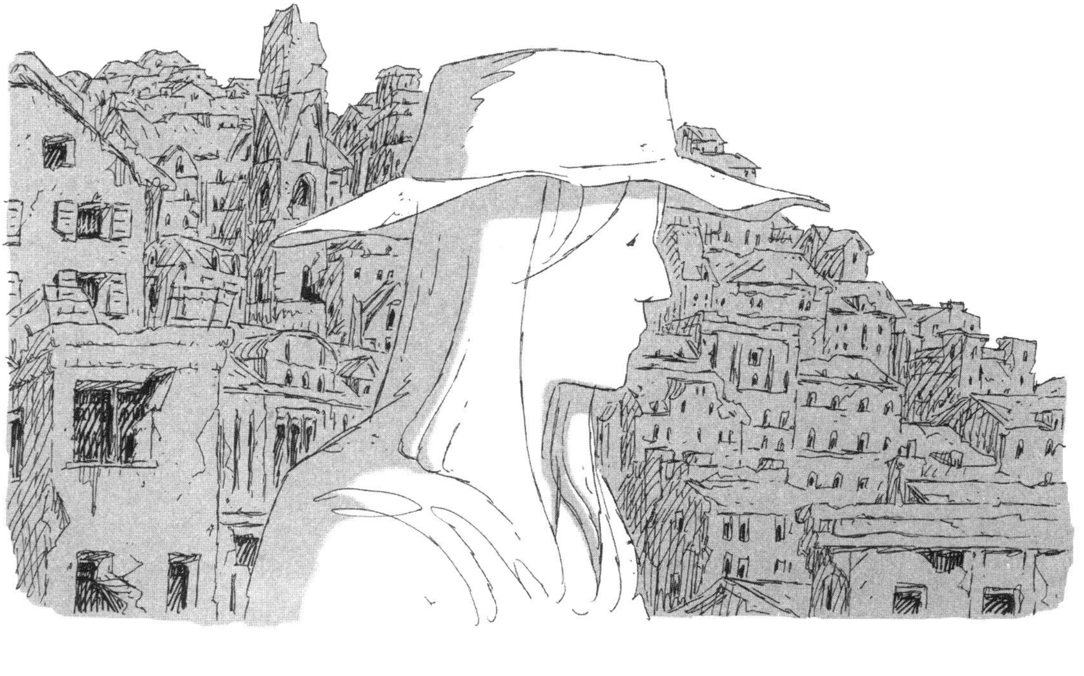

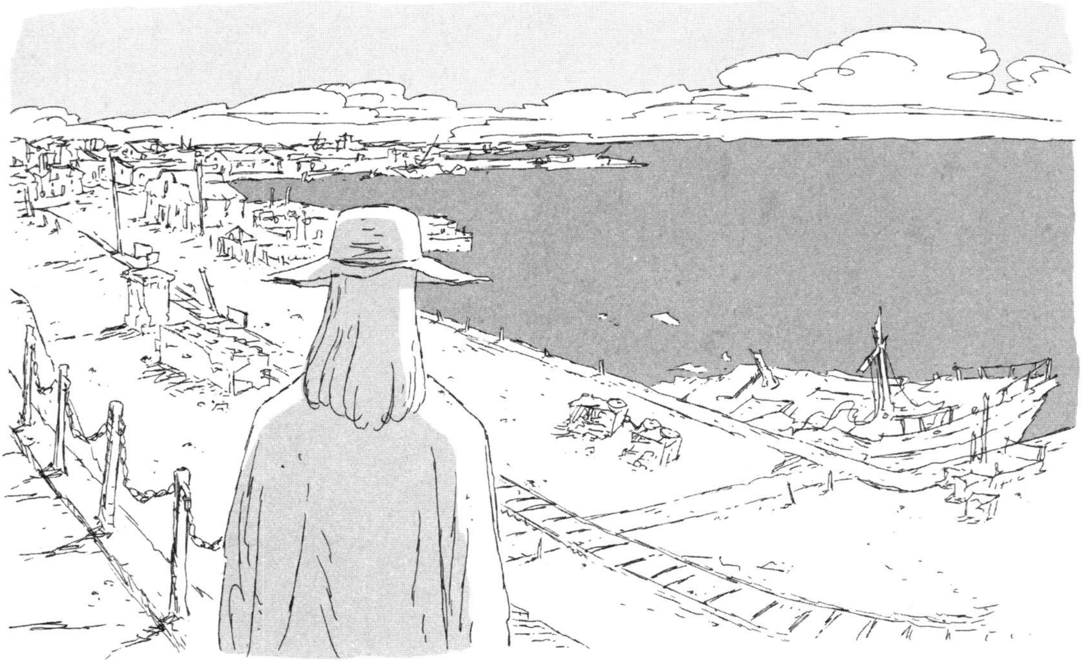

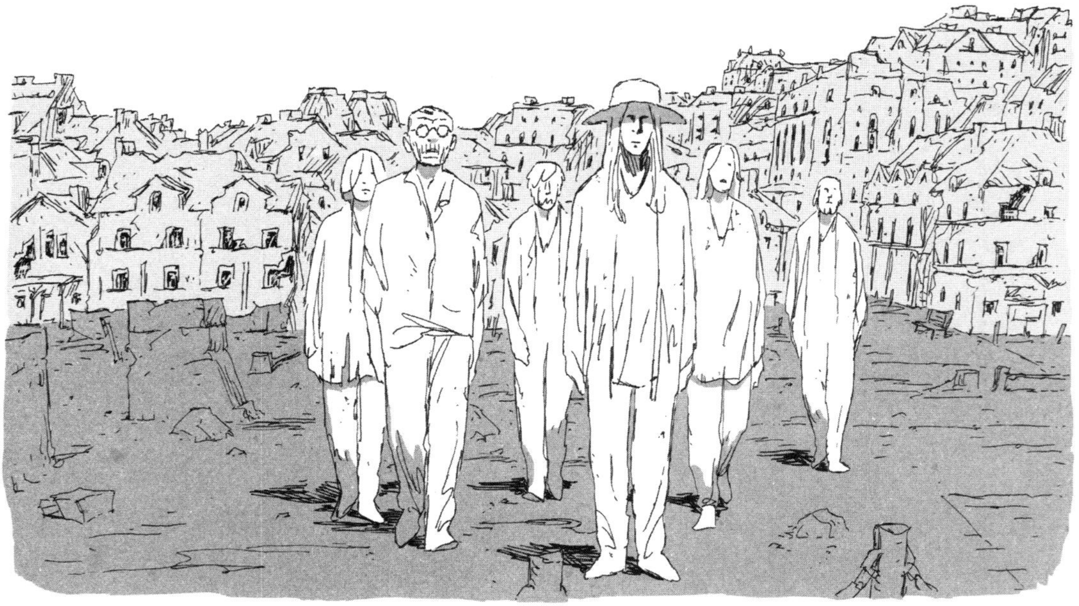

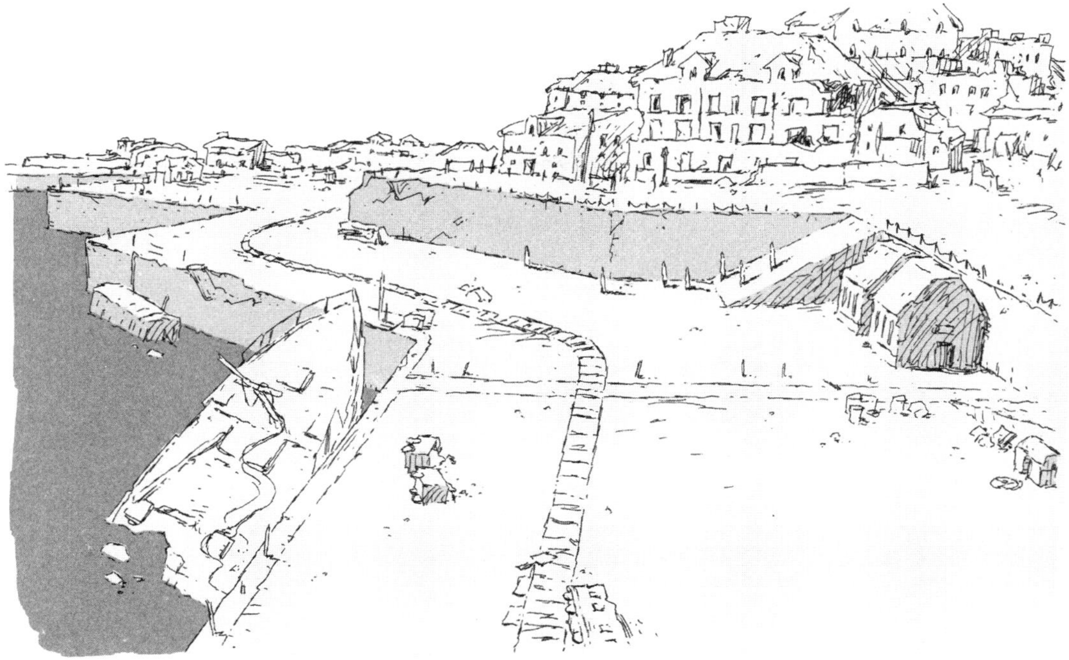

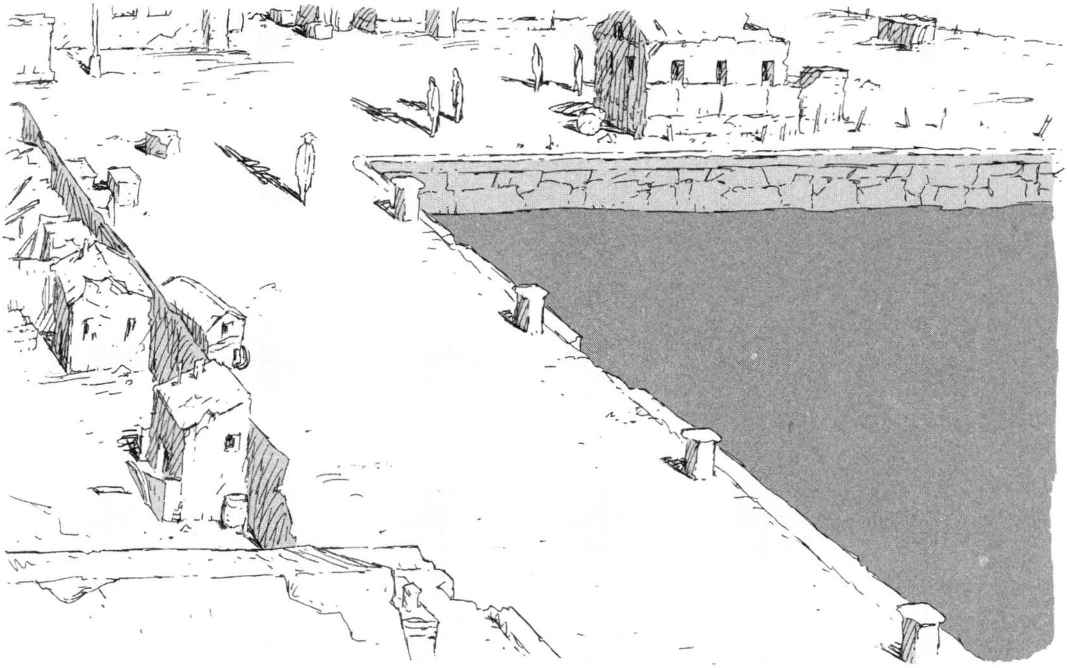

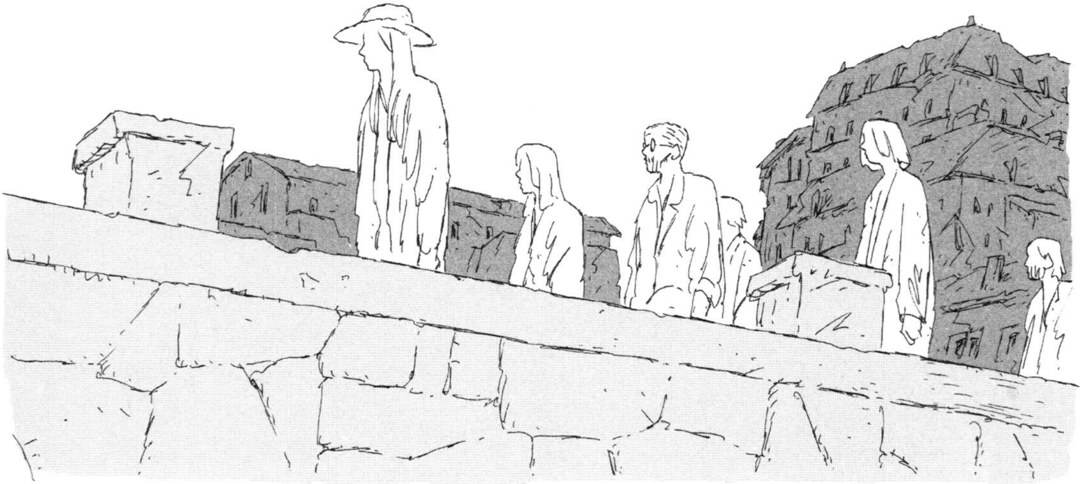

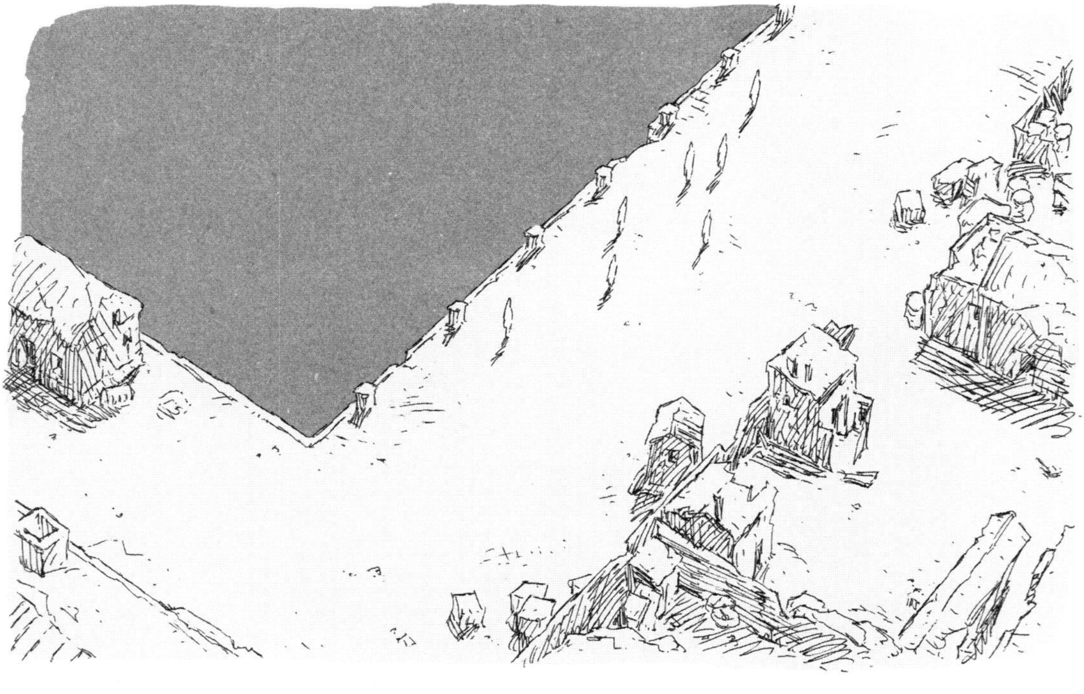

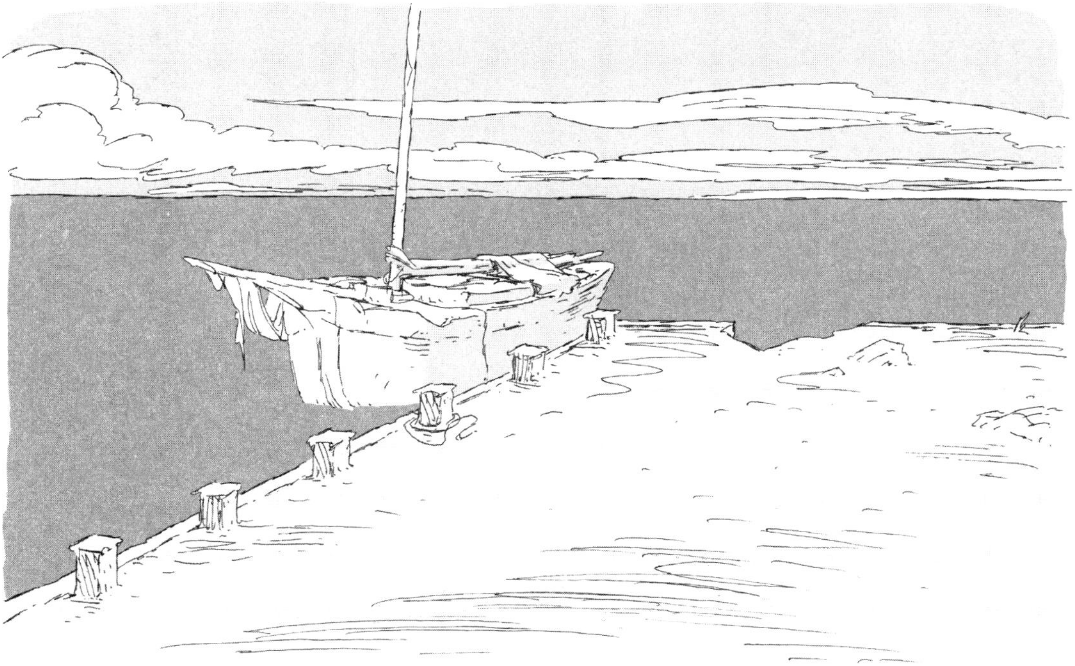

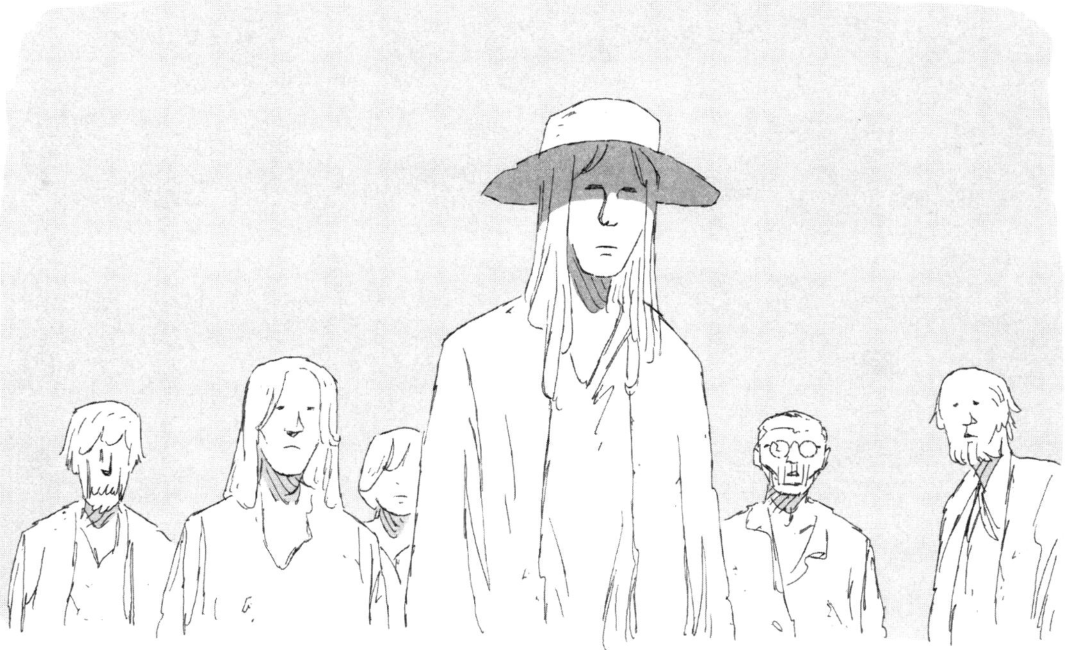

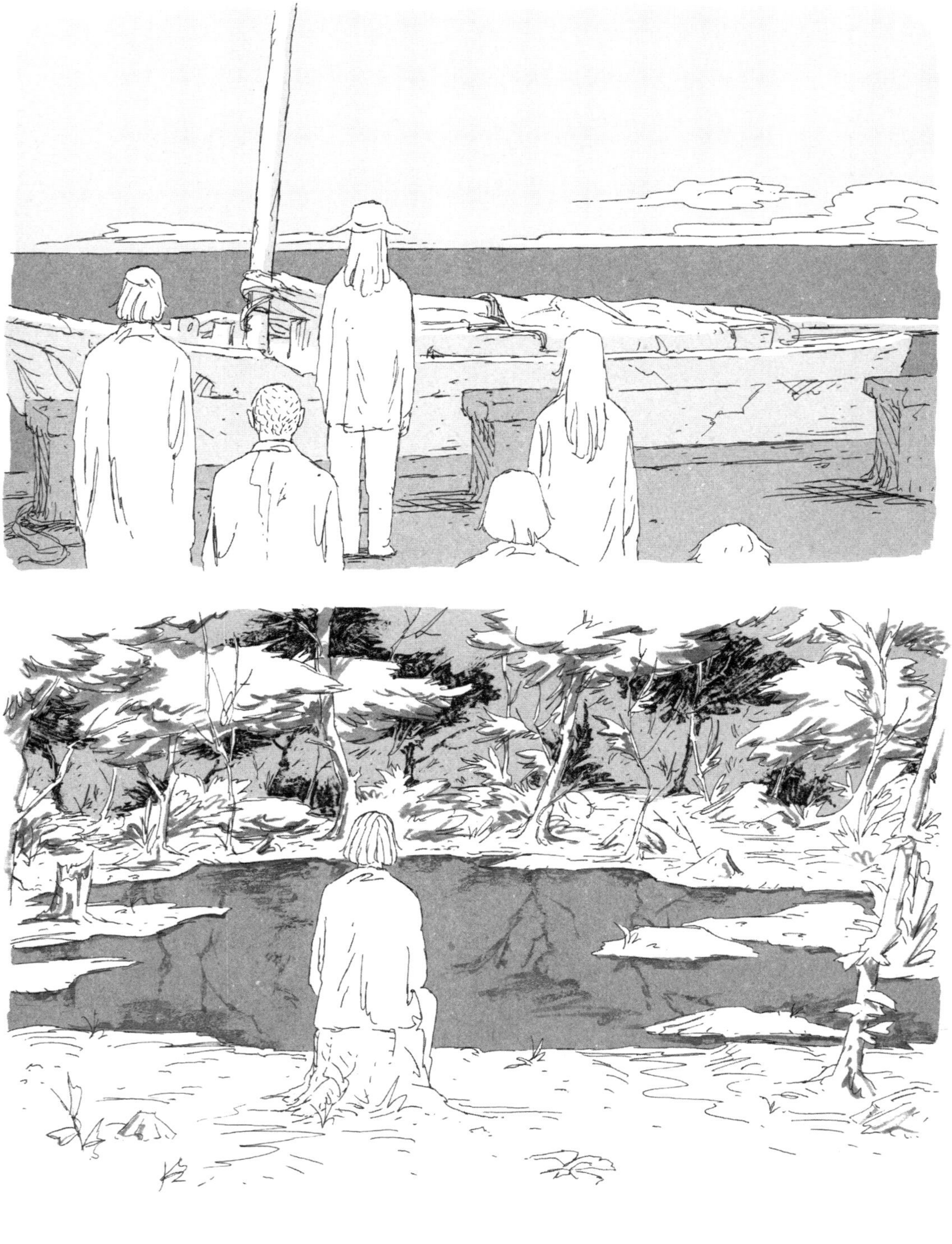

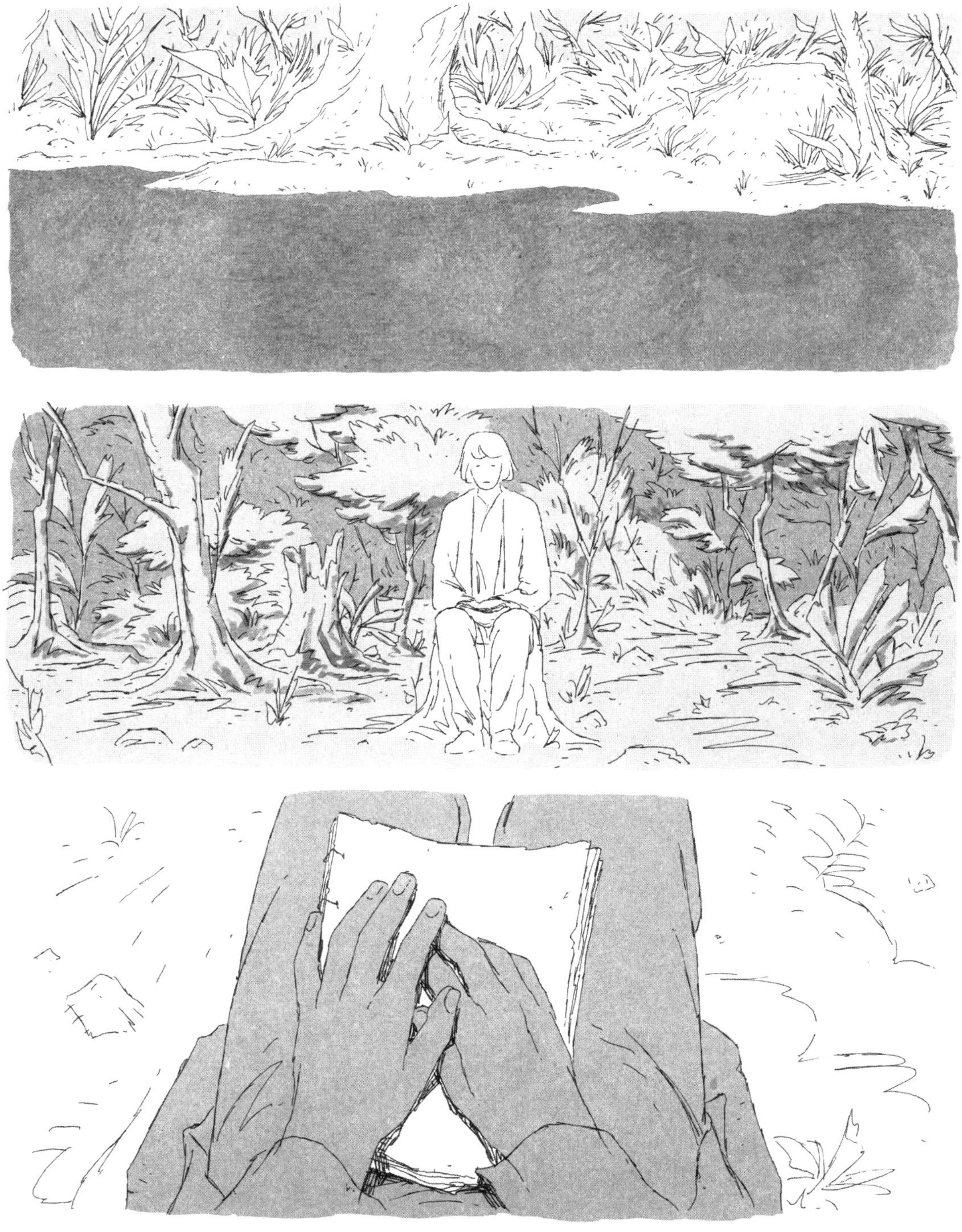

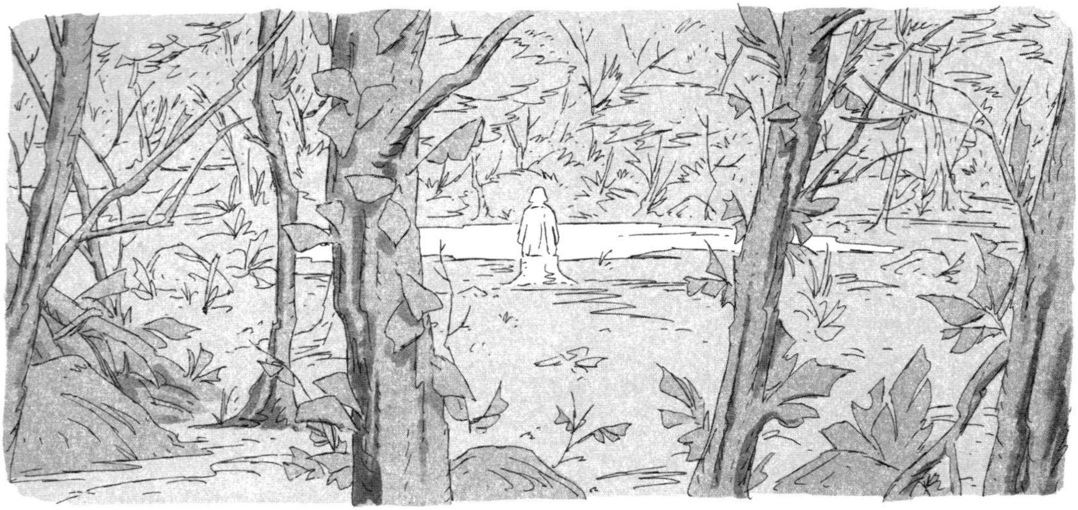

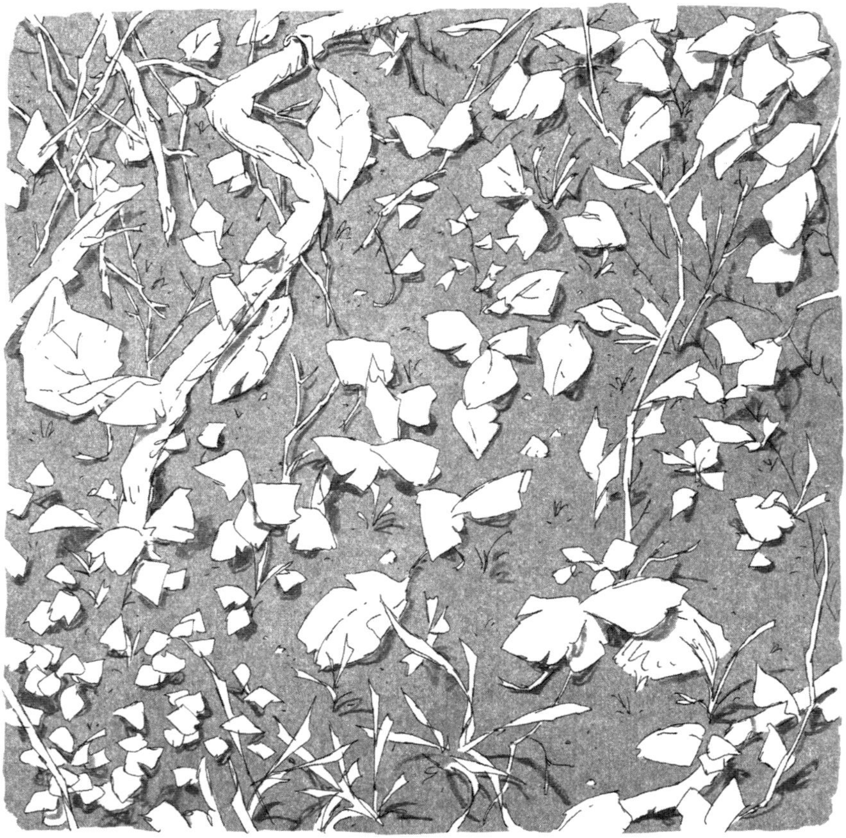

Thank you to Miki, Andy, Sal, Hartley, Guillaume, and my family.